The Education Papers: Women's Quest for Equality in Britain, 1850–1912

WOMEN'S SOURCE LIBRARY

Series Editors:
Dale Spender and Candida Ann Lacey

This series brings together some of the most important, but still too little known, written sources which document the history of women's struggles for liberation. Taken from the principal women's archive in Britain, The Fawcett Library, and reprinted in full wherever possible, these pamphlets and papers illustrate major debates on a range of issues including suffrage, education, work, science and medicine as well as making the words of individual women widely available for the first time. Each volume contains a historical introduction to the material and biographical details of those campaigners who sought to improve the social, economic and legal status of women. The series was devised in collaboration with Catherine Ireland and David Doughan of The Fawcett Library, both of whom greatly assisted in the selection and compilation of material.

Other volumes in this series:

Barbara Leigh Smith Bodichon and the Langham Place Group edited by Candida Ann Lacey
The Sexuality Debates edited by Sheila Jeffreys

Forthcoming volumes include:

Women's Fabian Tracts edited by Sally Alexander
The Non-Violent Militant: Selected Writings of Teresa Billington-Greig edited by Carol McPhee and Ann FitzGerald
Suffrage and the Pankhursts edited by Jane Marcus
The Lily edited by Cheris Kramarae and Ann Russo
The Revolution edited by Cheris Kramarae and Lana Rakow
Before the Vote was Won: Arguments For and Against Women's Suffrage, 1864–1896 edited by Jane Lewis
Sex and Social Order, 1660–1730 edited by Carol Barash and Rachel Weil

The Education Papers: Women's Quest for Equality in Britain, 1850–1912

Edited by
Dale Spender

WITHDRAWN

Routledge & Kegan Paul
New York and London

First published in 1987 by
Routledge & Kegan Paul Ltd
11 New Fetter Lane, London EC4P 4EE

Published in the USA by
Routledge & Kegan Paul Inc.
in association with Methuen Inc.
29 West 35th Street, New York, NY 10001

Phototypeset in Linotron Bembo
by Input Typesetting Ltd, London
and printed in Great Britain
by T. J. Press (Padstow) Ltd
Padstow, Cornwall

Library of Congress Cataloging in Publication Data

The Education papers.

(Women's source library)
Includes index.
1. Women—Education—Great Britain—History—
19th century.   2. Educational equalization—
Great Britain—History—19th century.   I. Spender,
Dale.   II. Series.
LC2042.E36   1987   376'.941   86–29632

British Library CIP Data also available
ISBN 0–7102–1126–0

Contents

Acknowledgments

Without the great generosity of David Doughan, the competent typing of Glynis Wood, the excellent research skills of Kelley Atkinson and the organisational aptitude of Candida Lacey, this volume would not exist.

Introduction

In 1792, in *Vindication of the Rights of Woman*, the classic analysis of educational inequality, Mary Wollstonecraft claimed that there could be no sexual equality without educational equality. In stating her case Mary Wollstonecraft made it clear that she not only believed sexual equality to be desirable and attainable – and inextricably linked with learning – she also set some of the terms for the sexual educational debate of the nineteenth and twentieth centuries when she insisted that both sexes be educated equally.

Does 'equal education' mean that girls and boys should have the *same* education? And if so, what sort of same education should they be given? Should girls receive the same education that boys have had for centuries, or should the needs and interests of girls be taken into account and the education of boys 'modified' so that it is equally appropriate for girls? Or does equal education mean equal educational *opportunity*? And what does this mean, anyway?

Or perhaps equal education may mean different education – but of equal duration, or equal status. For there have been those who have argued that as the two sexes have different roles to play in society they therefore have very different needs and that these should be reflected in very different educational provision. But while the education of girls might be different it would still be equal in that it was an equally useful, viable or appropriate education – for their sex.

As can be seen, there were (and are) many interpretations of *equal education* and they can lead to very different outcomes. This is why the question of what an equal education might be dominated the debates of the nineteenth century and continues to be a controversial and crucial concern even today. And when Mary Wollstonecraft raised the issue of equal education and the consequences it would have for the sexes and society she was by no means the first to formulate the framework.

It comes as something of a surprise – because such information has been suppressed and this is itself another aspect of educational inequality – to find that there were critiques of sex role conditioning even before Mary Wollstonecraft's protest. In 1790, Catherine Macaulay, who was acutely aware of the role education played in the construction of male supremacy, had also taken the stand that there was no need to resort to biological explanations to account for the ostensible supremacy of the male sex. Wherever and whenever significant intellectual sex differences emerged, she argued in *Letters on Education*, they could be readily explained in terms of differences in education. And so too did Catherine Macaulay contend that when the two sexes received an equal education the outcome would be intellectual equality.

The principles were much the same in the eighteenth century as they are today. The apparent intellectual supremacy of men was used as a justification for the greater power and authority of men, and while there were some who saw the advantages enjoyed by men as inevitable and natural there were others who saw such advantages as 'man-made' and who sought to end the preferential educational treatment males provided for their own sex.

But if the principles were much the same in the eighteenth century the context certainly was not. For while today, theoretically, women have the same access as men to education, this was not the case in the eighteenth century when there was a stark contrast between the educational opportunities available to women and those available to men.

Quite simply men were allowed formal education and women were not. In such a context there was little need for educational debate. The issue was primarily one of quantity rather than quality. The undisputed strategy for those who were interested in the welfare of women and justice in society was to call for educational provision for women which was equal to that provided for men.

That in the eighteenth century men were allowed learning and women were not was demonstrable: that this was a relatively recent development was also evident. For again, what is not widely recognised nor fully appreciated is that there was a decline in the education of women after the sixteenth century – and there is more than one reason for this deterioration.

Firstly there was a shift in attitude towards 'learned ladies' after the sixteenth century with a marked increase in hostility to women who would be educated. So only the brave – like Mary Wollstonecraft – could take the taunts and torments that were directed against the intellectual woman, and it is therefore understandable that the number of educated females should be very small. Such antagonism towards intellectual women, however, had not always prevailed. In the sixteenth century, while it had by no means been common, it had certainly been possible for a woman to be educated without causing undue offence. Sir Thomas More, for example, was just one father who believed that learning could agree equally with both sexes and that his daughter should be as well-educated as any son (see Antonia Fraser, 1984: 122).

Attitudes, however, were not all that had changed for the worse over the centuries: there had also been changes – for the worse – in terms of the facilities that were available for the education of girls.

When Henry VIII outlawed numerous religious orders, educational provision for both sexes was drastically reduced but the full significance of these closures has not always been realised, partly because they constituted only a temporary inconvenience in the education of boys and therefore attracted little attention. But these closures represented far more than a perturbation in the education of girls.

When the educational provisions of the Roman Catholic institutions came to an end, 'compensatory measures' were soon taken to remedy any of the deficiencies experienced by boys; no comparable steps were taken to repair the damage done to the education of girls. The consequences were critical, as Antonia Fraser has pointed out: 'The disappearance of convents at the time of the Reformation had deprived English girls not only of convenient places of local learning, but also of a pool of women teachers in the shape of the nuns themselves' (pp. 123–4).

With no schools and no teachers – and no training places for teachers, for women were not allowed to enter universities – the educational situation for girls was grim and seemed to afford few prospects for improvement when Mary Wollstonecraft made her demand for women's rights – and placed education at the centre of her concerns.

For Mary Wollstonecraft there was no mystery about why women were excluded from education. She saw such deprivation as part of the deliberate construction of women's 'weakness' and dependency. For her, the key to liberation lay in literacy and learning. Such an analysis is not so far removed from some of the understandings about power and supremacy that prevail today.

That the subordinate members of a society are not to be well-educated – or not educated at all – has been the policy of many a ruling elite in many different cultures. That literacy can be dangerous in those who are ruled has been the deeply-held conviction of many of those who have done the ruling. This is why 'the masses', the working class, were so long denied education in England (see Raymond Williams, 1975): this is why it was illegal in the United States to teach slaves to read and write; this is why for so many centuries women were excluded from formal education.

It is also why the nineteenth century witnessed the emergence of the organised movement for women's education. Such a movement was not without individual contributions, of course. There had been a series of intellectual and responsible women who had protested at the inequitable and iniquitous educational provision and who prepared the way for the nineteenth-century women's movement and who laid the foundations for the education debates.

There had been Aphra Behn (1640–89), for example, the great restoration playwright who had from the public stage denounced the disadvantages that men had devised for women. And there had been the philosopher, Mary Astell (1668–1731), who had insisted that women would never receive the right education from the hands of men and who was the first to advocate the establishment of a women's university – where women could be in charge of their own education.

There had been the anonymous 'Sophia, A Person of Quality' who, in 1739, in her publication *Woman Not Inferior to Man*, had exposed the false logic of male supremacy when she had taken up the issue that education was wasted on a woman: 'It is a very great absurdity to argue that learning is useless to women, because, forsooth, they have no share in public offices' she commented. For, 'Why is learning useless to us? Because we have no share in public offices. And why have we no share in public offices? Because we have no learning' (p. 27).

And of course there had been Catherine Macaulay (1731–91) and Mary Wollstonecraft (1759–97) who had also made their own critical contributions to the nineteenth-century campaign for women's education.

With this long tradition of analysis and debate – and with the education of women in such an impoverished and pitiful state at the beginning of the nineteenth century – the emergence of an increasingly organised women's movement for educational equity is not at all surprising. What is (perhaps) surprising is the degree of entrenched resistance that the movement encountered. For there was a struggle, a battle – some would say a revolution (see Margaret Bryant, 1979) – when it came to the attainment of women's educational rights.

4

Mary Wollstonecraft had argued – forcefully – that when educational inequalities were removed, sexual inequalities would be eliminated, and it seems that many accepted the accuracy of her analysis. This is why those who wanted sexual equality put so much energy into the struggle for educational equality: and why those who did *not* want sexual equality offered such entrenched resistance to the extension of education to women.

The education battle itself (as distinct from some of the debates) was fought on a single front: it was waged between those who wanted women to be educated and those who did not. And it was characterised on one side by the claim that education would lead to women's independence and that this would be good for women and for society; and on the other side by the assertion that if education did lead to women's independence it would mean ruin for women and the destruction of society.

Some of the same old arguments that had been exposed as false by 'Sophia' were advanced, yet again, to support the case for women's 'ignorance' and dependence.

So it was argued (often by educational and scientific experts) that for physical or mental reasons, women were not capable of being educated; or else it was argued that education would be wasted upon women who would only get married and have babies and therefore put their education to no good use; or even more blatantly it was argued that education would make women unfit for their roles as wives and mothers.

In their answers to all these objections the campaigners for women's education were united. There was no doubt they wanted *more* education for women and they were prepared to fight for it: where there was doubt was not in terms of quantity, but quality.

Within the ranks of the women's education movement there were debates about what the education was for, about what education – and educated women – should be. Among those who looked to education to promote sexual equality there were those who believed that women would only enjoy the same status and influence as men when women received the *same* education as men. This was the philosophy of Emily Davies and some of the other women who were instrumental in founding Girton, the first women's college at Cambridge.

As part of her long-term policy for women's independence and sexual equality – and part of her short-term policy to have women and their education taken seriously – Emily Davies insisted that the students at Girton should undertake the same education as men. For she knew the dangers of deviating from the male norm: she knew that any departure from the established male pattern would be seen not merely as a difference, but as a deficiency. And if it was not going to be said that women were unable to meet the educational standards of men, it was mandatory that women should have the same education as men.

But for those who were involved with the establishment of Newnham – the other women's college at Cambridge – the argument of the *same* education was considered neither convincing nor sound. They did not want to see women subjected to the same education as men, partly because they didn't think men's education was particularly good. Instead, the supporters of Newnham sought to use the opportunity of forming a new college to devise a new and more desirable form of education – for women, and for men. Why should women do what men had done, they asked? Why should women replicate male mistakes? Why not bring to education the benefit of women's insights and enrich and improve the entire educational process and product?

The debate on women's education at Cambridge (a debate well covered by Rita McWilliams-Tullberg, 1975) encompasses some of the philosophical differences which persist to this day, for there is still no consensus as to whether *equal* educational opportunity for the sexes can only be achieved by providing them with the *same* education.

When it comes to the issue of educational *quantity* it is clear that the nineteenth-century women's movement met with considerable success. What is now acknowledged is that, technically, women have the same opportunities as men in that, in contrast to earlier times, educational institutions are equally open to them. Objections to women's full participation in all areas are still raised and there are occasional instances when hormone levels or brain size are again cited as reasons for women's exclusion from specific subjects. But, in general, it can be agreed that women won the battle for equal educational entry. But there are other battles which women did not win.

Women did not win the battle for educational control. They did not win the battle to be in charge of their own education – nor to influence that of men. So while men opened the doors of their educational institutions to women they continued to provide for women the education that they had devised as the best education for men.

In this context it could be that the two sexes are receiving the *same* education but that it is by no means *equal*. For if it is an education about men, if it is an education that concentrates on and affirms male experience, it is not an education that equally resources the sexes. Instead, it is an education that structures inequality by enhancing the image of men, at the expense of women.

It is a common assertion that education is controlled by men: in 1978 Eileen Byrne stated that in the 'government of education' 97 per cent of the positions were held by men. One consequence of this decision-making-monopoly of men is that the educational theory and practice which they produce reflects the needs and interests of men. Wherever the needs and interests of women are different, argues Eileen Byrne, they are frequently unacknowledged, unknown and unmet.

This could well mean that educational institutions now cater no more for women than they did in the past when women were not permitted entry. This could well mean that if the different needs and interests of women are to be met, special provision must be made for them. And there has been a history of 'special provision' for women. From domestic science to women's studies the underlying rationale has been that women are different from men, that they have different requirements – and that this calls for a different education (see Mary Cathcart Borer, 1976; Sara Delamont and Lorna Duffin, 1978). This was a development that Emily Davies dreaded: she would have predicted dire consequences.

There is some evidence which suggests that she was right to do so. For the special educational needs of women have also been used to support and maintain sexual inequality and have therefore been the source of heated debate.

Clearly, any educational philosophy which begins with the reality of sex differences and which then attempts to educate for sexually differentiated ends, will do little to alter the *status quo*. It is not the ideal philosophy for those seeking to bring sexual inequality to an end. While it may seem (superficially) sensible to insist that because women are primarily responsible for the home and family they should be educated with this goal in mind, it must also be recognised that such a practice can result in women being educated for little else, and that in the end they can be limited, not liberated by their education (see Carol Dyhouse, 1981 for further discussion).

The case for the 'special needs' of women was one which was repeatedly put forward in the nineteenth century as reformers – for many reasons – reacted against the idea that women should be educated like men. It was a case that influenced educational provision and employment opportunities. And it was a case that was not without substance. For women did have very different responsibilities from men and to ignore their requirements was to deny their experience and their needs. But sadly, any attempt that was made to meet women's needs could be used to channel women away from the prestigious subjects favoured by men, or else to brand the women – and their education – as inferior to that of men.

So whether women have had the same education as men or whether they have been provided with something different, the verdict seems to be that women have not enjoyed an equally valuable or equally validated education as that experienced by men. So education has not (yet) led to the development of the society that Mary Wollstonecraft desired – one in which there is sexual equality.

This could, of course, be a failure of education itself: it may be that the eradication of sexual inequality cannot be achieved by educational means, and that alternatives are required.

Or it could be that the fault lies within the power configurations and that there will be no equal educational provision until sex inequality is eradicated and women have an equal share in educational policy and decision-making.

Or it could be that there are no cause and effect links between education and sex equality and that to put the two together – as women have done for centuries – is to introduce a false premise into the debate.

But what can be stated with some assurance is that there has been no end to the educational debate. Since the seventeenth century women have sought education and they have done so on the grounds that it would assist their own self realisation and help to end the dominance of men. In such a philosophy there is still room for much educational debate.

Dale Spender
June 1986

REFERENCES

Astell, Mary (1694), 'A Serious Proposal to the Ladies' reprinted in Katharine M. Rogers (ed.), *Before Their Time: Six Women Writers of the Eighteenth Century*, Frederick Ungar, N.Y., pp. 28–38.

Behn, Aphra, see Angeline Goreau (1980), *Reconstructing Aphra: A Social Biography of Aphra Behn*, The Dial Press, N.Y.

Borer, Mary Cathcart (1976), *Willingly to School: A History of Women's Education*, Lutterworth Press, London.

Bryant, Margaret (1979), *The Unexpected Revolution: A Study in the History of the Education of Women and Girls in the Nineteenth Century*, University of London Institute of Education.

Byrne, Eileen (1978), *Women and Education*, Tavistock, London.

Davies, Emily, see Barbara Stephen (1927), *Emily Davies and Girton College*, Constable, London.

Delamont, Sara and Duffin, Lorna (eds) (1978), *The Nineteenth Century Woman: Her Cultural and Physical World*, Croom Helm, London.

Dyhouse, Carol (1981), *Girls Growing Up in Late Victorian and Edwardian England*, Routledge & Kegan Paul, London.

Fraser, Antonia (1984), *The Weaker Vessel: Women's Lot in Seventeenth Century England*, Weidenfeld & Nicolson, London.

Macaulay, Catherine (1790), *Letters on Education*, reprinted 1974, ed. Gina Luria, Garland Publishing, N.Y.

McWilliams-Tullberg, Rita (1975), *Women at Cambridge: A Men's University – though of a Mixed Type*, Victor Gollancz, London.

'Sophia, A Person of Quality' (1739), *Woman Not Inferior to Man*, facsimile reprint, 1975, Bentham Press, London.

Williams, Raymond (1975), *The Long Revolution*, Penguin, Harmondsworth, Middlesex.

Wollstonecraft, Mary (1792), *Vindication of the Rights of Woman*, reprinted, Miriam Kramnick (ed.), 1978, Penguin, Harmondsworth, Middlesex.

George J. Romanes

Mental Differences Between Men and Women

(1887)

In his *Descent of Man* Mr Darwin has shown at length that what Hunter termed secondary sexual characters occur throughout the whole animal series, at least as far down in the zoological scale as the Articulata. The secondary sexual characters with which he is chiefly concerned are of a bodily kind, such as plumage of birds, horns of mammals, etc. But I think it is evident that secondary sexual characters of a mental kind are of no less general occurrence. Moreover, if we take a broad view of these psychological differences, it becomes instructively apparent that a general uniformity pervades them – that while within the limits of each species the male differs psychologically from the female, in the animal kingdom as a whole the males admit of being classified, as it were, in one psychological species and the females in another. By this, of course, I do not mean that there is usually a greater psychological difference between the two sexes of the same species than there is between the same sexes of different species: I mean only that the points wherein the two sexes differ psychologically are more or less similar wherever these differences occur.

It is probably due to a recognition of this fact that from the very earliest stages of culture mankind has been accustomed to read into all nature – inanimate as well as animate – differences of the same kind. Whether it be in the person of Maya, of the pagan goddesses, of the Virgin Mary, or in the personifications of sundry natural objects and processes, we uniformly encounter the conception of a feminine principle coexisting with a masculine in the general frame of the cosmos. And this fact, as I have said, is presumably due to a recognition by mankind of the uniformity as well as the generality of psychological distinction as determined by sex.

I will now briefly enumerate what appear to me the leading

features of this distinction in the case of mankind, adopting the ordinary classification of mental faculties as those of intellect, emotion, and will.

Seeing that the average brain-weight of women is about five ounces less than that of men, on merely anatomical grounds we should be prepared to expect a marked inferiority of intellectual power in the former.[1] Moreover, as the general physique of women is less robust than that of men – and therefore less able to sustain the fatigue of serious or prolonged brain action – we should also on physiological grounds be prepared to entertain a similar anticipation. In actual fact we find that the inferiority displays itself most conspicuously in a comparative absence of originality, and this more especially in the higher levels of intellectual work. In her powers of acquisition the woman certainly stands nearer to the man than she does in her powers of creative thought, although even as regards the former there is a marked difference. The difference, however, is one which does not assert itself till the period of adolescence – young girls being, indeed, usually more acquisitive than boys of the same age, as is proved by recent educational experiences both in this country and in America. But as soon as the brain, and with it the organism as a whole, reaches the stage of full development, it becomes apparent that there is a greater power of amassing knowledge on the part of the male. Whether we look to the general average or to the intellectual giants of both sexes, we are similarly met with the general fact that a woman's information is less wide and deep and thorough than that of a man. What we regard as a highly cultured woman is usually one who has read largely but superficially; and even in the few instances that can be quoted of extraordinary female industry – which on account of their rarity stand out as exceptions to prove the rule – we find a long distance between them and the much more numerous instances of profound erudition among men. As musical executants, however, I think that equality may be fairly asserted.

But it is in original work, as already observed, that the disparity is most conspicuous. For it is a matter of ordinary comment that in no one department of creative thought can women be said to have at all approached men, save in fiction. Yet in poetry, music, and painting, if not also in history, philosophy, and science, the field has always been open to both.[2] For, as I will presently show, the disabilities under which women have laboured with regard to education, social opinion, and so forth, have certainly not been sufficient to explain this general dearth among them of the products of creative genius.

Lastly, with regard to judgment, I think there can be no real question that the female mind stands considerably below the male. It is much more apt to take superficial views of circumstances calling for decision, and also to be guided by less impartiality. Undue influence is more frequently exercised from the side of the emotions; and, in general, all the elements which go to constitute what is understood by a characteristically judicial mind are of comparatively feeble development. Of course here, as elsewhere, I am speaking of average standards. It would be easy to find multitudes of instances where women display better judgment than men, just as in the analogous cases of learning and creative work. But that as a general rule the judgment of women is inferior to that of men has been a matter of universal recognition from the earliest times. The man has always been regarded as the rightful lord of the woman, to whom she is by nature subject, as both mentally and physically the weaker vessel; and when in individual cases these relations happen to be inverted, the accident becomes a favourite theme for humorists – thus showing that in the general estimation such a state of matters is regarded as incongruous.

But if woman has been a loser in the intellectual race as regards acquisition, origination, and judgment, she has gained, even on the intellectual side, certain very conspicuous advantages. First among these we must place refinement of the senses, or higher evolution of sense-organs. Next we must place rapidity of perception, which no doubt in part arises from this higher evolution of the sense-organs – or, rather, both arise from a greater refinement of nervous organisation. Houdin, who paid special attention to the acquirement of rapidity in acts of complex perception, says he has known ladies who, while seeing another lady 'pass at full speed in a carriage, could analyse her toilette from her bonnet to her shoes, and be able to describe not only the fashion and quality of the stuffs, but also to say if the lace were real or only machine made.' Again, reading implies enormously intricate processes of perception, both of the sensuous and intellectual order; and I have tried a series of experiments, wherein reading was chosen as a test of the rapidity of perception in different persons. Having seated a number of well educated individuals round a table, I presented to them successively the same paragraph of a book, which they were each to read as rapidly as they could, ten seconds being allowed for twenty lines. As soon as time was up I removed the paragraph, immediately after which the reader wrote down all that he or she could remember of it. Now, in these experiments, where every one read the same paragraph as rapidly as possible, I found that the palm was usually carried off by the ladies. Moreover, besides being able to read quicker, they were better able to remember what they had just read – this is, to give a better account of the paragraph as a whole. One lady, for example, could read exactly four times as fast as her husband, and could then give a better account even of that portion of the paragraph which alone he had had time to get through. For the consolation of such husbands, however, I may add that rapidity of perception as thus tested is no evidence of what may be termed the deeper qualities of mind – some of my slowest readers being highly distinguished men.

Lastly, rapidity of perception leads to rapidity of thought, and this finds expression on the one hand in what is apt to appear as almost intuitive insight, and on the other hand in that nimbleness of mother-wit which is usually so noticeable and often so brilliant an endowment of the feminine intelligence, whether it displays itself in tact, in repartee, or in the general alacrity of a vivacious mind.

Turning now to the emotions, we find that in woman, as contrasted with man, these are almost always less under control of the will – more apt to break away, as it were, from the restraint of reason, and to overwhelm the mental chariot in disaster. Whether this tendency displays itself in the overmastering form of hysteria, or in the more ordinary form of comparative childishness, ready annoyance, and a generally unreasonable temper – in whatever form this supremacy of emotion displays itself, we recognise it as more of a feminine than a masculine characteristic. The crying of a woman is not held to betray the same depth of feeling as the sobs of a man; and the petty forms of resentment which belong to what is known as a 'shrew,' or a 'scold,' are only to be met with among those daughters of Eve who prove themselves least agreeable to the sons of Adam. Coyness and caprice are very general peculiarities, and we may add, as kindred traits, personal vanity, fondness of display, and delight in the sunshine of admiration. There is also, as compared with the masculine mind, a greater desire for emotional excitement of all kinds, and hence a greater liking for society, pageants, and even for what are called 'scenes,' provided these are not of a kind to alarm her no less characteristic timidity. Again, in the opinion of Mr Lecky, with which I partly concur:

> In the courage of endurance they are commonly superior; but their passive courage is not so much fortitude which bears and defies, as resignation which bears and bends. In the ethics of intellect they are decidedly inferior. They very rarely love truth, though they love passionately what they call 'the truth,' or opinions which they have derived from others, and

hate vehemently those who differ from them. They are little capable of impartiality or doubt; their thinking is chiefly a mode of feeling; though very generous in their acts, they are rarely generous in their opinions or in their judgments. They persuade rather than convince, and value belief as a source of consolation rather than as a faithful expression of the reality of things.

But, of course, as expressed in the well-known lines from *Marmion*, there is another side to this picture, and, in now taking leave of all these elements of weakness, I must state my honest conviction that they are in chief part due to women as a class not having hitherto enjoyed the same educational advantages as men. Upon this great question of female education, however, I shall have more to say at the close of this paper, and only allude to the matter at the present stage in order to temper what I feel to be the almost brutal frankness of my remarks.

But now, the meritorious qualities wherein the female mind stands pre-eminent are, affection, sympathy, devotion, self-denial, modesty; long-suffering, or patience under pain, disappointment, and adversity; reverence, veneration, religious feeling, and general morality. In these virtues – which agree pretty closely with those against which the Apostle says there is no law – it will be noticed that the gentler predominate over the heroic; and it is observable in this connection that when heroism of any kind is displayed by a woman, the prompting emotions are almost certain to be of an unselfish kind.

All the aesthetic emotions are, as a rule, more strongly marked in women than in men – or, perhaps, I should rather say, they are much more generally present in women. This remark applies especially to the aesthetic emotions which depend upon refinement of perception. Hence feminine 'taste' is proverbially good in regard to the smaller matters of everyday life, although it becomes, as a rule, untrustworthy in proportion to the necessity for intellectual judgment. In the arrangement of flowers, the furnishing of rooms, the choice of combinations in apparel, and so forth, we generally find that we may be most safely guided by the taste of women; while in matters of artistic or literary criticism we turn instinctively to the judgment of men.

If we now look in somewhat more detail at the habitual display of these various feelings and virtues on the part of women, we may notice, with regard to affection, that, in a much larger measure than men, they derive pleasure from receiving as well as from bestowing: in both cases affection is felt by them to be, as it were, of more emotional value. The same remark applies to sympathy. It is very rare to find a woman who does not derive consolation from a display of sympathy, whether her sorrow be great or small; while it is by no means an unusual thing to find a man who rejects all offers of the kind with a feeling of active aversion.

Touching devotion, we may note that it is directed by women pretty equally towards inferiors and superiors – spending and being spent in the tending of children; ministering to the poor, the afflicted, and the weak; clinging to husbands, parents, brothers, often without and even against reason.

Again, purity and religion are, as it were, the natural heritage of women in all but the lowest grades of culture. But it is within the limit of Christendom that both these characters are most strongly pronounced; as, indeed, may equally well be said of nearly all the other virtues which we have just been considering. And the reason is that Christianity, while crowning the virtue of chastity with an aureole of mysticism more awful than was ever conceived even by pagan Rome, likewise threw the vesture of sanctity over all the other virtues which belong by nature to the female mind. Until the rise of Christianity the gentler and domestic virtues were nowhere recognised as at all comparable, in point of ethical merit, with the heroic and the civic. But when the ideal was changed by Christ – when the highest place in the hierarchy of the virtues was assigned to faith, hope, and charity; to piety, patience, and long-suffering; to forgiveness, self-denial, and even self-abasement – we cannot wonder that, in so extraordinary a collision between the ideals of virtue, it should have been the women who first flocked in numbers around the standard of the Cross.

So much, then, for the intellect and emotions. Coming lastly to the will, I have already observed that this exercises less control over the emotions in women than in men. We rarely find in women that firm tenacity of purpose and determination to over-come obstacles which is characteristic of what we call a manly mind. When a woman is urged to any prolonged or powerful exercise of volition, the prompting cause is usually to be found in the emotional side of her nature, whereas in man we may generally observe that the intellectual is alone sufficient to supply the needed motive. Moreover, even in those lesser displays of volitional activity which are required in close reading, or in studious thought, we may note a similar deficiency. In other words, women are usually less able to concentrate their attention; their minds are more prone to what is called 'wandering,' and we seldom find that they have specialised their studies or pursuits to the same extent as is usual among men. This comparative weakness of will is further manifested by the frequency among women of what is popularly termed indecision of character. The proverbial fickleness of *la donna mobile* is due quite as much to vacillation of will as to other unstable qualities of mental constitution. The ready firmness of decision which belongs by nature to the truly masculine mind is very rarely to be met with in the feminine; while it is not an unusual thing to find among women indecision of character so habitual and pronounced as to become highly painful to themselves – leading to timidity and diffidence in adopting almost any line of conduct where issues of importance are concerned, and therefore leaving them in the condition, as they graphically express it, of not knowing their own minds.

If, now, we take a general survey of all these mental differences, it becomes apparent that in the feminine type the characteristic virtues, like the characteristic failings, are those which are born of weakness; while in the masculine type the characteristic failings, like the characteristic virtues, are those which are born of strength. Which we are to consider the higher type will therefore depend on the value which we assign to mere force. Under one point of view, the magnificent spider of South America, which is large enough and strong enough to devour a humming-bird, deserves to be regarded as the superior creature. But under another point of view, there is no spectacle in nature more shockingly repulsive than the slow agonies of the most beautiful of created beings in the hairy limbs of a monster so far beneath it in the sentient as in the zoological scale. And although the contrast between man and woman is happily not so pronounced in degree, it is nevertheless a contrast the same in kind. The whole organisation of woman is formed on a plan of greater delicacy, and her mental structure is correspondingly more refined: it is further removed from the struggling instincts of the lower animals, and thus more nearly approaches our conception of the spiritual. For even the failings of weakness are less obnoxious than the vices of strength, and I think it is unquestionable that these vices are of quite as frequent occurrence on the part of men as are those failings on the part of women. The hobnailed boots may have given place to patent-pumps, and yet but small improvement may have been made upon the overbearing temper of a navvy; the beer-shop may have been superseded by the whist-club, and yet the selfishness of pleasure-seeking may still habitually leave the solitary wife to brood over her lot through the small hours of the morning. Moreover, even when the mental hobnails have been removed, we generally find that there still remains what a member of the fairer sex has recently and aptly designated mental heavy-handedness. By this I understand the clumsy inability of a coarser nature to appreciate the feelings of a finer; and how often such is the case we must leave the sufferers to testify. In short, the vices of strength to which I allude are those which have been born of rivalry: the mental hide has been hardened, and the man carries into his home those qualities of insensibility, self-assertion, and self-seeking which have elsewhere led to success in his struggle for supremacy. Or, as Mr Darwin says, 'Man is the rival of other men; he delights in competition, and this leads to ambition which passes too readily into selfishness. These latter qualities seem to be his natural and unfortunate birthright.'

Of course the greatest type of manhood, or the type wherein our ideal of manliness reaches its highest expression, is where the virtues of strength are purged from its vices. To be strong and yet tender, brave and yet kind, to combine in the same breast the temper of a hero with the sympathy of a maiden – this is to transform the ape and the tiger into what we know ought to constitute the man. And if in actual life we find that such an ideal is but seldom realised, this should make us more lenient in judging the frailties of the opposite sex. These frailties are for the most part the natural consequences of our own, and even where such is not the case, we do well to remember, as already observed, that they are less obnoxious than our own, and also that it is the privilege of strength to be tolerant. Now, it is a practical recognition of these things that leads to chivalry; and even those artificial courtesies which wear the mark of chivalry are of value, as showing what may be termed a conventional acquiescence in the truth that underlies them. This truth is, that the highest type of manhood can only then be reached when the heart and mind have been so far purified from the dross of a brutal ancestry as genuinely to appreciate, to admire, and to reverence the greatness, the beauty, and the strength which have been made perfect in the weakness of womanhood.

I will now pass on to consider the causes which have probably operated in producing all these mental differences between men and women. We have already seen that differences of the same kind occur throughout the whole mammalian series, and therefore we must begin by looking below the conditions of merely human life for the original causes of these differences in their most general form. Nor have we far to seek. The Darwinian principles of selection – both natural and sexual – if ever they have operated in any department of organic nature, must certainly have operated here. Thus, to quote Darwin himself:

Amongst the half-human progenitors of man, and amongst savages, there have been struggles between the males during many generations for the possession of the females. But mere bodily strength and size would do little for victory, unless associated with courage, perseverance, and determined energy. . . . To avoid enemies or to attack them with success, to capture wild animals, and to fashion weapons, requires reason, invention, or imagination. . . . These latter faculties, as well as the former, will have been developed in man partly through sexual selection – that is, through the contest of rival males – and partly through natural selection – that is, from success in the general struggle for life; and as in both cases the struggle will have been during maturity, the characters gained will have been transmitted more fully to the male than to the female offspring. . . . Thus man has ultimately become superior to woman. It is, indeed, fortunate that the law of the equal transmission of characters to both sexes prevails with mammals; otherwise it is probable that man would have become as superior in mental endowment to woman as the peacock is in ornamental plumage to the pea-hen.

Similarly, Mr. Francis Galton writes:

The fundamental and intrinsic differences of character that exist in individuals are well illustrated by those that distinguish the two sexes, and which begin to assert themselves even in the nursery, where all children are treated alike. One notable peculiarity in the woman is that she is capricious and coy, and has less straightforwardness than the man. It is the same with the female of every species. . . . [Were it not so] the drama of courtship, with its prolonged strivings and doubtful success, would be cut quite short, and the race would degenerate through the absence of that sexual selection for which the protracted preliminaries of love-making give opportunity. The willy-nilly disposition of the female is as apparent in the butterfly as in the man, and must have been continually favoured from the earliest stages of animal evolution down to the present time. Coyness and caprice have in consequence become a heritage of the sex, together with a cohort of allied weaknesses and petty deceits, that men have come to think venial, and even amiable, in women, but which they would not tolerate among themselves.

We see, then, that the principles of selection have thus determined greater strength, both of body and mind, on the part of male animals throughout the whole mammalian series; and it would certainly have been a most unaccountable fact if any exception to this rule had occurred in the case of mankind. For, as regards natural selection, it is in the case of mankind that the highest premium has been placed upon the mental faculties – or, in other words, it is here that natural selection has been most busy in the evolution of intelligence – and therefore, as Mr Darwin remarks, we can only regard it as a fortunate accident of inheritance that there is not now a greater difference between the intelligence of men and of women than we actually find. Again, as regards sexual selection, it is evident that here also the psychologically segregating influences must have been exceptionally strong in the case of our own species, seeing that in all the more advanced stages of civilisation – or in the stages where mental evolution is highest, and, therefore, mental differences most pronounced – marriages are determined quite as much with reference to psychical as to physical endowments; and as men always admire in women what they regard as distinctively feminine qualities of mind, while women admire in men the distinctively masculine, sexual selection, by thus acting directly as well as indirectly on the mental qualities of both, is constantly engaged in moulding the minds of each upon a different pattern.

Such, then, I take to be the chief, or at least the original, causes of the mental differences in question. But besides these there are sundry other causes all working in the same direction. For example, as the principles of selection have everywhere operated in the direction of endowing the weaker partner with that kind of physical beauty which comes from slenderness and grace, it follows that there has been everywhere a general tendency to impart to her a comparative refinement of organisation; and in no species has this been the case in so high a degree as in man. Now, it is evident from what has been said in an earlier part of this paper, that general refinement of this kind indirectly affects the mind in many ways. Again, as regards the analogous, though coarser, distinction of bodily strength, it is equally evident that their comparative inferiority in this respect, while itself one of the results of selection, becomes in turn the cause of their comparative timidity, sense of dependence, and distrust of their own powers on the part of women, considered as a class. Hence, also, their comparative feebleness of will and vacillation of purpose: they are always dimly conscious of lacking the muscular strength which, in the last resort, and especially in primitive stages of culture, is the measure of executive capacity. Hence, also, their resort to petty arts and pretty ways for the securing of their aims; and hence, in large measure, their strongly religious bias. The masculine character, being accustomed to rely upon its own strength, is self-central and self-contained: to it the need of external aid, even of a supernatural kind, is not felt to be so urgent as it is to the feminine character, whose only hope is in the stronger arm of another. 'The position of man is to stand, of woman to lean;' and although it may be hard for even a manly nature to contemplate the mystery of life and the approach of death with a really stoic calm, at least this is not so impossible as it is for the more shrinking and emotional nature of a woman. Lastly, from her abiding sense of weakness and consequent dependence, there also arises in woman that deeply-rooted desire to please the opposite sex which, beginning in the terror of a slave, has ended in the devotion of a wife.

We must next observe another psychological lever of enormous power in severing the mental structures of men and women. Alike in expanding all the tender emotions, in calling up from the deepest fountains of feeling the flow of purest affection, in imposing the duties of rigid self-denial, in arousing under its strongest form the consciousness of protecting the utterly weak and helpless consigned by nature to her charge, the maternal instincts are to woman perhaps the strongest of all influences in the determination of character. And their influence in this respect continues to operate long after the child has ceased to be an infant. Constant association with her growing children – round all of whom her affections are closely twined, and in all of whom the purest emotions of humanity are as yet untouched by intellect – imparts to the mother a fulness of emotional life, the whole quality of which is distinctively feminine. It has been well remarked by Mr Fiske that the prolonged period of infancy and childhood in the human species must from the first 'have gradually tended to strengthen the relations of the children to the mother,' and, we may add, also to strengthen the relations of the mother to the children – which implies an immense impetus to the growth in her of all the altruistic feelings most distinctive of woman. Thus, in accordance with the general law of inheritance as limited by sex, we can understand how these influences became, in successive generations, cumulative; while in the fondness of little girls for dolls we may note a somewhat interesting example in psychology of the law of inheritance at earlier periods of life, which Mr Darwin has shown to be so prevalent in the case of bodily structures throughout the animal kingdom.

There remains, so far as I can see, but one other cause which can be assigned of the mental differences between men and women. This cause is education. Using the term in its largest sense, we may say that in all stages of culture the education of women has differed widely from that of men. The state of abject slavery to which woman is consigned in the lower levels of human evolution clearly tends to dwarf her mind *ab initio*. And as woman gradually emerges from this her primitive and long-protracted condition of slavery, she still continues to be dominated by the man in number-less ways, which, although of a less brutal kind, are scarcely less effectual as mentally dwarfing influences. The stunting tendency upon the female mind of all polygamous institutions is notorious, and even in monogamous, or quasi-monogamous, communities so highly civilised as ancient Greece and pagan Rome, woman was still, as it were, an intellectual cipher – and this at a time when the intellect of man had attained an eminence which has never been equalled. Again, for a period of about 2,000 years after that time civilised woman was the victim of what I may term the ideal of domestic utility – a state of matters which still continues in some of the continental nations of Europe. Lastly, even when woman began to escape from this ideal of domestic utility, it was only to fall a victim to the scarcely less deleterious ideal of ornamentalism. Thus Sydney Smith, writing in 1810, remarks: 'A century ago the prevailing taste in female education was for housewifery; now it is for accomplishments. The object now is to make women artists – to give them an excellence in drawing, music, and dancing.' It is almost needless to remark that this is still the prevailing taste: the ideal of female education still largely prevalent in the upper classes is not that of mental furnishing, but rather of mental decor-ation. For it was not until the middle of the present century that the first attempt was made to provide for the higher education of women, by the establishment of Queen's College and Bedford College in London. Twenty years later there followed Girton and Newnham at Cambridge; later still Lady Margaret and Somerville at Oxford, the foundation of the Girls' Public Day Schools Company, the opening of degrees to women at the University of London, and of the honour examinations at Cambridge and Oxford.

We see, then, that with advancing civilisation the theoretical equality of the sexes becomes more and more a matter of general recognition, but that the natural inequality continues to be forced upon the observation of the public mind; and chiefly on this account – although doubtless also on account of traditional usage – the education of women continues to be, as a general rule, widely different from that of men. And this difference is not merely in the positive direction of laying greater stress on psychological embellishment: it extends also in the negative direction of sheltering the female mind from all those influences of a striving and struggling kind, which constitute the practical schooling of the male intellect. Woman is still regarded by public opinion all the world over as a psychological plant of tender growth, which needs to be protected from the ruder blasts of social life in the conservatories of civilisation. And, from what has been said in the earlier part of this paper, it will be apparent that in this practical judgment I believe public opinion to be right. I am, of course, aware that there is a small section of the public – composed for the most part of persons who are not accustomed to the philosophical analysis of facts – which argues that the conspicuous absence of women in the field of intellectual work is due to the artificial restraints imposed upon them by all the traditional forms of education; that if we could suddenly make a leap of progress in this respect, and allow women everywhere to compete on fair and equal terms with men, then, under these altered circumstances of social life, women would prove themselves the intellectual compeers of man.

But the answer to this argument is almost painfully obvious. Although it is usually a matter of much difficulty to distinguish between nature and nurture, or between the results of inborn faculty and those of acquired knowledge, in the present instance no such difficulty obtains. Without again recurring to the anatomical and physiological considerations which bar *a priori* any argument for the natural equality of the sexes, and without remarking that the human female would but illustrate her own deficiency of rational development by supposing that any exception to the general laws of evolution can have been made in her favour – without dwelling on any such antecedent considerations, it is enough to repeat that in many departments of intellectual work the field *has* been open, and equally open, to both sexes. If to this it is answered that the traditional usages of education lead to a higher average of culture among men, thus furnishing them with a better vantage-ground for the origin of individual genius, we have only to add that the strong passion of genius is not to be restrained by any such minor accidents of environment. Women by tens of thousands have enjoyed better educational as well as better social advantages than a Burns, a Keats, or a Faraday; and yet we have neither heard their voices nor seen their work.

If, again, to this it be rejoined that the female mind has been unjustly dealt with in the past, and cannot now be expected all at once to throw off the accumulated disabilities of ages – that the long course of shameful neglect to which the selfishness of man has subjected the culture of woman has necessarily left its mark upon the hereditary constitution of her mind – if this consideration be adduced, it obviously does not tend to prove the equality of the sexes: it merely accentuates the fact of inequality by indicating one of its causes. The treatment of women in the past may have been very wrong, very shameful, and very much to be regretted by the present advocates of women's rights; but proof of the ethical quality of this fact does not get rid of the fact itself, any more than a proof of the criminal nature of assassination can avail to restore to life a murdered man. We must look the facts in the face. How long it may take the woman of the future to recover the ground which has been lost in the psychological race by the woman of the past, it is impossible to say; but we may predict with confidence that, even under the most favourable conditions as to culture, and even supposing the mind of man to remain stationary (and not, as is probable, to advance with a speed relatively accelerated by the momentum of its already acquired velocity), it must take many centuries for heredity to produce the missing five ounces of the female brain.

In conclusion, a few words may be added on the question of female education as this actually stands at the present time. Among all the features of progress which will cause the present century to be regarded by posterity as beyond comparison the most remarkable epoch in the history of our race, I believe that the inauguration of the so-called woman's movement in our own generation will be considered one of the most important. For I am persuaded that this movement is destined to grow; that with its growth the highest attributes of one half of the human race are destined to be widely influenced; that this influence will profoundly react upon the other half, not alone in the nursery and the drawing-room, but also in the study, the academy, the forum, and the senate; that this latest yet inevitable wave of mental evolution cannot be stayed until it has changed the whole aspect of civilisation. In an essay already alluded to, Sydney Smith has remarked, though not quite correctly, that up to his time there had been no woman who had produced a single notable work, either of reason or imagination, whether in English, French, German, or Italian literature. A few weeks ago Mrs Fawcett was able to show us that since then there have been at least forty women who have left a permanent mark in English literature alone. Now, this fact becomes one of great significance when we remember that it is the result of but the earliest phase of the woman's movement. For, as already indicated, this movement is now plainly of the nature of a ferment. When I was at Cambridge, the then newly established foundations of Girton and Newnham were to nearly all of us matters of amusement. But we have lived to alter our views; for we have lived to see that that was but the beginning of a great social change, which has since spread and is still spreading at so extraordinary a rate, that we are now within measurable distance of the time when no English lady will be found to have escaped its influence. It is not merely that women's colleges are springing up like mushrooms in all quarters of the kingdom, or that the old type of young ladies' governess is being rapidly starved out of existence. It is of much more importance even than this that the immense reform in girls' education, which has been so recently introduced by the Day Schools Company working in conjunction with the University Board and local examinations, has already shaken to its base the whole system and even the whole ideal of female education, so that there is scarcely a private school in the country which has not been more or less affected by the change. In a word, whether we like it or not, the woman's movement is upon us; and what we have now to do is to guide the flood into what seem likely to prove the most beneficial channels. What are these channels?

Of all the pricks against which it is hard to kick the hardest are those which are presented by nature in the form of facts. Therefore we may begin by wholly disregarding those short-sighted enthusiasts who seek to overcome the natural and fundamental distinction of sex. No amount of female education can ever do this, nor is it desirable that it should. On this point I need not repeat what is now so often and so truly said, as to woman being the complement, not the rival, of man. But I should like to make one remark of another kind. The idea underlying the utterances of all these enthusiasts seems to be that the qualities wherein the male mind excels that of the female are, *sui generis*, the most exalted of human faculties: these good ladies fret and fume in a kind of jealousy that the minds, like the bodies, of men are stronger than those of women. Now, is not this a radically mistaken view? Mere strength, as I have already endeavoured to insinuate, is not the highest criterion of nobility. Human nature is a very complex thing, and among the many ingredients which go to make the greatness of it even intellectual power is but one, and not by any means the chief. The truest grandeur of that nature is revealed by that nature as a whole, and here I think there can be no doubt that the feminine type is fully equal to the masculine, if indeed it be not superior. For I believe that if we all go back in our memories to seek for the highest experience we have severally had in this respect, the character which will stand out as all in all the greatest we have ever known will be the character of a woman. Or, if any of us have not been fortunate in this matter, where in fiction or in real life can we find a more glorious exhibition of all that is best –

the mingled strength and beauty, tact, gaiety, devotion, wit, and consummate ability – where but in a woman can we find anything at once so tender, so noble, so lovable, and so altogether splendid as in the completely natural character of a Portia? A mere blue-stocking who looks with envy on the intellectual gifts of a Voltaire, while shutting her eyes to the gifts of a sister such as this, is simply unworthy of having such a sister: she is incapable of distinguishing the pearl of great price among the sundry other jewels of our common humanity.

Now, the suspicion, not to say the active hostility, with which the so-called woman's movement has been met in many quarters springs from a not unhealthy ground of public opinion. For there can be no real doubt that these things are but an expression of the value which that feeling attaches to all which is held distinctive of feminine character as it stands. Woman, as she has been bequeathed to us by the many and complex influences of the past, is recognised as too precious an inheritance lightly to be tampered with; and the dread lest any change in the conditions which have given us this inheritance should lead, as it were, to desecration, is in itself both wise and worthy. In this feeling we have the true safeguard of womanhood; and we can hope for nothing better than that the deep strong voice of social opinion will always be raised against any innovations of culture which may tend to spoil the sweetest efflorescence of evolution.

But, while we may hope that social opinion may ever continue opposed to the woman's movement in its most extravagant forms – or to those forms which endeavour to set up an unnatural, and therefore an impossible, rivalry with men in the struggles of prac-tical life – we may also hope that social opinion will soon become unanimous in its encouragement of the higher education of women. Of the distinctively feminine qualities of mind which are admired as such by all, ignorance is certainly not one. Therefore learning, as learning, can never tend to deteriorate those qualities. On the contrary, it can only tend to refine the already refined, to beautify the already beautiful – 'when our daughters shall be as corner-stones, polished after the similitude of a palace.' It can only tend the better to equip a wife as the helpmeet of her husband, and, by furthering a community of tastes, to weave another bond in the companionship of life. It can only tend the better to prepare a mother for the greatest of her duties – forming the tastes and guiding the minds of her children at a time of life when these are most pliable, and under circumstances of influence such as can never again be reproduced.

It is nearly eighty years ago since this view of the matter was thus presented by Sydney Smith:

> If you educate women to attend to dignified and important subjects, you are multiplying beyond measure the chances of human improvement by preparing and medicating those early impressions which always come from the mother, and which, in the majority of instances, are quite decisive of genius. The instruction of women improves the stock of national talents, and employs more minds for the instruction and improvement of the world: it increases the pleasures of society by multiplying the topics upon which the two sexes take a common interest, and makes marriage an intercourse of understanding as well as of affection. The education of women favours public morals; it provides for every season of life, and leaves a woman when she is stricken by the hand of time, not as she now is, destitute of everything and neglected by all, but with the full power and the splendid attractions of knowledge – diffusing the elegance of polite literature, and receiving the homage of learned and accomplished men.

Since the days when this was written, the experiment of thus educating women to attend to dignified and important subjects has been tried on a scale of rapidly increasing magnitude, and the result has been to show that those apprehensions of public opinion were groundless which supposed that the effect of higher education upon women would be to deteriorate the highest qualities of womanhood. On this point I think it is sufficient to quote the opinion of a lady who has watched the whole course of this experiment, and who is so well qualified to give an opinion that it would be foolish presumption in anyone else to dispute what she has to say. The lady to whom I refer is Mrs Sidgwick, and this is what she says:

> The students that I have known have shown no inclination to adapt masculine sentiments or habits in any unnecessary or unseemly degree; they are disposed to imitate the methods of life and work of industrious undergraduates just as far as these appear to be means approved by experience to the end which both sets of students have in common, and nothing that I have seen of them, either at the University or afterwards, has tended in the smallest degree to support the view that the adaptation of women to domestic life is so artificial and conventional a thing that a few years of free unhampered

study and varied companionship at the University has a tendency to impair it.

So far as I am aware, only one other argument has been, or can
be, adduced on the opposite side. This argument is that the physique of young women as a class is not sufficiently robust to stand
the strain of severe study, and therefore that many are likely to
impair their health more or less seriously under the protracted
effort and acute excitement which are necessarily incidental to our
system of school and university examinations. Now, I may begin
by remarking that with this argument I am in the fullest possible
sympathy. Indeed, so much is this the case that I have taken the
trouble to collect evidence from young girls of my own acquaintance who are now studying at various high schools with a view to
subsequently competing for first classes in the Cambridge triposes.
What I have found is that in some of these high schools – carefully
observe, only in *some* – absolutely no check is put upon the
ambition of young girls to distinguish themselves and to bring
credit upon their establishments. The consequence is that in these
schools the more promising pupils habitually undertake an amount
of intellectual work which it is sheer madness to attempt. A single
quotation from one of my correspondents – whom I have known
from a child – will be enough to prove this statement.

I never begin work later than six o'clock, and never work
less than ten or eleven hours a day. But within a fortnight
or so of my examinations I work fifteen or sixteen hours.
Most girls, however, stop at fourteen or fifteen hours, but
some of them go on to eighteen hours. Of course, according
to the school time-tables, none of us should work more than
eight hours; but it is quite impossible for any one to get
through the work in that time. For instance, in the time-
tables ten minutes is put down for botany, whereas it takes
the quickest girl an hour and a half to answer the questions
set by the school lecturer.

These facts speak for themselves, and therefore I will only add
that in many of those high schools for girls which are situated in
large towns no adequate provision is made for bodily exercise, and
this, of course, greatly aggravates the danger of over-work. In
such a school there is probably no playground; the gymnasium, if
there is one, is not attended by any of the harder students; drill is
never thought of; and the only walking exercise is to and from the
school. Let it not be supposed that I am attacking the high school
system. On the contrary, I believe that this system represents the

greatest single reform that has ever been made in the way of education. I am only pointing out certain grave abuses of the system which are to be met with in some of these schools, and against which I should like to see the full force of public opinion directed. There is no public school in the kingdom where a boy of sixteen would be permitted to work from eleven to eighteen hours a day, with no other exercise than a few minutes' walk. Is it not, then, simply monstrous that a girl should be allowed to do so? I must confess that I have met with wonderfully few cases of serious breakdown. All my informants tell me that, even under the operation of so insane an abuse as I have quoted, grave impairment of health but rarely occurs. This, however, only goes to show of what good stuff our English girls are made; and therefore may be taken to furnish about the strongest answer I can give to the argument which I am considering – viz. that the strength of an average English girl is not to be trusted for sustaining any reasonable amount of intellectual work. Upon this point, however, there is at the present time a conflict of medical authority, and as I have no space to give a number of quotations, it must suffice to make a few general remarks.

In the first place, the question is one of fact, and must therefore be answered by the results of the large and numerous experiments which are now in progress; not by any *a priori* reasoning of a physiological kind. In the next place, even as thus limited, the inquiry must take account of the wisdom or unwisdom with which female education is pursued in the particular cases investigated. As already remarked, I have been myself astonished to find so great an amount of prolonged endurance exhibited by young girls who are allowed to work at unreasonable pressure; but, all the same, I should of course regard statistics drawn from such cases as manifestly unfair. And seeing that every case of health impaired is another occasion given to the enemies of female education, those who have the interests of such education at heart should before all things see to it that the teaching of girls be conducted with the most scrupulous precautions against over-pressure. Regarded merely as a matter of policy, it is at the present moment of far more importance that girls should not be over-strained than that they should prove themselves equal to young men in the class lists. For my own part, I believe that, with reasonable precautions against over-pressure, and with due provision for bodily exercise, the higher education of women would *ipso facto* silence the voice of medical opposition. But I am equally persuaded that this can never be the case until it becomes a matter of general recognition among those to whom such education is entrusted, that no girl should ever be allowed to work more than eight hours a day as a *maximum*; that even this will in a large proportional number of cases be found to prove excessive; that without abundant exercise higher education should never be attempted; and that, as a girl is more liable than a boy to insidiously undermine her constitution, every girl who aspires to any distinction in the way of learning should be warned to be constantly on the watch for the earliest symptoms of impairment. If these reasonable precautions were to become as universal in the observance as they now are in the breach, I believe it would soon stand upon the unquestionable evidence of experimental proof, that there is no reason in the nature of things why women should not admit of culture as wide and deep and thorough as our schools and universities are able to provide.

The channels, therefore, into which I should like to see the higher education of women directed are not those which run straight athwart the mental differences between men and women which we have been considering. These differences are all complementary to one another, fitly and beautifully joined together in the social organism. If we attempt to disregard them, or try artificially to make of woman an unnatural copy of man, we are certain to fail, and to turn out as our result a sorry and disappointed creature who is neither the one thing nor the other. But if, without expecting women as a class to enter into any professional or otherwise foolish rivalry with men, for which as a class they are neither physically nor mentally fitted, and if, as Mrs Lynn Linton remarks, we do not make the mistake of confusing mental development with intellectual specialisation – if, without doing either of these things, we encourage women in every way to obtain for themselves the intrinsic advantages of learning, it is as certain as anything can well be that posterity will bless us for our pains. For then all may equally enjoy the privilege of a real acquaintance with letters; ladies need no longer be shut out from a solid understanding of music or painting; lecturers on science will no longer be asked at the close of their lectures whether the cerebellum is inside or outside of the skull, how is it that astronomers have been able to find out the names of the stars, or whether one does not think that his diagram of a jelly-fish serves with admirable fidelity to illustrate the movements of the solar system. These, of course, I quote as extreme cases, and even as displaying the prettiness which belongs to a child-like simplicity. But simplicity of this kind ought to be put away with other childish things; and in whatever measure it is allowed to continue after childhood is over, the human being has failed to grasp the full privileges of human life. Therefore, in my opinion the days are past when any enlightened man ought seriously to suppose that in now again reaching forth her hand to eat of the tree of knowledge woman is preparing for the human race a second fall. In the person of her admirable representative, Mrs Fawcett, she thus pleads: 'No one of those who care most for the woman's movement cares one jot to prove or to maintain that men's brains and women's brains are exactly alike or exactly equal. All we ask is that the social and legal status of women should be such as to foster, not to suppress, any gift for art, literature, learning, or goodness with which women may be endowed.' Then, I say, give her the apple, and see what comes of it. Unless I am greatly mistaken, the result will be that which is so philosophically as well as so poetically portrayed by the Laureate:

> The woman's cause is man's: they rise or sink
> Together, dwarf'd or god-like, bond or free.
>
> .   .   .   .
>
>   Then let her make herself her own
> To give or keep, to live and learn to be
> All that not harms distinctive womanhood.
> For woman is not undevelopt man,
> But diverse: could we make her as the man,
> Sweet Love were slain: his dearest bond is this,
> Not like to like, but like in difference.
>
> Yet in the long years liker must they grow;
> The man be more of woman, she of man;
> He gain in sweetness and in moral height,
> Nor lose the wrestling thews that throw the world;
> She mental breadth, nor fail in childward care,
> Nor lose the child-like in the larger mind;
> Till at the last she set herself to man,
> Like perfect music unto noble words.
>
> .   .   .   .
>
> Then comes the statelier Eden back to men:
> Then reign the world's great bridals, chaste and calm:
> Then springs the crowning race of human kind.
> May these things be!

NOTES

1 'This is proportionally a greater difference than that between the male and female organisms as a whole, and the amount of it is largely affected

by grade of civilisation – being least in savages and most in ourselves. Moreover, Sir J. Crichton Browne informs me, as a result of many observations which he is now making upon the subject, that not only is the grey matter, or cortex, of the female brain shallower than that of the male, but also receives less than a proportional supply of blood. For these reasons, and also because the differences in question date from an embryonic period of life, he concludes that they constitute 'a fundamental sexual distinction, and not one that can be explained on the hypothesis that the educational advantages enjoyed either by the individual man or by the male sex generally through a long series of generations have stimulated the growth of the brain in the one sex more than in the other.'

2 The disparity in question is especially suggestive in the case of poetry, seeing that this is the oldest of the fine arts which have come down to us in a high degree of development, that its exercise requires least special education or technical knowledge, that at no level of culture has such exercise been ostracised as unfeminine, that nearly all languages present several monuments of poetic genius of the first order, and yet that no one of these has been reared by a woman.

Founding of Queen's College

(1850)

Queen's College was opened on the 1st May, 1848. It was an offshoot from the Governesses' Benevolent Institution; which is a Society having for its design to benefit an important and very interesting class of our countrywomen, not only by affording assistance to them when in difficulty, sickness and old age, but by raising the standard of their accomplishments and thus entitling them to higher remuneration. With a view to these latter objects, the conductors of that Institution were led to the plan of examining into the attainments of governesses in quest of situations, and granting certificates of approval to those who could stand the test. But they soon discovered that 'to do any real good they must go farther; they must fit the governesses for their examination; they must provide an education for female teachers'. Finally, they came to the resolution that it was expedient to extend that instruction beyond the governess in fact and the governess in prospect, to all and sundry who might choose to avail themselves of it.

The result has been the establishment of Queen's College in its present form; an institution, namely where lectures are given in the various branches of female education, according to the enlarged requirements of the present day, in classes open to all ladies of twelve years old and upwards, on payment of a moderate fee per quarter. About two hundred and fifty are understood to be now on the list of pupils, the number in each class averaging about twenty, and the number of classes which each individual attends varying at pleasure . . . There are preparatory classes for young ladies from nine to twelve years of age; and also evening classes for governesses already engaged in the duties of their profession. In these last the instruction given is entirely gratuitous: 'they have been attended by above seventy ladies engaged in tuition, for the most part every evening: many of them at the head of schools, some connected with public institutions, some governesses of considerable standing'.

'Queen's College', *Quarterly Review*, vol. 86, 1850

Barbara Leigh Smith Bodichon

An American School

(1858)

'In a shop where we went to buy a pair of gloves, I entered into conversation with the shopman, – quite a gentleman he was, – and asked a great many questions about the common schools, which he answered to my satisfaction, for you know, perhaps, that Ohio is remarkable for its schools, and Cincinnati for the excellent school books there published.

The shopman said, "Call on Mr Cady, he is a director of the schools, and will be happy to show you everything;" and "right away," as they say, we went to Mr Cady's house, a quaker-like little man, who received us in the heartiest manner in his drawing-room, and was "enchanted to show us the institutions of his country." We went to the intermediate school, for there are three grades of schools, – the lowest, intermediate, and high school: age is not the qualification for admission, but attainment. The building of the intermediate school was about as large as four middle-class English houses, containing six large clean rooms, and six teachers, three men and three women. I should have said it was magnificent for a school, but Mr Cady says it was the first built and the meanest building they have. We went into Miss D'Orfeuille's room first. Please let me present Miss D'Orfeuille to you, an elegant young lady, well dressed, black hair and eyes, very striking looking, almost beautiful; her father was French, and she has something of the south in her. Her pupils are nice looking, all dressed well enough to keep out the cold; the boys look of a rougher class than the girls, because American girls have indescribable airs and graces, and expansive crinolines; their ages were from eleven to sixteen, and one boy even seventeen or eighteen; – average, twelve.

Miss D'Orfeuille was giving them a lesson in history – as usual, the history of America, for in this intermediate school they study

34

no other. In the high school they begin with English history and study general history after. They seemed interested and knew a great deal.

Then we went to another room, and were received by the principal of the school, Mr Masson, one of those nervous active-brained teachers one knows so well, a man whose whole soul was in the work. He was asking questions in mental arithmetic of a large class of boys and girls, questions in interest and compound interest, and it was marvellous the way in which they were answered by both boys and girls. I said to Mr Masson, "Do you find any difference in boys and girls?" "No, none whatever, they learn exactly the same things, and are, comparing all the boys with all the girls, exactly the same in capacity." Now this is very valuable testimony, for Mr Masson has taught some thousands of boys and girls. This was his experience; his theory was, that if girls went into the highest branches of mathematics they would fail. Of this he had no proof.

I went into another room of eighty or ninety girls and boys taught by a young woman, and then went down to Miss D'Orfeu-ille, who quite fascinated me, and heard fifteen or twenty girls read their compositions, some were good – one especially, describing different homes, the drunkard's home was very strongly delineated with very black colouring. But it is a mistake to make the children write compositions. Abstracts of reading are much better. As soon as the children left, I had a long chat with Miss D'O., when she said the girls were not so good as the boys to teach, and she found them less quick at arithmetic. I said, "I believe you like teaching boys best, even when they are less quick than girls." "Certainly I do," she said. "That is why your girls are not so forward." "Well perhaps it is, but you see the girls have no reason to be quick at calculating interest or at book-keeping, they will not make any use of their knowledge." I then asked "what their professions would be?" She said, "those who did anything would be teachers. I get ninety five pounds a year, some lady teachers one hundred pounds, Mr Masson two hundred and fifty pounds; women who do exactly the same work as men, get half the pay. The subjects taught in the school, are singing, reading, writing, arithmetic, geography, history, and composition. There are few diagrams used, and no pictures nor maps on the walls. The history and geography lessons are learned at home, so many pages to a lesson."

I remarked a want of general lessons and knowledge of common things. I thought of Mr Shields and how superior his school is to all others, known to me, in this respect. The twelve-year-old children can calculate interest in the most astounding manner. Mr

Cady, a business man could not follow them at all. I cannot tell you how it rejoiced my heart to see this school, and to know there are hundreds like it; to see children of rich men and the very poor sitting side by side. In New York those parents who can afford to send their children to private schools often do, but here rarely, because the private schools are not so good as the common schools. In the evening at seven we went to the evening high school, where young men and women go, who are employed in the day. We looked into a classroom where there were fifty or sixty men and boys, women and girls, – one man must have been forty, and some boys only twelve or thirteen, – they were having a grammar lesson. I must remark that the children here answer in much better English generally than English children in British schools. But no class of children in England can be compared to these. These schools are the true democratic element here. It is impossible to over-estimate the effect on the people in the next two generations. I believe if we do not bestir ourselves, we shall be left very *very* far behind America in virtue and happiness.'

Frances Power Cobbe

The Education of Women, and how it Would be Affected by University Examinations

(1862)

The subject of the education of women of the higher classes is one which has undergone singular fluctuations in public opinion. There have been times when England and Italy boasted of the literary attainments of a Lady Jane Grey and a Vittoria Colonna, and there have been times when the Chinese proverb seemed in force, and it was assumed that 'the glory of a man is knowledge, but the glory of a woman is to renounce knowledge.' For the last half-century, however, the tide seems to have set pretty steadily in the direction of feminine erudition. Our grandmothers understood spelling and writing, Blair's Sermons and long whist. Our mothers to these attainments added French and the pianoforte, and those items (always unimportant in a woman's education), history and geography. In our own youth we acquired, in a certain shadowy way peculiar to the boarding-schools of that remote period, three or four languages and three or four instruments, the use of the globes and of the dumb-bells, moral philosophy and Poonah-painting. How profound and accurate was this marvellous education (usually completed at the mature age of sixteen) it is needless to remark. A new generation has appeared, and he who will peruse the splendid curriculum of one of the Ladies' Colleges, of Bedford Square, or Harley Street, for instance, will perceive that becoming an accomplished young lady is a much more serious affair now than it was in 'the merry times when we were young.'

The question has now arisen, This wider and deeper education, how far is it to go? Have we reached its reasonable limit, or shall we see it carried much farther? If it be found desirable to push it into higher branches of study and greater perfection of acquirements, how will this best be accomplished? In particular, the grave query has lately been mooted, 'Will those University examinations

37

and academical honours, which have long been reckoned all-powerful in advancing the education of men, be found equally efficacious in aiding that of women? Ought they to be opened to female competition, and a Free Trade in knowledge established between the sexes? Or, on the contrary, does there appear just cause why this door, at all events, should for ever be closed to the possible progress of women?'

Before offering a few suggestions on this subject, I crave permission to make some general observations on the present condition of young women of the higher classes, and their special wants at this moment. A knowledge of these wants has alone induced me to obey the request to give such little aid as may be in my power to their efforts after a better state of things. Few indeed can be unaware that they are passing through a transition period of no small difficulty, and that there is urgent need for revision of many of the old social regulations regarding them. No class has felt more than they the rise in the atmosphere of modern thoughts; and where their mothers lived healthily enough in closed chambers, they are stifling. New windows must be opened to the light, new air of heaven admitted, and then we shall see bloom in women's cheeks, and light in their eyes, such as they have never worn before.

The miseries of the poor are doubtless greatest of all, but there are other miseries beside theirs which it behoves us also to consider. The wretchedness of an empty brain is perhaps as hard to bear as that of an empty purse, and a heart without hope as cheerless as a fireless grate. As society is now constituted, no inconsiderable portion of women's lives are aimless and profitless. There are Eugénie Grandets by hundreds in all our towns, and Marianas in Moated Granges in the country, whose existence is no better than that of 'the weed on Lethe's banks,' and yet who were given by Providence powers whereby they might have become sources of happiness to all around them. For (let us hope it will some time or other be recognised) there *are* purposes in the order of Providence for the lives of single women and childless wives, and they too are meant to have their share of human happiness. Most people prefer to ignore their existence as a class to be contemplated in the education of women, but it is as vain to do so as it is cruel. All of us know enough of those hapless households where the wife, having no children and few home duties, undergoes the most deplorable depreciation of character for want of employment of heart and mind; and her nature, if originally weak and small, shrivels up in petty vanities and contentions; and if strong and high, falls too often blasted by the thunderstorms of passion accumulated in the moveless and unwholesome atmosphere. All of us know those other households, none less hapless, where grown-up daughters, unneeded by their parents, are kept from all usefulness or freedom of action, frittering away the prime of their days in the busy idleness of trivial accomplishments; till, when all energy to begin a new course is gone, the parents die at last, and each one sinks into the typical 'Old Maid,' dividing her life henceforth in her small lodgings, between *'la médisance, le jeu, et la dévotion.'*

All this is pitiful enough. We may laugh at it; but it is not the less a miserable destiny, and one, moreover, which it is often almost impossible for a young woman to shake off. If she be a Roman Catholic, she may leave her home and go into a nunnery in all honour and credit; but the exchange is perhaps no great gain. If she be a Protestant, friends, parents, neighbours, and all her little world cry out lustily if she think of leaving her father's roof for any end, however good or noble, save only that one sacred vocation of matrimony, for which she may lawfully leave a blind father and dying mother, and go to India with Ensign Anybody. These curiosities of public opinion need surely to be set right. Let me plead with those men and women whose lives are rich and full, whose every hour has its duty or its pleasure, who can say,

> How beautiful it is to be alive!
> To wake each morn as if the Maker's grace
> Did us afresh from nothingness derive,

to think of these poor, narrow, withered existences, and not say, 'How can we keep women just what we would like – images set up in a niche?' but, 'What can we do to give to a vast number of our fellow-creatures all the joys of a useful and honourable life?' Again, there are numbers of young women who are free, so far as the wishes of their parents go, to devote themselves to practical usefulness. But the employment of women of the upper classes is one of the most difficult of achievements. At nearly every door they knock in vain; and, what is worse, they are sometimes told they are unfit for work (even for philanthropic work), *because* they are not soundly educated, or possessed of steady business habits. Yet when they seek to obtain such education, here again they meet the bolted door!

It is needless to go on farther. Enough has been said, I trust, to show that young women (both those possessed of the means of independent maintenance, and those desiring to support themselves by intelligent labour) are sadly in need of some further improvements in their condition. Among the ways in which it may be possible to effect such improvements, a high education manifestly stands foremost – a great good in itself, and needful for nearly all further steps of advance. On this subject also I must say a few words, and notably, to refute some popular misconceptions regarding it.

The idea that there is a natural incompatibility between classical studies and feminine duties, and that a highly-educated lady is necessarily a bad wife and mother, is indeed an idea venerable from its antiquity and wide diffusion. 'I would rather make women good wives than teach them Latin,' is a favourite species of apothegm, whose parallel, however (for all the sense it possesses), might be found in saying, 'I would rather make women good wives than make them eat their breakfasts!' Storing the mind with declensions, or the mouth with tea and toast, are neither of them, in the nature of things, antithetic to becoming a careful housewife and an affectionate companion. As Sydney Smith remarked, 'A woman's love for her offspring hardly depends on her ignorance of Greek, nor need we apprehend that she will forsake an infant for a quadratic equation.' *A priori*, the thing is not probable, and actually we see that a very different doctrine holds good. Few of us, I think, would fail to cite in their own circles the best cultivated women as precisely those whose homes are the happiest, who exercise therein that spirit of order and love of beauty, and, above all, that sense of the sacredness of even the smallest duties, which comes of true culture of mind. These private examples of moral excellence in studious women we cannot often quote on such occasions as the present. I may be permitted, however, to name two of them who have become household words among us all, and both of whom it has been my rare fortune to know very intimately. They are examples respectively of the two great lines in which a woman's virtue may be best displayed: the home duties of the wife and mother, and the out-of-door duties of the philanthropist.

The woman whose home was the happiest I ever saw, whose aged husband (as I have many times heard him) 'rose up and called her blessed' above all, and whose children are among the most devoted, was the same woman who in her youth outstripped nearly all the men of her time in the paths of science, and who in her beloved and honoured age is still studying reverently the wonders of God's Creation – that woman is Mary Somerville.

And the woman whose philanthropy has been the most perfect, who has done more than any beside to save the criminal and vagrant children of our land, and whose whole time and heart are given to their instruction, that woman is the same who taught

Homer and Virgil as assistant in her father's school at eighteen – that woman is Mary Carpenter.

We now proceed a step farther in our argument. After the examples cited, it may perhaps be assumed as proved that a high education does not in itself unfit women from performing either domestic or philanthropic duties; but that, on the contrary, it is a thing to be desired on every account. Our next position obviously is this: If a high education is to be desired for women, ought it not to be sought for them in those same university studies and honours which have so long proved efficacious in the case of men? Here another objection straightway rises up against us: 'A *high* education (it is said) may be desirable for women, but not a *University* education; for that would be to assimilate the training of the two sexes, and any step in such a direction must be fatal, as tending to obliterate the natural differences between them.'

A most weighty objection indeed would this be, were it founded on fact.

No *man* can possibly less desire any obliteration of the mental characteristics of the two sexes, than does every woman who has an intelligent care for the welfare of her own. But is such erasure indeed *possible*? Is it not clear enough that the Creator has endowed men and women with different constitutions of mind as of body? and need we be under the slightest apprehension that any kind of education whatever will efface those differences? Education is, after all, only what its etymology implies – the educing, the drawing out, of the powers of the individual. If we, then, draw out a *woman's* powers to the very uttermost, we shall only educe her *womanliness*. We cannot give her a man's powers any more than we can give a man a woman's brilliancy of intuition, or any other gift. We can only educe her God-given *woman's* nature, and so make her a more perfect woman. These differences will, I affirm, come out in every line of woman's expanding powers – in study, quite as much as in all beside. If a woman apply herself to Art, it will be a fresh type of beauty she will reveal. If she devote herself to philanthropic labours, she will not work like a man, from *without* – by outward legislation, but as a woman, from *within* – by the influence of one heart on another. Not by force of will, not by despotic volition does a woman ever do any good. She has abandoned somewhat of her womanhood when she exerts such powers. Even in teaching a class of little children, she rules not by authority, but by winning each little heart to voluntary submission. And in every other work it is the same. Her true victory must ever be an inward one, – a greater and more perfect victory, therefore, than was ever gained by conqueror's sword. And in matters of study it will be the same. Woman learns differently from man; and when she is able to teach, she teaches differently and with different lessons. If ever the day arrives when women shall be able to deal worthily with the subjects of our highest interests, we shall all be the better, I believe, for completing man's ideal of religion and morals by that of woman, and learning to add to his Law of Justice her Law of Love, and to his faith in God's fatherly care, her faith in His motherly tenderness, – that blessed lesson forgotten too long: that 'as a woman hath compassion on the son of her womb, even so the Lord hath pity on us all'!

The differences between men and women are co-extensive with their whole natures. A man and a woman are *parallel* to each other, but never *similar*. He is the right hand of humanity, and she is the left. They are *equivalents* to each other, but never *equals*. He is the pound in gold, and she is the twenty shillings in silver. All these differences are innate, unchangeable, ineradicable. It is a perfect caricature of them to represent that some kinds of knowledge are fit for men, and other kinds for women. As well might we say that some kinds of food were fit for one and not the other. It is not *in the truths to be acquired*, but in the *assimilation* of those truths in the mind which receives them, that the difference consists. It is as absurd to try to keep a woman feminine in mind by making her learn French because a man learns Latin, as it would be to try to keep her so in person by making her eat mutton because a man eats beef! Endless are the absurdities of this kind extant among us. Men ought to be well-informed: let women, then, know nothing but trivial accomplishments. Men ought to be strong and healthy: let a woman's cheek (as Burke expresses it) display the charming *morbidezza* of partial disease. A man ought to be brave: let a woman be instructed to dread all things in heaven and earth, from thunderstorms to spiders. Thus it is fondly imagined we are helping providence to keep women women, and securing the universe against the disorder of their turning into men. Not, however, by narrowing and clipping every faculty – not by pinching her in mental stays, shall we make a true woman. Such processes produce dolls, not women; figures very suitable to be set up in haberdashers' shops, to show off bonnets and crinolines, but not such forms as sculptors copy as types of womanly beauty. Our affair is to give nature its fullest, healthiest play and richest culture, and then the result will be what the Lord of Nature has designed – a true woman; a being, not artificially different from a man, but radically and essentially, because *naturally*, different – his *complement* in the great sum of human nature, not a mere *deduction* from his own share of that sum.

If these views be true, it follows that the highest education we can give will never efface, in the slightest degree, the natural characteristics of a woman's mind. Another argument, however, is here urged against us. It is said,

> Let it be granted that you will not make women *masculine* by teaching them Greek and Euclid; yet, it may still appear that Greek and Euclid are very inappropriate studies for women – useless in themselves, if not detrimental in the way supposed. A woman's mind has natural *affinities* to the lighter studies, and *repulsions* to the heavier ones. Let us have an entirely different course of studies, suited to the feminine soul, and then, perhaps, the form of a University education may be beneficial.

Now, that anyone will aver that the subjects of study in any one university are actually the very best possible subjects for women, or even for men, I do not suppose we shall find. But the point is, Who is to decide what is fit for a woman's brain save the owner of the brain herself? Who has a right to decree that the curriculum for the *goose* ought not to be the same as that which collegiate wisdom has appointed for the *gander*? If we were told that soldiers, artisans, or any other class of the community had sought instruction in arithmetic, or any such study, we should hardly think it our business to lay down the law for them: 'This is fit for you to learn, and this is unfit; your Bœotian brains may have *affinities* for the multiplication table, but they have certainly *repulsions* for the rule of three.' The proof of this particular description of pudding lies exclusively in the eating!

It may be found, indeed, hereafter, that opening up other studies for examination than those at present used, and leaving the option among them free, may be a desirable change, specially beneficial to women. This is quite possible; but in any case the highest masculine studies ought to be left free to a woman, *if* she feel the power and perseverance to undertake them. As Herbert Spencer remarks, 'That a woman has *less* powers than a man, is a poor argument why she should be forbidden to use such powers as she *has*.' It is a grave mistake to assume that what we judge is the proper pursuit for women in general is the proper one for each in particular, and that we have any just authority to crush individuality displayed in the choice of unusually arduous studies.

The three great revelations of the Infinite One – the True, the Beautiful, and the Good – are all alike in sanctity in themselves.

To devote life to the pursuit of any one of them is a noble thing. With respect to the Good we all feel this, and admit that to promote the virtue and happiness of our neighbours is a holy destiny for man or woman. And again, with respect to the Beautiful, we in a degree admit the same for women; and if they display the gifts of Jenny Lind, or Mrs Browning, or Rosa Bonheur, or Harriet Hosmer, we permit them to study music, or poetry, or painting, or sculpture. But with respect to the True, the rare and noble love of it, the readiness to devote life to its acquirements in abstract and abstruse studies – this is a thing we can hardly bring ourselves to sanction in a woman. Most women care only for the concrete and the personal, and the widest generalizations of philosophy too often interest them only as they concern the small affairs of their families and neighbours. Therefore, *because* few women rise to the love of abstract truth, *no* women are to be permitted to do so? This is utterly absurd. Instead of striving to bring all to the same dead level, we should welcome heartily all earnest devotion to Truth, Beauty, or Goodness, and rejoice in every diversity of gift whereby women may bring their special characteristics into play, and so enrich us all.

If I may hope that by these observations I have removed, in a measure, the objections to women pursuing the solid studies of a university education, I may now proceed to the positive side of the argument, which seems to have received far too little attention from men; namely, that the natural constitution of the female mind renders a solid education peculiarly desirable, and even necessary, to bring out all womanly powers and gifts in proper balance and usefulness. I verily believe that a *man* can infinitely better dispense with sound mental training than a woman. Among the essential differences between the mental constitutions of the two sexes, one of the most obvious is the preponderance in the latter of the intuitive over the reasoning faculties. As it has been facetiously expressed, 'When a man has laboriously climbed up step by step to the summit of his argument, he will generally find a woman standing before him on the top. But of how she got there, neither he nor she can give the smallest explanation.' This rapid intuition of women may or may not prove a defect. Properly trained and balanced by that carefulness of truth which comes of conscientious study, it is no defect at all, but a great advantage; but unregulated quickness is a peril and misfortune. Jumping at conclusions is a favourite species of feminine steeplechase, with whose sad results we are probably all too familiar. I recollect an instance of it, in which that imperviousness to reason, which affords apparently so much pleasure to spectators when manifested by young ladies, must have been rather trying to the person principally concerned. It happened that an elderly lady, a 'true woman' on weak-minded principles, discovered that the gentleman in whose house she resided had kindly paid the insurance for her personal property along with his own at his fire-office. Rousing herself in great indignation, she exclaimed, 'He insure my property? He insure *getting my property after my death*? No such thing! I meant to leave him a good legacy, now I will do nothing of the kind – I will alter my will and leave him nothing at all!' Vainly did the unfortunate gentleman endeavour to explain that fire insurances did not insure inheritance of property. Vainly did his friend, a Queen's Counsel of eminence, who had convinced a hundred juries, argue for hours with that irate old lady. Her will was altered, and the legacy revoked! I should like to know the sincere opinion of that gentleman on the desirability of giving a better cultivation to the reasoning faculties of women.

Again, women need solid mental training, not only to amend their reasoning and open their minds to argument, but also to correct the terribly inaccurate and superficial knowledge they now usually think sufficient. If the ladies of the present day proceed in geography too far to ask the celebrated query of one of their grandmothers, 'Was Hyder Ali an island or a continent?' and if in physical science they no longer (like another old lady) confine their knowledge of flowers to the Aurora Borealis and the delirium tremens, yet abundance of them are to be found whose ideas of Hyder Ali are of the most hazy description, and whose physical science might be expressed in the exhaustive analysis of another lady: 'Plants are divided by botanists into monandria, bulbous roots, and weeds.' Modern languages are excellent studies, especially for us women, to whom enforced silence, whether in England or on the Continent, is not supposed to be particularly tasteful. Often have I rejoiced for myself and my fellows, in finding ourselves all over Europe and the East, not only chattering away gaily on our own account, but able to assist our countrymen out of the multitudinous dilemmas to which their ignorance consigned them. Indeed, if any one particular branch of education be liable to the charge of giving to ladies an inconvenient degree of independence of, and even power over the lordly sex, it is precisely this one of modern languages, which on all hands is given as our *specialité*. A certain old saw concerning the 'Grey Mare,' and her superiority to her masculine companion in harness, is never so forcibly brought to recollection as when we behold the intelligent mother of a family at a railway station or hotel door in Italy or Germany, making all needful payments and arrangements with the utmost fluency and *savoir faire*; while at the rear of her brood of pretty chickens comes Paterfamilias, able to do nothing except carry the umbrellas and 'Bradshaws' of the party.

But these same delightful modern languages, does their acquirement afford any mental training similarly beneficial to that which a boy's mind undergoes over his Latin grammar? Speaking from my own sad experience, I must avow it does nothing of the kind, and that it is possible to talk three or four of them while remaining in pristine innocence regarding the cases and tenses of any one.

Lastly, the one noble science which would be the very best corrective of the slovenliness of female instruction, the science of geometry, is nearly utterly neglected. I verily believe that to gain only the idea of what constitutes a mathematical demonstration, and how mathematical reasoning proceeds, would be to many of our minds a clearing up of fog and haze which would brighten the rest of our days.

Now to bring woman's education out of the stage of imperfection in which it stops, it seems evident that some test and standard of perfection is needful. And this test to be sought and applied must be made a goal to which women will strive as ensuring some sort of prize. Scholarships and similar rewards are already used with much benefit at Bedford and other ladies' colleges. But the prize which naturally belongs to perfection of attainment is simply its *recognition*, – such public and secure recognition of it as shall make it available for all subsequent purposes. Herein will women find (as men have long found) the sufficient stimulus to strain up to that point, without which, in fact, education must ever be most incomplete. What the education of Oxford and Cambridge would be were there no such things as 'Little-go' and 'Great-go,' no examinations or strivings for degrees, women's education has hitherto been – nay, it has been worse, for it has been stopped at an age earlier than the collegiate education of men begins, and all the best years of study have been lost to her. We would now alter these things. We would obtain for women the right to such academical honours as would afford a sufficient motive and stimulus for thorough, accurate, and sustained study by young women past mere girlhood, and able to acquire the higher branches of knowledge. This *general* and great benefit would be the first object – the raising for *all* women the standard of education. But, beside this general utility, we believe that great special use would accrue to certain classes of women (and through them to the community) from thus opening to them the benefit of university education.

First, as regards those intending to be governesses. Here will be first provided an exceedingly high standard, held out with due encouragements for those who seek the chief places in the profession. An entirely new class of instructresses will, we believe, be thence created. Secondly, mothers, whether themselves well taught or ignorant, will know on what they depend when they engage such governesses; and not, as now, find themselves constantly deceived by shallow pretence, and references to ill-judging employers. Thirdly, and above all, a few dozen *accurately* trained governesses would, I am convinced, do much to revolutionize the present state of female education in the country, by giving to their pupils the same habits of solid and accurate study they have themselves acquired. The slovenly lessons, the half-corrected exercises, will then, we hope, be at an end; and the young lady's schoolroom become a mental gymnasium, where health and soundness of mind will be gained for life, instead of what it now is too often – a place where ineradicable habits are acquired of mental scrambling and shuffling, of shallowness and false show. And again, these certificates will be of importance as preliminary steps to the introduction of women into the medical profession. On this great subject I have no space worthily to speak, and can therefore only refer to it as one of the improvements most to be desired. Such little experience as I have myself had of such matters has lain among a class the most piteous assuredly in the community – the sufferers from incurable disease. I can only record my conviction that a large number of women among them would have been saved from agonizing deaths had they been able in the first stages of their disorder to obtain the advice of female doctors. There are other employments beside those of governesses and physicians – clerkships, secretaryships, and the like, to which the admission of women will be universally facilitated by the proposed degrees. These matters are, however, sufficiently obvious to require no discussion.

I hope I have now in some measure demonstrated – first, that some improvement is needed in the condition of young women, and that a better education is one of the stages of such improvement. Secondly, that a high education does not make women *less* able and willing to perform their natural duties, but better and more intelligently able and willing to do so. Thirdly, that to assimilate the *forms* of a woman's education to that of a man by means of examinations and academical honours, and also the *substance* of it by means of classical and mathematical studies, will in nowise tend to efface the natural differences of their minds, which depend not on any accidental circumstances, to be regulated by education, but on innate characteristics given by the Creator. Fourthly, that there are many positive benefits, general and particular, to be

47

expected from such Examinations and Honours, such classical and mathematical studies being opened to women.

Now it happens that there is one institution in this country which seems especially qualified to afford the advantages we have supposed – namely, the London University. In the older universities the rule of collegiate residence necessarily excludes women; but in London, the examinations being open to all, wheresoever educated, there is no reason why young ladies studying in the various female colleges, or in their homes, should not be admitted to share all the benefits of the institution.

As most of my readers are no doubt aware, the proposal that women should be thus admitted has been lately under debate in the Senate of the University – the occasion of a new charter offering a convenient opportunity for the change. A clause (it was suggested) should be inserted, extending the present terms, 'all classes and denominations of her Majesty's subjects, without any exception whatever,' to that *small* class, including half the human race, to which her Majesty herself belongs. This proposition, after much debate, was negatived, but only by the casting-vote of the chairman. Not unreasonably, therefore, may we hope that on the next occasion a fresh consideration will be given to the case, and another decision obtained. That so startling a proposal received on its first suggestion the votes of ten members of the Senate out of twenty, is much more surprising than that it should have been ultimately rejected. The long list of eminent names which has been obtained in favour of the movement, is guarantee for an amount of public opinion which may well inspire confidence in eventual success.

Should it so prove, and the University of London open its doors to women, the time will not be far distant when the innovation, which some may now regard as a derogation from its dignity, will be boasted of as no inconsiderable claim to public gratitude and respect. Those inequalities of the two sexes which place women at a disadvantage during ages when might makes right, are altered in happier times, when the strong heart is seen to be worth as much as the strong head. The tide has turned for women, and by and by the credit of helping their progress will not be lightly esteemed. Even were this otherwise, however, the University of London would hardly suffer, I think, from following in the course of the schools of Alexandria, where the martyr Hypatia held the first chair of philosophy then existing in the world; or in that of the University of Padua, where women learned and taught by the side of Galileo, Petrarch, and Columbus.

In conclusion, I would venture to make one appeal: do not let us in this, or any other matter connected with women's claims, allow ourselves to be drawn aside by those prejudices which on both sides distract us. To a woman of refined feeling, that popular ogress, the strong-minded female, is so distasteful, that she is inclined rather to leave her whole sex to mental starvation than contribute to the sustenance of one specimen of the genus. To a man with a spark of fun in his composition, the temptation to perpetrate jokes about Mistresses of Arts and Spinsters of Arts is perfectly irresistible. But, after all, refined women will best prevent the growth of strong-mindedness, in its obnoxious sense, by bringing their own good taste to help their sisters, whom the harsh struggles of life under a woman's disadvantages have perhaps somewhat hardened and embittered. And men who laugh at the absurdities (incident, alas! in some mysterious way to all the doings of women), will also in graver moments feel that there is another side to the subject, not a ludicrous one; and that the answer of the poor frogs to the boys in the fable might often be made by human sufferers: 'throwing stones may be fun to you, but it is death to us.' To aid a woman in distress was deemed in the old days of chivalry the chiefest honour of the bravest knight; it is assuredly no less an honour now for wise and generous men to aid the whole sex to a better and nobler life, and to the developing more perfectly, because more fully and freely, that womanhood which God has also made in His own image – a divine and holy thing.

Mary Carpenter

on

The Education of Pauper Girls

(1862)

The education of the female sex is one of the most important problems of the present day. If, at *all* times, it is essential to the well-being of the human race that those to whom is committed its early nurture should be duly prepared and educated for those important duties, at the present day, when female emigration is pointed to, on the one hand, as the only means of relieving society of an enormous and unprofitable surplus of female labour; and on the other, we are warned that untrained and helpless women are as little wanting at the Antipodes as here, it is especially evident that women, in order to do their true life's work in any station, in any part of the globe, *must be educated.*

But for this simple proposition to be practically adopted by the country, we must wait at least for another generation to pass, and only hope that all the mistakes of this present one, – all the difficulties and trials consequent on them, all the lessons which have been given by the experienced, and forgotten as soon as received by the thoughtless, – that all these may have had some small due effect; we can only hope that when we are gone our words may be remembered. But with respect to the girls who are the subject of this paper, we need not wait for them or their parents or friends to be convinced that our views are sound and ought to be carried out. *They*, the next generation, the mothers of the one that follows, are in our hands, the hands of society, to be trained as the most enlightened educationists of the day may deem best. We see enormous evils round us which we cannot remedy, we behold multitudes of young girls springing up in our midst to misery and ruin, and we cannot stretch out a helping hand to save them, for they have low, ignorant parents, who know nothing and care little about their daughters' true education. Some, perchance, have sunk so low, and been so ill-trained, that the law interferes and takes them out of the hands of their parents; and we stand on this bad foundation to raise a good superstructure, in a reformatory. But the workhouse girls are our own charge; *we* have the sole responsibility of them; the Government is not sparing in its allowance to their teachers, devoting some £30,000 annually that workhouse children may be well trained. The parents cannot interfere. There is no criminal taint to be washed out. We have every opportunity in our hands of rearing up another generation of wives and mothers, far better than the present, or of preparing a better race of female emigrants to our colonies, and *we are* NOT *doing it*. Whether we ask commissioners on education, or inspectors, or visitors of workhouses, or governors of gaols, we shall have the same mournful answer from all. However they may differ in other matters, they will agree in this, – that bad as is the education and training usually given to boys in ordinary workhouse schools, the girls receive one even less calculated to fit them for the duties of life; and the exceptions to this general experience will only be where there has been some special influence exerted to counteract the evils of the system. We require thus to study closely what is the cause of the evil, and to consider how it may be removed.

Let us first endeavour to ascertain what kind of education should be given to pauper girls.

We use the term *pauper* girls because it is the common one to designate the class before us; but we would wish to see it altered. Children ought never to be considered as paupers; they have committed no act of their own which should degrade them. Children *must* always be dependent on others for their support; nature assigns to the parent the support of them, society discharges to the child a duty which the parent cannot, or does not, perform. All human beings in a free and Christian country should be regarded as entering the world free and unstained by any acts of others, – all equal in the sight of the Creator. We must divest ourselves therefore of the idea that a child, because in a workhouse, is less *entitled* to care than the highest in the land. We are then now to consider how best to train young girls for whose education we are responsible, – young girls who are to be fitted to maintain themselves honestly, and to take their proper place in society. Let us think of them simply as young girls, not as pauper girls.

Every girl should be so learned as to be *able* to fill the duties of a *home*: whatever else may be superadded, this is essential; and the requirements of a home are so varied, that to fulfil them well she must, in learning to discharge them, have learned what will enable her to turn her hand easily to varied branches of industry, should such be needful. The girl is especially adapted by nature for a *home*. The boy loves to roam – he delights in enterprise, in action; though he generally treasures the love of his mother in a sacred recess of his heart, yet his affections are not bound up in his home – he does not pine for it; though he may long to return to the scenes of his early sports, yet he longs still more to rove over the world. The girl is totally different. The affections have large sway over her whole being. Nature has given her varied scope for them in the true home. She is the object of the tender love of the parents, and of her brothers and sisters, and love is constantly awakened and called out by her position in the family. She has the babies to fondle and nurse like a little mother herself; she has a thousand household cares to attend to, and learns cooking practically while she helps to get her father's dinner; and if the eldest girl feels herself a very important help in the house, after going regularly to a good day-school, and learning needlework, and enough of reading, writing and arithmetic for all common purposes, she is prepared at fourteen to take her humble position in life as a little servant, or her mother's helper and right hand, and to fill it with credit. A real good home is infinitely better than any school for the education of girls, – even a second-rate or a third-rate one is preferable. There her true nature is developed, and unless she is thus prepared to fill its duties well in after life, all other teaching is comparatively useless.

Now, though it is impossible for us by any artificial contrivances or ingenious mechanism to equal, still less to surpass, the training which the Heavenly Father, through His all-wise natural orderings and arrangements, would have given to the girl, yet we must always have before us the true and perfect prototype, if we would discharge towards these children the duties which are thrown upon us by the inability of their natural guardians to discharge them. We are not to think of them as a number of pauper children who must be taken care of at as little expense as possible, but as young girls who, when grown to womanhood, will be the bane or blessing of the next generation, and whom we must prepare for their part in life to the best of our ability, as fulfilling a solemn duty.

It is then essential, in the first place, that the *home element* shall be made as much as possible an essential one in every institution for the reception of *all* young girls, whether orphans, or deprived from whatever cause of the care of their parents. With the *home* must also be combined the school. We have already spoken of the peculiar excellence of the training obtained in the home; that received in a school is hardly less important. No one who has studied a good school can fail to have observed of what immense value it is to the child, independently of the amount of knowledge acquired. That indeed is obtained in a far superior way, under the present enlightened modes of instruction, to what a child could meet with at home; but besides, the faults of character are more easily and effectually corrected, and the tendency is checked which the very excellence of a home is apt to foster – to regard *self* as of undue importance. No one can go into a well-managed infant school without observing all this, and perceiving that these children are being better educated than is usually the case in the nurseries of the rich, where young children are often left under the care of a nursemaid but little acquainted with the principles of education, and who is anxious to purchase peace and quiet by yielding to, and thus fostering, the capricious tempers of her charge. The school for the *infant* department of pauper girls and boys combined, may then be much like an ordinary infant school, managed by a kind, loving, and trained teacher, but it must be supplemented by a motherly and sisterly care when the school-hours are over. Every infant requires to feel that it is the object of *individual love* and tenderness. If this is wanting, and if the little creature is not shielded from all injurious sights and sounds which would produce an ineffaceably bad impression on its young senses, and if its weak and probably diseased constitution is not carefully studied and strengthened; if all this is not done for the pauper infant, as we would do it for our own, we shall not only have much to eradicate as it grows older, but it will be impossible for any after instruction to counteract the ill effects of the first neglect.

The young girl leaves the infant school perhaps at eight years old, or younger. It is possible, though *barely probable* that in a large infant school, if under the care of a motherly matron who infuses her spirit into all the officials, the want of a true home may be supplied to a certain extent to the *young* child; and the judicious development of its faculties, with discipline of its passions and self-will, and loving culture of its affections, may prepare it well for the next stage – the juvenile department. But in this the want of the true home-training is especially felt, and cannot be supplied in a very large establishment. As we have already stated, the girl must be prepared for the varied duties of a home. The boy has his different faculties called out, and his individual powers and tastes developed in many ways in the industrial occupations which he may be engaged in, even if placed in a large institution. Agricultural work affords a boundless variety and exercise of his different powers; his natural energies, and even his destructive tendencies,

53

may be so exercised on the materials of industrial work as to train them well and turn them to good account. He may be happy and do well. But a girl in a large institution is in a perfectly different position, and I would beg to lay great stress on this point. Her work is not varied in the same manner, and washing and house-work poorly take the place of gardening, carpentering, and other trades. If the institution is large, the managers usually endeavour to economise labour by the introduction of washing machines, wringing machines, drying closets, and other contrivances, which are most valuable if the object is to save labour, but most injurious if the object is to train the girl. She must leave such a laundry not only utterly incapable of going through the necessary processes in an ordinary house, but what is worse, with her mind quite unpre-pared to use its faculties in actual life. The dormitory work does not teach girls how to perform the housemaid's ordinary duties; and the cooking is necessarily on so large a scale, and so managed, that few comparatively out of only one hundred girls can learn it at all, and even these may be quite unacquainted with the way to boil a potato, or make a common family pudding. In a large school for several hundred girls I have seen the kitchen provided with such conveniences for cooking, that even the potatoes were steamed in large trays, and there was nothing in it to give one an idea of a common kitchen; the girls were not even employed to bake the bread, – an admirable industrial occupation, most useful to girls in many respects; the laundry was chiefly filled with women, who of course could get through the work quicker than girls, and thus they lost the opportunity of learning; even needlework, the woman's special and peculiar art, loses in these large establish-ments. In the one I have alluded to, a contract was entered into for the clothing; and though the girls made their own clothes and the shirts of the boys, they never learnt to mend either, or acquired the valuable art of keeping themselves neat and tidy with old and patched clothes, – a most important one for young persons in the humble walks of life. In another large boarding-school for girls, very fine needlework is taught; and thus it may be supposed that a means of earning a livelihood is put in the girl's hands; first-rate needlework is produced in the school, which adds to its funds; but yet the girls are not trained to be good needlewomen, because, in order to procure more quickly well-made articles, each girl learns one part of it only, and may thus be entirely confined to making the wristbands of shirts without learning to make the other parts or to put together a whole garment. All experienced visitors whose opinions I have heard respecting the first institution of which I have spoken, have all been much struck, as I have myself, with the heavy, dull look of the girls in it, nor have I ever been able to hear that they are sought for or valued as servants, admirable as is the order and arrangement of the institution. Neither of the two is a Workhouse School; both are under the exclusive management of gentlemen. All girls then, from the time they leave the infant school until within a year of their being likely to go out to service, should be placed in schools not too large to admit of a distinct family feeling and family management. Nor should these schools be mere sub-divisions according to age, learning, etc., of a large number. If it *is* necessary to congregate many in one locality, let them be divided (as is done with full success at Lancaster, U.S.) into genuine family homes, where the different ages and varieties of temper of the girls may prevent the injurious monotony; where there may be real home duties which even the youngest may learn to perform, and where home affections may be cherished. With such an arrangement all the separate homes might unite in one common schoolroom, and thus all the advantages of economy and superior classification be obtained. The size of these homes may vary from twenty to thirty, but should not exceed forty girls. After the girls have gone through this ordinary home and school training, it would be highly desirable that they should be placed where they can obtain more special training for their future work in life – in separate homes, where they should have somewhat more liberty, and have more preparation for the particular mode of life they are intended for. Mrs Way has admirably carried out this plan in her Brockham Home for Workhouse Girls of about fourteen years of age. In some districts homes connected with factory work might be valuable, but they should still exercise a parental tutelage over the girls. In all cases where the girls are actually put out to earn their own living, a friendly interest in them should still be maintained; and there should be a home to which they can return during temporary loss of employment, as in Miss Twining's Industrial Home. These prove that girls must still feel that they have friends, that they are not uncared for; that there are those who grieve when they do wrong, and rejoice at their successful career.

Such, I believe, is a brief statement of what ought to be the education of workhouse girls. I need not say that it is *not* of this character in our country. There are doubtless some few and exceptional cases, where the country workhouse, under the management of some benevolent and judicious guardians, aided by lady visitors, becomes a true home. But these exceptions only prove the rule. Even in well-managed workhouse schools, quite separated from the adult paupers, the girls look listless, and in a very inferior condition to the boys: this I have myself observed; nor, if the principles here laid down are admitted, is it at all difficult to assign the reason for this. If there is any connexion between the workhouse for adult paupers and that for children, none can tell what contamination is the consequence; what influences are imbibed, even by young children, who are placed for care with female paupers, it may be of the lowest character. A pauper element is infused into them from earliest childhood, – an element devoid of all that is good, or would defend from evil in the female sex. Hence the appalling fact which was revealed in a recent Parliamentary return, that during the ten years ending 31 December 1860, 1,736 young girls returned to the workhouse – being double the number of boys; and 1,896 returned, not from misconduct, but to become a burden on the country. In January 1859, there were (as stated in the Poor Law Report, p. 189) 12,353 illegitimate pauper children. This awful fact speaks for itself. Are we going to rear up these twelve thousand infants as we reared their mothers? and as we reared the multitudes of wretched girls who did not return to the workhouse, but found their way to penitentiaries and gaols? Such facts ought to be widely known by the country, and then we believe that the country would demand an *entire alteration* of the whole system. No palliatives will avail to cure a system which is based on an entirely false principle. No home feeling can exist in any institution in which voluntary Christian effort does not infuse some of that love which was appointed by the Creator to be the very atmosphere of childhood. No guardians appointed to administer poors' rates ought ever to manage schools for the children. No men, however wise and good, ought to superintend institutions for young girls. The children ought all to be separated from adult paupers, and begin life anew free from reproach; and the management of them should be committed to benevolent and enlightened women, under whose direct control all officials should be placed.

We shall be told that it will be impossible to find voluntary workers among the female sex who will undertake so enormous a work, as that of managing schools for all the pauper girls in the country. A similar difficulty was made ten years ago, when we, the voluntary workers, asked the Government to give into our care the criminal children, who were becoming an increasing burden to the country in gaols. The Government gave us the needed authority and pecuniary aid, and there has been no lack of managers or teachers adapted to the work. Women have been making a rapid advance during the last ten years in the power of working for themselves and others. Numbers of ladies have already devoted themselves to workhouse visiting, and will doubtless be ready to take the less painful and difficult work of managing the schools for young girls.

Now, such a change in the present order of things may be effected, I stated in a paper read before another section of this Association last year, entitled 'What shall we do with our Pauper Children?' I also stated it in my evidence before the Poor Law Committee last year. It does not fall within the province of the present paper to discuss it; but only, after considering the principles of the education of pauper girls, to express the strong conviction that this cannot be carried out efficiently, either as regards the country or the children, except by voluntary benevolent and Christian agencies, combined, as in the case of schools for juvenile delinquents, with inspection and pecuniary aid from the Government.

Jessie Boucherett

Endowed Schools: Their Uses and Shortcomings

(1862)

It is recommended in the Report of the Royal Commission on Education, that the funds of all ancient charities found to be useless or mischievous in their action should be placed at the disposal of certain commissioners to be applied to the purposes of education. The annual income of the charities included in this description and recommended to be abolished, amounts to no less than £101,113 9s. 3d.[1]

If, therefore, the proposed plan should meet the approbation of Parliament, the principles by which the yearly distribution of so large a sum are to be regulated will become a matter of no little moment.

One of the objects which it is intended to promote by these means is the establishment of endowed or assisted schools to meet the wants of those portions of the community which are the least provided for by existing institutions, but which yet require educational aid. This principle is perfectly just. A large sum being unexpectedly added to the funds devoted by the nation to the purposes of education, it is right to bestow the bonus on those who have hitherto received little or nothing from the public, but who are not the less in want of help.

The justice and reasonableness of this proposition will recommend itself to every one, but some difficulty will perhaps be found in deciding which is the class that comes the most under this description. It is for the object of clearing up this point that these pages have been written and the tables, to be found further on, compiled.

The working classes seem at the first glance to have the strongest claim, but we are told on high authority that they are already so well provided with National Schools that there is a strong probability of their becoming more intelligent than the class immediately above them,[2] and the Commissioners themselves and the general public seem to be of opinion that they have lately received a higher education than is likely to be of use to them in their humble station. The upper classes being wealthy, have of course no need of help. The portion of society then which most requires assistance must be sought for among the various sections of that large division called the middle classes.

Some of these, however, are already at least tolerably well provided from existing endowments; let us then take a brief review of the present condition of middle class education, with a view of discovering whether there are any sections which, though in want of help, receive as yet little or none. But first we will specify what are the benefits which endowed schools do, or at least ought to confer.

The benefits which proceed from endowed schools are twofold. First there is the direct good done of providing those educated in them with useful instruction, and secondly there is the indirect but more widely spread good which they effect by raising the standard of education generally.

Before deciding on the subject of new endowments, we must make up our minds which of these purposes we consider to be the most important. If the object we set before us is to provide every tradesman or other person above making use of a national school with the means of giving his children a good education at a rate below prime cost, then the number of schools required will be very large and the requisite sum of money beyond that to be placed at the disposal of the Commissioners. But if our object is to provide a certain number of well-conducted schools as models, found to offer at the same time a good education to those who will hereafter become teachers in private educational establishments, then the number of schools required would be much smaller and the expense far less heavy. If the amount of money at command were unlimited, it would perhaps be desirable to attempt the first object, but this is not the case. A hundred thousand a year cannot provide education below prime cost for all who would be benefited by receiving it; we must choose therefore, whether we will provide for some one section in this manner, wholly neglecting the others, or whether we will divide the benefit equally among all, by giving to every section model schools and places of education, where the teachers of private schools can be trained.

The first course would be manifestly unjust. To educate one portion of the community highly out of public money, while leaving another portion equally in want of assistance wholly

County	Number of Grammar Schools	Number of Scholars	Male	Female	Other Endowed Schools	Number of Scholars	Male	Female
Bedford	2	211	204	7	26	2,230	1,503	727
Berks	3	139	139	. . .	40	1,943	1,244	699
Buckingham	4	762	762		25	1,398	927	471
Cambridge	4	225	225		42	3,654	2,278	1,376
Chester	20	1,082	1,037	45	47	3,430	2,119	1,311
Cornwall	4	69	69		25	1,166	667	499
Cumberland	33	2,147	1,587	560	82	3,625	2,339	1,286
Derby	13	791	688	103	75	4,078	2,733	1,345
Devon	10	303	303		70	4,208	2,846	1,362
Dorset	7	370	365	5	26	1,269	880	389
Durham	10	576	520	56	46	4,259	2,784	1,475
Essex	14	369	369		54	3,815	2,298	1,517
Gloucester	16	833	833		89	6,187	3,510	2,677
Hereford	4	263	222	41	44	2,551	1,504	1,047
Hertford	14	1,225	1,044	181	25	1,421	920	501
Huntingdon	4	169	169		21	1,258	872	386
Kent	14	634	634		65	4,886	3,068	1,818
Lancaster	54	4,204	3,643	561	158	13,554	8,330	5,224
Leicester	8	400	400		46	3,368	2,082	1,286
Lincoln	23	1,267	1,242	25	108	7,267	4,513	2,754
Middlesex	16	3,681	3,681		61	9,975	6,183	3,792
Monmouth	3	136	136		24	1,601	807	794
Norfolk	7	270	227	43	44	3,033	1,978	1,055
Northampton	11	382	377	5	77	4,050	2,737	1,313
Northumberland	8	574	454	120	57	4,146	3,339	1,807
Nottingham	6	348	344	4	52	3,082	2,067	1,015
Oxford	9	583	583		42	2,431	1,466	965
Rutland	2	86	86		13	589	383	206
Salop	9	399	392	7	40	2,245	1,279	966
Somerset	7	311	311		49	2,576	1,513	1,063
Southampton	10	416	393	23	49	2,279	1,292	987
Stafford	18	741	738	3	65	4,092	2,385	1,707
Suffolk	11	465	457	8	55	3,057	2,066	991
Surrey	9	869	869		37	3,538	1,931	1,607
Sussex	4	193	193		28	1,569	999	570
Warwick	19	2,114	1,849	265	73	5,625	3,316	2,309
Westmoreland	29	1,507	1,139	368	39	1,819	1,206	613
Wilts	5	179	169	10	40	2,283	1,346	937
Worcester	15	898	664	234	70	5,251	3,425	1,826
York	88	4,711	4,011	690	390	21,552	13,714	7,838
Total	547	34,902	31,528	3,374	2,419	161,360	100,849	60,511

unaided, is an injustice that can never be committed intentionally, but it is one into which we may easily be led unless we become well instructed in the facts of the case, know how the existing schools are distributed, which classes they benefit, and which they leave unassisted.

With the view of making this part of the question clear, the preceding table has been compiled from Kelly's county directories and the Census of 1851, Education Department.

The united income of these schools amounted to £400,000,[3] a sum so large that the additional £101,000 a year, though considerable in itself, is comparatively small. In some of the higher kind of grammar schools boys receive an education which fits them for college at a cheap rate; and the sons of ill-beneficed clergy and poor professional men, of farmers and the upper class of tradesmen, often avail themselves of the advantages here offered, sometimes boarding and lodging with the head master. In other schools a good commercial education is given at a rate so far below prime cost that the poorest tradesman can afford to send his sons if within reach of a walk. As a general rule the common endowed schools are but little superior to ordinary national ones, and the class of children that frequent them only a shade above those of labouring men. But in some of these noble establishments the orphan sons of poor tradesmen are gratuitously received, boarded, clothed, educated, and finally apprenticed to any trade they wish to learn; thus these children are protected from the evil influences which would otherwise surround their poverty and helplessness.

Doubtless in many instances these schools are ill-managed and fail to produce the good effect they ought, but this partial failure is owing to want of superintendence and is not caused by the poverty of the endowments, for in some of the instances of inefficiency cited by the Commissioners the pay of the master is very large.[4]

Under proper regulations these schools would be wealthy and numerous enough to provide all the classes whom they are intended to benefit with good model schools and good training places for private masters; and even now, imperfect as is their management, they have a great effect in these respects and raise the standard of education among these favoured classes considerably above its natural level.

But a study of the table will show that these benefits are unequally divided, and that some sections are almost entirely excluded from all share in the advantages. For instance, in the common endowed schools it will be seen that the number of girls educated in them is small compared to the boys, the number being – Boys, 100,849; Girls, 60,511.

The number of male and female children existing in every class being the same, we must conclude either that there are more boys' schools than are wanted, or that there are not enough for girls. It having never been stated that the former is the case, it is impossible to avoid coming to the conclusion that there is a great deficiency in the latter respect.

This deficiency ought therefore to be made up out of the new fund and the number of boy and girl scholars brought to about the same before any new schools for boys of this class are built and endowed.

In the list of scholars at Grammar schools, the difference is still greater, the number of boys being 31,528 and of girls 3,374, barely a tenth.

The reason here is evident: these schools were founded for the purpose of giving a cheap classical education, a kind of teaching which would have been of no use to girls, and from which they were therefore excluded; and though the classical education has now become very generally a secondary object, comparatively few boys going eventually to college, yet the foundations being as a general rule originally intended for boys only, they are rightly kept exclusively for them.

But this exclusion from all means of obtaining a good education falls heavily on the sisters of the boys who are taught at these schools, for girls of this rank can seldom or ever be provided for by their parents, but must after their father's death, and sometimes before, earn their bread for themselves, until they marry; and if they do not marry, for all their lives, and must lay up something for their old age.

Among women of the labouring classes a good education is of comparatively little importance, for health and strength are of more service to a labourer's daughter than knowledge or intelligence; but in the middle ranks, a woman cannot become a domestic servant: she would feel that to do so was a degradation; and even if she did not, she would not possess the requisite physical powers from want of early training.

Her livelihood must be earned then, if earned at all, by intelligence; and to all who gain their bread by the exercise of their mental powers a good education is the first necessary, and the privation of it a most serious injury.

Private schools for girls are not only worse than boys' endowed schools, but are very inferior to boys' private ones.[5] The reason of this is, that there exist scarcely any places where girls of the middle classes can be trained as teachers. A boy who is intended to become a private teacher can get well taught at an endowed school for a very small expense, but a girl who is intended to become a teacher can only learn at a private school and at a considerable expense; consequently the teachers are themselves untaught. Now the question is, shall the new fund be applied to building more and more schools for boys who are already well supplied with model schools and training places for masters, or shall it be applied to building and endowing a few middle class girls' schools in every county, where teachers for private schools may be instructed, and where a good system of teaching shall be maintained as an example to others? To show how hardly this exclusion from educational endowments acts, let us take the not unusual case of a tradesman's family being left orphans. It is then strange to see the sons taken into a good Blue-coat school, tenderly nurtured, carefully trained, and finally put in the way of earning an honest livelihood, while the daughters are left to rough it in the world as best they may, or are consigned to the contaminating atmosphere of a workhouse. Surely these poor orphan girls have the first claim to public help, at least if the rule is to hold good that those who are the most in want of assistance are the fittest objects for receiving it!

There is another class who suffer severely from want of education. It frequently happens that the incomes of the country clergy are very small, sometimes amounting to only £80 or £100 a year: it is impossible for such clergymen to provide fortunes for their daughters, who must therefore, unless they marry, depend on their own exertions for support. These young ladies are particularly well suited, by birth and position, to become governesses in private families and in schools of a higher grade, but isolated as they are in country villages, they have no means of obtaining good instruction, for their fathers cannot possibly afford to send them to even a tolerable boarding school.

Thus they are compelled to go out into the world to earn their livelihood in some way or other, without having received any education to assist them.

If they become governesses, they receive low salaries and are unable to lay by for their old age.

Workhouse visitors tell us that large numbers of women 'who have seen better days,' are to be found in the wards; probably not a few are of this class, and it is certain that many clergymen's daughters are supported by the Corporation of the Sons of the Clergy on pensions varying from £10 to £20 a year.

To remedy this hardship, I would suggest that a large endowed boarding school ought to be erected in every county, to which the daughters and orphans of the clergy who have less than £200 a year should be sent free, and to which the less poor clergy and men of other professions might also send their daughters on paying a sufficient sum to cover their expenses, and leave a little profit over; say £25 a year. There ought also to be at least one school for girls in the chief town of every county, answering to the Blue-coat boys' schools, where tradesmen's orphans might be received gratis, and to which the townspeople might send their daughters cheaply, as day scholars, and where a useful commercial education should be given, such as would enable the pupils hereafter to become saleswomen, clerks, and bookkeepers, or, if so inclined, teachers in private schools.

If the principle laid down at the beginning be admitted – namely, that those classes who are the most in want of assistance, yet receive but little from existing endowment, are those who ought to be helped, then a fair claim for these poor girls has been shown, for they certainly want help more than any other class in the community and as certainly receive but little; in some counties positively none.[6]

If any scruple be felt at applying money left originally for general purposes to the special object of improving the condition of women, the reader must remember that the land left to these charities, now called mischievous and useless, was left as much for the benefit of women as of men. Some of it was given in order to distribute bread among the poor, not excluding women, some to provide coals at stated seasons without distinction of sex, some to provide lodging and food for wayfarers whether men or women. Many of these institutions have been abused, others have been made useless by the advance of civilization, and without doubt they require reform. Still the intention of the founders to help all who require help, without partiality or favour, should be respected; and as the female population is more numerous and more distressed than the male, women have hitherto enjoyed the larger share of the bounty. If then these charities are abolished and boys' schools are erected with their wealth, women will be great losers. At the very least one half of this money belongs to women, as it was intended for their benefit by the founders; and if less than half is spent upon them, common fairness will be disregarded as well as the founders' wishes.

But perhaps it may be said that such an injustice can never be contemplated, and that the evil deprecated is imaginary. Unhappily this is not the case. At this moment a school is in the course of erection,[7] to be built and endowed at the recommendation of the

Charity Commissioners and with the sanction of the Court of Chancery, out of the proceeds of land left originally to provide shelter for wayfarers, and subsequently used to build almshouses and give pensions to old men and women. This school is to be exclusively for boys. The evil, therefore, is not imaginary. A precedent has been established for diverting funds, originally left for the equal benefit of men and women, to the exclusive use of men. This precedent may possibly be generally followed if vigorous efforts are not made to attract attention to the subject.

But setting aside all considerations of justice and humanity, it may be shown that this exclusion of women from the means of obtaining a good education is disadvantageous to the community at large. A great diversity of religious opinions prevails among tradesmen, and inconveniences are consequently found to arise at schools on the subject of religious instruction. These difficulties are very frequently evaded (at private day schools at least) by the simple expedient of giving none at all. Now when it is remembered that the parents, and more especially the mothers, have themselves received no religious instruction from the same cause, the evil becomes serious. Doubtless many of the children attend Sunday schools, or accompany their parents to church or chapel, but the instruction thus received can only be of a very slight nature, and is apt to be forgotten during the week.

Thus two dangers arise: first of the children growing up altogether irreligious, and secondly of the more seriously inclined running into every kind of fanaticism and religious extravagance from having no real knowledge to guide them. But serious as is the evil with regard to men, with regard to women it is far worse, because the home religious teaching of the children generally falls to the mother's lot.

It is often said that the moral feeling of the smaller trading classes has reached a very low point; that they not unfrequently use false weights and even put unwholesome adulterations into the food they sell; the women, too, are notoriously harsh mistresses towards their maid-servants.

Now may not this general low tone of feeling be fairly ascribed to the entire absence, or miserable nature of the religious instruction received by the girls, which causes them when they become mothers to fail in impressing on their children as strongly as they ought the duty of behaving honestly towards all, and of showing kindness to their dependents?

If this be not the cause, it is at least a singular coincidence that the class in which moral feeling is at the lowest ebb, is also that which receives the least religious instruction.

These moral deficiencies have been perceived by the clergy, who in order to remedy the evil are now making great exertions to get up more and more good schools for boys; but I do not believe they will succeed in their object unless they include girls in their efforts. The Rev. J. S. Howson, of Liverpool, says on this subject:

Why do I single out girls of the middle classes as subjects for special consideration? Partly because they have been more overlooked than the boys, partly because I believe the condition of their education to be worse than that of the boys, partly because the agencies now set in motion for raising the standard and improving the quality of the education of the classes in question are almost inoperative on the female half of them. . . . But there is another reason why this subject should be closely and separately considered. The girls are more important than the boys. The power of woman is really the greatest power in the country. This power is all the greater because it is not openly and visibly exercised; it is the power not of force but of influence. It is not merely that the mothers of each generation are the most influential instructors of the next, – not merely that while we men are occupied with a thousand employments that take us away from our homes and children, the influence of woman is exercised continually and at that period of life when impressions are most easily received. This is not all. The influence is continuous over the men themselves. It is exercised, whether felt or not, at each part of the whole social machine.

If any question in the whole world is suitable for the consideration of an Association for Social Science, it is the inquiry into the kind of education which our women receive in their girlhood.[8]

Now, if this be in any degree true, is it wise to exclude women from an equal share of educational endowments? Would it not be a mistake as well as an injustice to devote the new fund to the exclusive use of men who already enjoy more than two-thirds of the present endowments? That to do so would be contrary to the wishes of the founders of the old charities, and cruel towards those numerous single women, who, though debarred from the means of good education, are yet compelled to try to earn their bread in callings requiring intelligence, has already been shown. The attention of all who have at heart the interests of humanity and social improvement should be directed towards the disposal of this £101,000 a year, which if rightly and justly expended, may be the means of bestowing such great and lasting benefits on the whole community, by raising the moral tone of a large but corrupt class, and by affording to numbers of necessitous and industriously disposed persons the means of earning an honest livelihood, from which they are at present debarred by the want of the necessary education.

NOTES

1 Abstract of the Royal Commissioners on Education. G. Herbert Skeats. P. 109.
2 See Mr Gladstone's speech at Oxford. *The Times*, 23 November 1861.
3 At Abbas Milton there were no scholars on the foundation, though the income of the school was £199 10s. At Plympton there is frequently only a single pupil, although the income is £220. At Wotton-under-Edge there is a free grammar school the income of which is £536, the scholars ten in number. At Coventry there are seven endowed schools with an aggregate income of £2,808; the number of boys educated in them is estimated at 350. Several other instances are quoted in the Commissioners' Report.
4 Edinburgh Review, July 1861. Popular Education, page 34, and Abstract of the Royal Commissioners on Education, page 100.
5 *The Times* early last December in animadverting on boys' private schools stated that the only subjects well taught in them were 'penmanship and arithmetic.' But this blame is in fact high praise, as these are precisely the two essentials of a middle-class education. The boy who can write and reckon well and quickly can earn his bread, even if his knowledge of history and geography is rather vague. In girls' schools nothing is well taught, not even 'penmanship and arithmetic;' indeed, if they were, there would be small ground for complaint. Many girls leave school writing a scarcely legible hand, and unable to add up a bill of parcels with correctness. A girl who had been several years at a 'seminary for young ladies' and wished to become a bookkeeper, was asked if she knew arithmetic well, and replied that she did, having been as far as Practice at school, but on examination it appeared that she could not multiply correctly. This is one instance out of many that could be quoted.
6 See table of Grammar Schools. The common endowed schools would be useful to a lower class than those here spoken of. The following counties contain no superior endowed schools to which girls can be sent: – Berks, Buckingham, Cambridge, Cornwall, Devon, Essex, Gloucester, Huntingdon, Kent, Leicester, Middlesex, (containing sixteen boys' Grammar Schools with 3,681 scholars), Monmouth, Oxford, Rutland, Somerset, Surrey, Sussex. Thus in none of these counties is there the means of training teachers for private middle class schools. In many other counties the number of female scholars in endowed schools does not amount to ten.
7 This school is in Lincolnshire. Twelve almshouses and their inmates,

male and female, will still be maintained; but all the rest of the fund is to be devoted to this boys' school. The cost of building is estimated at £3000, and the salaries of the masters will be £160.

8 Transactions of the Social Science Association, 1859. Page 309.

Josephine Butler

The Education and Employment of Women

(1868)

The economical position of women is one of those subjects on which there exists a 'conspiracy of silence.' While most people, perhaps, imagine that nearly all women marry and are supported by their husbands, those who know better how women live, or die, have rarely anything to say on the subject. Some social problems as this are certainly painful; they may or may not be insoluble; they must not be ignored.

The phrase 'to become a governess' is sometimes used as if it were a satisfactory outlet for any unsupported woman above the rank of housemaid. When we see advertisements in the news-papers, offering 'a comfortable home,' with no salary, as a sufficient reward for accomplishments of the most varied character, we sometimes wonder at the audacity of employers; but when we learn that such an advertisement, offering the situation of nursery governess, *unpaid*, was answered by *three hundred women*, our surprise has in it something of despair.

The truth is, that the facts of society have changed more rapidly than its conventions. Formerly muscles did the business of the world, and the weak were protected by the strong; now brains do the business of the world, and the weak are protected by law. The industrial disabilities of women, unavoidable under the earlier *régime*, have become cruel under the later. There is neither the old necessity of shelter, nor the old certainty of support.

The census of 1861 gave nearly six millions of adult English women, distributed as follows:

Wives	3,488,952
Widows	756,717
Spinsters over 20	1,537,314
	5,782,983

The census also gives the numbers of women who work for their own subsistence, as follows:

Wives	838,856
Widows	487,575
Spinsters (above or under 20)	2,110,318
	3,436,749

In the first place, then, it appears that marriage, as a means of subsistence (to say nothing of the indecorum of looking forward to it in this light) is exceedingly precarious in two ways. The proportion of wives to widows and spinsters in 1861 was just about three to two, while of these wives themselves nearly one in four was occupied in other than domestic duties, either as her husband's coadjutor, as in farm-houses and shops, or, of necessity, as his substitute in cases of his desertion, or helplessness, or vice. In the second place, the number of widows and spinsters supporting themselves, which in 1851 was two millions, had increased in 1861 to more than two millions and a half. The rapidity of the increase of this class is painfully significant. Two and a half millions of Englishwomen without husbands, and working for their own subsistence! This is not an accident, it is a new order of things. Of the three and a half millions of women – wives, widows, and spinsters – engaged in other than domestic occupations, it is probable that scarcely a thousand make, without capital, and by their own exertions, one hundred pounds a year. The best paid are housekeepers in large establishments, a few finishing governesses, and professed cooks. 43,964 women are returned as outdoor agricultural labourers – a fact worthy of remembrance when it is said that women are too weak to serve in haberdashers' shops. Women, refused admission to such shops on the pretext that they are not strong enough to lift bales of goods, have been afterwards traced to the occupations of dock porters and coal-heavers. In practice the employments of women are not determined by their lightness, but by their low pay. One newspaper still scoffs at the desire of women to be self-supporting: but starvation is a sufficient answer to sneers. As a favourable symptom of the last few years, I may add that 1822 women are returned as employed by the post-office. 213 women are returned as telegraph-clerks. It is instructive to note the way in which the salary of these women telegraph-clerks has fallen. When the telegraph companies were first formed, the pay of a female clerk was eight shillings a week, to be increased by a shilling yearly, until it reached fourteen shillings a week. So great, however, has been the competition of women for these situations, that the pay has been reduced to five shillings a week, a sum on which a woman can scarcely live unassisted. In France the women telegraph-clerks have met with a worse fate. The government took the management of the telegraphs, and dismissed the women, because they had no votes to bestow on the government candidates. The exclusion of women from the suffrage has been called a harmless injustice; but there is no injustice which is not liable to become an injury.

At present the principal employments open to women are teaching, domestic service, and sewing. I come to consider the remuneration of the highest profession open to women.

In 1861 there were 80,017 female teachers in England, of whom the majority were governesses in private families. It is difficult to ascertain the average salary of governesses, because the Governesses' Institutions in London and Manchester, which are the chief sources of information on the subject, refuse to register the applications of governesses who accept salaries of less than £25 a year. The number of this lowest class may be guessed from the fact that for a situation as nursery governess, with a salary of £20 a year, advertised in a newspaper, there were five hundred applicants; as I have already stated, three hundred applied for a similar place with no salary at all. To return to the higher class. The register of the last six months at the Manchester Governesses' Institution shows an entry of –

54	governesses who asked for			£30 and under, per annum.		
20	„	„	„	40	„	„
19	„	„	„	50	„	„
17	„	„	„	60	„	„
10	„	„	„	70 and upwards.		

These sums, it must be remembered, are expressions of what governesses wish to receive.[1] Taking nursery governesses into the account, and remembering that the above statistics refer only to the higher ranks of the profession, it is probably not too much to say that from 0 to £50 a year is the salary of nine governesses in ten. Situations offering more than £50 are the prizes of the profession, but are generally such as to compel a serious outlay on dress and personal expenditure. It is difficult to imagine how the majority of governesses manage to scramble through life, when we remember that their position involves several journeys in the year, that they must sometimes provide for themselves during holiday seasons, and that must always dress as ladies. Miserable must be their means of providing for old age or sickness, to say nothing of claims of affection or of charity throughout life, or the means required for self-culture.[2]

Probably there are few portions of society in which more of silent suffering and misery is endured than among female teachers, and in the class which supplies them. Charitable people who have opened little 'Homes' for decayed governesses can tell histories of struggling lives and crushed hopes which it saddens one to hear. The reports of Bethlehem Hospital and other lunatic asylums prove that not a few poor governesses find their way thither. Some are found in Penitentiaries among the fallen. Inquiry shows that insufficient food while out of situations, added to the mental trials of an unloved and isolated being, have driven some of these governesses to opium or to strong drink, until, penniless and degraded, they have sought a refuge among penitents where there was nothing to pay. 'Her funds are exhausted, and she earnestly seeks a re-engagement;' words such as these, taken from an advertisement in *The Times*, headed – 'To the benevolent', are no unfrequent symptom of a deep and wide distress. Some determined women there are who have devoted to self-culture as much of their pittance as could be spared from the barest needs of life, and of whom it is known that, night after night when they went to bed, they have tied a band round their waist to keep down the gnawings of hunger. One such I know who has risen by her force of character to almost as high a place as it is at present possible for a *woman* to occupy in the educational world, but who is not yet free from sufferings entailed by years of mental anxiety and bodily privations. An insufficiency of the necessaries of life is not the bitterest complaint of many of these sufferers, who by their lives protest that man does not live by bread alone. 'Worse than bodily privations or pains' (I quote the words of one of them) 'are these *aches and pangs of ignorance*, this unquenched thirst for knowledge, these unassisted and disappointed efforts to obtain it, this sight of bread enough and to spare, but locked away from *us*, this depressing sense of a miserable waste of powers bestowed on us by God, and which we know we could have used for the lessening of evil and the increase of the happiness of our fellow-creatures.'

The desire for education which is widely felt by English women, and which has begun to find its expression in many practical ways, is a desire which springs from no conceit of cleverness, from no ambition of the prizes of intellectual success, as is sometimes falsely imagined, but from the conviction that for many women to get knowledge is the only way to get bread, and still more from that instinctive craving for light which in many is stronger than the craving for bread. 'Amongst the wealthier classes' – I give the words of one who has much knowledge of that of which she speaks –

women are better provided for materially, though even here
they are often left to the mercy of the chances of life, indulged
and petted whilst fortune smiles, left helpless to face the
storm of adverse circumstances; but here, more often than
elsewhere, one meets with those sad, dreary lives, that have
always seemed to me amongst the worst permitted evils of
earth, –

> A wall so blank
> My shadow I thank
> For sometimes falling there –

is true of many a life. Even sharp misfortune is sometimes a
blessing in a life of this sort; something to do, and leave to
do it. I do not say that any possible education, any freedom
of career, any high training of faculty, would spare *all* this
waste; some part of it is of that sad mystery of life which we
cannot explain, and for the unveiling of which we can only
wait and pray. But I am quite sure that much of it is altogether needless, and comes from the shutting up in artificial
channels of those good gifts of God which were meant to
flow forth freely and bless the world. If I could only tell, as
I have felt it in my own life, and in the lives of other women
whom I have loved, how wearily one strains the eyes for
light, which often comes not at all!

God knows it all, and if men do not know it, it is because
they have been, I will not say they are, cruelly and criminally
thoughtless. I wish some of those men who talk as if they
imagined our life a delightful one, could but be women for
one little year, and could feel the dreariness I speak of, feel
too the intense longing to be up and doing, helping in the
world's work which is God's work, and know the depressing
effect of that inaptitude, which is the want, not of capacity
or of faculty, but of training. The serious work of life needs
all the help that women as well as men can bring to it, and
for helpfulness something more than goodwill is needed.
Always have my own ignorance and helplessness been the
hindrances to that for which I would have freely given my
life; and I know that other women feel in just the same way:
I have heard and known too much of thoughtful women not
to be sure of this. Confessions of this kind, the simplest and
frankest confessions of ignorance, and of why that ignorance
is painful, have been made to me many a time by women
whom the world pleases to think clever, but who are too
true-hearted to believe the world.

It is not as luxury that we crave knowledge, but as bread of life for ourselves and others. We want it that we may distribute it to others, with helpful hands and words of blessing. We want it as the lever by which we may help to raise the world. If we thought only of gratifying vanity, there are easier and shorter ways to that end. Whilst men are a little too apt to depreciate the intelligence of women as a class, they are apt to over-rate the intelligence of individual women whom they may happen to know and esteem. Many a woman is credited with power merely because she has never been brought to the test of performance.

For the amelioration of the condition of female teachers two things are necessary: the first is to raise the intellectual status of qualified teachers, and to accord a juster social recognition to their profession; the second is, to find other occupations for those who are unfit to teach, and only take to teaching because they can do nothing else.

The first of these objects will be materially advanced –

First – By the establishment of places for a higher education than schools can offer, such as the projected College for women. Mr Bryce, in his interesting 'Report on Schools in Lancashire,' says, 'The teachers cannot be greatly blamed for this' (i.e. inefficient teaching), 'since it is the result of the inadequate provision now made in this country for the instruction of women. Conceive what schoolmasters would be, if there were in England no Universities, or any foundation schools either of the higher or the lower grade, and if the private schools, by which alone education would then be supplied, were to lose the reflex influence and the stimulating rivalry of these public institutions. This is exactly what the state of the teachers of girls is now.'

Secondly – By the accordance of University certificates to women, provided always that these University certificates possess intrinsic value, declare a due amount of knowledge and of capacity to teach, and are given 'with scrupulous care to none but deserving persons.'

Governesses would, I hope, not be the only women who would avail themselves of these privileges. Everything is good which tends to break down the line of social demarcation which still, to a great extent, separates governesses from other ladies, as once it separated school-masters from other gentlemen; and it is greatly to be desired that women with a real talent for teaching, whatever their social position, should actually teach for a few years, and raise the profession of governesses, as the profession of schoolmasters has been raised, by an infusion of disinterested zeal and the energy of a voluntary choice.

Any effort in the cause of governesses is important, not only as it affects individuals at this moment engaged in the profession, but still more in its bearing upon the future of all English girls and women, through the prospect which it holds out of an improved education for the daughters of the middle classes, who, more and more, will have to maintain themselves. And if we think how much honour and dignity ought to attach to the office of a teacher (rightly understood) we should, from the highest motives, be anxious to raise the character and social standing of those who seek that office. For this question of woman's education is far from being one of intellectual progress merely; it is a question of deep moral import, and enters far into the heart of society, affecting the best interests of men as well as those of women. Mr Francis Newman says, 'the increased influence of women' (through education chiefly) 'will keep in check the liquor traffic, and other abominations which men too readily excuse.' The connection of this question of woman's education with some of the most grievous of social problems is closer than might be supposed. De Tocqueville asked an American gentleman why open immorality, such as England has to show, was so rare in New England: the answer was, 'because of the greater respect which men have for women, the women who are their equals in society.' It will not be for themselves alone that enlightened and educated women will demand respect; they will claim it also for poor women, whom it is too often deemed a light matter to injure in the worst way, and even for the fallen, who through the voice of their happier sisters shall yet demand, not only compassion, but the respect due to every human being, however clouded with misery and sin.

When, on the other hand, we consider the best means of relieving the profession of Governesses by drafting its incompetent members into other occupations, the whole question of the employment of women rises before us, a painful and even a terrible problem. Three principal obstacles stand in the way of such an enlargement of woman's opportunities. These are –

(1) Prejudice of employers and of the public.
(2) Combinations among workmen to exclude women from their trades.
(3) Defective education and training of the women themselves.

I will consider these in order –
(1) Prejudice is slowly dying out, but indifference remains. Educated men who can help, who *would* help if they knew the

need, have not yet learnt that need. I do not blame them with any bitterness. There has been enough already of bitterness on the one side and of levity on the other. But an acknowledgment of past error lies at the base of every true reform. Let that be acknowledged here, which every thoughtful observer must see, that through all ages of the world's history the more powerful sex have been liable to use their power carelessly, not for protection only, but for pain. So comes it that at this day just and chivalrous men find themselves, (as Lord Palmerston said of the Emperor of Russia), 'born to a heritage of wrong and oppression.' They cannot, if they would, at once alter the structure of the society around them. But even of these just men I complain that they *do not see*. If they saw, they would act; and ought they not to see? Our best men too often know nothing of the lives of any women except those with whom they are immediately connected, and whom they guard in comfort and ease. They do not think of those who sit in cold and want outside. Many a tender-hearted but not large-hearted man, on hearing some hint of hardships among women outside his own circle, thanks God that *his* dear wife or daughter is exempted from them, and so dismisses the subject. When once such men are brought to see and to feel, we invariably find them *more* indignant than women themselves, who are well schooled in patience. Much of this misery is strange and unknown to men, and was certainly never designed by them. The old social order has changed, giving place to the new, but women have fallen out of line with the onward movement, fettered by their own cowardice and the careless selfishness of men. Custom and use press heavily on women, they endure long before they dare to think whether the system under which they suffer is a right or a wrong one, whether their burdens be removeable or no – whether, in short, they have fallen into the hands of God or man. Even when they are fully persuaded that their burdens are removable, they have no voice to raise. They are unrepresented, and the interests of the unrepresented always tend to be overlooked.

(2) The exclusion of women from trades is in most cases notoriously based upon a coarse selfishness. Take the instance of the china painters at Worcester.

It appears that both men and women are employed in this art, but that the women having excited the jealousy of the men by surpassing them in skilful execution, and consequently earning better wages, were by them forcibly deprived of the maulsticks on which it is necessary to rest the wrist while painting. Thus the women are at once rendered incapable of any fine work, and can only be employed in the coarser kinds of painting. The masters submit to this tyranny, though to their own disadvantage, being probably afraid of a strike or riot if they resist, and the women are forced to yield from the fear of personal violence from their less skilful but heavier-fisted rivals.

This story appeared in the *Edinburgh Review* for 1859, and it is surprising that it did not excite more general indignation. The conduct of the Apothecaries' Company is worse than that of the china painters, inasmuch as doctors have not the excuse of indigence to justify their exclusiveness. The *Daily News*, in a recent article, concludes an account of some of the proceedings of that body with these words:

> We recommend these facts to the good people who think that coercion, restriction, and the tyranny of combination are peculiar to any one class of society. It will be a great day in England when the right of every individual to make the most of the ability which God has given him, free from interested interference, is recognised, and to that goal we are surely advancing; but our progress is slow, and it is very clear that it is not only in the lower ranks of the community that the obstructive trades' union spirit is energetically operating.

The chivalry, or the justice of educated men could scarcely be brought to bear upon a subject where chivalry and justice are needed more. In this matter, of the bad effects of trades' unions, much may be hoped for from the known character of working men themselves, as a class. They are not wanting in justice, in tenderness of heart, and in a shrewd perception of right and wrong when they are placed before them: but they need enlightenment and instruction – and they wait for it – from those who are their superiors in education and trained intelligence. Untold good might be done, and much future misery averted, if those among our leading men who have the ear and the confidence of working-men would (themselves first instructed) bring before them fairly and patiently, such subjects as these. Economics lie at the very root of practical morality, and it is to be hoped that men of influence, and genius, and experience of life, will address themselves gravely to the task of instructing the working classes on this most grave subject.

The common objection brought before the Society for promoting the Employment of Women, is that a risk would be thus incurred of decreasing the employment of men. Now, in the first place, this is by no means certain. No one proposes to interfere with the men at present working at any trade; but while the demand for young men at high wages in the colonies continues practically unlimited, it may be questioned whether the admission to a sedentary employment at home is not a pitfall as often as an advantage. Many a young man would be healthier and happier at some manly trade in Canada or Australia, than in standing behind an English counter or plaiting straw. To take only the trades connected with women's dress and such matters, the census of 1861 gives the following numbers of *men* employed in trades, some of which would seem as distinctly appropriate to the one sex, as soldiering and sailoring to the other.

	Males.
[3]Mercers, Drapers, and Linen Drapers	45,660
Hair Dressers and Wig Makers	10,652
Haberdashers and Hosiers	4,327
Straw Hat and Bonnet Makers	1,687
Washermen and Laundry Keepers	1,165
Stay and Corset Makers	884
Milliners and Dress Makers	803
Artificial Flower Makers	761
Berlin Wool Dealers	63
Artists in Hair – Hair Workers	42
Baby Linen Makers	13
	66,057

Disabilities of sex are parallel to disabilities of creed, and the economical results are likely to be the same. Silk weaving was driven *into* England by the revocation of the Edict of Nantes, and I believe that now several light trades are being driven *out* of England by the industrial proscription of women. 'But supposing,' says Miss Boucherett, 'that the competition for employment were so great that whatever was added to the prosperity of one sex must be deducted from that of the other, is it just that the whole of the suffering thus caused should be laid upon the weaker half of humanity? How great a contrast is there between the spirit of Christianity, and the course of conduct too frequently pursued in this our country!'

'Be just before you are chivalrous,' many a woman is tempted to exclaim, when she finds every door through which she might pass to a subsistence, closed in her face with expressions of deference. Signs have not been wanting which have justified the saying 'that a selfish disregard of the interests of women, and indifference to their sufferings, is the great national sin of England, – and all national sins, if unrepented, meet with their punishment sooner or later.'

(3) The defective training of the women themselves is the most serious of all the hindrances which I have been considering. Here it is that the vicious circle returns upon itself. These women cannot teach, because they are so ill educated, and again, they are so ill educated that they can do nothing *but* teach.[4] Many a woman rejected from the shop-till or housekeeper's room for ignorance and inefficiency, is compelled to offer herself among the lowest class of nursery governesses, or, failing all, to embrace the career, the avenues to which stand ever wide open, yawning like the gates of hell, when all other doors are closed.

The fault of this defective training lies mainly with the middle-class parents who, as the Endowed Schools Commissioners say plainly enough, educate their daughters to get husbands, and for nothing else.

Education was what the slave-owners most dreaded for their slaves, for they knew it to be the sure road to emancipation. It is to education that we must first look for the emancipation of women from the industrial restrictions of a bye gone age. In the meantime I may surely say that no lover of his country, of justice or of God, can see this misery unmoved. 'He looked for judgment, but behold oppression, for righteousness, but behold a cry.'

I sometimes hear it said 'I am weary of this question of the rights, or the wrongs, of women.' Undoubtedly there are many who are quickly weary of any thought which is perplexing or painful: nevertheless the facts remain the same – that women constitute one half of the human race, that whatever affects them, for good or evil, affects not one half, but the whole of the human race, and that the *primary* education of all generations of men rests in the hands of women.

There are two classes of advocates of the improvement of the education and condition of women. The one class urge everything from the domestic point of view. They argue in favour of all which is likely to make women better mothers, or better companions for men, but they seem incapable of judging of a woman as a human being by herself, and superstitiously afraid of anything which might strengthen her to stand alone, prepared, singlehanded, to serve her God and her country. When it is urged upon them that the women who do and must stand alone are counted by millions, they are perplexed, but only fall back on expressions of a fear lest a masculine race of women should be produced, if we admit any theories respecting them apart from conjugal and maternal relationships.

On the other hand, there are advocates who speak with some slight contempt of maternity, in whose advocacy there appears to me little evidence of depth of thought, or tenderness, or wisdom, and which bespeaks a dry, hard, unimaginative conception of human life. They appear to have no higher ideal for a woman than that of a *man* who has been 'tripos'ed,' and is going to 'get on in the world,' either in the way of making money or acquiring fame. They speak of women as if it were a compliment to them, or in any way true, to say that they are like men. Now it appears to me that both these sets of advocates have failed to see something which is very true, and that their ears are deaf to some of the subtle harmonies which exist in God's creation – harmonies sometimes evolved from discords – and which we are much hindered from hearing by the noise of the world, and by our own discordant utterances.

The first class of advocates do not know how strong Nature is, how true she is for the most part, and how deeply the maternal character is rooted in almost all women, married or unmarried: they are not, therefore, likely to see that when a better education is secured to women, when permission is granted them not only to win bread for themselves, but to use for the good of society, every gift bestowed on them by God, we may expect to find, (as certainly we shall find,) that they will become the *more* and not the *less* womanly. Every good quality, every virtue which we regard as distinctively feminine, will, under conditions of greater freedom, develop more freely, like plants brought out into the light from a cellar in which they languished, dwarfed and blanched, without sun or air. The woman is strong in almost every woman; and it may be called an infidelity against God and against the truth of nature to suppose that the removal of unjust restrictions, and room given to breathe freely, and to do her work in life without depression and without bitterness, will cause her to cast off her nature. It will always be in her nature to foster, to cherish, to take the part of the weak, to train, to guide, to have a care for individuals, to discern the small seeds of a great future, to warm and cherish those seeds into fulness of life. 'I serve,' will always be one of her favourite mottos, even should the utmost freedom be accorded her in the choice of vocation; for she, more readily perhaps than men do, recognises the wisdom and majesty of Him who said – 'I am among you as he that serveth.' In Him, – 'in Christ Jesus,' says the apostle, 'there is neither Jew nor Greek, there is neither bond nor free; there is neither male nor female.' It has been the tendency of Christianity, gradually and slowly, to break down all unfriendly barriers between races, and to extinguish slavery; and last of all it will – this is our hope – remove disabilities imposed by the stronger portion of society upon the weaker.

What do we lose by the abandonment of national exclusiveness? Is labour demoralised because slaves are free? Does *service* cease when servitude is at an end? Common sense alone, without the help of historical knowledge, might lead us to suppose that women will not do their *special* work in the world worse, but better, when justice shall be done them.[5] It is in the name of *Christ* that the removal of burdens and disabilities is preached: much wisdom might be learned regarding some of these matters if people would look more closely at this, and note that this is the Person in whom all virtues which are considered essentially womanly, as well as those which are considered essentially manly, found their perfect development. A little meditation on this double truth – that in Christ all distinctions are done away, and that in Him, nevertheless, were exhibited in perfect beauty the distinctive virtues of the feminine character – would suggest some lessons which the world has been very slow to learn, would tend to remove groundless fears regarding the consequences of the abandonment of many unreasonable and unchristian theories which prevail, and to counteract the materialistic doctrine which has sunk too deep into the heart of our so-called Christian community, a doctrine which amounts to this, that 'the weaker races, classes, persons must struggle on unaided, and if they are trampled down and die out, the fact proves that it is better for the world that they should perish, so only a stronger and higher stock will remain;'[6] a doctrine of which we see the fruits in our wickednesses in Asia, etc., and which takes its stand on a supposed 'law of nature' that the weak must go down.

The tone in which certain foolish popular writers speak of unmarried and childless women betrays both coarseness of feeling and ignorance. They speak of these women as having altogether missed their vocation, and as necessarily dwarfed in affection and motive, because they have not performed certain physical functions. We are all mothers or foster-mothers. The few exceptions to this rule – the cases in which the maternal feelings are weak or wanting – are to be found among mothers of families as well as among childless women. I have known many unmarried women in whom all the best characteristics of maternity are stronger than in some who are actually mothers. It would be wise of the State to avail itself of this abundance of generous womanliness, of tender and wise motherliness which lives in the hearts of thousands of women who are free to bring their capacities to bear where they are most needed. The country counts by tens of thousands its orphan and outcast children, in workhouses, and in the streets of our great cities. These orphans have lately been called 'the children of the State:' for the care of these children of the State alone, mothers and nurses of the State are needed, women who must be free to some extent from domestic ties of their own. These workhouse children are not likely to grow up to be useful to the country or other than dangerous classes, while they are left wholly to the mercy of vulgar, uneducated people.[7]

Leon Fauchat exclaimed, when told of crimes committed in our country against children − 'Est-il possible que ces choses soient permises par une nation qui a des entrailles!' 'Take heed that ye offend not one of these little ones,' are words of most solemn import: when women begin to deserve and acquire more weight in the community, the warning contained in them will be better understood. The interests of children will not remain unrepresented any longer than women remain so. I say this with certainty, knowing the nature of woman. It will not be left to an indignant father, or philanthropist, or to an impassioned poetess, at long intervals to translate in the ears of the public the inarticulate cry of the children:

> They are weeping in the playtime of the others,
> In the country of the free,
> For the man's grief abhorrent, draws and presses
> Down the cheeks of infancy.
>
> They look up with their pale and sunken faces,
> And their look is dread to see,
> For they mind you of their Angels in their places,
> With eyes meant for Deity:
> 'How long,' they say, 'how long, O cruel nation,
> Will you stand, to move the world, on a child's heart,
> Stifle down with a mailed heel its palpitation,
> And tread onward to your throne amid the mart?
> Our blood splashes upwards, O our tyrants,
> And your purple shows your path;
> *But the child's sob curseth deeper in the silence*
> *Than the strong man in his wrath.*'

The ears of my reader would not endure to hear what I could tell, what my eyes have seen, of outraged innocence, of horrors and miseries endured among the children of the poor. I am not unmindful of the benevolent enterprise there is in our country, the orphanages, schools and homes springing up everywhere. God be thanked for these! but they do not yet meet the evil; and we must remember that stone walls do not shut out crime, nor regulations confer blessing; these institutions themselves fail in their purpose unless the compassionate motive which originated them be sustained in a constant and abundant flow. The histories of many charities in foreign countries and at home prove that institutions devised by loving hearts for protection and blessing, have become, for lack of the constancy of the internal impulse, neither more nor less than 'habitations of cruelty.' What I here complain of is the thriftless waste of good feelings, of emotion – emotion which on the one hand is ill trained, and consequently takes a false or unreal direction, and on the other is wearing itself out, unclaimed. Tears shed over sentimental works of fiction or some imaginative woe might well be bestowed on the realities around us. Surely there is room enough among *them* for the promptings of a mighty compassion! Surely there is cause enough *here* for tears! 'Mine eye runneth down with rivers of water for the destruction of the daughter of my people.'

And there is other work on every side waiting to be done by women – the work of healers, preachers, physicians, artists, organisers of labour, captains of industry, etc., while on the other hand women are waiting to be prepared for service, and ready to bridge over, as they alone can, many a gulf between class and class which now presents a grave obstacle to social and political progress.

The second kind of advocacy of the rights of women, of which I spoke, may be said to be simply a reaction against the first. It is chiefly held by a few women of superior intellect who feel keenly the disadvantages of their class, their feebleness, through want of education, against public opinion, which is taken advantage of by base people, their inability, through want of representation, to defend their weaker members, and the dwarfing of the faculties of the ablest and best among them. These women have associated little with men, or at best, know very little of their inner life, and do not therefore see as clearly as they see their own loss, the equal loss that it is to men, and the injury it involves to their characters, to live dissociated from women: they therefore look forth from their isolation with something of an excusable envy on the freer and happier lot, which includes, they believe, a greater power to do good, and imagine that the only hope for themselves is to push into the ranks of men, to demand the same education, the same opportunities, in order that they may compete with them on their own ground. They have lost the conception of the noblest develop-ment possible for both men and women; for assuredly that which men, for the most part, aim at, is not the noblest, and yet that is what such women appear to wish to imitate; they have lost sight of the truth, too, that men and women were made equal indeed, but not alike, and were meant to supplement one another, and that in so doing – each supplying force which the other lacks – they are attracted with a far greater amount of impulse to a common centre. When St Chrysostom preached in Constantinople, that 'men ought to be pure, and women courageous,' he was treated as a dangerous innovator, a perverter of the facts of nature, a changer of customs. I hope that many such innovators will arise, who will shew forth in practice the possibility of the attainment of a common standard of excellence for man and woman, not by usurpation on either hand, nor by servile imitation, but by the action of each upon each, by mutual teaching and help. The above misconception, like many other errors, results from men and women living so dissociated as they do in our country; hence comes also all that reserve, and incapacity for understanding each other which has existed between the sexes for so many generations, those false notions about women which are entertained in society, and great injury to the work, and happiness, and dignity of man and woman alike: for it may be truly said that many of the most serious evils in England are but the bitter and various fruit of the sacreligious disjoining of that which God had joined together, the disunion of men and women, theoretically and practically, in all the graver work of life.

The following account of the School of Art, in Newman Street, London, is interesting, as affording some illustration of this subject. Mrs Heatherley writes,

This School was begun on the separate principle, about twenty-three years ago, by Mr James Mathews Leigh. I first knew the place in 1848, when I studied as an amateur. Mr Leigh, whilst agreeing to the idea of mixed classes as a theory, always declared that the men's conduct and conversation would render it impossible for any lady to come amongst them, and they were certainly very rough in manner when, after Mr Leigh's death, we took the school. We were warned that we should be ruined by introducing the mixed system. Very soon both parties found the convenience of studying in the Gallery every day, instead of having to take their places on alternate days. Finding it succeed, at the end of 1861 we admitted ladies to the evening school: there are about two hundred students in the course of the year. Great individual freedom is allowed, and a most friendly feeling exists amongst the students. Every one who knew the place before the admission of women agrees that there has been great improvement; quite another tone prevails. We have never had to dismiss anyone for conduct that was disapproved. From here went the first ladies to the Royal Academy, one of whom, a girl of about twenty-one, gained the gold medal, last December, for the best historical picture. As a general rule, where there are equal facilities, the women are the most successful. The Academy ceased to admit them when their numbers reached about twelve, and now takes them in only when the time of studentship of others expires. They made this change at the end of two years, without giving any notice here or at any other school, to the great disappointment of a number of girls. This I think is an act of hardship, as there has been shown positively that no incompetence exists. Unless there be chances offered to women of being able to follow a profession, parents will invest in consols, as a general rule, rather than in a superior education. The mention of our school may be useful, because there are doubts in many minds as to the expediency of free intercourse between young people, and facts are better than theories. The more that is done to bring young men and women together in a rational manner, the sooner we may hope to arrive at a social state less immoral than the present.

I am persuaded that anyone who will candidly and carefully consider the histories of separate communities of men or women, for educational or other purposes, must see that the evils attendant on such a system as they represent outweigh its conveniences. The arrangement is for a given period, but not so the evils which accompany it, for they – and of this men are not ignorant – too often leave their effects, I may say their curse, throughout life. The objection rises at once of the difficulty of adopting any other arrangement than the present, which may be called an unnatural one. This objection will be more effectually met by facts than by reasoning, and in time facts will speak for themselves, while up to the present they attest that whenever the experiment of a different system has been tried, the difficulties have been found to be very much less than it was believed they would be, before the trial was made.

To conclude this part of my subject, although I grant that too much stress cannot be laid upon the improvement of the education of women who will be actually the mothers of a future generation, yet I wish, on the one hand, that persons who only look at it from this point of view would take more into account the valuable service our country might command if it but understood the truth about the condition and feelings of its unmarried women, and that a more generous trust were felt in the strength of woman's nature, and the probable direction of its development when granted more expansion, while on the other hand I should like to see a truer conception of the highest possibilities for women than is implied in the attempt to imitate men, and a deeper reverence for the God of nature, whose wisdom is more manifested in variety than in uniformity. It cannot be denied that a just cause has sometimes been advocated by women in a spirit of bitterness. Energy impeded in one direction, will burst forth in another; hence the defiant and sometimes grotesque expression which the lives and acts of some few women have been of the injustice done to them by society. This will cease, and while it lasts, it ought to excite our pity rather than our anger. It must be remembered that it is but a symptom of a long endured servitude, a protest against a state of things which we hope will give place to a better. It is folly to regard it as the natural fruit of that of which we have scarcely seen the beginning. Acts of violence on the part of a long oppressed nation are not the offspring of dawning liberties, but of a doomed tyranny. Again, no important reform can be carried without a measure of attendant confusion. Evil agencies are the most vigilant for destruction at the beginning of a great and good work, and many lives have to be consumed in its inauguration. Any evils which may at first attend a social reform ought not to alarm us: they are transient; they are but the breakers on the bar which must be crossed before we launch into deep waters, but the 'noise and dust of the wagon which brings the harvest home.'

There is a near future and there is a far future; there are plans for the near future and plans for the far future. The world is full of plans for the near future; not so of plans for the far future. There are people who do just what comes first to their hand to do, there are others who do all for a near future, others again who do all for a far off end. The first and the last have much in common; it is the second aim, which when exclusively pursued, misleads. Plans and schemes for the near future gain and obtain with most people; not unfrequently they wither away like untimely fruit: those who look afar off prevail, yet not they, but rather He prevails in them, who taught them to stretch their vision to the distant horizon, and enables them to bear with composure the disappointment of present hopes.

Some say, 'in order to insure success for this or that movement, you must have a scheme beforehand, a well-planned system, a fixed principle of action, else you will be blown hither and thither.'

Without offering any opposition to such a theory, there are others to whom there appears but one principle of action, – to fix the eyes on the far future, and to do today the work of today; each day to undo the heavy burdens as they come to their hand, each day to break some link of the chains which bind, and to let some who are now oppressed go free, God guiding these efforts to the desired end.[8] They have more faith in that which grows from within than in that which is planned from without, and built according to the preconceived plan. Such plans or schemes as must be adopted by them are made as elastic as possible, so that the builders can avail themselves, at each step, of experience gained, and be ready to correct or undo any part of the work without sacrificing the whole; they are content with the light which falls on the path immediately at their feet, and with the fairer light in the distance. Perhaps it is by such a principle of action that we can best supply 'the needs of the times,' and it is the possibility of adopting such a principle in times of need that alone can ensure permanence in usefulness for the venerable institutions of the country. What such institutions generally do is to resist all movement, or if they admit any change, it is only to crystallise anew in an altered form. Almost all true help is special; and crystallised institutions seldom have help to give for great and special necessities. But there are times when an impulse, having its origin in the *hearts* of men, is found to be stronger than custom and use; if it cannot work within the established bounds, or by existing machinery, it will work without them. Somehow or other difficulties vanish before such an impulse, and much is accomplished which before was held to be impossible.

I cannot conclude these remarks without expressing the gladness and gratitude with which I am filled when I see the earnest spirit in which some of the best and most thoughtful men are beginning to consider these matters; and I venture especially to acknowledge the kindness of men in high educational positions themselves, whose sympathies have lately been enlisted on behalf of the women-teachers whose struggles, and sorrows, and social disadvantages I have tried to indicate. Mr Maurice says, very truly, 'Whenever in trade or in any department of human activity, restrictions tending to the advantage of one class and the injury of others have been removed, there a divine power has been at work counteracting not only the selfish calculations, but often the apparently sagacious reasonings of their defenders.' If we were not assured that there is indeed a divine power at work in all these things which some of us have so deeply at heart, we should lack the only stimulus which enables us to work on, to live and to die for that which we hold to be right and true; for 'except the Lord build the house, their labour is but vain that build it.'

NOTES

1 Miss Strongitharm states in respect of the Governesses' Institution at Manchester – 'Remember that those who register here are the favourable specimens of the class, the governesses who accept salaries under £20 – and their name is Legion – being excluded by the Rules of the Institution, and that the salaries asked by no means represent in most cases, the salaries obtained – a governess being often too glad to get a home on almost any terms.'

2 The condition of governesses in schools is, on the whole, better than in private families; they have more companionship and independence, and, except in the very poor schools, are better paid.

3 Census for England and Wales. Vol. ii. Occupation of people: summary tables.

4 'In one of Jerrold's sketches, Mr Isaac Cheek is asked, "What can you do?" Now, as Isaac had not dined for three days, he thought himself justified in saying – "*Anything.*" Hunger thus conferred the cheap diploma of omnipotence: why not of omniscience too? In a bitter moment I have been tempted to say that a governess is too often a poor lady who knows nothing, and teaches everything for nothing.' – *Dr Hodgson.*

5 'I have preached,' says Theodore Parker, 'the equivalency of man and woman – that each in some particulars is inferior to the other, but, on the whole, mankind and womankind, though so diverse, are yet equal in their natural faculties; and have set forth the evils which come to both from her present inferior position. . . . But I have thought she will generally prefer domestic to public functions, and have found no philosophic or historic argument for thinking she will ever incline much to the rough works of man, or take any considerable part in Republican politics.'

6 F. Newman.

7 I have spoken of the incompetency of a vast number of teachers, an incompetency sometimes natural, more often the effect of want of training. But I believe it is widely acknowledged that women generally have a great aptitude for teaching boys as well as girls. Mr Bryce, in his Report, says, 'The bright point in this otherwise gloomy landscape is that women are naturally skilful teachers, and that they are, as far as my observation goes, zealous and conscientious teachers. Whenever I happened to hear the teaching of a lady of good ability who had herself been thoroughly educated, its merits struck me as at least equal, and probably superior, to those which would be found in the teaching of a man of the same general capacity and education. Women seem to have more patience as teachers, more quickness in seeing whether the pupil understands, more skill in adapting their explanations to the peculiarities

of the pupils' minds, and certainly a nicer discernment of his or her character. They are quite as clear in exposition as men are, and, when well trained, quite as capable of making their teaching philosophical. I must confess myself to have been also impressed by the interest which they so often took in their pupils, and their genuine ardour to do their best for them.'

8 'Is not this the fast that I have chosen? to loose the bands of wickedness, to undo the heavy burdens, and to let the oppressed go free, and that ye break every yoke; is it not to deal thy bread to the hungry, and that thou bring the poor that are cast out to thy house?' – Isaiah lviii, 6,7.

Letter to the Mayor of Liverpool

(1867)

To the Worshipful the Mayor of Liverpool

Sir,

I thank you for the kind reception which you gave to my letter addressed to you in March. I write once more to say that the generous promises of support which I have received encourage me to persevere in the effort which I described to you; and at the same time I wish to define more clearly what the class of women is which this work, with others, I hope, which may succeed it, is destined to benefit. It is the class of those who have not yet overstepped the line which separates innocence and guilt, but who, surrounded by a corrupt moral atmosphere and destitute of honest resources, are liable to become at any moment a passive burden on the public, or a positive plague – supported by the rates, or by theft, or by an alternative more shameful still. It is acknowledged that this class has not been sufficiently considered in Liverpool.

It is a common remark among those who are trying privately to succour the poor, that when a girl is simply *in danger* it is very difficult to offer her effectual help. For want of sufficient preventive agencies whose aid they may invoke charitable persons are sometimes actually obliged to wait till the man or woman whom they would fain assist has claimed the attention of the community by some overt act of crime or despair. The Matrons of several Penitentiaries have told me that they have frequently to refuse applicants for admission because amidst all their wretchedness they have abstained from making a profession of vice. The Matrons add, that it is much to be wished that such applicants could be directed to some Refuge of a more general kind.

In this town we have Refuges for discharged prisoners, Reformatories, Penitentiaries, and the like, which unite instruction with sternness, and render discipline instrumental to moral renovation and subsequent restitution to society. This is a noble work, and there is great need of all existing Refuges for fallen women; there is great need of more. But we must be aware that our charitable efforts on the one hand may be made to swell the inducements which the poor already have to do evil, unless they are balanced on the other hand by equally earnest efforts on the behalf of those who, comparatively speaking at least, have resisted temptation. And while in London, and in most towns, as much has been done for protection as for rescue, in Liverpool this has not been the case.

If these destitute women do not become criminals they become paupers. For most of them the Workhouse practically means the oakum-shed, which, thus replenished, becomes a problem too difficult for the ablest and most benevolent of Workhouse Governors, and involves, as we have seen, a moral atmosphere and a type of occupation directly destructive of self-dependence and self-respect. The despondency of the pauper is the most sluggish of social sores.

But no argument is needed to enforce the economy of prevention, – to show the advantages of a conception of charity which aims at employing the experience and education of the higher classes to direct the energies of the lower, which comes from the head and the heart rather than from the pocket. For indeed schemes like these – recently started, but surely spreading – have been found more nearly self-supporting than any others which strike as deeply at the roots of misery and crime. Yet money they do need, and it is money well spent. For the results are not such as political economists need fear. We shall not foster dependence by helping women to help themselves. We shall not foster indolence by organizing industry.

The causes which have produced this mass of female destitution are not new, nor peculiar to Liverpool. Working women will obviously be worse off than working men if the proportion between the number of occupations open to women and the number of occupations open to men is less than the proportion between the number of women and the number of men seeking support from these occupations. And

in point of fact almost everywhere, except in certain manufac-
turing centres, the number of openings offered to women
has hitherto been not only absolutely but relatively smaller
than the number of openings offered to men, and consequently the trades to which women are admitted have been
almost always overstocked. There is no radical cure for this
disproportion till men shall cease to consider sex as a disqualification *per se* for occupations for which women are practically fit. In the mean time the condition of the working
woman, almost always worse than that of the working man,
becomes *very much* worse when her disadvantages are aggravated by local circumstances.

Liverpool, the queen of seaports, shares the miseries as
well as the glories of a people whose home is on the deep.
Women here exceed men in number, and of these women
an unusually large percentage have to support themselves.
Sudden failures of dockyard employment, deaths at sea, and
the virtual widowhood and orphanage of the families of many
sailors who are *not* dead – causes like these leave unsupported
many women who have married too young to have had any
opportunity of learning a trade or practising for domestic
service. It is mainly to such widows and orphans that I would
offer an Industrial Home.

No doubt some of them have homes already. 'In No. 13,
Robertson-street,' says Dr Trench in his report on the health
of Liverpool in 1866, 'seven adults and three children slept
in a room of 594 cubic feet, and in No. 17 of the same street
ten adults live in a room of 600 cubic feet. In No. 13 in 5
Court, Hawke-street, seven adults occupied a room of the
same dimensions. The number of six adults in a room of 600
cubic feet is very common. In all cases where adults are
spoken of, there is a mixture of sexes, and therefore an
offence against moral and hygienic law.'

'The contact of home influences' is sometimes spoken of
as a blessing to be preserved at any cost. Does this mean the
physical, continuous, and compulsory contact of dissolute
adults?

Enough of horror. But let no man think that I am
proposing a work which he can innocently leave undone.

Industrial Homes such as I desire to see established would
not be, strictly speaking, Industrial Schools, for girls would
not be received under sixteen years of age. But young women
would be taught to work, subjected to a needful discipline,
and at the same time exposed to elevating and religious

influences, so that their moral and industrial training would go on at once.

Those whose hearts are warm in any matter are loth to think that they have said enough. But here I cannot bear to add any formal appeal. When the very stones cry out I need not interpret. Nor can I suppose that I speak to men unwilling to hear. Where the poison-weeds of crime and misery grow so rank I must believe that God has planted in many hearts their antidote, Pity.

I remain, Sir, yours faithfully,
JOSEPHINE E. BUTLER

Letter to Mr Bryce on Examinations for Governesses

(1868)

My dear Mr Bryce,

It is natural that Oxford men, who are kindly disposed to join a scheme which aims at raising the status and testing the capacities of governesses, should wish first to understand from whom the demand for such a scheme arises, and how many women would be likely to avail themselves of opportunities of examination.

The demand comes from the higher class of schoolmistresses and governesses themselves, from women personally familiar with the present disorganisation of their profession, with the perplexities of the employer and the hardships of the employed. I will explain through what channel it is that these women have made their wishes known. Last summer a society was formed, called 'The North of England Council for the Higher Education of Women.' This is a body composed of representatives from Leeds, Liverpool, Manchester, Newcastle, and Sheffield. In each of these places there is an association of schoolmistresses and others interested in the education of girls, and the leading members of these local associations are deputed to the North of England Council.

The first act of this Council was to invite Mr Stuart, Fellow of Trinity College, Cambridge, to deliver educational Lectures to women and girls in Leeds, Liverpool, Manchester, and Sheffield, which he did in the autumn of last year to an audience of nearly six hundred in the four towns, most of whom were examined on paper by the Lecturer. Mr Pearson, Fellow of Oriel College, Oxford, and Mr Hales, Fellow of Christ's College, Cambridge, have consented to deliver similar courses, in the above-mentioned towns and in Bradford, during the ensuing spring.

But the first general meeting of the Council was at Leeds, October 31st, 1867, and one of their first resolutions was, that it was desirable that members of the Universities of Oxford and Cambridge should be invited to institute examinations, in which women above eighteen years of age might obtain certificates of general proficiency, or of proficiency in special subjects.

As President of the Council referred to, it is my duty to prefer this request to members of the Universities, and to explain the reasons which led the Council to make it. As I have said, those reasons are in the interest both of employer and employed.

The schoolmistresses on the Council are accustomed to the bitter complaints of parents, who say that it is intolerable, but that it is necessary, to catechise a lady governess as they would not catechise a housemaid. There exists in Manchester a Society for the Employment of Women. Some of its warmest supporters are persons who have been converted to its objects by governess-hunting alone. What they have been compelled to learn of the miserable incompetence of crowds of women who, (however poorly remunerated,) are driven into the ranks of teachers from the want of other work has impelled them to help on a movement which aims at filling up the gap hitherto existing between teaching and domestic service as feminine avocations.

On the other hand, it is noticeable that while the position of schoolmasters has been greatly improved during the last fifty years, mainly through the large infusion amongst them of University men, the position of schoolmistresses and female teachers in general has undergone no corresponding improvement. This seems to be in great measure owing to the want of any recognised test, like a University degree, by which the competent female teacher may be distinguished from the incompetent. In the absence of such a distinction the status and remuneration of the whole class is in danger of being adapted to the deserts of its least worthy members.

In France, Germany, Switzerland and the United States there are systems for examinations for female teachers, and in France no woman may open or assist in a school without a certificate of competency. This is in effect to transform the occupation of the female teacher from a trade into a profession. Miss Clough, the Secretary of our Council, is preparing a short account of the French and German systems. The American system is described in Mr Fraser's report on American schools, in a Blue Book supplementary to the report of the Endowed Schools Commissioners. About sixty or eighty governesses are examined every six months in Berlin alone, and there are Boards of Examiners in all the provincial capital towns in Prussia.

We are but slowly becoming aware in England how far we are behind many other civilized countries in some such important matters as these. Repeated attempts have however been made by those interested in female education to introduce some such examinations into England. All these schemes were discussed at a meeting held in London on December 14th, 1867, and it was decided that none of them exactly met the existing need.

You tell me that the first impression of some people is that the Cambridge Local Examinations offer all that is wanted for women. These are a great boon and they have been very gratefully received, but we had never worked for them if we had intended to stop there. They are only open to girls under eighteen, and are necessarily much too elementary to meet the requirements of the professed teacher. What would be thought of appointing a master at Eton or Harrow on the strength of his having passed one of the Local Examinations? If an examination of so elementary a character as this really represented the highest tide-mark of possible feminine attainment and ability in this country, the decadence of England would not merely be at hand but completed, and neither technical education, nor extension of franchise, nor any other popular remedy could any more bring life out of death. Happily however feminine intelligence is not absolutely starved out by the absence of due culture, satisfactory tests, and worthy recognition: some women at least are just as much impelled as some men to seek pure truth for the love of it; why should they not be ten times as many more than they are? I do not know which is the greater loser, the individual missing her worthy development, or society missing her best help.

Mr Markby, Secretary to the Syndicate for conducting the Cambridge Local Examinations, testifies to the severity with which the restriction of age is felt. 'The repeated refusals,' he says, 'which I was obliged to give to young women who requested admission to our Examinations were the most painful part of my duty. In the early part of last year letters came from all quarters asking us to waive our rule, and pressing on us the value of a certificate on which the public would rely to ladies seeking a livelihood by teaching. . . . The impression the letters made on me was due not so much to their actual number as to their being evidently representative of a widely felt want. Many came from local Secretaries, the rest almost invariably from persons who took interest in the education of women – very few from young women who wanted an answer for themselves alone. Therefore, although of course each presented a particular case on which a reply was to be given, it was clear that the reply was expected to apply to all such as might come under the notice of the writer. Indeed I was often told so. . . . I am certain from what I have seen that if a good scheme of examination can be set on foot and time given, we shall have as many women candidates for honours as we get now at Cambridge or Oxford. More than twenty-one per cent of the whole number of girls that went in last year got one or more distinctions in special subjects, and I assure you that these distinctions imply considerable proficiency. . . .'

These extracts touch on the probable number of candidates for a higher examination. Several persons have applied to members of our Council, asking to be informed of the proposed examinations as soon as anything is made public, some with a view to the advantage of their daughters, some to that of their governesses, and some girls who have this year passed the senior local examination are anxious to begin working at once for a higher one for which they have begun to hope. A collection of the names of candidates for the first examination will be made by us as soon as anything can be said positively as to the precise form the examination will take. I have little doubt that our Council could guarantee fifty candidates for the first examination, with a prospect of increasing numbers. A high standard, which is here so especially desirable, would necessarily for a time at least limit the numbers, but then it would be a permanent advance that would have been made, and the interests of education would be better served by an examination which only a few women would pass at first, than by one which a crowd could manage just to get through.

I ought to add that the University of London holds out hopes of an extension of some examinations to women. I sincerely hope that these will be most useful, especially in London and the South of England, but I do not think them likely to satisfy the needs of the North. The North is the most advanced part of England in its desire for education; it is more accessible to Scotchwomen than London is, and no one who knows Manchester can deny that it deserves to be made a centre of such examinations as these. Would it be well in any way to connect the proposed University Board with the North of England? In any case the two schemes may well exist together. There will be work for both. For the desire which our Council expresses is neither fleeting nor fanciful: it is a desire felt very deeply by very many women, and which will yet gain strength as it gains hope.

I add a list of the Cambridge men who have kindly consented to join the proposed Board, and warmly thanking you and other friends at Oxford for the interest you take in our wishes and plans,

I remain,
My dear Mr Bryce,
Yours very sincerely,
JOSEPHINE E. BUTLER

The Rev. PROFESSOR KENNEDY.
The Rev. PROFESSOR LIGHTFOOT.
The Rev. PROFESSOR KINGSLEY.
PROFESSOR ADAMS.
PROFESSOR CAYLEY.
PROFESSOR FAWCETT.
PROFESSOR LIVEING.

The Rev. J. ROBY I. TODHUNTER	Fellows of St. John's College.
The Rev. R. BURN	Fellow and Tutor of Trinity College.

J. L. HAMMOND
    H. JACKSON
    F. W. H. MYERS
    H. SIDGWICK
    J. STUART
	Fellows of Trinity College.

The Rev. J. VENN	Fellow of Caius College.
The Rev. T. MARKBY	Secretary to the Syndicate for conducting Local Examinations.
H. PEILE	Fellow of Christ's College.
H. D. WARR	Fellow of Trinity Hall.

Emily Davies

Special Systems of Education for Women

(1868)

Among the controversies to which the movement for improving the education of women has given rise, there is one which presses for settlement. The question has arisen and must be answered – Is the improved education which, it is hoped, is about to be brought within reach of women, to be identical with that of men, or is it to be as good as possible, but in some way or other specifically feminine? The form in which the question practically first presents itself is – What shall be the standards of examination? For though there are still a not inconsiderable number of places of so-called education, into which no examiners from without are allowed to penetrate, the persons by whom these establishments are kept up are pretty certain to disapprove of any change in the existing practice, and are not likely to be troubled with perplexing questions as to the direction in which the reforming tendency should work. The controversy may therefore be assumed to be between two parties, each equally accepting examinations as 'valuable and indispensable things' alike for women and for men – each equally admitting that 'their use is limited,' and that they may be abused.

Of these two parties, one regards it as essential that the standards of examination for both sexes should be the same; the other holds that they may without harm – perhaps with advantage – be different. The controversy does not lie between those on the one hand who, believing men and women to be exactly alike, logically hold that all the conditions to which they may be subjected ought to be precisely similar, and those on the other who, regarding them as completely unlike, cannot believe that anything which is good for one sex can be anything but bad for the other. No rational person takes either of these clearly-defined views; but between the two there is a kind of cloudland, in whose dimness it is not always easy to see the way to wise action. It may do something towards clearing away the haze to endeavour to give some answer to the questions – Why do you ask for a common standard? Do you want to prove the intellectual equality of the sexes? – or their identity? If you desire to improve female education, why not strive after what is ideally best, instead of trying to get things for women which have produced results far short of perfection in men?

The abstract questions as to equality and identity may be quickly dismissed. The advocates of the 'common' principle – those who hold what may be called the *humane* theory – altogether disclaim any ambition to assert either. As to what may be expected as the statistical result of comparison by a common standard, there may be much difference of opinion. If it should be to show a general average of somewhat inferior mental strength in women, a fact will have been discovered of some scientific interest perhaps, but surely of no very great importance. That complete similarity should be proved seems in the nature of things impossible, even if there could be any reason for attempting it; for supposing it to be a fact, it is not the sort of fact which could be brought to light by the test of an examination. A comparison between male and female novelists, or male and female poets – if one may venture to apply such epithets to 'the double-natured' – would be a better criterion, for those who are curious in such matters, than any which could be devised by examiners. In a discussion of practical policy, these considerations may be set aside as matters of chiefly speculative interest.

We come down, therefore, to the narrower and more hopeful inquiry – Which is best, to extend methods of education admitted to be imperfect, or to invent new ones presumably better?

The latter course is urged on the ground that there are differences between men and women which educational systems ought to recognise; or supposing this to be disputed, that at any rate the conditions of women's lives are special, and ought to be specially prepared for; or there is a latent feeling of repugnance to what may appear like an ungraceful, perhaps childish, attempt to grasp at masculine privileges – an idea which jars upon a refined taste. Considerations of this sort, resting mainly upon sentiment or prejudice, can scarcely be met by argument. It is usually admitted that we are as yet in the dark as to the specific differences between men and women – that we do not know how far they are native, and to what extent those which strike the eye may have been produced by artificial influences – that even if we knew much more than we do about the nature of the material to be dealt with, we should still have much to learn as to the kind of intellectual discipline which might be most suitable. Nor have we as yet any trustworthy evidence – scarcely so much as a plausible suggestion – as to the manner in which the differences of the work in life to which men and women respectively are said to be called, could be met by corresponding differences in mental training. The arbitrary differences established by fashion seem to have been directed by the rule of contraries rather than by any intelligent judgment. Practically, what we come to is something like this – People who want to impose a special system have some theories as to the comparative merits of certain studies, which they feel a friendly impulse to press upon others at every convenient opportunity; or they have a vague impression that as certain subjects and methods have been in a manner set apart for women ever since they can remember, there is most likely something in them which distinguishes them either as suitable to the female mind, or as specially useful to women in practical life. To discover how much of truth there may be behind this opinion would be a tedious and difficult task. It may be enough to remark that experience seems to be against it. It is precisely because the special system, as hitherto tried, has proved a signal failure, that reform is called for.

There are other advocates, however, of independent schemes, who take up a totally different ground. They only half believe, or perhaps altogether repudiate, the female mind theory; and they are prepared to go great lengths in assimilating the education of the sexes. But they say –

(1) Male education is in a very bad state – therefore it is not worth while to spread it.
(2) Rightly or wrongly, it *is* different from that of women. It would be useless to examine people in things they have not learnt; and women do not as a rule learn Latin and Greek and Mathematics. We must recognise facts.

By all means let us recognise facts. But let us remember also that facts are created things, and mortal. There are old facts, of a bad sort, which want to be put an end to, and there are new and better facts, which may by wise measures be called into being. And speaking of facts, let this be considered – that however bad the education of men may be, that of women is undoubtedly worse. On this point the Report of the Schools Inquiry Commission speaks very distinctly. After adverting to the general deficiency in girls' education, which 'is stated with the utmost confidence and with entire agreement, with whatever difference of words, by many witnesses of authority,' the Commissioners observe that 'the same complaints apply to a great extent to boys' education. But on the whole, the evidence is clear that, not as they might be but as they are, the girls' schools are inferior in this view to the boys' schools.' And if this is the evidence as regards the school period, during which girls are receiving more or less regular and systematic instruction, it is likely to be still more unanimous and emphatic as to the later stage, during which men are, in however antiquated and foolish a manner, as the reformers tell us, at any rate in some sort taken in hand by the universities, while women are for the most part left altogether to their own resources. It will probably be admitted, without further argument, that to make the education of average women only as good as that of men, would be a step in advance of what it is now.

But is this intermediate step an indispensable one? Are we obliged to go through a course of wandering along paths which have been found to lead away from the desired end? Cannot we use the light of experience, and, avoiding exploded errors, march straight on to perfection by the nearest road? To a great extent, Yes. There is no reason, for example, to imitate boys' schools in their excessive devotion to physical sports; or in the exclusion of music from the ordinary school routine; or to take up methods of teaching of which the defects have been discovered. Again, looking to the higher stage, no one would wish to reproduce among women either the luxurious idleness of the lower average of university men, or the excessive strain of the competition for honours which is said to act so injuriously on the studious class. But these are evils from which women are pretty securely guarded by existing social conditions. There is at present not much fear that girls will take too much out-of-door exercise, that they will give too little time to music, or that governesses will blindly model their teaching on the plans in vogue in boys' schools. Fashionable young ladies are not in danger of idling their time away at college, and the studious are not tempted by valuable rewards attached to academical distinction. It is not in its weak points that male education is likely to be imitated by women.

The immediate controversy turns, as has been said, upon examinations – examinations regarded as a controlling force, directing the course of instruction into certain channels; pronouncing upon the comparative value of subjects, fixing the amount of time and attention bestowed upon each, and to some extent guiding the method of teaching; wholesomely stimulating; and aptly fulfilling its great function of plucking. What are the conditions required to produce the right kind of controlling force? We want authority – that no one disputes. We want the best subjects encouraged. What they are, the most competent judges have not yet settled; but most people, perhaps not all, will agree that when they have made up their minds their verdict ought to be acted upon. We want an examination which can be worked beneficially. To adopt an examination so radically bad that it could not in itself be made an improving exercise, might be defensible, perhaps even justifiable, taking a very enlarged view of contingent moral influences. But it would be a difficult case to defend, and no one has taken it in hand. We want an examination for which candidates will be forthcoming. Finally, we want an examination which will sift. We do not want to have certificates of proficiency given to half-educated women. There are examinations which will do this already within reach.

Authority; wise choice of subjects; so much skill in the construction of questions that at any rate they do not invite shallow and unthorough preparation; practicability; and due severity – these are requisites which most people will agree in regarding as essential. But the agreement does not go much farther. As to authority, what constitutes it? Is it the personal reputation of the examiners, or is it their official position? Or is it the prestige acquired by prescription? Or has the quality of the candidates anything to do with it? It is as to the two last points that opinions differ. We can agree so far as this, that an examination by men of high repute will carry more weight than one by men unknown, and that an examination by an official body such as a university, will be more readily believed in than one by any self-constituted board, however respectable. But supposing these two points secured, is a new examination conducted by competent examiners appointed by a university all that is to be desired? Will an unknown standard, having expressly in view candidates drawn from a limited and notoriously illiterate class, be worth much as regards authority? Mr Matthew Arnold remarks that 'High pitched examinations are the result, not the cause, of a high condition of general culture, and examinations tend, in fact, to adjust themselves to studies.' There is much reason to expect that such a scheme as has been supposed would from the outset be, whether justly or unjustly, regarded as in some way accommodated to the inferior attainments of the class, and that starting with small repute, it would have to contend with the natural tendency of all things to justify their character. The most highly cultivated women would not care to submit themselves to an ordeal in which to fail might be disgrace, but to pass would be no distinction. The mere fact of its special character would in itself repel them. That the greatest of female novelists should have taken the precaution to assume a masculine *nom de plume* for the express purpose of securing their work against being measured by a class standard, is significant of the feeling entertained by women. Right or wrong, wise or foolish, here is at any rate a fact to be recognised, and a fact having a manifest bearing on the question in hand. An examination limited to a class, and with which the *élite* of that class will have nothing to do, is not likely to command very high respect.

As regards the choice of subjects and the practical manipulation, so to speak, it appears that if we are to have an examination stamped by official authority, we must go to the old authorities for it, and these authorities may be supposed to have already done their best, according to their lights, in devising the existing examinations. University examiners are human, and no doubt make mistakes, but if they are incompetent to direct the education with which they are familiar, why should they become suddenly wise when they enter upon a field unknown to them by experience, but as regards which they are but too well supplied with theories? It may be said that the new work would probably fall into the hands of new men, who would start with more advanced ideas, and that they might be able to carry through for women what they cannot get for men. But the counsels of inexperience are not always the wisest, and supposing the case to be as represented, it seems to be merely a question of a very short time. At the universities the generations succeed each other more rapidly than anywhere else. The young men of today will be the governing body a few years hence, and will then be able to carry out their ideas for both men and women. If the new thing proposed is better than what men have already, women do not wish to monopolise it.

The questions of practicability and severity may be taken together. A medium is required between a test so far out of reach that no one will go in for it, and one so loose that it fails to discriminate. And here we must not forget that, though without any fault of their own, the great majority of women *are* very imperfectly educated, and it is therefore impossible, in the nature of things, to devise any test which can at once embrace the great mass and yet be sufficiently exclusive. There are a few educated women. We want to find them. We may be very sorry that other women, perhaps equally intelligent and willing, have not had the chance of being educated too. We are bound to do all we can to bring education within their reach. But we are not bound to perpetuate the evils with which we are struggling, by certifying competent knowledge where it does not exist.

And it is not, except perhaps to some small extent, that the education of women has taken a different line, and that they do know some things thoroughly well, if only they had the opportunity of showing it. The defectiveness of female education tells all the way through. The schools are indeed improving, but then it is to be observed that the best girls' schools are precisely those in which the 'masculine' subjects have been introduced, and by which therefore the imposition of a feminine test is least likely to be desired. The real question of practicability therefore seems to be not what would exactly fit female education as it is, but what it may be made to fit itself to, within a reasonable time and without great inconvenience and difficulty.

On this question much valuable evidence is to be found in the Reports of the Schools Inquiry Assistant Commissioners. Mr Giffard says,

> If I were to sum up the impressions I derived from my visits to girls' schools, I should say (1) that the mental training of the best girls' schools is unmistakeably inferior to that of the best boys' schools; (2) that there is no natural inaptitude in girls to deal with any of the subjects which form the staple of a boy's education; (3) that there is no disinclination on the part of the majority of teachers to assimilate the studies of girls to those of boys; (4) that the present inferiority of girls' training is due to the despotism of fashion, or in other words the despotism of parents and guardians.

Other evidence to the same effect abounds. Any one who knows well the better class of teachers of girls will endorse Mr Giffard's statement as to their willingness to adopt innovations. There is no insuperable difficulty in getting teaching of any subject where there is a sufficient demand for it. It would probably be easier to get first-rate teaching in classics and mathematics than in, say modern languages, because they are the subjects which have hitherto been chiefly cultivated by highly educated men. And though a test which would at first exclude the great majority of ordinary women may have an appearance of rigour almost amounting to cruelty, it is consoling to know that there are already open to women many opportunities of bringing to the test such elementary or fragmentary knowledge as circumstances may have enabled them to pick up. The Society of Arts gives examinations not to be despised, in a great variety of subjects, and the machinery for conducting them brings them within easy reach. The Government Department of Science and Art gives certificates of competency to teach in various branches of science and art. The Royal Academy of Music gives examinations and a diploma. The Home and Colonial School Society holds examinations for governesses which include, besides the ordinary subjects of instruction, such as modern languages, music and drawing, the special qualifications required by governesses in schools, namely, teaching power, and governing power. It cannot be truly said that female teachers have no means of showing competency, and that those who are willing rather to work gradually for radical reform than to catch hastily at half measures, are sacrificing the present generation for the sake of shadowy advantages in a distant future.

The kind of result which is likely to follow from an adaptation of a female examination to the *examinees*, may be conjectured from the advice given by a schoolmistress in reference to the Cambridge Local Examinations. Complaining of the vexatious demand for a degree of attainment in arithmetic not commonly reached in girls' schools, she remarked briefly, 'I would have all that expunged.' The suggestion that one advantage of these examinations might consist in the pressure brought to bear in favour of unpopular subjects, was met by the rejoinder, 'But why press an unpopular subject which is of no use in after life?'

The tendency of examinations to adjust themselves to studies is a consideration of great importance. At present the weak points in the education of men are the comparatively strong points in that of women, and therefore less need attention. It is where men are strong that women want stimulus and encouragement – and it may be added, they need this only, in order to produce satisfactory results. The Cambridge Local Examinations furnish a case in point. In the first examination to which girls were admitted, 90 per cent of the senior candidates failed in the preliminary arithmetic. Fortunately, the standard was fixed by reference to an immense preponderance of boy candidates, and it was understood that the girls must be brought up to it. Extra time and probably better teaching, aided by greater willingness on the part of the pupils, who had been made aware of their deficiency, were devoted to the unpopular and 'useless' subject. In the next examination, out of the whole number of girls only three failed in it.

Other reasons for desiring a common standard, of a more subtle character, can scarcely be apprehended perhaps in their full force without personal experience. Probably only women who have laboured under it can understand the weight of discouragement produced by being perpetually told that, as women, nothing much is ever to be expected of them, and it is not worth their while to exert themselves – that they can write lively letters, full of graphic description and homely touches, but that anything like original research or profound learning is not for them to think of – that whatever they do they must not interest themselves, except in a second-hand and shallow way, in the pursuits of men, for in such pursuits they must always expect to fail. Women who have lived in the atmosphere produced by such teaching know how it stifles and chills, how hard it is to work courageously through it. Every effort to improve the education of women which assumes that they may, without reprehensible ambition, study the same subjects as their brothers and be measured by the same standards, does something towards lifting them out of the state of listless despair of themselves into which so many fall. Supposing that the percentage of success attained by women should be considerably less than that of men, the sense of discouragement thus engendered would be as nothing compared with the general self-distrust produced by having it taken for granted that they are by nature disqualified to stand the ordinary tests. To make the discovery of individual incompetence may be wholesomely humbling or stimulating, as the case may be, but no one is the better for being told, on mere arbitrary authority, that he belongs to a weak and incapable class. And this, whatever may be the intention, is said in effect by the offer of any test of an exclusively female character. No doubt there are university men whose opinion of their own education is so low that they can honestly propose a special standard for women with the intention and expectation of its being better than anything that has been known before, and an example to be imitated in male examinations. But this idea is so new and so bewildering to the outside world, that it is simply incomprehensible. The statement of it is regarded as irony.

If it were otherwise – supposing that in the future the relative positions of men and women as regards Learning should be reversed – the arguments in favour of common standards would be changed in their application, but would remain substantially the same. There would still be the same reasons for desiring that in all departments of study boys and girls, men and women, should walk together in the same paths. Why should they be separated? And the whole specialising system has a tendency, so far as its influence goes, to separate – to divide where union is most to be desired. The easy way in which it is often taken for granted that, as a matter of course, men care for men and women for women – that a certain *esprit de corps* is natural, if not positively commendable – must surely arise from a most inhuman way of looking at things. Conceive a family in which the brothers and sisters form rival *corps*, headed by the father and mother respectively! If on the small scale the spectacle is revolting, surely it ought to be no less so in the great human family. In the rebellion of the best instincts of human nature against such a theory, we have a security that it will never prevail. But sympathy may be checked even where it cannot be destroyed; and to put barriers in the way of companion-

ship in the highest kinds of work and pleasure, is to carry out in
the most effectual way the devices of the dividing spirit.

But when all has been said that can be, or that need be, said in
favour of common standards, it may still be urged – All this is
very well, but can you get them? What university is likely to open
its degree examinations to women? Would it not be well to try
some judicious compromise?

To those who are aware that women have at this moment free
access to the degrees of several foreign universities, to say nothing
of historic precedent, the idea of extending those of our own
country is not so very startling. We see in the papers from time
to time notices of ladies who have taken the degree of Bachelière-
ès-Sciences, or Bachelière-ès-Lettres, at Paris, Lyons, or elsewhere;
and three English ladies are now studying for the medical degree
at the University of Zurich, without hindrance or restriction of
any sort. In England the only university which could at present
be reasonably asked to open its examinations to women is that of
London. The condition of residence imposed by the old universities
must exclude women until they are able, by means of a college of
their own, to offer guarantees as to instruction and discipline
similar to those which are required at Oxford and Cambridge. It
is probable that within no very distant period the opportunity of
complying with this essential condition will be within reach of
women, and there is reason to hope that the examinations of the
University of Cambridge may then be substantially, if not in name
– and this last is a secondary consideration – as accessible to women
as they are to men. But when this shall arrive, the wants of non-
resident students will remain to be supplied; and here it is manifestly reasonable to look to the one English university which
undertakes this particular work. The question has been before the
University of London for some years, and a supplemental charter
has been obtained, empowering the university to institute special
examinations for women. The first step taken under this charter
has been to draw up a scheme for a general or testing examination
for women parallel with the matriculation examination for men;
and by a curious coincidence, the subjects found specially appropriate to women are, with a few exceptions, precisely those which
had already been laid down as specially proper for men. Greater
option is given in the section of languages; for some inscrutable
reason, one book of Euclid instead of four is considered enough
for women, and by way of compensation physical geography is
thrown in; English *Literature* is added to English language; and a
choice is permitted between chemistry and botany. It will be
observed that, except three books of Euclid, nothing which is

considered good for men is *omitted*, the only substantial difference being that women are allowed greater freedom in selection. Whether this gift of liberty is better than guidance need not here be discussed. As to the level of attainment to be exacted, no official announcement has been made. It is confidently asserted that it will be in no way inferior, as regards difficulty, to the parallel matriculation examination; and as the subjects prescribed will, for a time at any rate, exclude ordinary half-educated women, it seems likely that the assertion will be justified.

Here then seems to be a fair case for compromise. To begin with, we have the authority of a university which is growing in public estimation and importance, which is recognised as the great examining board for all students whose circumstances preclude college life, and which year by year is acquiring more of that dignity which belongs only to age. Then, looking at the examination itself, and especially at the programme of subjects prescribed, it cannot be denied that it is admirably suited to the education of women in its present state of transition. Modern languages and English literature have their place by the side of classics, mathematics, and physical science. Taking the Schools Inquiry Commissioners as a guide – and there could scarcely be a better – we find that in their chapter on 'Kinds of education desirable,' their recommendations show a remarkable correspondence with the course laid down in the London programme. Some provision will no doubt be required to bring the requisite instruction within reach of women; but here we come upon one of the advantages of community of subjects. It is certain that as young men all over England are continually preparing for this examination, there must be people employed in teaching them, and by a little arrangement, the same teachers may be made available for their sisters. One of the benefits contingent on the use of such an examination is, that it may lead to the extension of good teaching. It is, of course, also possible that women may become the prey of the crammers, but probably not at all to the same extent as their brothers – the inducement to an unstudious woman to go through an examination merely for the sake of a pass being comparatively small. The matriculation examination is taken up by a large proportion of male students as their one and final test, and as such it will no doubt be made immediate use of by women.[1] If it should be found that the machinery works well, that the demand which has been alleged on the part of women is real, and if the students, by passing creditably this first stage, establish their claim to the complete university course, there is little doubt that it will ultimately be acknowledged. The step which has already been taken may be regarded as a tentative effort in the right direction, and public opinion is not likely to permit backsliding.

NOTE

1 It is estimated that nearly one-half of the undergraduates go no farther than matriculation. Taking the year 1865 as a specimen, it appears that there were 616 candidates for matriculation and only 309 for the degree of Bachelor in the various faculties. The average age of candidates for matriculation has varied from seventeen years and eleven months to twenty years and ten months. In the years 1863–5 it was over twenty years.

Home and the Higher Education[1]

(1878)

Before entering upon any of the matters which more particularly claim our attention at such a meeting as this, I wish to offer my thanks to the association for the opportunity and the inducement given to me to make acquaintance with its work. It seems very desirable that the labourers in various parts of the educational field should be cognisant of each other's work, the objects sought and the methods employed, the experiments set on foot, the successes and the failures, that we may learn from each other, and acquire something like a common stock of experience. For those who are chiefly occupied at what may be called a somewhat central position, it is a great gain to know, not only in the imperfect way that things are picked up from notices in the newspapers, but thoroughly, by close inspection, the details of important educational enterprises in various parts of the country; and I feel that I have added substantially to my own small stock of useful knowledge by studying the Reports of this association. Feeling this, it has occurred to me that there might be some reciprocity in the matter, and that it might not be useless for me to state very briefly my impression as to the work going on in Birmingham. Putting it in the briefest form, I should say that the quality appears to me to be better than the quantity. I notice with pleasure the solid character of the subjects taken up – as e.g., Latin, Greek, Algebra, Geometry, Trigonometry – and the favourable reports of the teachers on the progress made, and I confess that, for my own part, I would rather, in the interests of sound education, hear of small classes of real students, who genuinely respond to thorough teaching, than of large audiences flocking to popular lectures, listening with interest for the moment, and going away with some 'general ideas,' perhaps, but without having really mastered any part of what has been put before them. Still, while recognising the excellent quality of the work, and the value of quality as compared to quantity, one cannot but feel that in this great town the number of students might have been expected to be larger. It is evident that great zeal has been shown in providing the means of cultivation, but it does not appear that the young people of the place have, in any considerable number, shown a corresponding zeal in the use of the means.

Such an observation suggests inquiry as to the causes of the apparent apathy, which I am afraid is by no means confined to Birmingham, and I shall ask you presently to consider whether one of these causes may not consist in some errors in our general domestic policy – some mistakes in our internal family arrangements – and whether it might be possible to institute some not too revolutionary changes, which, on the part of the home, might from within meet half-way the efforts from without of this and kindred associations. If in dealing with such a subject what I have to say must be of a very simple and homely nature, I shall beg to be forgiven for the sake of the practical bearing which will, I hope, be found in any observations or suggestions that I may venture to make.

Before, however, going further, I wish to make one or two remarks on some points as to the classes and examinations held at Birmingham, regarded in connexion with the general provision of higher education for the upper and middle classes of this country.

I observe that considerable prominence has been given to the agency of the Cambridge Higher Local Examinations, and that classes have been organised with a special view to these examinations, as well as, I am glad to see, for preparation for the London University Examinations.

I observe further, that while a good many of the ladies who have attended classes have obtained a Higher Local Certificate, the young men have declined to present themselves for that examination; the explanation suggested by your Committee in their Report for last year, being that the standard is too high for them. This might lead a bystander to the conclusion – agreeably flattering to women – that at Birmingham women are better educated then men. It is not likely, however, that any one who knows a little of the general state of the higher education of women, will rashly accept such a conclusion. For myself, being perhaps of a suspicious turn, I was not prepared to believe the flattering tale without investigation, and I find on inquiry that, as might have been expected, there is another explanation, i.e., that the ladies who have taken these examinations are not in quite the same circumstances as the young men who have kept aloof from them – that they are not young women in business, having only their evenings and holidays unemployed, but for the most part, either govern-esses, whose daily work turns upon examination subjects, or ladies of leisure, the sisters of men who are, or might be, university graduates. It appears, therefore, that what has been done in these examinations ought rather to be regarded as a stepping-stone to higher things, than as a permanent resting-place. I cannot be satisfied for women to accept, and I do not believe that they will accept, permanently, a lower standing in the educational world than that of men, and I would invite the ladies who have done well in the Higher Local Examinations, to take a step forward, and occupy their natural place by the side of their brothers.

A few years ago such an appeal would have been manifestly futile. It would have been answered, with indisputable force –

> All the Universities are closed to women. However much they may desire an education corresponding with that of their brothers, and however ready they may be to comply with all the conditions of a University course, the opportunity is denied them. Nothing at all parallel with the University education of men, is within reach of women.

Some years ago, as I have said, this would have been unanswer-able. But things have happily changed. One great university, that of London, is, as we all know, at this moment taking the necessary steps for extending all its degrees, just as they are, to women, and I suppose that in the course of this year the way will be perfectly open. This is a boon for which those who are interested in education, are deeply indebted to the wise and courageous members of the university who have taken up the question, fought our battle, and carried it through to a successful issue. I hope that women will pay their share of the debt of gratitude in the most practical form, by entering in large numbers on the path thrown open to them, and I feel the more sanguine as to the place that Birmingham may be expected to take in this forward march, as this Association has already had experience in carrying on classes for preparation for the London Examinations, and it is abundantly evident that there will be the most cordial readiness to provide all that is needed for women in this direction. With regard to the establishment of a Local College, as suggested in the Report that we have just heard, it appears to me that steps towards it have already been taken by the formation of classes of adult students, and I see no reason why this course should not be continued, on, as we hope, an increasing scale, postponing any decision as to the form that further developments may take, until a considerable body of students has been gathered and larger experience gained.

A hope has been expressed, in which we must all concur, that before long Oxford and Cambridge may follow the example of the University of London, and open their degrees also to women. There are many who hold that degrees conferred like those of the University of London on the results of examinations, without conditions as to a course of instruction and discipline, fail to recognise an essential part of the best university education. Those of us who take this view, must labour and hope for the admission of women, under fit conditions, to the high privileges of our old universities. I cannot myself expect that so great a step as the formal opening of Oxford and Cambridge degrees will be taken just yet, but in the meantime we must thankfully acknowledge the warm sympathy that has been shown, and the advances in this direction that have been already made. By the friendly aid of members of the University of Cambridge, so generously and unfailingly afforded that we have learnt to rely upon it with confidence, it is now possible to offer to women a Certificate precisely corresponding in substance with the Cambridge B.A. Degree. The Girton College Degree-Certificate – so called in order to indicate its distinctive character – is conferred on exactly similar conditions to those imposed on a graduate of the University of Cambridge. In order to be a Cambridge B.A., it is necessary to reside for a prescribed period, either at a college or as an unattached student, under instruction and discipline, as well as to pass certain prescribed examinations. Similarly a candidate for a Girton Degree-Certificate is required to reside at the college for the period prescribed for regular undergraduates by the university, under instruction and discipline – the instruction being given by distinguished members of the university – and also to pass examinations in the same papers, at the same time, and under the same examiners as those for undergraduates. The examinations are not held formally under the authority of the university. It is a favour on the part of the examiners, and occasionally one may not see his way to taking part in it. In that case his papers are looked over by a colleague. The essential point of obtaining a judgment in accordance with the university standard is thus secured.

The case being thus, as I have stated, that women have now fairly put before them the opportunity of obtaining a real University education, it appears to me that claims are established on the public and on parents. I would put it as a public question, whether those who have to appoint teachers of girls, either in schools or families, ought to be permanently satisfied with any lower standard than they demand for the teachers of boys. I say *permanently*, for I am well aware that for some time it will be impossible for all the teachers that are wanted to produce any qualification equivalent to a university degree, and I should be sorry to seem to forget that there are personal gifts of greater importance than a mere academical qualification. We need to be on our guard against attaching too high a value to degrees and certificates. But this applies to both men and women. All that I urge is that where it would be said, as in the case of masterships in the great schools for boys, that any one not a graduate could scarcely be thought of, we should at least look forward to saying the same thing as to a mistress-ship – that it should not be said that a teacher of boys must of course have a degree, but for a teacher of girls a Higher Local Certificate will do.

To parents also I would appeal, and would ask them to recognise the simple fact that their daughters no less than their sons need all that a complete and thorough education can do for them, and that where it would be a matter of course to send a boy to the university, it should be equally a matter of course to do as much for a girl. I know that here the difficulty will often arise, that whereas a clever boy may be sent to the university by the help of the scholarship which he is sure to win, very little assistance of this kind is provided for women. The difficulty is real, but I think not insuperable. If time allowed, I believe it could be shown that even on purely commercial principles, to give a girl a university education is not a bad investment of capital, but I must not enter upon detail and will say no more on this point. I am afraid, indeed, that in speaking at all of such education as involves residence in college, I may seem to have wandered away from the specific business of this meeting, and also from the point which I began by proposing to bring specially under consideration, that of the organisation of home life with a view to the promotion of higher education. But I venture to think that what I have urged bears, not remotely, on our immediate business. I believe that though comparatively few women may be able to go to a distance for their education, these few will exercise an important influence on those who are left at home, and that the college life may react upon home life and aid in producing just those modifications which are needed in order to bring it into happier relations with the circumstances of modern society. Here, indeed, I feel that I tread on dangerous ground. The mere suggestion that our sacred, time-honoured, happy English homes can have anything to learn from such an upstart, new-fangled institution as a college for women, must I fear, be felt to be an audacity, if not an outrage. But there are times and places at which audacious things may be said. Birmingham is perhaps not an unsuitable place, and I hope it may prove that the present is not an unsuitable occasion, when I explain in what sense I regard the influence of the college on the home as likely to be beneficial. I must emphatically disclaim at the outset, any desire to turn homes upside down, putting the young people in the first place and making the comfort and convenience of the parents subordinate to that of the children. Such a subversion of the fit order of things is far from being the object in view. I must premise also that I should be very sorry if in anything I may have to say, there should be found the least semblance of a charge against parents of harshness or severity. On the contrary, I suppose there never was a time when young people were made so much of, so petted and fussed over, one may say, as they are now. If we listen to schoolmasters and mistresses and college tutors, we hear far more of laxity of home discipline and of excessive anxiety on the part of parents for the health and comfort and pleasure of their children, than of any tendency to harshness. But the misfortune is that the kindly indulgence and the sacrifices that parents are willing to make are so much in the direction of luxury and amusement – the piling up of enjoyment – and so little concern is shown comparatively for higher interests. A college, on the other hand, by the mere fact of its existence, asserts the claims of the higher life and undertakes to provide for them. It is from this point of view, as dealing with the needs of our higher nature, that I venture to hope for some good results from a more general familiarity with college life. My idea is that there are certain principles, if I may so call them, underlying and governing the organisation of a college – that the same principles, with obvious limitations, ought to underlie and govern the organisation of a household of young people – that they are often forgotten or put aside in our ordinary home arrangements, and that therefore a salient example of their application may, without being minutely followed, be of use in calling attention to them and suggesting attempts to carry them out in varying forms according to varying circumstances. What these principles are, I would state briefly thus – that the strengthening and development of character by a discipline combining subordination to rule with a considerable amount of self-government, is one of the main objects to be kept in view by those who are responsible for the direction of the young during the intermediate stage between boyhood or girlhood and manhood or womanhood, and further – that the strengthening of the mind by studies of a bracing nature and its enrichment by the acquisition of knowledge, are among the *duties* of life, and that therefore devotion to study, within reasonable limits, is not an abnormal thing, to be admired, or wondered at, or tolerated, or condemned, as our prejudices may dictate, but simply to be expected as a matter of course, from any well-conducted young person. Acting upon these principles, a system of discipline is established, laying down certain general rules which must be obeyed, but at the same time throwing upon the students much of the responsibility of self-guidance, allowing, within necessary limits, much freedom in the choice of friends and companions, and in such matters as e.g. the management of health, relying upon the student's own good sense and self-control in the place of minute direction from above. Similarly as to studies – the best teaching is provided and advice is at hand but much latitude of choice is allowed both as to subjects and the apportionment of time, the arrangement of the general daily routine simply securing that whatever the study may be, it can be carried on under such conditions as shall make it most wholesome and fruitful. In a college, as is well known, a student has the inestimable advantage of being free from disturbance, able not only to read in peace, but to 'think things out' – to carry on sustained thought, without liability to the worry and distraction of casual interruption. This great boon – the power of being alone – is perhaps the most precious distinctive feature of college life, as compared with that of an ordinary family. But a college supplies also the stimulus of sympathy and companionship, and this, not only in study, but in healthy physical sports. This last is an advantage we cannot afford to despise, looking upon it as an aid towards the development of a vigorous *physique*, the sound body fit for the habitation of the sound mind.

Now, how far is all this applicable to young people living at home? I believe that many of the advantages of a college might, in a greater or less degree, be attainable in a well ordered home, if only parents, and especially mothers, will give their earnest attention to the solution of the problem before them, and, above all, if they will give the reins to their imaginations, allowing themselves to picture a domestic interior somewhat different to what we see every day – a development of the family ideal which shall make room for, and even cherish, individuality. Such an expansion, by the mere fact of its allowing free play to individual tastes and energies, might do much to remove the jars and discords which too often mar the full flow of family harmony. Parents do not seem always to realise what is coming upon them when their young people leave school for good; no longer children at home for the holidays, but young men and women entering upon the business of life – a new element, requiring a new place to be made for it. Young men are, no doubt to a great extent provided for. They are put into a business which takes them out of the house all day, and employs the largest part of their time, and the great point of regular systematic occupation is thus secured. But as to girls, it is often taken for granted that they will shake into their places, whether there is a place for them or not, – and that they will find something to do, or, in other words, that they will invent a scheme of life for themselves and stick to it, without help or guidance. Surely this is expecting from them what is beyond their years. In an admirable work on education lately published – 'The Action of Examinations,' by Rev. H. Latham – a passage occurs which bears so aptly on this point that I take leave to quote it. 'Self direction,' says Mr Latham, 'is a quality which is not expected early in life; youths, we know, even though they may be ready to apply themselves to work when it is given them, can rarely find work for themselves and set themselves to it.' This is the view of an experienced college tutor as to young men; why should we expect young women to be different? Experience, I believe, testifies that in this respect they are very much alike. It is not so much that youth fails in inventiveness. It is common enough for girls, on leaving school – supposing that they have been at a good school, and have had their minds awakened and stirred – to draw up very neat and elaborate plans for carrying on their studies at home. They begin, perhaps, full of ardour and hope, but the end is most often disappointment and failure. They break down, partly from missing the stimulus of habit and companionship, partly from the want of support and encouragement from their superiors. It may be rejoined, perhaps, that they started on a wrong tack, that instead of aiming at self-improvement, they ought to have tried to make themselves useful. It is doubtful whether they would prosper better in this direction. In many parts of the country, girls are taken from school very early, even as early as sixteen, expressly on the theory that they are to be useful at home, and this sounds reasonable enough. It sounds well, when we hear that a girl is to be her mother's right hand, and so on. But before we can be sure that it is as good as it sounds, we want to know more exactly, of what use she is to be at home, and whether her mother wants a right hand. For if the mother has already two very good hands of her own, it may be that another is not wanted and that being super-fluous, it may grow weak and flaccid from insufficient exercise. I do not mean to assert that usefulness at home is a mere fiction. What I urge is that before household duty is fixed upon as a girl's sole function, there should be serious consideration as to whether there is enough of it adequately to occupy and develop her energies, and also whether a long period, perhaps many years, exclusively devoted to it is likely to be the best preparation for any future that may be in store for her. If such a case can be made out, then, regarding the household as a place of business, there may be the same sort of reason for giving a girl a place in it that there is for putting a boy into an office. Only, it should be done with as much deliberation and purpose in the one case as in the other. There may be some analogy too, even in details. I understand that when a youth goes into an office, he is not expected to wait about all day, on the chance of something turning up. He is not told that he will find something to do, if he really wishes it, or that he is to look about him and watch for opportunities of making himself useful. He has his appointed post, his own desk and his stool, and regular work cut out for him. And when he has learnt the business, he receives a salary and is recognised as doing work of appreciable importance. As a rule, there is not the same order in the conduct of household business, so far as the young ladies are concerned. It is usual for the whole family to congregate in one room, each being alike the victim of every interruption, every one carrying on her individual occupation in suspense, so to speak, liable at any moment to be called off from it for something else, trifling or important, as the case may be. Naturally enough, these half occupied people prey upon each other. Gaiety is of course, to many, the most absorbing pursuit, but there are besides, various pernicious practices by which even very quiet people manage to get rid of a great deal of time. One, largely prevalent, called 'dropping in,' which means paying little insignificant visits at all hours of the day, is specially noxious. There used to be another terrible institution, known as 'spending the day,' which meant going to your neighbour's house at one o'clock and staying till ten, with nothing to do for the whole of those nine hours but to sit and chat, with perhaps a bit of fancy work, in your hand. This is, I believe, dying out, but there still remains the custom of receiving visitors for several days or weeks, during which they are expected to be constantly entertained from morning till night. The process is wearisome enough for the guests, and terribly demoralising to the poor hostesses, who conceive themselves obliged by hospitality to make this sacrifice of the order and continuity of their daily occupations. By way of indemnity they return the visits, thus securing to themselves a double loss. Unfortunately the young people belonging to circles in which these customs prevail, are almost powerless against them. They can scarcely make any effectual resistance without giving offence, or even pain, and incurring the reproach of being unsociable and illnatured. Attempts to make a stand against wholesale interruptions are pretty sure to be met by expressions of surprise and regret, if not actual remonstrance. It is really pathetic to hear of the efforts that well-disposed young women will make to do something better with their lives – how they will join an essay society, or a society for the encouragement of home study, or a reading society – I have heard of one which compels its members under penalties to read for a certain time every day – these things being resorted to not only as a defence against their own idleness and desultoriness, but also as something of the nature of 'an outward and visible sign,' something which can be held up to relations and friends as a plea for the concession of a little slice of quiet time.

If the faithfulness of this picture is admitted, as I think it will be, at least in part and allowing for exceptions, it may still be said, How can it be helped? A mother cannot be running after her girls all day, setting them to work at every turn; what can she do? What have you to suggest? I would ask her to remember the first principle that the young need a framework within which to use their reasonable liberty, and also that other principle that mental culture is a duty, and not a mere fancy or indulgence. I believe that if these principles are laid to heart, modes of applying them will be found, but I will venture, with submission, to throw out one or two practical hints as to details. Would it be possible for the mistress of a household, when planning her daughter's place in it, to fix upon certain definite service to be expected from her, be it much or little, and having laid down what is required, to leave it to the daughter's discretion, subject of course to the general convenience, to do it at her own time, it being understood that when this regular work is done, the rest of her time is at her own disposal? Or, if this is thought impracticable, could certain hours be fixed upon – something corresponding to a man's office hours – and set apart for domestic or social claims, and the rest be considered her own? If this could be arranged, then I would ask further that if she chooses to give her own time to study, it may be treated with so much respect as that it shall be possible to pursue it in quiet and comfort, not in the midst of the family circle, – and that a certain warmth of approval may accompany it, so that the student may go to it with an untroubled conscience. I would lay stress on this point of the untroubled conscience, because I am afraid that much of women's work of this sort is done with an uneasy mind, a haunting doubt as to whether they are not selfishly pleasing or benefiting themselves, when they ought perhaps to be doing something for other people. It is easy to see how such questionings must take the heart out of the work, making it dull and spiritless, even if there be no grave injury done to the moral sense.

I have spoken of the conditions of home life chiefly as they affect the women who are expected to find in it their sphere, but I wish to add a word with reference to the young men whom this association specially desires to aid. I am afraid that in doing so I may seem to be taking a leaf out of the book of those great statesmen and orators, who, when asked to speak at such a meeting as this, deliver a long discourse entirely occupied with the interests of boys or men, and, at the end, throw in a word or two for women, just to show that they are aware of their existence and have a friendly feeling for them. Women may be tempted sometimes to feel a little aggrieved at this sort of treatment, but it seems to me only natural. The orator speaks of what he knows, and there is generally the compensation that though he may have been only thinking of men, his instructive utterances are equally applicable to women, who need feel no scruple in profiting by them. Similarly, though I have spoken primarily of what I know best, I venture to hope that what I have said will be found to be, in principle, susceptible of a wider application. I have urged the need of guidance, of sympathy, of encouragement, and of such recognition of the worth of intellectual and spiritual culture as shall lead to the greatest facilities being given for its pursuit in the details of domestic arrangements. Surely all this applies to young men as well as to women. They, too, are human, they need the warm breath of social and domestic approval to counteract the chilling influences which surround us all, and against which we have to maintain a continual struggle. They, too, need to be reminded that it is not the whole duty of men to produce money, any more than it is of women to distribute it – that there is a higher life, always liable to be choked by the cares and the pleasures of the material, visible world around us. Does not the apathy that we have to contend with arise mainly from a too exclusive devotion to comfort and pleasure? and is not this lower sort of life, with its petty aspirations and aims, too often fostered and encouraged by the low tone of social and domestic opinion? We do not, it seems to me, sufficiently estimate the immense weight of social and domestic opinion, or fully realise all that we should gain if this vast force could be brought to pronounce decisively on the side of the higher life, by recognising the duty of mental and spiritual cultivation for both men and women. Hitherto it has often been cold and indifferent, when not positively hostile. Let us hope that through the united efforts, in all parts of the country, of such missionaries of culture as the founders of this association, social and domestic opinion may be gradually leavened and converted, or – to put it in another form – the social and domestic conscience enlightened and stimulated. To contribute towards the realisation of this aim, though it may sound somewhat vague, is to my mind of deeper and wider import than any of the details of effort, though these are necessary and must not be neglected. I can but congratulate the people of Birmingham on having among them this association, so well deserving of their confidence, living and working and expressing emphatically before the world their sense of the value of culture. And I venture to predict, as well as warmly to wish for the association, a future worthy of the devotion and the public spirit which led to its formation, and with which it has been carried on.

NOTE

1 The following paper contains the substance, with some alterations and additions, of an address given at the Annual Meeting of the Birmingham Higher Education Association, 21 February 1878.

Dorothea Beale

Address to the National Association for the Promotion of Social Science

(1865)

I believe I may take it for granted, at least in an address to this Association, that the question has no longer to be argued, whether education, in the fullest sense of the word, is desirable for girls, but that the aim is simply to discuss what methods are best. One great object of such associations is (in the firm belief that nothing has been created in vain) to bring into activity, and render available for the good of the community, all resources hitherto comparatively unutilised. Grant, therefore, that woman has been endowed with mental and moral capacities, and we must also grant that it was intended these should be cultivated and improved 'for the glory of the Creator and the relief of man's estate;' that we are bound to render to Him 'both thanks and use.'

And here let me at once say that I desire to institute no comparison between the mental abilities of boys and girls, but simply to say what seems to be the right means of training girls, so that they may best perform that subordinate part in the world, to which I believe they have been called.

First, then, I think that the education of girls has too often been made showy, rather than real and useful – that accomplishments have been made the main thing, because these would, it was thought, enable a girl to shine and attract, while those branches of study especially calculated to form the judgment, to cultivate the understanding, and to discipline the character (which would fit her to perform the *duties* of life), have been neglected; and thus, while temporary pleasure and profit have been sought, the great moral ends of education have too often been lost sight of.

To the poorer classes the daily toil and struggles of their early life do, to some extent, afford an education which gives earnestness, and strength, and reality; and if we would not have the daughters of the higher classes idle and frivolous, they too must be taught to appreciate the value of work. We must endeavour to give them, while young, such habits, studies, and occupations, as will brace the mind, improve the taste, and develop the moral character. They must learn, not for the sake of display, but from motives of duty. They must not choose the easy and agreeable, and neglect what is dull and uninviting. They must not expect to speak languages without mastering the rudiments; not require to be finished in a year or two, but impatiently refuse to labour at a foundation.

I feel that the following paper may seem egotistical; there will be many to differ from me in principles and practice, but your object in asking me to write on the system pursued in our college was doubtless to elicit not only a theoretical but a practical answer to the question proposed in this department, I will speak as briefly as possible of the *matériel* principles and method pursued in our college.

I am sure it is but little suspected by many, how greatly the mere rudiments of education have been neglected, whilst a fair external show has been made. I will illustrate my meaning from my own experience. I must premise that it is my practice, when a pupil enters, to ask her to write on some historical or geographical subject. I set an easy sum in the last rule which she professes to have learned, and give a few tenses of French verbs, etc., as the case may be. These papers, for the last few years, I have carefully preserved, and arranged them according to the age of the writers. I will not speak of those written by junior pupils, from whom of course we expect many faults, but take those written by pupils above 15 years of age; of these I have 47. I turn first to the arithmetic, a subject professedly taught in all schools, with what success you will judge by the following table. For various reasons, five did no sums.

No. of Pupils who professed
to have learned

Fractions	7	sums set	all wrong.
Rule of Three or Practice	17	,,	all wrong.
Comp. Long Division	11	,,	10 wrong.
Comp. Short Division	1	,,	wrong.
Comp. Multiplication	4	,,	all wrong.
Simple Multiplication	2	,,	both right.

We next take the French, a study which, in a girl's education, occupies an important place, and may therefore fairly be considered a test. Three were not to learn the language, and we may charitably hope they were perfect, for only three out of the remaining 44, were able to write correctly the few tenses set. One of 17 years old, and another 15, failed to write a single word correctly; nine failed, even in '*avoir*' and '*être.*'

Lastly, as regards English spelling, I think there are only five of the 47 papers which contain no error, four are marked as *very bad*, five as bad in this respect. We must remember, too, that these errors appear, not in a dictation containing difficult selected words, but in a few lines written on a given subject. Of the general style of the papers, the writing, the composition, both in English and French, and the interesting historical and geographical facts brought to light, I am sure that none can form an adequate idea but those who have enjoyed the privilege of seeing them. I have carefully erased the names of the authors, and, should it serve any useful purpose, shall be ready to produce their works.

Those who are unacquainted with our college will of course think that our pupils must come from a very low class. To show that this is far from being the case, I add a list which I drew up from our nomination book, a few months ago, for the Schools' Enquiry Commission.

Daughters of officers in the army, about	·27
Private gentlemen	·27
Clergymen	·20
Medical men	·8
(Or, including military, 17)	
Civil service	·6
Lawyers and barristers	·4
Bankers	·2
Naval officers	·1
Various, as merchants, manufacturers, surveyors, &c.	·5
	1·00

I have a set of papers written by girls much younger in St Paul's district school here, which are greatly superior.

Certainly, if we looked for brilliant results, we should be discouraged, and the difficulty of teaching pupils of 15 to 18, who are ignorant of the rudiments of an ordinary education, and yet could not be taught in a class with those many years their juniors, is very great; it obliges us to have a large staff of teachers, so that they may be instructed in that which we must take it for granted is known to the class.

We may well ask how is such a state of things possible? How is it that the daughters of the higher middle class are more ignorant and untrained than the children of the national schools? I think one cause is that parents have too often trusted, when they should have inquired; they frequently spend from £100 to £200 a year on sending their daughters from home; during the holidays they hear the piano, they see the drawings (not always the pupils' own) but how often do they institute any inquiry into the progress made in any other branches; or, if unable to undertake it themselves, how rarely do they care that there should be a system of examination to see whether the work is properly done. They are afraid of popular outcry, afraid of the excitement, afraid that their children should take a low place, forgetting that (if the examination be conducted without any of the improper excitement of publicity) it is also a test and means of moral training, since those who work from the right motives simply do their best, and are not over anxious about results. I do not desire that there should be a system of competitive examination, but a general testing of the work done, and if this cannot be responded to in a quiet lady-like manner, it does not speak well for the moral training of the school.

Another cause is that girls are often placed in an inferior school, or under incompetent governesses, or allowed to work in a desultory way until they are 14 or 15. Plans and governesses and schools are changed for a passing fancy, and then they are sent to one with a high reputation, this it is thought will be enough for them, 'as they are not required to be learned ladies.'

I ask whether a boy educated on this plan would be good for much; would he or would he not be likely to have acquired habits of lazy self-indulgence? And is a girl so trained likely to prove a diligent and wise and thoughtful woman?

Lastly, a girl usually leaves school altogether, and too often throws aside serious occupations at an age at which her brother enters on his college life. When she is just beginning to see the use of much she had previously found dull and monotonous, when, more than at any previous time, a taste for good reading and useful pursuits might be developed.

Before proceeding, I may perhaps presume upon my somewhat wide educational experience to say something upon the relative advantages of the home, school, and college system. For some years I was educated by governesses at home, I have been at school in London and Paris. For one year I was head teacher in a boarding school of 100 pupils; for seven years I was teacher at Queen's College, London; for seven years I have been principal of the Ladies' College, Cheltenham. Both in London and on the continent, especially in Germany (where it is most usual for the pupils to live at home and attend school) I have taken every opportunity of inquiring into different systems, and my verdict is decidedly in favour of the college system, that is to say, when, and only when, the internal arrangements of the college, and the moral training of the pupils are in the hands of a lady. Of course I must expect to be regarded as a prejudiced person, but it does seem to me that a system which combines home life with school discipline, which brings a girl into contact with many, without necessarily making her the intimate companion of any, which gives her opportunities of observing character before she is called upon to judge in the battle of life, whilst parents are able to correct what is wrong, and to confirm what is right in those judgments, must be one more generally suitable than either of the others.

Of course when children are educated at home, and an anxious mother daily sees and suffers from her children's faults of temper and disposition, she will be tempted to think she had better give up the training into other hands, and send them away. Doubtless this is sometimes wise, often unavoidable; but how frequently, without necessity, is the burden of parental responsibility temporarily cast aside, only to press with tenfold weight in later years. How many parents have learned bitterly to regret that they removed a daughter from the divinely appointed influences of home, and severed by long separation those bonds of affection which might have checked the young in the hour of temptation, and been the support and comfort of their own declining years.

Should there be no college in the neighbourhood, still I consider that the college system offers greater advantages than a boarding school usually can, when the boarding-houses are such as we have endeavoured to make them. Too often in a school, the mistress, fatigued with the morning's teaching, is glad to leave the children alone, or to the care of inexperienced teachers; she is ignorant of what goes on during the greater part of the day. The lady appointed by the council to be the head of the boarding-house, has the morning hours free, but she is required to devote herself to the care of the pupils whenever they are not at the college.

Either she herself, or one of the college governesses, invariably accompanies them to and from college. She has to see that the hours of preparation are observed, and that exercises and lessons are properly prepared. I need hardly add that she must be a lady in manners and education, and willing to consult and co-operate with the principal in all things relating to the physical, intellectual, and moral good of the pupils. I by no means maintain however, that our system is suited for all without exception; when I find one for whom I consider it unsuited, I am the first to desire her removal.

And here I may perhaps notice a few points in which I consider the college system offers advantages, and some in which ours differs fundamentally from other ladies' colleges. First, we take many precautions before admitting a pupil, and the council exercises a double veto.

A shareholder is liable to be balloted for; when he has a share he may nominate one pupil, but only subject to the approval of the council. A nomination paper must be sent in stating the name, address, and profession of the father, giving references, etc.; if the council are not perfectly satisfied, the child may be excluded.

The college, although governed by a committee of gentlemen, is, as regards internal administration, strictly under female management. When this is not the case, the manners of the pupils must suffer; besides, there are innumerable apparently trifling details, which are yet important in a girl's education; many lessons of daily life that only a woman can teach.

An institution of this kind can offer guarantees for the character of the education given, which private institutions cannot; and it can secure the services of gentlemen who would not spend their time in private teaching.

The members of the council having no pecuniary interest, are simply anxious for the good of the institution; they have no views of profit, and are therefore always ready to make grants to the full extent of the income for any object likely to improve the education or the efficiency of the college. They endeavour to secure the services of the best teachers; they give them by capitation fees an interest in the success of the institution, and they select annually examiners of the highest character to examine and report upon the instruction given.

In 1863 and 1864 the examination, which had previously been undertaken by gentlemen residing in Cheltenham, was conducted by Sidney Owen, Esq., Historical Lecturer at Christ Church, Oxford, and University Examiner. Some extracts from his long and able report, I have placed in your hands. This year he was too much engaged at Oxford to be able to take part in our examination, which was conducted by the following gentlemen:

Scripture	Rev. John Eaton, late Fellow and Tutor, Merton College, and Public Examiner, Oxford.
History	Rev. W. Newman, Fellow and Lecturer on History, Balliol College, and Public Examiner, Oxford.
Natural Science	Prof. Ramsay, F.R.S., F.R.G.S., and Examiner, London University.
Astronomy	Prof. John Phillips, M.A., LL.D., F.R.S., F.G.S., etc., Oxford.

Geography – Physical and Political	R. Etheridge, Esq., F.R.S.E., F.G.S., Royal School of Mines, London.
Mathematics	W. Esson, Esq., M.A., Fellow of Merton College, and Public Examiner, Oxford.
English Language and Grammar	Dr Ernest Adams, Ph.D., F.L.S., Manchester.
English Literature	Rev. U. W. Bayly, M.A., Cheltenham College.
French	T. Pagliardini, Esq., St. Paul's School, London.
German	Dr Schrader, Ph.D., Bonn.

Copious extracts from their reports have been printed, and the whole may be read by any parents of pupils on application to the Hon. Sec.

In a large institution girls are enabled to measure their own powers in a way impossible in home tuition, and thus much conceit is rooted out; and when the moral tone in a school is high, an influence for good is exercised, and the character is strengthened.

Where the constitution is fairly good there can be no question that the regular walks are beneficial to health, and the objection as to going backwards and forwards, at first considered so serious, is now much less frequently heard.

I must now add a few words on the special constitution of our college, and some warnings suggested by experience. First, the machinery of proprietary colleges is somewhat complicated, and it is liable to get out of order. Thus for example, if the shareholders agitate, when a measure does not at once commend itself to their judgment, they may interfere with the efficiency, and endanger the existence of the institution. Secondly, none must attempt to carry out reforms in education, unless they have faith enough in their own system to work on quietly for a time, in the face of popular opposition, and unless they have capital to fall back upon.

The capital of the college at its opening, January 1854, was about £2,000; in December 1858, the estimated assets, as shown by the balance-sheet, were £901, giving a loss of £1,100 during the first five years, or an average deficit of £220 per annum.

During the first two years after my appointment the average deficit was about £91, and the assets were reduced by December 1860, to £719. The council then decided to raise the terms, and this, together with the gradual and steady increase in the number of pupils, has placed the finances in a satisfactory condition. The average number of regular students has been as follows:

1859	72
1860	78
1861	99

1862	117
1863	126
1864	122

The assets last December were £1,646, showing an average surplus on the last four years of £232 per annum.

There are altogether 150 shares held by 107 shareholders, who have the right of nominating one pupil upon each share, and attending the annual meeting. The executive council is appointed by the general meeting, and consists of a president, vice-president, and seven members. Any vacancies occurring in the course of the year are filled up by the council, and the appointment must be confirmed at the general meeting. The council has the entire control of the finances, the reception or rejection of nominations, the appointment or dismissal of teachers, and all that relates to the external government, and to the admission of pupils.

The principal is responsible for the internal government, with which the council never interfere, and although the council appoints teachers, the principal recommends; in other words, the council merely reserve to themselves a veto.

The pupils are arranged in three divisions, and on their entrance it is determined by examination to which they shall be assigned.

There are nine regular English teachers, one French governess, and one German. Lessons are also given by professors in natural science, astronomy, English literature, physical geography, English language, French, drawing, music, and dancing.

To avoid the vexatious extra charges which often form so large an item in school bills, the council have made the terms inclusive of all subjects which belong to the course of study and are suitable for class teaching. The only extras are, therefore, music, singing, and dancing lessons. The terms for Division I. are 22 guineas; for Division II., 17; and for Division III., 12.

Division I. includes four classes. The average age of the pupils is from 15 to 18 or 19; it usually contains nearly 40 pupils; last year an average of 39. The majority of these take the ordinary course of study, but others, for whom regular school routine is no longer necessary, are allowed to select special subjects. The upper and lower first are under the immediate care of the principal; the upper and lower second, of her sister. Division II. contains six classes, the pupils varying in age from about 11 to 16. Division III. contains two classes of little children from about 6 to 12.

Each governess has the sole management of the one or two classes assigned to her, not only to carry out the general discipline of the college, but to make herself acquainted with the character and abilities of each of her pupils, and to meet any special difficulties as far as may be. Thus, one may be backward in French; in that case she is not allowed to join the German class, but extra French work is given instead. Another may not wish to learn drawing; the vacant hours will then be filled up by some other study. Another, being backward in English, but forward in French, it is arranged, if possible, for her to attend a higher class. Another, not being in good health, or being less quick than others, is unable to accomplish as much as her companions, and some one study is dropped.

Every variation from the rule is entered in the time-table given to each pupil by her governess, and thus there is as much care and thought given to each as there would be in a small school. Of the evening time-tables I will speak presently, but I may perhaps add here that every parent is specially requested to inform the principal should the work given appear to be too much. Whenever this is found to be the case, the amount is diminished. When pupils were required to attend twice a day, and prepare their lessons in the evenings, complaints of this kind often occurred; now they are scarcely ever heard.

I have only to a small extent assigned special subjects to special teachers, but rather kept to the public school plan of committing to the care of one teacher, say, on an average, 12 to 20 pupils (in Division I. sometimes more, in Division II. always less). The class governess has of course assistance in drawing, French, and German. She invariably gives the Scripture lessons, and is responsible for the intellectual and moral condition of her class; in all cases of difficulty she consults with and appeals to the principal. Her pupils are immediately under her eye. A general supervision is however exercised by the principal; she rarely leaves the school-room, where nearly all the classes are assembled, and her attention would be attracted by any irregularity, or want of submission and attention.

The pupils below Division I. are brought into immediate contact with the principal by receiving from her, besides occasional lessons and examinations, a Scripture lesson once a fortnight, and she is kept informed of the character and work of each pupil by a frequent inspection of the exercise-books (which are brought to her by the class governesses once a fortnight) and by reading each week, in the presence of the pupils and the class teachers, the marks obtained.

And here I may say, that we regard the education of these children as worthy the best efforts of our minds, and not as mere routine work. This I would impress not only on my coadjutors here, but upon all our profession. The physician, the barrister, labours at his work, and thinks no effort too great to promote the benefit of those who consult him; but our office has been despised, and the training of children has consequently suffered. To sit so many hours in the schoolroom has too often been considered sufficient, whilst the labour of thought has been evaded, and reading neglected.

We have no punishments, in the ordinary sense of the term. Too often, when arbitrary punishments are attached to certain offences, a child learns to regard the punishment or fine as in some sense a compensation – to think she may disobey, provided she is willing to pay the price. Our punishments are, as far as may be, the necessary consequence of a fault of omission or commission. Thus for example, if a lesson is imperfectly learned, we do not add to it, but there necessarily follows the trouble and inconvenience of preparing it at another time, as the teacher has no leisure to hear it again during the morning hours; the delinquent must go to the principal, and write her name in a book kept for the purpose; she must return in the afternoon, take her place in a certain set of desks, and remain there until the lesson is finished. Or again, if confidence is forfeited by an underhand act, then a place is assigned, not in any way prominent, but still more immediately under the teacher's eye. This is felt, and rightly, to be a serious matter, for it expresses that the child is not trusted. She knows that we cannot trust one who has given us cause for distrust, until indeed time has shown repentance; and she knows we cannot pretend to trust, when we do not. The special treatment of moral offences, such as falsehood and wilful disobedience, is a subject on which I cannot enter here. Of course, in every case, we lay the matter before the child, show the wrong and its consequences, and I believe, when the teacher is really in earnest and cares for the child, that such a conversation rarely fails to have the right effect. We generally find we can, without punishment, bring the pupil to acknowledge and repent the wrong; but if a child, after repeated attempts, is still found not to be trustworthy, it is better she should leave.

Except the prizes assigned by the examiners once a year, we have no tangible rewards. The weekly marks are simply read. They have no influence upon prizes, nor even on place in class, which is given once for all at the beginning of a quarter on the marks gained at the written examination.

Once a year however, prizes are given to the pupils in each class who obtain from the examiners the highest number of marks. I was opposed to this custom, I did not think it necessary to make pupils work, they seemed as earnest and painstaking before prizes were given as since. I felt it was better they should work from the love of knowledge, or a simple sense of duty; but the council took another view, and as there is much to be said on their side of the question, I yielded. In life, prizes must be to a great extent the reward of thoughtful industry, and it seems to me that on the one hand we may thereby teach the children to put success at its true value, and point out to them that it is at the bar of our own conscience alone that we must stand approved or condemned; that on the other hand they may learn to bear disappointment patiently. I do not find that prizes create any feelings of jealousy or ill-will, nor can I blame a child who looks forward with pleasure to carrying home to her parents this proof that she has tried to do as they would have her. It appears to me a matter of less importance than is usually supposed, and in any case can affect only a few pupils at the head of a class. Stimulants to exertion however, are rarely needed. There are very few who are not interested and earnest in their work, and our difficulty is more frequently to check too great zeal, and to insist upon the observation of those limits we place to the time devoted to study than to demand more.

Reports of attendance, progress, and conduct, are sent home quarterly, and upon these are also entered from the 'late and return books' the number of times a pupil has failed in punctuality, or brought a lesson imperfectly prepared. The little children of Division III. take home a book of their marks every week. As regards the details of instruction, I may perhaps mention some special points; first, as already said, nearly all the classes are held in one large schoolroom, it is 69 by 30 by 18; it opens at one end into the dressing-room, through which the pupils enter, and at the other into a supplementary room (20 by 30), where drawing and calisthenic lessons are given. This large room is lighted by 16 windows, it is heated by hot air, but there are also two open fire-places which help to change the air, and several ventilators. The rooms look upon the garden and south-west, thus the aspect is warm, but in summer we are not troubled with the morning sun. Besides these rooms there is one in which the first class often assembles, one specially devoted to the little ones, and four used occasionally.

The hours are from 9·10 till 12·55 for all, except during November and December, when the classes meet later. A few minutes' interval is allowed about 11 o'clock; the junior classes take a turn in the garden if the weather permits; in all cases the lessons are so arranged as to afford sufficient rest and variety, e.g., all have a calisthenic lesson twice a week; part of another morning is devoted to drawing; music lessons make a change from the class teaching, and the younger pupils have also some needlework. The afternoon hours for preparation of lessons (except on half holidays) are from 2·45 till 4·15. Two governesses are always in attendance, and all whose parents prefer it may, without extra charge, prepare their lessons at college. Many who live near do so, others are glad to be spared the fatigue of returning. Those who are backward in any particular subject, those who require 'finishing,' and have no good foundation laid, those who require teaching how to learn, are glad to come. All who have returned lessons are necessarily present, but occupy different seats.

We take advantage also of the afternoon hours to pursue special studies not included in the regular course, e.g., Latin and Greek. There are also music lessons and extra drawing lessons, sketching classes out of doors, or concerted music classes.

To return to the morning hours. Every pupil has one particular desk assigned to her, in which she is always to be found, except when in class; her seat is always near her class teacher; great quietness of manner and voice is insisted on, and as there are sometimes nine classes going on at once, this is strictly necessary for the community, as well as desirable in itself; having her pupils around her the teacher has ample opportunity of observing their conduct, of checking faults of manner, etc. During school hours, and in the dressing-rooms, no speaking is allowed without permission. To those unacquainted with our college this rule will probably appear absurdly strict. I had at first many doubts about its expediency, but I have found it valuable.

First, it is a great means of teaching self-restraint; and surely one thing that women should learn is 'to keep silence' when they feel inclined to speak. Second, it helps to form a habit of strict obedience, of conscientious regard for little things. The rule would be dangerous, if permission were not granted within reasonable bounds, but it prevents gossiping, and enables girls to attend a large school without being exposed to the temptations often incident thereto.

Those who prepare their lessons at home are provided with a card, on which the evening work for each day is entered. It is arranged by each class governess at the beginning of the quarter, and the approximate time required is entered – it is then sent home to the parents, who supply the hours at which the preparation is to begin and finish. The hours fixed may of course be departed from at the option of the parents if necessary, but the card forms a guide, and we desire to be informed, should the time spent in preparation much exceed or fall short of that assigned; such alterations are then made as may be considered necessary. A dawdling child is perhaps invited to come in the afternoons, that she may learn how to work – something may be taken off the work of one who is naturally slow, and greater excellence or more work is required from those who are too rapid. As regards the lessons given in school, they are not strictly lectures in geography, history, etc., some book is taken as a guide, the pupils are thoroughly examined on the passage set, and the teacher then proceeds with the lessons, giving as far as possible the results of recent travels, the most important points from voluminous histories, etc. In the higher class notes are sometimes taken, and the lecture written from them; sometimes the pupils are not allowed to write during the lesson, but a few heads are given, and the subject worked out from these. The notes of every lecture, as well as all exercises, are thoroughly corrected, and signed by the teacher responsible for the correction. For Euclid and the theory of arithmetic no book is allowed, lest the proposition should be learned by heart – the pupils are, as far as possible, led to find out the demonstration for themselves – should they be unable, it is given *viva voce*, and written in the teacher's presence; sometimes it is necessary to go over the proof many times before it is understood, but only new pupils are found to yield to the temptation of saying 'Yes' when they do not understand, as this method is sure to bring ignorance to light. German is made with us to occupy in some degree the place which Latin takes in a boy's education. Great attention is paid to the declensions and grammar, interlinear translations are written, and a pupil who betrays a tendency to inexactness, is required even in the higher classes to construe. Every one must have a word-book when preparing translation, and enter those not previously known; in the higher classes this is divided into three columns, one for the word – the second for the derivation or root – the third for the English; before the translation lesson is begun, the teacher ascertains whether these words have been learned. For pronunciation certain small portions, usually of poetry, are selected, and repeated by the teacher until the pupil has caught the accent; a few lines treated in this careful way are more useful than many pages read in the ordinary manner. Exercises are written as usual, and corrected by the teacher, who marks a number against each fault. Before writing a fresh exercise, the paper is folded in two – in one column the sentence in which a mistake has occurred is copied correctly, the words that were wrong are underlined, and the number of the fault written against it – in the other the rule that was broken is written out.

A portion of a lesson is devoted once a week to the explanation of those faults which are not the result of carelessness. The difficulty of taking a study by no means universal, as a principal subject, has been to a great extent obviated by fixing what are called simultaneous hours, so that pupils from various English classes can attend the same German. The regular class teachers assist, both with French and German.

Spelling and arithmetic are the two subjects which perhaps cause us most trouble, owing to the almost incredible deficiencies of pupils who come to be finished. The plan we pursue is the following. We give dictation scarcely at all, and then only after preparation, since writing a word incorrectly for the first time is very likely to fix it in the memory. We let young children copy a good deal from books; the middle classes learn poetry by heart, and write it from memory once or twice a week; this teaches them, besides spelling, habits of great accuracy, attention, and neatness. Throughout the college, to the very highest class, every pupil who makes a mistake in note-books, examination papers, etc., is required to write out one column of the word misspelt. In difficult cases, special private lessons are given in the afternoons, or at spare times, on derivations.

In order to make sure that the lessons are understood, it is our practice, in all except the lowest division, to give every week a written examination in some one subject. This we find most useful, but it involves a great deal of labour to the teacher. It gives the pupils facility in composition, and since they are required to write on subjects in which they are interested, it teaches them the value of exact knowledge, for vague sentences are valued at less than nothing; also it shows the teacher how far she has been understood. An hour is always devoted to the giving out and thorough criticism of these examination papers in the presence of the class, and errors of matter, style, and spelling are dwelt upon. Every quarter, throughout the college, there is a general examination, which lasts a few days. Every year external examiners are appointed, as before mentioned.

Music is taught in the usual way, by private lessons; but there are also classes for the practice of concerted music, to which only advanced pupils are admitted. There may be from 4 to 12 performers, two to each piano; thus the pupils are enabled to obtain an intimate acquaintance with those works of the great masters (as Cherubini, Bach, Haydn, etc.) which are usually performed by an orchestra, and this promotes also, decision, accuracy, and facility in reading. Twice a year we have a musical examination, i.e., each pupil is required to play some one piece in the presence of her companions and as many parents as wish to attend; no strangers are admitted.

Drawing is taught from copies and models. Frequently in the course of the summer sketching parties are formed, and lessons given by the master out of doors. Once a year drawings are submitted to an examiner, and prizes awarded; but no drawings are sent in which have been touched in the slightest degree by a master.

We have a room specially fitted up for calisthenic exercises, and an experienced teacher attends two mornings in the week. This we consider very important for the health of growing girls.

In conclusion, I sincerely hope that the inquiry into the important subject of girls' education, which has been instituted by the Royal Commissioners, and the discussions of this Association, may be productive of much good. I believe that all who have any real acquaintance with the subject see the necessity for some sort of inspection, and differ only about the mode. I do not think the plan for admitting girls to the same examination with boys in the University local examination a wise one; the subjects seem to me in many respects unsuited for girls, and such an examination as the one proposed is likely to farther a spirit of rivalry most undesir-able. I should much regret that the desire of distinction should be made in any degree a prime motive, for we should ever remember that moral training is the end, education the means; the habits of obedience to duty, of self-restraint, which the process of acquiring knowledge induces, the humility which a thoughtful and compre-hensive study of the great works in literature and science tends to produce, these we would specially cultivate in a woman, that she may wear the true woman's ornament of a meek and quiet spirit. As for the pretentiousness and conceit which are associated with the name of 'blue-stocking,' and which some people fancy to be the result of education, they are only an evidence of shallowness and vulgarity; we meet with the same thing in the dogmatic conceit of the so-called 'self-educated man,' who has picked up learning, but has not had the benefit of a systematic training and a liberal education.

I am sure that a great reform is needed, I believe that the faults of manner and character which some imagine to be the evidence of over-education, are the results of ignorance, and that in well-educated women, as in men, we shall find the results of a right education to be gentleness of manner, unselfishness, humility, and a more cheerful and entire obedience to rightful authority; not pride of intellect, but a subduing sense of the great responsibility which all God's gifts involve.

I fear we have but small cause for self-gratulation, when we look at the kind of literature most in demand at our lending libraries, and remember that girls are the greatest readers of sensation novels; but little cause for saying we need no reform, when we look at the revelations of domestic life in the newspapers. As a mere question of bodily health too, I am sure the subject demands consideration; for one girl in the higher middle classes that suffers from over work, there are, I believe, hundreds whose health suffers from the feverish love of excitement, from the irritability produced by idleness, frivolity, and discontent.

This subject – I mean the influence of a right education upon bodily health – merits more consideration than it has hitherto received, and it is now attracting much attention in Germany. It is argued that since mental emotion in some cases is able to produce death, in others disease, and in all of us temporary functional disturbance, then we are acting unwisely in attacking the symptoms only; we must 'minister to the mind diseased.' I will not add more on the subject now, but commend it to the consideration of the section.

It has been well said that every teacher ought to be a physiologist, for while on the one hand a system of overtasking the powers cannot be too strongly deprecated, on the other serious evils (especially in the case of girls) have resulted from a hasty recommendation to throw aside for a long period all study, when a temperate and wisely regulated mental diet was really required. I am persuaded, and my opinion has been confirmed by experienced doctors, that the want of wholesome occupation lies at the root of much of the languid debility of which we hear so much after girls have left school. The two are closely connected: *mens sana in corpore sano.*

I had wished, in conclusion, to say something on the subject of female education in relation to its historical aspects, but I will only quote the words of one who has thought far more deeply and laboured much longer in the field than I have done.

There are a few endowed schools where girls are fed and clothed, and taught to read and write indifferently; and a few schools have been lately established and maintained by public subscription where orphan girls can obtain superior instruction; but the numerous foundations of ancient endowment for the religious and intellectual education of young females, scattered over the country in the middle ages, were all swept away at the dissolution of religious houses in the sixteenth century. The great ecclesiastical foundations for men were reformed and re-established on an improved system, but the rich endowments for the benefit of women were either seized by court favourites or transferred to schools and colleges for men, and our sex to this day have not recovered from the fatal blow. For a few years the women educated in these ancient schools added lustre to the England of Elizabeth. Their French might be the French of 'Stratteforde atte Bow,' rather than that of Paris (and perhaps they were none the worse for that), but their acquirements kept pace with those of their brothers. The next century witnessed an eclipse, and the ignorance of the following ages led, by an easy descent, to the profligacy of many succeeding generations. It is only since the accession of Queen Victoria that there has been any encouraging prospect of revival. I most heartily wish success to all who are willing to befriend the good cause of superior female education, which was an object of my heart's desire in the last century, and was the dream of my early childhood.

Frances Buss

Evidence to the Schools Inquiry Commission

(1865)

Do you think any means could be taken for improving the class of schoolmistresses by any system of certificates, or in any other mode? – I think most strongly that every one who teaches ought to go through some course of training in the art of teaching after having received a certificate of attainment . . . I only know of one place at the present moment where a governess of the middle class can get training, and that is at the Home and Colonial.

[Dr Storrar:] From what sources do you usually draft your assistants? – We have tried to get them from those who have been educated in the school and subsequently trained in the Home and Colonial. By that means we have secured a certain amount of power of teaching.

Have you been able to get a sufficient supply from your own school? – Not always, on account of the difficulty of age. Of course the girls are too young at 20 or 21 to be entrusted with the charge and moral training of a large class . . . My belief is that we should do better with certificated mistresses trained in the National schools, than with such mistresses as we can get.

[Lord Lyttelton:] You are not allowed to have certificated mistresses? – No; Government will not allow it. It does occasionally happen that one can get a mistress who has been trained, but who has fallen short of the certificate, or who from change of circumstances has resigned a Government school.

How have they done with you? – They generally do extremely well, in so far that they are able to govern the children and impart a good English education, but they are very deficient in accomplishments. In such cases we are obliged to supplement French and higher drawing by some other teacher. . . . We find it answers extremely well with the young children, where accomplishments are not so necessary. . . . For them, I do not think there is any better teaching than is given by the Government trained mistresses, and that if we can secure one of those mistresses she is perfectly capable of making the teaching interesting, discarding text books almost entirely, and making the teaching oral.

You attach great importance then to getting rid of the habit of merely learning bits of books by heart? – Yes. All our teaching for years past has been almost entirely oral, that is to say, we do not use text books and do not set lessons to be learnt, except in facts, such as geographical names, which must be committed to memory.

Do you mean that you give what are called gallery lessons, and then call upon the children to reproduce them; or do you mean that you take a book and require the girls to master it and catechise them upon it? – In the lower classes we require the teachers to draw up sketches of their lessons, as they would have to do in the National schools, to make the lesson oral, and to reproduce the teaching from the children by rapid questions, of course combining with these a certain amount of home lessons. The teaching of the more advanced pupils necessarily involves books. In languages and literature, for instance, there must be books to be read, but as a rule we entirely discard lessons from mere text books.

[Lord Lyttelton:] How many teachers have you? – We have 11 governesses in daily work and 19 assistants, making a total of 30 for 200 pupils.

It cannot be denied that the picture brought before us of the state of middle-class female education is, on the whole unfavourable . . . want of thoroughness and foundation; want of system; slovenliness and showy superficiality; inattention to rudiments; undue time given to accomplishments, and these not taught intelligently or in any scientific manner; want of organisation . . . a very small amount of professional skill, an inferior set of school books, a vast deal of dry, uninteresting work, rules put into the memory with no explanation of their principles, no system of examination worthy of the name . . . a reference to effect rather than to solid worth, a tendency to fill rather than to strengthen the mind . . .

Findings of the (Taunton) *Schools Inquiry Commission*

Transactions of the National Association for the Promotion of Social Science: The Education of Girls

(1865)

Dr Hodgson,
It is for those who object to the equalisation of the instruction of boys and girls to show in what respects the two ought to differ, and in what respects the characters of the two sexes are so widely distinct as to involve the necessity of a separate education for each. . . . Now let us ask ourselves for a moment what are the subjects, if any, on which boys should, and girls should not, be taught. I have not been able to hear from anyone the suggestion of even a single subject. . . . I would draw no line of demarcation, so as to limit the extent of knowledge which either boy or girl may acquire. I would throw open the portals of knowledge freely to both. Let each sex acquire what it can. Circumstances will draw a line of demarcation: so will ability and opportunity. There is no necessity for our drawing any other line, and there is extreme injustice in our doing so. I would apply to those differences between the male and female sex, the very same principle I would apply to the different classes of society, the rich and the poor. I say it is unwise and unjust to fix any arbitrary limit to the education the poor are to get. Their poverty already more than sufficiently limits it; and it is for us rather to try and extend the amount of instruction than to endeavour arbitrarily and intentionally to limit it. So with the female sex, I say, let us throw open the gates through which the temple of knowledge is to be entered, and let us allow fair play to every one who enters it, being satisfied that difference of capacity, difference of means, difference of opportunity, will fully maintain that inequality of knowledge, that difference of mental state which I confess is desirable . . .

Dr Hancock,
It appears to me that the reason of the neglect of the education
of girls in the upper and middle schools is that we do not
carry out with regard to them the principles which prevail
in other departments of education. With regard to the poorer
classes, wherever the government recognises the necessity of
interfering it interferes equally. Wherever they found boys'
schools they found girls' schools; and in every parish school
founded by the state over the three kingdoms both sexes are
taught alike. But when we come to the middle and upper
schools it is otherwise. . . . If we hold that universities and
grammar-schools are unnecessary, abolish them; but if they
are maintained as advantageous to men, we ought to give
the same advantages to women. . . . Now I think this
inequality in our educational system produces some very
unsatisfactory results. We live in an age when men's opinions
are modifying and changing, and it is a serious disadvantage
when, in the same family, the women are not educated
equally with the men. We labour under the disadvantage of
the men having more advanced views than the women.

Mr Joseph Payne,
Where we have to deal with a common mind, both the
subjects taught and the mode of teaching must be in a great
degree common. We are not teaching a different, but the
same kind of human being. The mind has properly no sex.
It is the mind of the human being, and consequently there
must be of necessity a similarity in the instruction of both
sexes.

Elizabeth Sewell

from

Principles of Education

(1865)

The aim of education is to fit children for the position of life which
they are hereafter to occupy. Boys are to be sent out into the
world, to buffet with its temptations, to mingle with bad and
good, to govern and direct. The school is the type of the life they
are hereafter to lead. Girls are to dwell in quiet homes, amongst a
few friends; to exercise a noiseless influence, to be submissive and
retiring. There is no connexion between the bustling mill-wheel
life of a large school and that for which they are supposed to be
preparing . . .

   This idea, of making a boy's attainments the standard by which
to measure the girl's is indeed obviously unfair. . . . Not one girl
in a hundred would be able to work up the subjects required for
an Indian Civil Service examination in the way which boys do.
Her health would break down under the effort: and health is the
obstacle which, even under the most favourable circumstances,
must stand in the way of a girl's acquiring the intellectual strength
which at this age is so invaluable to a boy. He had been tossed
about in the world, left in a great measure to his own resources,
and been inured to constant physical exertion. He has been riding
and boating and playing at cricket, and both body and mind have
been roused to energy; and so, when he comes to study, he has a
sense of power which acts mentally as well as physically, and
enables him to grasp difficulties and master them. The girl, on the
contrary, has been guarded from over-fatigue, subject to restrictions with regard to cold and heat and hours of study, seldom
trusted away from home, allowed only a small share of responsibility; – not with any wish to thwart her inclinations, but simply
because, if she is not thus guarded, if she is allowed to run the
risks which to the boy are a matter of indifference, she will prob-

ably develop some disease which if not fatal, will at any rate be an injury to her for life. The question of health must be a primary consideration with all persons who undertake to educate girls. It will be a perpetual interruption to their plans for study and mental improvement, but it is one which can never be put aside.

Elizabeth Wolstenholme-Elmy

The Education of Girls, its Present and its Future

(1869)

We are, it appears, on the eve of great educational reforms. We have been told, and by voices we cannot disregard, that instead of being, as we fondly believed, amongst the first of European nations in matters of instruction, we are so far fallen behind the onward march of other nations that it is now the special shame of England to possess almost the worst instructed people in Europe. The unscientific temper and spirit of our upper and governing class, the Philistinism of our middle class, and the sordid and brutal ignorance of multitudes of our working people, have been conclusively shown to be due either to defects of education or to its still more melancholy absence. The cry is everywhere loud for amendment. Schemes of university reform and extension, schemes for the re-organisation of our secondary instruction, theories of very different degrees of merit as to the just plan and scope of a comprehensive system of national education, are now before the world. If the day of much talking is the precursor of the hour of action, then the hour of action is near at hand. And yet, even amongst our reformers themselves, there appears to be little agreement as to what we can and ought to do by instruction. One authority has very recently told us that the first object of all instruction should be to fit a *man* to earn his own livelihood. Another tells us that it is the function of education to correct all narrow, special, and professional tendencies. A third, that the primal and direct aim of instruction is to enable a man to know himself and the world, all other being at best but subordinate aims. Are these views really so antagonistic as those who hold them seem to believe? Is there not a meeting point in which all are reconciled? Is it not plain that honest industry is of itself a part, and a most important part, of the highest education; that genuine work is the most perfect method of culture? Surely it is time that the dignity of labour in this sense should be recognised, and that such instruction should be given to all as shall substitute living, thinking workmen for mere machines. The industrial and economic advantages of this are clearly enough perceived, and a more rational system of instruction is urgently demanded on these grounds. Of at least equal importance is the enormous intellectual gain both to society and to the individual workman. And again, is it as a matter of fact the case that the best workman, the one who has had the fittest training for his task, is in any true sense narrow, special, or professional? Is it not, on the contrary, the case that where the intelligence is the clearest and quickest within the range of the daily avocation, intelligence and sympathy will be widest and deepest beyond its bounds? Where mere routine enters the least into the daily order of life, the life outside that daily order will be most intense and vivid. And again, how can a man rightly choose his daily task unless he has first learnt to know himself and the world? Such knowledge, as Mr Arnold says, is 'the only sure basis for action.' Nothing else can secure for us that just economy of individual aptitude which is the key to all the success of the future. Nothing else can secure to us that wise use of special aptitudes which shall give to each man access by his own particular gateway to intellectual life and vital knowledge. Unless some such reconciliation be possible, our hope of securing an educated people is indeed a vain dream.

But in all these discussions we hear singularly little of the education of women. 'The air is thick,' says a Quarterly Reviewer, 'with schemes for the education of women;' but these schemes lie quite apart from the general discussion of the subject, and have been conceived in the interests of women by women themselves. In the remarkable volume of *Essays on a Liberal Education*, which we must regard as the manifesto of the most advanced educational reformers, one solitary paragraph is devoted to the education of girls, and to a casual plea that what they learn at all they should learn well. From Mr Arnold's interesting volume on the schools and universities on the Continent, we gather a shadowy notion that there are such things as girls' schools, that the teaching of the girls is on the whole the best where that of the boys is the best; but that everywhere and at all times it lags very far behind. Mr Arnold concludes his volume by the sketch of a very comprehensive plan of re-organisation for English instruction, but throughout that plan there is no expression of a wish that girls should partake of its benefits. On the contrary, if we are to judge of his intentions from a footnote elsewhere, he would seem to desire expressly to shut out girls from any scheme for the improvement of public or school instruction.

The Schools Inquiry Commissioners, whilst readily yielding to the representations that girls' schools fell naturally within the scope of their inquiry, and bestowing great pains and attention, both directly and through their Assistant Commissioners, on the investigation of the problem of female education, were yet unable to treat it otherwise than as a separate and secondary matter. We do not complain of these things. They are but natural, perhaps inevitable, in our present imperfect state of civilization, and they are only referred to here in order to show how necessary it is that women should speak for themselves, and claim to be considered, not as a separate community, but as a part of the whole. The aim and office of instruction are surely the same with women as with men. Their claim to right instruction rests on precisely the same grounds; their need of it is as great, perhaps greater; nor has it ever yet been proved that the nature of women is so radically different from that of men that the methods of instruction which we pronounce unscientific, uneconomical, and irrational in the case of men, can be pronounced scientific, economical, and rational when applied to women.

It will not come within the scope of this paper to consider the great problem of national education in its broad sense, including the instruction of all classes, and emphatically the elementary instruction of our wage-receiving class. All that need be said on this head is that when that question comes fairly before the nation, and the time for decisive action has come, as it must come very soon, it should be remembered that we are not one nation of Englishmen and another nation of Englishwomen, but one nation of English men and women, and that, as a matter of the soundest national policy and a means of the highest social well-being, it is imperative that Englishwomen should be as well instructed as Englishmen. But in the more limited part of the subject, with which alone we have here to deal, it is easy to show that, what for want of a better word we must call the secondary instruction of girls, is even more confused, more fragmentary, more worthless than that of boys, and stands in even more urgent need of a thorough and comprehensive re-organisation, whilst the higher education cannot as yet be said to have any existence. Its shadowy form floats before the public eye, as Carlyle pictures the German Adam to have done upon the stage 'going to be created.'

It is almost impossible to convey to any one who has had no experience in teaching girls any notion of the wholly unsystematic and confused state of their education. A lively, we *wish* we could say an exaggerated, sketch of some of its most striking defects is to be found in Mr Bryce's valuable report presented to the Schools' Inquiry Commission. The great majority of English girls are educated either at home with the help of governesses and masters, or at exceedingly small schools, whether day-schools or boarding-schools. Parents prefer these small schools because they believe they approach the most nearly to that which is their ideal of instruction for girls, and what in theory is very beautiful, home-education; but in nothing whatever is there a greater divergence between the theory and the actual, and in many cases the only possible practice, than in this matter of home-education for girls.

Before, however, entering upon the consideration of special defects of the education of girls as carried on at home and in these small schools or quasi-homes, it will be worth while to notice some defects which affect all schemes and methods of female education alike, and the correction of which must attend any considerable reform in mere organisation. The first of these defects which require reform concerns the parents, the second concerns the teachers. It is simply true as a general statement that English parents, who are apathetic and irrational enough about the education of their boys, are much more so when the education of their girls is in question. Here and there a mother devotes herself to the right training of her daughters, superintends judiciously the teaching both of governesses and masters, or supplements and sustains the efforts of the school teacher; and here and there a father interests himself in developing his daughter's powers, and is anxious that she should be a thinking creature and not merely an accomplished nonentity. But how few these cases are every teacher can bear melancholy testimony. In the wealthy classes frivolity and fashion rule. The mother devotes herself to society, and social duties and social pleasures are found incompatible with other obligations, whilst the girls themselves are too lightly and too early whirled into the same vortex. Fashion has stamped its approval upon certain external accomplishments and graces. The period during which social triumphs can be achieved is short and fleeting, and these accomplishments and graces, right enough and beautiful enough in their own place, must be purchased at the sacrifice of all else. Such a mother has simply no notion in what true education consists. It is not often that one can be found so simply ignorant and silly as the mamma who begged that her little daughter might not be troubled with the halfpennies and farthings in her arithmetic, because, as she said, 'she can have no use for it when she marries; her husband and her housekeeper will do all that.' But the spirit of that mother is found everywhere. The suppressed thought most frequently is, 'It will not help her to get married;' and thus we are brought round to the consideration, that the primary cause of the bad education of women is to be found in the bad education of men themselves. If we seek to improve the education of women, we must improve that of men. If we improve that of men, we shall sooner or later improve that of women also; but the advantage is greatest every way if the two reforms proceed hand-in-hand.

In the less wealthy middle classes the pressure of necessity is often very heavy, and the instruction of the girls is the first expense in which it is commonly thought curtailment is possible. As in the case of the wealthier classes the wish to make girls brilliant and attractive during a certain short period of their lives is answerable for much folly; so in this class the fact that the education of girls has no immediate commercial value is the great hindrance to a better education. We cannot appraise the value of a cultivated mind. Presumably, therefore, it has no value. A certain amount of education, or at least of instruction, is essential to a son's success in life, and, fortunately for boys, some of the subjects in which instruction is thus essential may be made educational instruments of no mean value. But what success in life is possible to a daughter? The son must make his own way in the world. The daughter must have hers made for her by somebody. It is thus that the question of education or no education is regarded. The period of a daughter's systematic instruction, if systematic instruction for girls *is to be found*, is perpetually interrupted and cut short at both ends. If there were no other plea than this for the free admission of women to industry, we should hold that this plea was sufficient. Industrial occupation is more than the supplement of education to women of this class. It is the only condition upon which they will be permitted to be educated. Other reasons, and ostensibly more urgent, there no doubt are, but this reason is in very truth the most weighty of all. Let us but consider how it works. A woman must remain ignorant because, to her, knowledge has no practical, that is, commercial value. She is idle because she is ignorant. She becomes frivolous or vicious because she is idle. And for how much of the misery of the world idle hands and wasted brains are responsible it would be hard to say. This we can only suggest as a point needing far graver consideration than is often given to it. So, too, it is worth considering how enormous a power for good all this energy might become if economised and trained. How to deal with these difficulties in the case of parents is the standing perplexity of teachers. We must confess that we see no hope for immediate reformation. It is only by the greater extension of education itself that education will come to be rightly valued, and in this way the task of the teachers of the next generation will be a far easier and pleasanter one than that of the teachers of today.

But if the teachers cannot reform the parents, they may at least reform themselves. Mr Bryce says: 'Teachers,' that is, women who teach, 'have two defects; they have not themselves been well taught, and they do not know how to teach. Both these defects are accidental, and may be remedied.' These are not slight defects. The charge against teachers could not well be graver than that they are ignorant and incompetent, and yet it is quite true that these defects are 'accidental, and may be remedied.' It is not the fault of the existing body of the teachers of girls that they themselves were badly taught. It is not their fault that they had no right training in teaching as an art, and have never been led to look upon education as the practical application of the highest science. But it will be their own fault if they do not discover these defects for themselves; if they do not apply the remedy, and if they do not make it impossible for such a charge to be justly brought against the teachers of the future.

The elder teachers can indeed do little more than perfect themselves by private study in the various subjects which they profess to teach, and aid the younger teachers by their experience, encouragement, and sympathy; but for the younger teachers facilities are already offered, or will shortly be offered, of which if they do not choose to avail themselves they will be foolish and almost criminal. Stimulants to private study, and direction in that study, are now accessible in most of our great towns, where the Lectures to women have been successfully established. Whatever shape these Lectures may ultimately take, and whatever their bearing upon the education of women in general, there can be no doubt of their great value to teachers, not merely, nor even chiefly, for the direct instruction which they afford, and for the suggestive lines of study pointed out, but by helping them to the best methods of teaching, by bringing them into contact with the best living teachers. Those who have had the opportunity of listening to Professor Huxley's lectures at the London Institution – lectures the mere syllabus of which is a most instructive lesson in teaching – will readily perceive of what immense value such aids must be to the teacher. But incidental aids of this kind will not alone suffice. It is absolutely necessary in the interests of education that teachers should secure the highest special training for their special work, and that they should master the secrets of combination and co-operation. Whilst a general high culture is essential to a teacher, it is equally necessary to do away with the superstition that any one person can teach any and all subjects equally well. Here more than anywhere else is it necessary that there should be that economy of individual and special aptitudes of which we have before spoken. It is not less necessary for women than for men, for girls than for boys, that those who teach should be 'masters of their business – that each shall be set to teach that branch which he has thoroughly mastered, and shall not be allowed to teach any that he has not.' But this presupposes that teachers will be prepared to submit themselves to definite tests of their qualifications, as well as to the specific training which is necessary. For women in general such tests of attainments have already been provided by the Universities of London and of Cambridge[1] in their recently-devised examination schemes. The Cambridge scheme in particular lends itself to the present necessities of teachers in a manner which will make their acceptance of it almost a matter of certainty. The examination falls too early this year – too soon, that is, after the publication of the scheme, and in relation to the usual distribution of the time of teachers – to afford any conclusive test as to their readiness to avail themselves of its provisions. If they should permanently refrain from doing so, the fact would have a painful significance.

Whether under the provisions of the Endowed Schools Bill *special* examinations for teachers will be devised, and if so, what form these examinations will take, it would be premature even to guess. But after all, no test of attainments, however necessary and however valuable, will suffice for the equipment of a teacher. It ought to be a recognised part of every teacher's duty to familiarise herself with the great educational experiments of the past, and with their results; with the experiments now being made in other countries; and, above all, with the experiments which are being made at home. Actual practice in teaching under the eye and direction of an experienced teacher would be invaluable, and some machinery by which this shall be made possible ought now to be recognised as a pressing educational necessity. It would not be difficult to point out ways and means of securing such training. How important this is every teacher who has blundered through many wrong methods, and who has felt the consequent vexation and disappointment, as well as the absolute loss to pupils, can abundantly testify. One other point may here be mentioned: it is more than ever desirable that those women who devote themselves to teaching should do so with deliberate intention. It is a matter of grave concern, that in the case both of men and of women who teach this should so seldom be done, and that the work of a teacher should be constantly taken up as a mere temporary occupation pending something better. No high professional skill can be hoped for so long as this is the case, and in no profession whatever can skill and experience be more desirable and important.

But however much may be done by an improvement of the qualifications of teachers themselves, we cannot look to this for the whole of the advance we desire. Without better organisation, without a better relation between all the parts of the scheme of our instruction, the ablest and most highly-qualified teachers will accomplish but little. The present general practice of education, either at home or in very small schools, is inconsistent with any *wide* diffusion of a more thorough instruction. No doubt this is the best thing possible in particular cases; but even in the best cases of the kind the waste of power is enormous.

The objections to education exclusively at home and to education in very small schools are so nearly the same that it may be convenient to treat of them together. The small school has indeed the disadvantages of home instruction, with some of its own super-added. The notion of many people on this subject is, that if mothers and governesses were what they should be, home education would be the perfect ideal of education for girls. Yet it is not too much to assert that education at home, understanding by education thorough systematic instruction, is in any but the very small minority of cases impossible. It is idle to deny the immense value of home influences. The ideal of girls' education, and of boys' also, appears to demand the just admixture of public instruction and of private and domestic influence. The problem is a difficult one, perhaps the more difficult because we do not yet appreciate its difficulty; but also one not incapable of solution. In the case both of the home and of the small schools, the first fatal defect is that one person must either teach many subjects to different pupils in different stages of progress, or that separate teachers must be engaged at an expense which is beyond the reach of any but the very wealthiest. A very small result is produced by an expenditure of power, of time, and of money, wholly incommensurate. Take the case of a governess in a family with three or four children of different ages. She is expected to teach something of perhaps a dozen different subjects to each of three or four pupils, each of whom requires separate and individual instruction. But individual instruction in such a case means no instruction at all. It means giving an infinitesimal fragment of time, and a divided and distracted attention to each of the pupils and subjects in turn; or if anything more real is aimed at, it is only accomplished at a cost of time, of labour, of brain, and of nerve, which no human creature should be asked to undergo. Even in the more fortunate case of the governess whose pupils are of much the same age and the same attainments, the effect is pretty sure to be depressing to the teacher, and monotonous to the pupils. The teacher's powers are never roused and stimulated as they are under the effort necessary for collective or class-teaching, and the pupils have no standard of comparison outside and beyond themselves. Moreover, we believe it to be mischievous to both teacher and pupil that the latter should be so exclusively under one predominant influence, and that the former should be so constantly in the attitude of a critical study of the same type of character, the same defects, or even of sympathy with the same excellences.[2] Of course when masters and other teachers are in attendance this evil is to some extent remedied, but then another difficulty arises. Unless the governess is sufficiently cultivated both to supplement and superintend this additional teaching, it fails to become education in the true sense, and remains mere instruction on detached and unrelated subjects. No doubt this is a defect of school teaching also in our present state of confusion; but it is one of the defects most easy to remedy. For the full development of character the free play of a variety of influences is most desirable. In a home of real refinement and cultivation a thousand subtle influences are daily brought to bear upon the children which are of the greatest importance, and which it is the height of folly to forego. The education of the feelings is here carried on, informally, but most effectually. This, which is *the* valuable part of home-education, ought not to be lost. To send a girl from such a home to a mere ordinary fashionable boarding-school is a high stretch of imprudence; but this is probably not necessary.

In the case of small schools all the difficulties of home instruction are found, if possible, in a somewhat aggravated form. Let us take the case, a very common one, of a school with from twelve to twenty pupils, their ages varying from six or eight to eighteen, and let us imagine what one, two, or even three teachers can do in such a chaos. For our present purpose it does not matter whether these schools are boarding-schools or day-schools. In the case of the cheap schools, the one or two teachers must suffice for the needs of all the pupils. In the case of the more expensive ones, a larger staff of teachers, either resident or visiting, is provided, but at a cost which makes the fees, though excessive to the parents, scarcely at all remunerative to the principal teacher. It would be interesting to learn what is the average rate of *profit* upon her capital of a schoolmistress, to say nothing of remuneration for her labour. If one could set the case of the very few who acquire a small independency over against that of the many who struggle on encompassed by difficulties, and of those who are utterly ruined, we should probably find that the average of profit was nothing at all. There are reasons for this in the present state of female education into which it is not necessary to enter, and it is only mentioned here to illustrate the wastefulness of our present educational confusion. But whether in the case of the less expensive or of the more expensive schools, this difficulty is added to most of the difficulties of home instruction, that not only are the pupils of all ages and at all stages of progress, but that they come and go in the most bewildering manner. A girl of sixteen will perhaps come to school and prove on examination more backward than another child of twelve. It is injurious to both to teach them together; to provide separate instruction is again to multiply difficulties. One would scarcely expect to be believed, if one gave the simple natural history of such a school, and showed how fitful and how irregular is the school instruction of most girls. We wonder much how many schoolmistresses ever framed a consistent course of study which should stretch over six years. We wonder still more how many have successfully carried it out in the case of even one pupil. Either those pupils who stay longest at school are sacrificed to those who casually come and go, or these latter, and these are the far greater number, must be sacrificed to the interests of the very few. The burden laid upon the teachers of small schools is indeed greater than anyone can bear, and it is no wonder that even able and earnest teachers begin to feel, after years of such experience, that the remedy is not in their own power. It is not in the power of any *one* teacher to remedy this evil, but it is within the power of combinations of teachers working together in the interests of education and working judiciously, with the aid of public recognition and encouragement, gradually to extinguish it.

The experiment of large schools for girls has already been successfully tried, and the results are conclusive as to the superiority of the system (so far at least as concerns day-schools), from whatever point of view we regard it. Their superior economy is obvious. But this economy cannot be estimated simply in terms of money. The school reacts upon the teachers, and their teaching becomes more spirited, energetic, and successful. The lower fees at which such schools can offer really good instruction, enable intelligent parents to avail themselves of the advantages of a longer school period, and in such schools alone have we as yet been able to reap the advantages of a graduated, systematised, and comprehensive course of instruction. Morally, we believe the gain to be also great. It is possible in such schools to substitute government by a healthy public opinion for government by a personal will; the free play of extensively varied influences is secured, a freedom which tends much more to the naturalness, independence, and variety of character than any system of more exclusive influences. Classification is easy, and the stimulus and support of companionship in study are more fully afforded.

The case of large boarding-schools is different and much more difficult. Perhaps the best that can be said of them is, that the inherent evils may by skilful teachers be reduced to a minimum, but it can never be considered very desirable to bring together great numbers of young people and to throw them into the intimacy of an English boarding-school, without far more careful oversight than it is easy to secure, whilst any approach to the system of perpetual espionage would be at once hateful to our English notions, and, as we believe, fatally mischievous to both teachers and pupils.

If these are the evils, what then are the remedies? We are not in Utopia, nor do we propose to shadow forth Utopian dreams, but sober, practical measures, which, if not possible today, may perhaps be so tomorrow. By connecting the home life with some one or other of the forms of collective instruction of which we shall hereafter speak, the home influences might be preserved, and another set of influences, little, if at all, inferior in value might be added. We want first, in every considerable town in England, a High School for girls – perhaps a High School and a Secondary school, under Municipal or Government control, which should offer the best possible education on very moderate terms. The school ought to be such that it should serve as a model to all those private establishments for which in the future, as at present, there will no doubt be abundant room. To such a school as this it would be very easy to attach all manner of appliances and apparatus in the way of lectures or special classes, which might be attended by pupils from private families or the smaller schools. If we could not in every town find a Professor Huxley who should make Physical Geography fascinating and simple to schoolboys and schoolgirls, and incidentally teach teachers how to teach, others might yet be found who would in their several ways perform a similar service.

Second, if the small schools, whether as day or boarding-schools, are to continue, teachers must find out for themselves some plan of co-operation which shall make their labour richer in results. If four or five teachers would work together and make of each small school one class, each working up to each in a graduated and progressive course of instruction, the matter would be simple enough. So far as the teachers are concerned, we believe this might be done at once. The difficulty is with the parents, who would be apt to suppose that teachers were working from interested motives, and whom it would be impossible to bind down by any formal agreement. If however such progressive classes or grade schools cannot be established, we see no remedy for the crying evil of the small school system, except in the gradual amalgamation and absorption of these schools themselves. Under a comprehensive national system this would be very easy, as a matter of private arrangement exceedingly difficult.

Third, as there will still remain many parents who cannot make use of the day-school, but either of choice or of necessity must send their daughters to study away from home, we would suggest the establishment, in various country districts, of schools corresponding to the high schools of which we have spoken, a central institution, that is to say, with its complete staff of teachers and professors, but in which there should be no resident pupils. The officers of the institution should not take boarders because their work in the actual school hours would be sufficiently exhausting, but boarding-houses should be opened, and regularly licensed, the only persons allowed to keep such boarding-houses being ladies (wherever circumstances favoured it, married ladies) of education and refinement. The number of boarders should in every case be limited, and the person licensed to the boarding-houses should stand in the relation of friend and private tutor to the boarders. By some such plan the gravest evils of large boarding-schools would be escaped, and the economical and social advantages of collective instruction be secured.

Fourth, we need the establishment first of one, and ultimately of many such institutions as the Hitchin College for Women. It would seem almost unnecessary to argue this point. If the education of women is ever to advance beyond its present low level, it must be by the creation of means which have never yet been employed. Systematic instruction for women in any way analogous to that which the universities supply to men, and which is likely in the future to be supplied more fully, and at more numerous centres, has never yet in England been offered to women. That there are many amongst us who would gladly have profited by this higher education we know too sadly. That there are now those eager and desirous to avail themselves of it, is perfectly certain; but whether such a demand exists or not, it is plain that it ought to exist and that we ought to set about creating it if it did not. Such provision is necessary in the first place for teachers; for the rhyme is as true today as it ever was:

> But little way her knowledge reaches.
> Who knows no more than what she teaches.

And yet, such is the irrationality of our present methods that we constantly find our teachers teaching what they do not know, and, most lamentable of all, wholly ignorant of their own ignorance. Now the very first step towards improving away these ignorant teachers is to send out as teachers as many women as possible of genuine attainments and high cultivation. Some such women there are to be found already amongst the ranks of teachers, but they have come by their attainments in almost every case by the slow and difficult process of self instruction. Possibly character may have been strengthened and faculty matured under the process, but at a cost both to themselves and others which they would thankfully have been spared. If such women could give the history of their own efforts and failures, we should find in these the very best plea for making the higher education easily accessible to women. Which of them could not tell a dreary story of efforts wasted upon wrong methods of study, of time lost in reading inferior books, which the slightest suggestions of greater knowledge or experience would have saved them? There is not one amongst them who is not conscious of painful gaps and short-comings, defects which are perpetual hindrances to her best and most earnest work. But this is not peculiar to women who teach. All those women who, from whatever cause, have been led actively to interest themselves in the pressing social questions of the day, must have felt the same miserable want of an instruction larger and deeper, and a mental discipline more bracing than has been permitted to them. The difficult social problems of today are not to be solved by mere native kindness of heart, still less by unassisted common sense. Never was there a time when there was so much work waiting to be done which demanded the highest faculty, perfected by the best possible training. Our schools cannot supply this want of good training. We have shown that they are not adequate to the work already imposed upon them. The cases are very few indeed in which by a special happy combination of advantages a woman can secure at home the systematic culture which is most desirable. It is not probable, indeed it is not possible, that such an experiment as this should supply all that is necessary for the higher education in an age of educational ferment and innovation like our own. But as *one* experiment, and a most valuable one, we earnestly wish it complete success.

Fifth, but for the multitude of women who cannot avail themselves of such an institution, or who would not if they could, who want systematic instruction brought to their own doors, or who have only time and opportunity for some measure of the higher culture, which fragment they would yet most highly prize – for these, for the young mothers seeking instruction, for the teachers engaged in their profession and wishing to continue their studies and to supplement their own fragmentary education – for all these we must look to the development of the Lecture system at work in many of our large towns. These courses of lectures, distinctly educational in character and supplemented by examinations, have already proved of essential service. Whether ultimately these lectures will develop themselves into genuine local colleges, offering the highest instruction attainable to women, whether they will form an important part of those educational agencies of the future which are to affect not only our women but our men, it is premature to say. Those who work most earnestly for them, and are most interested in their success, are of all people the most unwilling that they should be prematurely systematised, or should ever become crystallised or stereotyped. But we do see in these beginnings the germs of something far greater, of something indeed capable of almost indefinite expansion and development; for wherever the zeal to teach and the desire to learn have manifested themselves in a remarkable degree side by side, as they have done lately, in our lecturers and pupils, *there* is a vitality which is only struggling to invest itself with a form – there are the elements of organic growth, which our want of skill may thwart or distort, but cannot kill.

It would be wrong to bring this paper to a close without something more than a mere passing reference to the great educational measure of the day. The Endowed Schools Bill is not a source of unalloyed pleasure to some educational reformers, who would have preferred that it should have taken its place as part of a larger national scheme. But taken by itself as a part measure, and as a promise of the future, no one who cares for the real advance of education can afford to be indifferent to it. Least of all can women be so. If that measure, or any modification of it, whilst retaining the saving clauses which secure to women a share in its advantages, should ever become law, it will be the fault of women themselves, if they do not use it as the most powerful lever ever yet applied to raise the education of women. It will be their duty under the provisions of the temporary part of the Act to claim for girls, wherever grounds of right or of expediency can be shown, their share in any and all educational endowments, to insist that the necessities of girls shall not be forgotten. Forgotten, we say, since in the misappropriations of the past it is certainly not wilful injustice which has been at work. It is with this, as with much else that is painful in the position of women,

> Evil is wrought by want of thought
> As well as want of heart.

Since the Endowed Schools Bill was first brought before the House of Commons, a very important change has passed over it. Power was given to the Select Committee to which the bill was referred, to divide it into two parts. This has been done, and it is only the first and least important part of the bill which has passed the House of Commons, and will, it is hoped, speedily become law. This part of the bill will make possible a thorough reform and re-organisation of our Endowed Schools. It will lead to the right and economical use of educational funds which have been scandalously misapplied. It will bring up the existing Endowed Schools to a far higher level of efficiency. Let us hope that it may ensure the acceptance of a larger and broader system of culture than many of our Grammar Schools, adhering too servilely to the traditions of the past throughout a changing present, have hitherto found possible. But after all, we have here only the machinery for a temporary and partial improvement. Some schools will be immensely improved, the majority will be left pretty much where they are, and no machinery has been provided for securing the continued efficiency of even the improved schools. The most important part of the measure has been postponed; but will, no doubt, be brought forward next session, perhaps with modifications; but shorn, let us hope, of none of its most just and wise provisions.

The provisions for the establishment of an Educational Council, for the examination and registration of teachers, for the registration and inspection of schools, are primary necessities in the present state of education. This part of the measure concerns all schools, and not simply the Endowed Schools; and although no coercion can be employed in the case of private schools to enforce inspection and registration, a considerable amount of moral pressure can scarcely fail to be brought to bear upon them. The best and most earnest teachers of private schools know too well the advantages of external and impartial examination, to allow such opportunities to remain unimproved. No sacrifice of independence is involved, no proposal made to impose any rigid uniformity of subjects or of methods of instruction. That such uniformity could ever be desirable is improbable; in the present stage of educational theory and experiment, it would be fatally mischievous; but such uniformity it is not proposed to establish. Every private schoolmaster will be as free to make his own experiments, and to carry out his own methods then as now. Let us add, every private schoolmistress; for it is most important to observe that this part of the measure concerns women as *much* as men, teachers of girls as much as teachers of boys. The teachers of girls may be examined, girls' schools may be inspected, and the extent to which this is done will depend upon the teachers themselves. It is very much to be hoped that in any special schemes of examination that may be devised under the provisions of this bill, it will not be thought necessary to apply separate tests to men and to women, to girls' schools and to boys' schools. Far more desirable is it that a general scheme of examination should be devised, comprehensive enough for both, and elastic enough to suit individual specialities.

It is also very desirable that women should be directly represented on the proposed Educational Council. There are women in England, just as competent as any men who may be chosen, to deliberate on general questions of education, and to give practical effect to their deliberations. There are many who have given more serious attention to the education of girls, and more active help towards its improvement, than any man has yet done. If the counsel and assistance of such women be rejected, there is nothing to supply its place. And those men who care most about the right education of women, are the most ready to admit that they are not competent alone to solve the problem; that they need, at every step, the suggestion and the co-operation of women.

That this part of Mr Forster's great measure will have a powerful effect for good upon the education of girls, there can be no manner of doubt. To them it is much more important than any possible provision under this year's bill can be. In this year's bill the interests of girls were to some extent provided for by a judicious use of the personal pronouns. Their claim to *some* share in the educational endowments of the country was fully recognised. The Select Committee improved in this respect upon the original terms of the bill by giving greater prominence to the claims of girls. A new clause, Clause 12, was also introduced, providing that, in framing schemes under this bill, provision should be made, as far as conveniently might be, for extending to girls the benefits of endowments. By this clause, the claims of girls are fully admitted, but a wide discretionary power is left to the Commissioners under the terms 'as far as conveniently may be.'

Grave questions arise here as to the proportionate claim of girls and boys. A very interesting discussion took place on this clause in the House of Commons, on 14 June, when an amendment was moved by Mr Winterbotham, M.P. for Stroud, to the effect that the words 'equally with boys' should be introduced after the word 'girls' in this clause.

It should be noticed that the clause, even with Mr Winterbotham's amendment, does not necessarily imply that girls should take equal shares with boys in all existing endowments. As a matter of natural right it might be fairly argued that girls have a claim to a full half of whatever money is nationally devoted to educational purposes. The women of the country outnumber the men, and whatever may be said of girls in general, and of their need of and capacity for education, it is clear that in the class most largely affected by the Endowed Schools Bill, the educational needs of girls are, even as a question of simple industrial advantage, quite as great as those of boys. It is in this class that the enormous excess of unmarried women – women who must support themselves by their own independent exertions – is to be found. The practical exclusion of girls from the highest educational advantages offered to this class is in very many cases equivalent to a sentence of lifelong pauperism and dependence. It is to the last degree indecent that women should be dependent on marriage for a professional maintenance. It is highly inexpedient that they should be restricted to a few avocations for which it is presumed that the slightest possible education – or none at all – is adequate. Yet such is the practical result of the exclusion of girls from the higher education. It is not permissible to assert with Mr Beresford-Hope, that the education required for girls is less extended than that which ought to be imparted to boys, unless it can be conclusively shown that society as a whole, including that very important element the girls themselves, is the richer, the happier, the better for such restriction. It cannot be asserted that this has ever been shown. It is clear that men do not know the material destitution which so largely exists amongst this class of women. It is assumed in the face of the most patent facts that all women marry and are provided for by their husbands; whilst nothing is more plainly to be seen by those who will open their eyes, than these three things:

(1) That a very large minority of women do not marry.
(2) That of those who do marry, a very considerable proportion are not supported by their husbands.
(3) That upon a very large number of widows (more than one-third of the widows in the country), the burden of self-maintenance and of the maintenance of their children is thrown.

It is an absolute necessity of our present social condition that women should have as free admission to professional and industrial training as men; that there should be no monopoly of sex, and no protective duty on either side. Natural differences and natural fitnesses would then assert themselves, and men need not for one moment fear that in any work for which they have special natural advantages they will ever be driven out of the field by women. The injustice to women consists in appropriating to men all the artificial and acquired advantages of education and training. Of the economic gain to the community it is not necessary here to speak. But equality of education must precede equality of industrial training. The former is the foundation upon which the latter must rest. Experience has conclusively shown that in cases where it has been sought to give a sound industrial training to girls or women, their defective early education has always been the most miserable but the most effectual hindrance.

But admitting for a moment that no industrial advantages resulted to the country from the better education of women, that the women themselves can be materially provided for without any exertion of their own, that men are and ought to be the universal bread-winners, does it then in the least follow that a more restricted education will suffice for the needs of women, than would be found adequate to the necessities of men? It would rather then appear that the material burdens of society being borne by the men, to the women it should belong to provide for its moral and intellectual development. If we would have a rational and just morality, a religion free from bigotry and superstition, or the reality of intellectual culture diffused to any great extent throughout society, we must look for these results to the education of women.

Nor again is it for those who boast of the sanctity of our domestic institutions to admit that a slighter culture on the part of women than of men is the just basis of such institutions. The influence of the mother is probably the most real and pervading influence in the world. The influence of the wife can be far less accurately gauged, but it is an influence that not even the highest culture can afford to despise; it will degrade where it does not elevate. 'The possession of a wife, conspicuously one's inferior in intellect, is, like other privileges, attended with a few inconveniences, and, among the rest, with the occasional necessity of using a little deception.'[3] How profoundly true this is, and how fearful a source of demoralisation we have here, is painfully manifest to any acute observer of life.

The arguments or assertions which we have been dealing with were actually used by opponents of the claims of girls in the discussion on the Endowed Schools Bill; but those who held such language met, happily, with very little support or encouragement. It was remarkable how anxious nearly every one who spoke was to express sympathy with the advancement of women's education in general, and with the notion of giving girls a large share of the endowments. But there was an evident reluctance to admit any arithmetical equality of claim with boys.

Before discussing this point, it may be well to remember that from the enormous revenues of our ancient universities, women draw no educational advantage whatever; that in the liberal provision made for the higher education of men, no room has hitherto been found for a consideration of their claims. No institutions parallel to the nine great public schools have ever been founded for girls. Of the particular educational endowments contemplated by Mr Forster's Bill, girls have only a most insignificant share. The statistics furnished to the Schools' Inquiry Commission, show that about 3,000 girls are educated in what may be called public schools – that is, either proprietary or endowed schools. Of the 1,100 girls returned as under instruction in endowed schools, about 500 belong to the class which attends our national schools. The remaining 600, then, represent the class of girls corresponding to the class of boys who frequent our Grammar Schools. No doubt this enumeration is incomplete, and there remain schools which the diligence of the Assistant Commissioners did not succeed in bringing to light; but these figures show very plainly how insignificant is the help given to girls in the matter of education, and this inequality in the treatment of girls and boys is no modern novelty, although its evil results are, perhaps, more apparent now than at any earlier period. A claim for girls has frequently been preferred on historical grounds. It has been urged that the majority of endowed schools were intended for children of either sex indifferently, and that the appropriation of the schools to the sole use of boys has been an act of spoliation so far as regards the girls. No doubt this is true in a few cases; there are some plain instances of flagrant robbery of girls, but in four cases at least out of five the endowments were distinctly intended for the use and advantage of boys. The very same feelings and prejudices were at work in times past which are at work today, and which make it so difficult to obtain pecuniary assistance for any project which has in view the improved education of girls or women – any project, that is to say, which goes beyond the limits of sectarianism, or of a somewhat narrow philanthropy. Even in these directions, what is done for girls is in nothing like equal proportion to what is done for boys. But beyond these limits it is almost impossible, where girls are concerned, to obtain money for any educational purpose. Large sums are every year being appropriated in one way or another for the education of boys;

nothing or next to nothing is being contributed to that of girls. Let one case stand by way of illustration. A carefully devised plan, to which we have earlier referred in these pages, for giving to women some of the advantages of collegiate instruction and discipline, has now been before the public for about two years. It was designed that the institution, buildings, and apparatus having been once provided, should be on a self-supporting basis. It was calculated that the building and apparatus would cost somewhere about 30,000*l.*, and an appeal was made for assistance to an undertaking of a truly national character. Of the 30,000*l.* required, about 3,000*l.* have been promised; a sum of course wholly inadequate to the expense of erecting even the smallest building suitable for such a purpose. Students were readily forthcoming, and the College will open in October; but in a hired house with all the disadvantages and waste of power, so perfectly well understood by teachers, of buildings not originally adapted for educational purposes. We cannot help believing that if boys had been concerned, the necessary sum would have been subscribed in a single year. As it is now, so it has ever been, the interests of girls have been postponed, not of ill-will, but of indifference or forgetfulness, to those of boys. We prefer, therefore, to rest the claims of girls on grounds of justice and expediency, rather than on any grounds of historical precedent.

It has been assumed that the education supplied at home is amply sufficient for the needs of girls. It is not necessary to repeat the arguments already urged against this view, since it must be abundantly evident to all who will consider the facts, that as a question of expense alone, home education with the vast majority of girls is simply impossible. The sisters of Eton and Harrow boys may be taught at home, so far as expense is concerned, though even here they are probably at a serious disadvantage as regards solid instruction, but the sisters of the boys who attend our provincial grammar schools cannot be taught at home, and for them there is no provision except in the private adventure school, which may chance to be everything that could be desired, but is just as likely to be for educational purposes utterly worthless. These considerations bring us face to face with the question of the proportionate claim of girls and boys. Mr Forster remarked in the discussion on Mr Winterbotham's Amendment, that if they had to set to work to deal with a fresh fund, he quite agreed with his honourable friend that they ought to divide it between girls and boys, but at present the endowments were for the most part possessed by boys. He was very anxious that the Commissioners should consider, in the words of the clause, how far they could extend to girls the benefits of these endowments, but it would be quite impossible that they could do so equally, because that would be to deprive the boys of the education which they were already in the possession of.[4] Although it might be said that the fact of possession does not absolutely cover the right of continued possession, yet it is quite certain that nobody wants to deprive boys of any educational advantages to be derived from endowments. But is it quite necessary that what is given to the girls should be taken from the boys? Is there not room, if the Schools' Inquiry Commissioners can be trusted, abundant room for superior economy of management in many if not in most of these schools, and should all the advantage of this economy be appropriated to boys? Plainly it will be impossible, where the endowment is very small, to establish side by side with a school for boys a similar school for girls. One strong institution is much better than two weak ones, and in the general interests of education it is probably better that there should be one good school, even though boys should appropriate the advantages, than two feeble ones. But these are just the cases in which the experiment of mixed schools might be tried with advantage. If there cannot be the good school for boys and the good school for girls, it seems reasonable to conclude that the one good school ought to be equally for boys and girls. To many of us mixed education appears the only rational solution of our educational difficulties. It is not proposed to argue that a system of mixed education would be of unmixed advantage; it is quite sufficient to show that the balance of advantage is in its favour. On the economic ground the gain is plain. The expense of a double staff of teachers and a double set of school-buildings is at once saved. But the only objections to such an experiment rest on moral and social grounds. Why it should be considered so dangerous and doubtful for boys and girls or for men and women to share each other's serious pursuits whilst they are allowed freely to share each other's frivolities, is a matter of perpetual surprise to those who accustom themselves to look beyond the range of tradition or convention. The strong prejudices of English society on this point have worked very mischievously in many directions besides this of education.[5] Of the saddest results of the separate education and life of the sexes it is impossible here to speak; as a slighter, but still mischievous result, it is sufficient to notice the profound ignorance of each other's real nature and ways of thinking common to both men and women. Certain sides of each other's character are studied perhaps a little too closely and curiously; beyond these all is an unknown land of doubt and mystery, about which vague conjecture is safe and easy since explanation is impossible. We do not deny the charm of this sense of mystery and difference; what we complain of is, that artificial differences should be first created and then mistaken for those real, essential differences which are of the ordinance of nature, and which fit the sexes each to supplement and complement the other. Many a life has been wrecked upon mistakes arising out of this ignorance.

Women are perpetually excluded from the provisions of various kinds made for men, and no adequate separate provision is or can be made for them. The comparative advantage or disadvantage of a mixed system of education can only be determined by free experiment, and this experiment cannot be said to have been yet made in England under fair conditions. Such experiments as have been possible, have been pre-eminently successful. It certainly seems most natural that brothers and sisters should go to school together; that the schoolroom should be the expansion of the home-life into the life of society. Natural reasons against such community of education there would seem to be none, but rather every natural reason in their favour.

But whatever solution of present difficulties may be found, it is plain that the question of the higher education of women is a most urgent one, one which will not bear to be delayed. We plead the cause of women. We ask that the gifts of God may not be wasted, that women themselves may not be robbed of some of the purest joys of life, those of intellectual effort and achievement, and that society which needs their help so much may not be defrauded of their best and worthiest service. Give us knowledge, power, and life. We will repay the gift a hundred-fold. Set free the women who sigh in the dark prison-houses, the captives of ignorance and folly. Cruel tyrants are these; slay them! With yourselves, people of England, it rests to put an end to that reign of frivolity of which you say you are so weary. Help women to become wise, that they may be just and true, merciful and loving.

APPENDIX

So few men really understand the material destitution of women, that I am tempted to transcribe a few sentences from letters which have come to me within the last five days, simply premising that these are not picked selections, but specimens of cases hundreds of which could be cited if necessary, and such as are perpetually being brought before those women who interest themselves with the condition of their sex:

June 16*th*. – 'The negotiation respecting ★ ★ ★ ★ ★ falls quite through, I am sorry to say. The hours of work are all right, sixty-eight hours per week; but the salary offered is 30*l*. a year (for every purpose, including board), and the salary is of consequence to Mrs —. Can you suggest any other openings? She must emigrate to America as a civil service clerk.'

The lady of whom this is written is a widow (marriage the natural provision for women!); an educated woman in the true sense of the word, in the very fulness and maturity of her powers, and though a woman of the highest refinement, one possessed of that energy of character and natural faculty which fit her to act as a pioneer; a lady too who has abundantly proved her administrative capacity in unpaid work of the highest kind. Is it not melancholy that such remuneration should be considered adequate payment for the labour of such a woman?

Granted that she has been specifically trained to no industry, educated labour ought to be worth more than 2*d*. an hour, and the want of special training is the very grievance we complain of – the want of training, and the monopoly by men of those posts for which such women are abundantly well qualified. With such facts before us, and facts immeasurably worse than these, need we wonder that thousands of women feel that they are an incumbrance in this corner of God's universe, and pray passionately for leave to die?

Another letter:

June 17*th*. – 'I am so sorry that I was obliged to decline the appointment on the terms offered. It would be an idle expense for me to accept a post with a salary on which I could not live and dress myself. Is it not hard for a well-educated lady to begin on 11*s*. 6*d*. a week, less than many a factory girl of sixteen or seventeen receives for her manual labour? . . . If anything else occurs to you which you think might be suitable for me, I shall be very glad to hear of it; but of course I only mean if the employment is anything new, and for the benefit of our sex, as you have too much to do for me to trouble you otherwise.'

Another letter, also June 17th:

'Can you give me any suggestions about the employment of

women, or rather *ladies*, who have not enough to live upon, and have not been brought up to do anything? I know so many of that class who would be *thankful* to gain a few shillings a week. Miss King told me of the society in London, but I think something local is wanted. Here (a fashionable watering-place) we have a place where ladies can take their needle-work, but the chance is that it may remain there twelve months before it is sold; if not sold, it is returned, perhaps soiled, and the lady is out of pocket. Besides, work of that kind is *slavery*, the pay for it is so poor.'

You who have daughters, wives, and sisters, whom you guard tenderly from present evils, take care that you are not preparing for them graver evils when you are no longer able to provide for them. It would disgrace you, you think, that they should work now, at least outside their own homes, and for any but you. Have you prepared them for the chance, a very likely one, of having no home in which to work? Unless you have done this, cease to sneer at us who seek to make up for your neglect, and cease to wonder that we no longer regard you as a sufficient earthly providence for women. If your affection be anything more than that common form of selfishness which considers women as the mere playthings of men, you will look further into the future than you have yet done, and will prepare differently for the days which may come to all, which *will* come to many of your dear ones.

NOTES

1 More recently by the University of Dublin.
2 A friend writes: 'A master whom I knew got a boy or two removed from his own class into that of a master of a different temperament. His class, which had hitherto gone ill, went well. He said, "I felt I only had to *eliminate the personal equation*." But a governess such as you describe has no chance to eliminate the personal equation.'
3 The Mill on the Floss.
4 *The Times* report.
5 The experiment of mixed classes – boys and girls – was tried at Liverpool College in the summer of 1868, by the Principal, Rev. G. Butler. A course of lectures on the Schools of Painting was given by him to about 250 boys, the senior pupils of the three schools, and some of the pupils of the Royal Institution School, who attended voluntarily; also to upwards of 100 girls and their teachers. The girls took copious notes, as did the boys, and appeared much interested in the subject of the lectures. No inconvenience of any kind resulted from this experiment, nor did it appear to the pupils as at all strange or unnatural; and it is probable, that to boys living at home with their sisters, and attending

day-schools, companionship with girls in study, as well as in their daily life at home, would come easily and naturally. In the above instance, the influence of sisters engaged in the same study as their brothers, was found beneficial. – EDITOR.

Maria Grey

On the Special Requirements for Improving the Education of Girls

(1871)

The task I have undertaken this morning is to point out what are the special requirements for improving the education of girls of all classes above those attending the Public Elementary Schools. I have confined my remarks to the former, because there is abundant evidence to prove that their education is actually worse, and is far less adequately provided for than that of the lower class. These requirements appear to me to be:

(1) A truer conception by parents, and the public generally, of what education is, and what are its uses.
(2) The improvement of schools through a better organisation, and a system of inspection.
(3) The improvement of female teachers as a class.
(4) The giving to girls some healthy stimulus to exertion and self-improvement.

The first and most essential of these, as leading necessarily to all the rest, is a thorough change in the ordinary conception of the aim and purpose of a girl's education; I should rather say of the conception of education itself. So long as education is confounded with instruction, and is valued only for its pecuniary results in assisting the process of 'getting on' in the world, so long will the education of girls who have not to 'get on' – or, whose occupations when they are obliged to work for their own maintenance, are not supposed to require any great intellectual cultivation – will be considered of secondary importance to that of boys, and will continue to suffer from all the evils which affect it now.

If the true view of education were generally adopted, if it were understood to mean the drawing out and cultivation of all the faculties with which it has pleased God to endow His human creatures – intelligence, affections, will, conscience, the training of each individual to guide himself aright through the circumstances of life, to know his duty and to do it – it would be at once seen that education is as important to women as to men, to the poor as to the rich; that it is not a question how much or how little knowledge will enable the pupils to get creditably or successfully through life, but what kind of knowledge and what method of imparting it will best draw out intelligence, and form a sound judgment; what moral discipline will quicken conscience to see the right, and strengthen the will to do it when seen.

As no one – except, perhaps, a Saturday Reviewer – will deny that women have intelligence, affections, conscience, will, that they have occasions to exercise judgment, and a path of duty to discern and to tread, as difficult, perhaps, as their brothers', it follows that education in its only true sense, as moral and intellectual training, is equally indispensable to them, and must be conducted on the same principles and by the same methods.

I have dwelt on this point, because I hold it of vital importance to our commonwealth, and because in every discussion about education, the confusion of ideas respecting what education is, and what is to be expected from it, becomes painfully apparent.

Not long ago £60,000 were subscribed in the City, that schools might be established to produce a better race of city clerks; but if the training in those schools is directed only to give the technical instruction necessary to clerks, instead of forming habits of right thought and right action, and above all of unflinching loyalty to duty, the City will have spent its £60,000 in vain. It may get better bookkeepers, readier writers; it will not get the intellectual and moral trustworthiness which are required to make good clerks, as they are to make men good in any station in life.

It is this same moral and intellectual trustworthiness, the result of an education expressly directed to produce it, which we require for women. If in each case we examine why a woman fails as wife, as mother, as mistress, as servant, we shall find the cause of failure is not her want of this or that piece of technical knowledge, cooking or sewing, or housekeeping, but the want of habits of observation, thought, and method; of self-control, of conscientiousness. When her field of duty enlarges with a higher social position, or one involving greater responsibilities, she fails also for want of the larger knowledge, the higher cultivation required to comprehend wider relations, and to act wisely amidst various and conflicting claims. Therefore I ask, as the first requirement for improving the education of girls, that its object be held to fit them morally and intellectually, not for the matrimonial market, but to do their duty wisely and faithfully in that station of life whatever it may be, to which it may please God to call them.

The second requirement I have mentioned is, the improvement of Girls' Schools. The principal defects of these schools, as pointed out by the Schools Enquiry Commissioners, are 'that they are commonly too small, which not only tends to multiply them unduly, and increases the cost, but as is well known, makes them as instruments of instruction inferior to large ones;' – that they attempt to teach everything, and consequently fail to teach anything well; that their teachers, books, and methods, are generally very inferior; that being, with extremely few exceptions, private adventure schools, the mistresses are at the mercy of the parents, and must give, not the education they think best, but what the parents will pay for, and that the parents as a rule, are unwilling to pay for anything but accomplishments. It is the reform especially of the second and third grade schools, which is most urgent. In them the whole of the lower and middle middle-class girls are educated, i.e. – the whole of the future wives and mothers of the most influential class in the country, and the teachers not only of their own class, but of the classes above them.

The problem we have to solve is how to provide for them good schooling at such a reduction of expense as shall induce parents, too ignorant themselves to know what is good, to prefer the sound teaching which is also cheap, to bad teaching which is expensive.

This solution is sought by many in the extension of educational endowments to girls. But as aid from that source must come slowly and we have little power to hasten it, I think it more practical to consider what we can do for ourselves by private and voluntary efforts.

I must first premise that I do not enter into the question whether home or school education is the best for girls: – First, because my time does not allow of it, and secondly, because it only affects the small minority whose parents are rich enough to pay for a resident or daily governess. All the rest, that is the enormous majority, must be educated at school or not at all.

But taking the school education as a necessity, there is a great preponderance of evidence in favour of large day-schools as against boarding-schools, the scholars living at home or in boarding houses connected with the day-schools.

All the advantages considered by the Schools Enquiry Commissioners to attend boarding-schools, belong only to those which, like our great public schools, from their size, their social standing, their traditions, form each a little world in itself, exercising a strong influence over the pupil's character, and assisting his general education. No such schools exist for girls. Their boarding-schools are as a rule very small, and offer none of the advantages enumerated above. It is evident that there must be an enormous waste of teaching power, and consequently, of money, in these small schools. On this point I will quote a letter I have received from Miss Fish of the Stockwell Training College, in answer to my request that she would give me the benefit of her experience.

> The teaching of large numbers together is always more economical. Better teaching power can be procured, for teachers can be better paid. In a small school just the same number of classes is usually necessary as in a large one, for among twenty-five or thirty pupils there is just the same variety of attainment and ability as among sixty or a hundred. Where the young ladies' ages vary from seven, to sixteen or seventeen, probably about ten classes are necessary for ordinary lessons, if all are to be taught thoroughly; but the classification cannot be so good as this in a small school, because the proprietor cannot afford to pay a sufficient number of good teachers. It follows either that valuable time is lost, and slow progress made by the more intelligent, who are neglected in order that their duller or younger classmates may improve, or, and this is more frequently the case, the quick and bright whom it is always most pleasant to instruct, are taught to the exclusion of the others. I also think that schools should be large, because a teacher with many pupils is less dependent on individuals for support, and therefore less likely to pander to the wishes of foolish parents.

I may add to Miss Fish's statement, that another disadvantage of these small schools composed of girls of different ages, is, that a mistress perfectly qualified perhaps to teach young children, and to develop the faculties most active at that age, may be very incompetent to teach older girls, who require to have their powers of thought, judgment, and self-discipline called out and trained. If we remember that education properly so-called, consists in drawing out and training the mental and moral faculties, we shall perceive that each period of childhood and girlhood must have its special method of training, its special mental and moral food, and that the organisation of classes, and lessons in schools, should be regulated by these considerations alone.

What we want then are classes in which the pupils should be as nearly as possible of the same degree of attainment, large enough to secure the maximum of efficiency with the minimum of cost in teaching, combined with the moral and physical advantages of home life. It seems to me that this want might be supplied, partially at least, by some plan of organisation among the best of the existing schools themselves, which might be carried into effect through the associations of schoolmistresses, aided by the local associations for promoting the education of women, now formed or forming in many of our large towns, and which will, I hope, extend before long over the whole country. There are two directions this organisation might take. One is that suggested by Miss Davies in her little book on the Higher Education of Women, a book of which I must say in passing, that it contains more wisdom on this subject in a small compass than any other I know, and leaves little for others but to enlarge on the texts it supplies.

Miss Davies' plan consists – I quote her own words – in 'establishing in every favourable locality a thoroughly good day-school, and clustering round it boarding-houses of moderate size, according to demand. In places like Blackheath, Clapham, St. John's Wood, or in any locality where girls' schools congregate, this plan might be adopted, and would combine many of the respective advantages of large and small schools. The facilities for classification, companionship in study, healthy public spirit, and a general kind of *open-airiness* which go with large numbers, would be found in the school, and the boarding-houses would have the quietness and something of the domestic character which it is difficult to get in a household conducted on a very large scale.' A similar scheme was more fully elaborated by Miss A. Clough, in a paper sent by her to the Schools Enquiry Commissioners, and printed in the second volume of their Reports, p. 84. I would suggest that the boarding-houses in connection with the central school should vary in their scale of expense so as to meet the requirements and the means of scholars of different social positions. I think some such arrangement as this might meet the objection to girls of different grades of society mixing together outside the school-room.

Miss Davies says nothing of the means by which the central school is to be provided. Miss Ann Clough looks for them from Government help, or endowments, if private individuals will not provide them by subscription. And the outlay required for the buildings and furniture of good central schools would be considerable, always a most important consideration where feminine interests are concerned. I may mention as an instance of this, the pecuniary difficulties which the Camden Town School for Girls, started by the public spirit and energy of Miss Buss, has been struggling with from the beginning, though it already numbers

190 pupils, and would, if the first outlay could be covered, become as great a pecuniary as it is an educational success. The plan I venture, with much diffidence, to offer as an alternative, as requiring less outlay of capital, is the association of a certain number of the existing small schools into a group, each school agreeing to receive pupils only of a certain age, or rather standard of attainment, and the group of schools representing the divisions or classes of a large school, from one to another of which the pupils should pass according to their progress. Each school would still be governed independently by its own mistress as regards discipline and method of teaching, but the general course of study and the system of examinations for passing from one school to the other, would be laid down by the Committee of the Association together with all matters equally concerning the whole group.

Such of the Associated Schools as were boarding-schools, might still take in as boarders pupils of different ages, who would attend as day-scholars, the school representing the class in which their degree of proficiency should place them. By this means parents would still have the choice of placing their children under the care of the mistress in whom they might feel most confidence, and who might be admirably adapted for general supervision though incompetent to give efficient teaching.

I do not see why one or other or both these methods of organisation should not be carried into effect by voluntary co-operation, without waiting for the aid of endowments, which at the best can provide only model-schools in each district, and cannot supply the educational wants of the country. I am inclined to think that the solution of more than one knotty social problem of our day must be sought in co-operation, the combination of numerous small means, to produce the large aggregate of force, necessary to take the field successfully in any of the contests of modern life; and why should not co-operative societies for education answer as well as for any other object, provided the essential conditions of success, honesty and ability, are forthcoming in both cases alike? Moreover, I believe that any movement destined to benefit large classes must, to be permanently successful, prove not only self-supporting but remunerative.

As with the dwellings of the poor, so with the education of women. Both may receive an immense impulse from individual zeal and benevolence, but the one class will not be decently housed, nor the other decently educated, till it can be proved experimentally that the supply of decent dwellings and decent education can be made a sound commercial investment. I am glad to be able to add that soon after writing that sentence I received from Dr Bond,

Principal of the Hartley Institution, Southampton, the Prospectus of a proposed Ladies' College at Southampton, to consist of a junior, middle, and senior department, offering every advantage of instruction at a moderate cost, the funds to be provided by a Limited Liability Company, issuing a certain number of shares at £25. each bearing 5 per cent. interest, except where disposed of for the use of pupils.[1] It would not be a bad plan to establish Provident School Societies on the same principle as other Provident Societies, which by the payment of moderate instalments from the time of the child's birth, might secure the child superior schooling with much less strain on income.

Next in importance to the organisation of schools, is some provision for their examination. The advantage of examination by an external and independent authority is, I think, becoming daily more fully recognised. 'Bring the work to the light,' says Miss Beale, and those who are conscious their work is good, will be only too glad to have it so tested. The extension of the University Local Examinations to girls has conferred upon female education a benefit which can scarcely be over-estimated, by supplying it with a standard to work up to, a standard of accuracy, thoroughness and real mental discipline, which meets and corrects the special defects in the teaching of girls. I think it would be very desirable that the Ladies' Associations for promoting the education of women, which are now multiplying through the country, should direct their efforts more immediately to extending the Local Examinations, and bringing larger numbers under their influence, and only secondarily to establishing higher class lectures for ladies, which have failed, I am told, in several places after their first novelty had passed off, as Mechanics' Institutes failed, and for the same reason, the want of preparation for them by sound early training in those for whom they are intended. But what I desire specially to advocate now, is the examination of the schools themselves, with a view to test not only their results as shown by the picked scholars, likely to go up for the Local Examinations, but the average work of the school, its organisation, its methods, its discipline, and all other points which determine, when taken together, whether the school is a place of real or of sham education, whether, to use the imagery of the very analogous art of gardening, it is a forcing house, or a well cultivated garden, or a fallow field in which good and bad seed are dropped and grow up haphazard.

The examinations should be such as to exclude the possibility of cramming for them. As the object of the teaching should be to develop the faculties of the scholars and train them to think and judge rightly, to cultivate and enrich their minds, so the school examination should be directed to test how far that object has been attained, to what degree intelligence rather than memory has been exercised, and the principles underlying each study clearly apprehended.

Such an examination would not be competitive, and its average results would be an accurate measure of the educating power of the school.

The University of Cambridge has for some years past offered to examine schools, but the terms demanded, are beyond the reach of all but the comparatively wealthy. The College of Preceptors also examines schools, but its terms per pupil seem too high for the lower middle-class girls' schools which most need such testing of their work. I recommend, therefore, that every effort should be made on the one hand to induce the universities to extend their influence, and employ some of their wealth in establishing a staff of examiners of secondary schools on terms within the reach of the lowest grade, and on the other to devise means to induce the mistresses of girls' schools to desire and invite examination, by bestowing on examined schools certificates of competency, which should give them the advantage of a recognised stamp of merit over unexamined schools.

What I have said on the organisation and grading of schools, would be very incomplete if I left out of consideration any provision for carrying on the education of young women, to the higher stage represented in that of young men by their university career. No idea is more fatal to women, than that their education is finished with their school-life and that idleness is henceforth to be the privilege of all who can afford it. If their education has been worth anything it ought by that time to have taught them how to learn, and the value of knowledge; but knowledge will have been till then used only as a means of intellectual discipline. It now becomes for the first time, an end in itself, and the advantage of the college course following the school is that it offers or ought to offer to those who really desire them, facilities for the systematic pursuit of that end under first-rate instruction. Mr Matthew Arnold in his Report to the Schools Enquiry Commission, says, 'It is impossible to over-value the importance to a young man of being brought in contact with a first-rate teacher of his matter of study, and of getting from him a clear notion of what the systematic study of it means.'

It seems to me that this is of equal importance to a young woman who desires to pursue her studies instead of dropping them. It is the crowning of the edifice of education, the want of which according to Mr Arnold, 'not only tends to give us a want of scientific intellect in all departments, but it tends to weaken and obliterate in the whole nation the sense of the value and importance of human knowledge, to vulgarise us, to exaggerate our estimate, naturally excessive, of the importance of material advantages, and to make our teachers, all but the very best of them pursue their calling in a mere trade spirit, and with an eye to little except these advantages.' (See Report, Vol. vi. Schools Enquiry Commission, p. 635.)

What can more fatally increase these injurious tendencies than the exclusion of women from this completion of education, on the ground that, as women, they have no material advantages to gain by it? Till very lately this exclusion has been absolute. The College for Women now at Hitchin, is the first complete attempt which has been made to give to women desiring them the same advantages that the university offers to men.

I can only allude to it here, and the subject has been brought fully before you already, I hope not without practical results.[2] But this much I must say that no organisation of education for girls can be complete without the college, to supply the higher knowledge which the school-training has prepared the mind to desire and receive.

Let it not be supposed that I think every young woman should go to college, or that because I have mentioned the university course as the most complete form of the higher training which should follow on the school-life, I undervalue all other forms and the efforts made in other directions to attain the same end. I should be sorry, indeed, to see it become the fashion for young women, as it is for young men of a certain station in life, to go to college, whether they cared for its intellectual advantages or not, and pass through a three years' course, not of culture, but of very expensive idleness. Nor do I, by any means, think the course at our English universities a perfect one as regards study. But this is so fully recognised by our ablest university men, that reform cannot be far off, and the system has two advantages of special value to women, as meeting the two principal wants in their education: it concentrates attention on two or three subjects, and requires a thorough grounding in them; it subjects the knowledge acquired to definite tests of recognised value, which therefore bear to other tests the same relation as a coin of the realm to a fancy medal. I may add that, to those, who, like myself, believe mixed education will ultimately prove the best, both morally and intellectually, for both sexes, the college, and the local examinations which lead up to the college, recommend themselves as the most direct and assured steps towards it, by establishing the capacity of girls and young women to pursue the same course of study, and to bear successfully the same tests as boys and young men, and also by accustoming the public mind to the idea of both sexes working towards common objects, and being tried by a common standard.

At the same time I fully recognise that a college, such as that at Hitchin, were it as large and successful as I believe it will be in a few years, could meet the wants only of a picked few, and that there is abundant room and demand for all the other means of giving to women a higher culture now being tried, such as the classes for women in connection with the University of London, those instituted at Cambridge, and now connected with a boarding-house to receive students from a distance, the Higher Examinations for Women, the lectures or classes for ladies, now multiplying over the country. These are all moves in the right direction, and will I believe, instead of interfering with each other as is feared by some, meet different needs and different means and help, each in its degree, to rescue the best years of a woman's youth from elegant or vulgar frivolity, and from the pernicious idleness which is the mother of all mischief. I hope that it may also in time delay the period of marriage, and make it as preposterous for a girl as for a boy to marry at seventeen or eighteen, and to take upon herself, unripe as she is at that age in mind and body, the duties of wife, mother, and mistress of a household.

I pass now to the third requirement for improving the education of girls, i.e. a sufficient supply of good teachers. It is needless to multiply evidence of the present incompetency of teachers and governesses as a class. The question is, how are they to be improved? The two capital defects of the teachers of girls, according to Mr Bryce, are these, 'They are not themselves well taught, and they do not know how to teach.' The remedy for the first of these will be found in the improvement of girls' schools, and in general measures for raising the standard of their education. There are at present so few good cheap girls' schools, that it is practically impossible for the class whence the majority of teachers comes to get well taught themselves; and to have been well taught is the best lesson in teaching well. 'The best remedy for the defects of female teachers is,' says Mr Fearon, 'to provide all Englishwomen of the middle class with the opportunity of higher liberal education.' It is in this that the help of endowments, could it be obtained, would be most beneficial; by cheapening good education, and providing the means through exhibitions and scholarships for students of real ability to pass from the lower to the higher grade schools, and finally to college. As regards the advantages of special training institutions for teachers, the evidence is very conflicting.

The Schools Enquiry Commissioners do not recommend them for teachers in secondary schools, whether male or female, and one great objection to them for the latter is the great outlay they would require. Still teachers must be trained both in the theory and practice of their art. Here again I will quote Miss Fish, though obliged to curtail very much her exceedingly valuable remarks. The great necessity of such training can, she says, 'only be understood by teachers, or those who have paid great attention to the subject. Where it is necessary that some qualities should be possessed in an especial degree, surely there should be special training. . . . Really good teachers are much more rare than is generally supposed. . . . In most schools, even those reputed good, the larger number of girls, those who will never become brilliant scholars, those who require something more than the mere *presentation* of truth cannot be said to be educated at all. The lesson is put before all alike; the few who can, grasp it, the many go away with mental power as undeveloped as before.'

Teachers should be trained to most skilful, patient, and exhaustive questioning, and to become interested in the study of minds; interested in learning to understand each girl's mental peculiarities, in order to see intuitively the working of the thoughts within. A good teacher is able to perceive the precise step in the working of those thoughts, where the confusion, the difficulty occurs, and so to begin her teaching at the right point, to lead from the known to the unknown.'

Many girls, who would never become brilliant in scholarship, must, nevertheless, make wiser and more thoughtful mothers, and much more intelligent companions for their husbands, if their mental powers were thus skilfully educated through the whole course of their school life. If we could produce one generation of good teachers, there would be little more difficulty, for young teachers unconsciously imitate the best teaching they have seen, and that which they have most admired. How then are teachers to be trained to this difficult art, which, like every other art, has its two branches of theory and practice? I would suggest that student-teachers should as a rule form part of the staff of every large school or group of schools, that lectures on the theory of education should be given to them, and that a special examination should be added for them, to the general examination of the school.

With reference to these lectures, Miss Fish says:

I think, nay I am sure, that lectures on the theory of education will never make good teachers unless accompanied by daily practice; and such lectures are almost valueless to young teachers, unless given by some one who is constantly observing and criticising their teaching. The head-teacher, if competent for her duties, is the best person to give instruction in school management to those under her charge. Teachers could be well trained in schools on these conditions: first, that the head-mistress should be a first-rate teacher; second, there should be a sufficiently large staff of teachers (student-teachers and assistants) for the head-mistress to be able to superintend her student-teachers' work.

Criticism lessons are in my opinion of great value, particularly if the head-mistress herself shews the pupil-teachers how they could have done better what was badly done in the lesson. I believe that good teachers of secondary schools may be produced without the establishment of training colleges, if the two conditions I have mentioned be fulfilled, as they might easily be in large schools.

I should add to Miss Fish's recommendations the institution of lectures on the human nature the educator has to deal with, and the laws of the human mind, such as habit and association, through which he must work. It is possible to *instruct* well without the knowledge of these, but not possible, I think, to *educate*, and it is education we want to get.

With regard to the final examination of teachers by a constituted authority capable of conferring certificates of recognised value, joined to a system of registration, both of teachers and schools, the measures recommended by the Scholastic Registration Association seem to me to meet so exactly the wants of the case, that we cannot do better than strengthen its hands by every means in our power, only taking care to press the claims of school mistresses to be admitted on the same terms as school-masters, to the examinations and degrees instituted for teachers, whether by the universities, by the College of Preceptors, or by a Government Board.

All these measures would lead to the most important requisite of all for the improvement of female teachers, namely that they should take up teaching as a profession, prepare for it seriously, and look to it as the work of life. It is too well known that at present women take to teaching as almost the only way of supporting themselves which does not involve the loss of that intangible thing called gentility, and think they can take it up without any preparation at all. A truer estimate in the public mind of what education is, and of the great and difficult work the educator has to accomplish, would soon alter this pernicious practice. Teachers would be required to rise to the level of their task, and their social status would be raised by the operation of the same causes.

I look also to the increase of large Collegiate Schools, such as the Ladies' College at Cheltenham, and the North London Collegiate School – the head-mistresses of which hold a position both dignified and independent, as helping to raise female teachers as a class, by offering to them the prizes of professional merit.

I believe that in a few years a great career will be opened to women as teachers. It is the career for which nature has specially fitted them, and if we can place within their reach and induce them to add to the gifts of nature the preparation and cultivation necessary to fashion the raw material into the perfect instrument, I feel confident that we shall at no distant day see schoolmistresses holding as honoured and honourable a position as the schoolmaster.

This brings me to the last of the requirements I have mentioned for improving female education, i.e. that women should have an object to work for, and on this I must crave your patience to listen to a few words, for though not a portion of education it influences it throughout.

It is true that women have the highest object of all, the attainment of excellence for its own sake; but that, like the attainment of knowledge for its own sake, affects only the small minority of either sex, the upper 10,000 of the human race, who are alone capable of conceiving and pursuing a high ideal with a disinterested passion. The average – and it is always the average we must consider – are incapable of this, and require lower and more commonplace motives to stimulate them to exertion. These motives are supplied to boys by the necessity of working for their maintenance. They are brought up in the knowledge that they will have to choose a profession, and that their success in life will depend on their doing their work well, whatever it may be. Girls, on the contrary, of the classes we are dealing with, are brought up to think their education of no consequence, except as fitting them to take their place in their own social sphere. They are taught explicitly, or implicitly, that marriage is the only career open to them, and they learn but too quickly that success in that career does assuredly not depend on their efforts at self-improvement.

I must again record my profound conviction that so long as marriage is held out as the only aim of a girl's life, and her education regulated with the sole view of making her pleasing to marrying men, so long will all attempts at improvement fail, except with the few capable of rising above the average tone of thought and feeling. In season, and out of season, line upon line, and precept upon precept, must all who hold the higher and truer view urge upon parents, and upon society, that marriage should not be the first object of a woman's life, any more than of a man's: that girls should be trained from childhood, to the idea that they, like their brothers, must take their share of the work of life; that their education should prepare them by the formation of good intellectual and moral habits, to perform it well; – that they should be not only allowed, but induced to work for their own maintenance, where the circumstances of their parents make an independent provision for them impossible, and that when those circumstances place them above the necessity of working for a provision, they should hold themselves bound to help, and train themselves to help efficiently in doing the unpaid work of the world, where the harvest is so plentiful and the labourers so few.

How much women would gain in worth and dignity, how rapidly their education would improve, if such views were prevalent, scarcely need be pointed out. All the want of thoroughness, the showy superficiality which degrade it now, would disappear before the necessity of real preparation for real work, and the ends being clearly understood and accepted, the means would not long be wanting.

Let it not be supposed that I undervalue marriage, or that I want to broach some wild theory of feminine independence; so far from it, I hold that only in the union of man and woman is human life perfect and complete. I would not wish, even if it were possible, to make women independent of men, but neither do I wish them to sit in half-starved, or luxurious idleness, waiting, or worse still, planning for husbands by whom they are to be raised to the single dignity possible to them.

Mr Anthony Trollope, in one of his late novels, mentions as a true anecdote, that in a family of three maiden ladies, the youngest always took precedence of her sisters, and on a stranger asking the reason why, the elder sister meekly replied, 'Matilda once had an offer of marriage.' I would put an end to the state of society in which such an anecdote is not only possible, but where similar ones would be common, if people generally spoke and acted as they feel; a state of society in which it can be said with perfect truth of large numbers of women, in the words of one of the heroines of the same novel:

> They're just nobodies. They are not anything particular to anybody, and so they go on living till they die. . . . A man who is a nobody can perhaps make himself somebody, or at any rate he can try; but a woman has no means of trying.

She is a nobody, and a nobody she must remain. She has her clothes and her food, but she isn't wanted anywhere. . . . People put up with her, and that is about the best of her luck. If she were to die, somebody, perhaps, would be sorry for her, but nobody would be worse off. She doesn't earn anything, or do any good. She is just there, and that is all.

Is that a fate for a human being with a heart and soul and intellect, and the capabilities within her of using them, if allowed, in adding to her own welfare and that of others, a fate to be condemned solely because she is not born with the charm or the cunning to win a husband? I recommend the novel I have quoted to the consideration of all who think women have nothing to complain of, when they are neither beaten nor starved, and who advise them as their only wise policy, 'to rest and be thankful.'

My advice is very different. Let us be thankful indeed that there is, at last, a feeling awakening in the country, that the women who desire education ought to have it placed within their reach. Let us be thankful – we cannot be too thankful – to the many generous and able men who, in the spirit of true chivalry, are helping our weakness with their strength. Let us be thankful too that our own tongues are unloosed, and that we are not only allowed but invited, as I have been on this occasion, to plead our own cause before the public; but let us not rest – no, not for an instant – till we have won for women the right and the means to the highest culture of which their nature is capable – not that they may gratify an unwomanly spirit of selfish ambition and rivalry, but that they may become more worthy and more fit to do the noble work God has given them to do.

NOTES

1 This project has since been carried into effect. An Association for Education of Women has been formed in Hampshire, in association with the National Union, and the College at Southampton will very shortly be opened. Schemes are also on foot in other localities for establishing schools with funds raised by Limited Liability Companies.
2 This alludes to a meeting held for the College at Leeds, two days before this paper was read.

Maria Gurney

Are we to have Education for our Middle-Class Girls?

(1872)

Preface

A few words of preface are necessary to explain why the following paper, which is only the history of a special Institution, is published in the series issued by this Union. The Camden Collegiate Schools, of which it gives an account, are the best examples extant of the class of Schools which it is one of the objects of the Union to establish in every populous district. The system pursued in the Upper School has been tested by twenty-one years of experience; and the rapid increase of the Lower School establishes the fact that such Schools meet a great want, and, if opened under auspices which inspire confidence and give a guarantee of the quality of the teaching offered, are certain to be successful. The very extent of the need that must be met (some statistics giving the number of girls requiring secondary education, in England and Wales alone as 225,000), makes it evident that far the greater number of schools must be wholly self-supporting, and will therefore probably fall short either in cheapness or efficiency of the more favoured endowed schools. But all the more do we require a standard such as we may hope will be afforded by the schools established, or to be established, by the Endowed Schools Commission, and especially by these Camden Town Schools; which only require such an addition to their endowment as would enable the Trustees to complete them on the plan and scale stated in this pamphlet, to become models of the best and most encouraging kind, because possessing the prestige of established success. Their sphere of usefulness would be thus extended far beyond the immediate benefit of the pupils attending them; and it is on this ground that their claim on the liberality of the general public is justly rested, and that this statement of what they are and of what work they are doing, is put forth by the National Union for Improving the Education of Women.

This question has received a practical reply in the North of London, where such girls' schools as are eagerly desired for other places are already instituted, and are in good working order.

This great benefit to the neighbourhood, and through the neighbourhood to the whole of London, is not the work of a day, but is the result of the patient toil and perseverance of twenty-one years.

But although the North London Collegiate School has existed since 1850, it was only placed on its present basis, as a public school, at Christmas, 1870, when the Lower, or Camden School was founded. The two schools together now contain 470 pupils, and are of two grades – not divided for the sake of mere social inequalities, but for the convenience of different means and requirements. The fees, in the Higher School, range from nine to fifteen guineas per annum, in the Lower School from four to six guineas.

It may seem surprising that a good education can be offered at so low a price, because in England no public or national efforts have hitherto been made to educate the mass of girls between the 'young ladies' whose parents pay £80 or £100, or even £200 or £300 per annum for instruction principally in so-called accomplishments, and girls trained in elementary schools on payment of 1d or 2d weekly.

This apathetic indifference does not exist with regard to boys, nor does it exist in other countries. In America, every girl as well as every boy has the opportunity of a good public free education, both in elementary and secondary schools, whilst over the continent there exist 'Secundar' and 'Burgherschulen,' either free, or with fees ranging from about £2 to £10 annually.

The neglect with which middle-class girls' education has been hitherto treated in England was clearly evidenced by the report of the Royal Commissioners, from which important deductions have been drawn in a pamphlet entitled, 'Ancient Charities and Endowed Schools.'

The subject of this pamphlet lies at the root of our present question, and a few figures will suffice to show its bearings. The funds of those ancient educational charities found to be useless or mischievous in their action, are now placed under the Endowed Schools Commission, and amount annually to £101,113. How can this sum be best employed for the public good? Elementary

Schools now receive sufficient support from the public and from Government, but what is the present number and efficiency of Endowed Grammar Schools, the proper provision for the middle classes? A table compiled from the Census, shows the existence, in England, of 547 Endowed Grammar Schools, containing 31,528 boys, and 3374 girls, or ten times as many boys as girls. Also out of the meagre number of 3374 girls, 2179 belong to the Counties of York, Lancashire, Cumberland, and Westmoreland. The author of this pamphlet points the following moral from the inequality existing between boys and girls.

> To show how hardly this exclusion from educational endowments acts, let us take the not unusual case of a tradesman's family being left orphans. It is then strange to see the sons taken into a good Blue-coat School, tenderly nurtured, carefully trained, and finally put in the way of earning an honest livelihood, while the daughters are left to rough it in the world as best they may, or are consigned to the contaminating atmosphere of a workhouse.

Other facts can be cited in confirmation of this inequality. One example is mentioned in the same pamphlet of a school in Lincolnshire, built exclusively for boys, from money bequeathed for both men and women, 'to be spent on almsgiving, and on the assistance of wayfarers.' This instance does not stand alone. The equal claims of girls to an education similar to that of boys have not yet been acknowledged by any of those wealthy women of our country who might naturally be expected to make use of their money in the endowment of girls' schools, but who continue to pour it into the large funds already at the disposal of boys. A lady has recently given the sum of £4000 for the foundation of a scholarship at Brazenose, Oxford, for boys from the Manchester Grammar School, and has also largely assisted Owen College, while the need still exists of a middle-class school for girls in that wealthy city.

Public opinion is not yet alive to the want, although the day may be rapidly approaching when wealthy men and women will feel that they are supplying *the* greatest need of the present time by the founding of middle-class girls' schools.

The pamphlet before-mentioned, on the supposition that the money in the hands of the Commissioners will be spent on this object, and that it is yet insufficient for the establishment of *many* schools, recommends that this public money should be spent on a *few*, to serve as models, and for the training of teachers.

But model schools cannot supply the present want throughout

the country. Numerous schools are required, with further endowments, or other starting funds. Assuming such a starting fund, the scale of fees, both in the Upper and Lower Camden Schools, is fixed in accordance with the recommendations of the Royal Commissioners.

The estimate on which this scale is fixed is, that buildings and furniture once supplied, and a small endowment for repairs given, all middle-class schools ought to be able to meet their current expenses out of the pupils' fees. Similar plans may be followed in other schools, which will not only serve as models, but will gradually meet the pressing need for girls' education.

We now proceed to a more minute description of the two schools.

North London Collegiate School

This School, recently removed to 202, Camden Road, was commenced twenty-one years ago as a private enterprise by its present head-mistress, Miss Frances M. Buss, in conjunction with the Rev. David Laing, the well-known Secretary of the Governesses' Benevolent Institution. In its history may be found the germs of its constant and ever-widening success. The plans of teaching which up to the present time have been pursued with unflagging energy and enthusiasm, may be described by a quotation from a paper by Dr Hodgson. 'Such teaching as shall place the pupil *en rapport* with the world she is about to enter, and shall inculcate and inspire industry, frugality, self-dependence, self-control, a definite plan of life, the preference of the claims of the future to present enjoyment, and a steady self-advancement for the sake of others as well as for one's own.'

Such systematic training, and thoroughness in thought and study, produced their fruits. This was strikingly illustrated in 1863, when the experimental Cambridge Examination for Girls took place. Twelve junior candidates were presented direct from the usual routine of school life, all of whom passed the ordinary subjects without failure. They required *no* special preparation for the ordeal of a public examination, although such examinations were then new events in the history of girls' education.

From the band of steady working pupils thus formed, Miss Buss has little difficulty in selecting her trained teachers, and their gratitude to her led indirectly to the present development of the

schools, from private to public schools. This arose from the
following incident.

Two years ago a number of these pupils asked permission to
present a testimonial to Miss Buss. This she declined, unless it
could be presented in such a form as to benefit the schools, and
thus the public. Her pupils, entering into her spirit, were not
damped in their ardour; they collected the sum of £230, which
became the nucleus of the new enterprise. Twenty pounds spent
on a clock was all that she would accept of the testimonial; the
remaining sum was devoted to the founding of a scholarship for
a public object, and the word *public* became the key-note of changes
which she had long revolved in her mind. She resolved that her
private interest should give way to the general good in the establishment of a public school for girls, to be placed in the hands of
trustees, and that the testimonial should found the first scholarship
in perpetuity, under the new system.

In this enterprise Miss Buss had a definite object in view, not
alone that of maintaining a large school; this could have been as
well accomplished had the school remained in her own hands, for
she had already two hundred pupils in Camden Street, and no
premises could be found which would accommodate a much larger
number.

Her objects were twofold; firstly, to give *permanency* to the
school by forming it into a public institution; secondly, and
especially, to benefit the pupils by instilling into their minds higher
and wider views of life, through the medium of an early *esprit-de-
corps*. As children even they should become members of a public
body, and so gradually learn their duties to the State. They might
thus be aided to catch the spirit which has been sung –

> Then none was for a party,
> Then all were for the State.

The infusion of a public spirit into the minds of girls has often
been desired; such a wish was recently expressed by Mr Broderick
in an admirable speech delivered at a meeting of the National
Union for improving the Education of Women. With Miss Buss
action quickly followed thought; her scheme was organized and
soon carried to a successful issue.

The North London Collegiate School, established in 1850,
retaining its old name, and all its pupils, was removed into new
and better premises in the Camden Road. Two boarding-houses,
at different rates of payment for pupils at a distance, remained in
connection with it. Miss Buss transferred her private interest to a
board of trustees, by whom a trust-deed was framed, which

reserved the power of establishing other grade-schools in the neighbourhood.

In the necessary fittings and furniture of the new premises large expenses were incurred. Friends interested in the cause of education, have already collected about £500, in order that a debt may not hang over the school at its commencement. They also share the desire of the founders that future gifts, with any additional money which may accrue from increased fees, shall after the requisite buildings have been obtained be devoted strictly to educational purposes, i.e. towards the founding of scholarships and the increasing of educational advantages in the school. For these objects there is yet ample scope; no limit can be assigned where education is concerned, and meanwhile the further want of thoroughly suitable school premises must await an opportunity.

As it now is, the North London Collegiate School offers a picture rarely to be equalled of active and cheerful life. A description of it has been already published, from which the following extract is taken.[1]

> The North London Collegiate School in Camden Road occupies an unpretending building, which at first sight appears only a private house, but well rewards an inspection. The Secretary's entrance-room contains several boards, on which are inscribed the already numerous names of successful competitors in various public examinations. One hundred and twelve pupils have passed the Cambridge, College of Preceptors, School of Art, and other examinations; during the past year alone eight have obtained honours in the Cambridge examinations, and two in the London University examination for women. One pupil also passed the London University examination for women, with high honours, in the previous year.
>
> From this room a long and winding passage leads to a most attractive school-room capable of holding 120 girls. The aspect of this room is remarkably pleasant, the bright young girls are arranged at long reversible desks, and separate classes are divided by curtains, on the plan of elementary schools. A dark staining of wood on walls, floors, and desks, below the large windows, which open on sky and foliage, gives an air of brightness and refinement to the whole room. The children can here write undisturbed by one another, or may be collected for a general lesson, while the long passages give them a convenient space for the musical gymnastics, which form a part of every day's work.

Upstairs the house is equally well-arranged, one long room stretching from end to end, while two smaller class rooms on each floor, are prepared for separate classes. This division is suitable to the instruction given; the whole school is divided into eight large sections for English teaching, these are again subdivided into classes for Arithmetic, French, Latin, Mathematics, etc. The teaching is principally oral, and besides the visiting teachers, both masters and mistresses, who come to give instruction in certain subjects, Miss Buss has the advantage of clever mistresses, whom she has herself trained to teach, and who pursue her system. There are more than 200 girls in attendance, all occupied in earnest work, and this with the quietude which only a perfect organisation can give. Their ages range from 6 to 18, with fees varying according to age, from 9 to 15 guineas per annum. Girls of very various stations in life attend the school, the only test of admission being respectability and good conduct.

Last summer, examinations were held in school, and prizes were subsequently distributed at a public meeting, held on July 15th, 1871, at St. George's Hall, Langham Place. The Earl of Dartmouth presided; in addition to the ordinary school prize lists, special prizes were presented – given by the Countess of Dartmouth, the Countess of Hardwicke, the Marchioness of Camden, the Rev. J. Back, the Vicar of St. Pancras, the Rev. H. Sinden, the Rev. Charles Lee, Mrs Laing, and the old Pupils. Special mention was also made of Miss Greatbatch's eminent success at the London University Examination, and of Sir Sterndale Bennett's commendation of her thorough knowledge in Harmony and Counterpoint.

There had been special encouragements to study by the gift of valuable prizes for various subjects from friends of the school.

The following is a list of the scholarships and prizes offered for the ensuing year.

Presentations

The Laing Scholarships There are six Scholarships in the gift of Mrs David Laing, each tenable from year to year, at her discretion. These were founded in 1860, and 17 girls have been already educated, wholly or in part. These Scholarships cover the school fees, but their tenure depends on satisfactory reports of progress and conduct.

The Reid Scholarships The Trustees of Mrs Reid's Fund offer, annually, a scholarship tenable for two years, at Bedford College. This scholarship is decided by an examination.

The Gilchrist Trustees have kindly offered a grant of £25 for a year, to aid the higher education of certain girls. Two are preparing, by means of this grant, for the approaching Examination for Women, conducted by the London University.

Prizes are awarded in every class for the different subjects of study.

The following are additional prizes:

> The Hardwicke Prize for general diligence, by the Countess of Hardwicke.
> The Countess of Dartmouth's Prize of £5 for the first student in French.
> The Marchioness of Camden's Prize for the first student in French.
> Mrs Newmarch's Prize of £5 for the best Original Letter on a given subject.
> Mrs Harvey Lewis' Prize of £5 for acquaintance with the Laws of Health.
> The Vicar's Prize for the best English Essay.
> The Rev. John Back's Prize for Scripture.
> Mrs D. Laing's Prize for the best specimen of Plain Needlework.
> The Rev. Charles Lee's Prize for Harmony.
> The Rev. H. Sinden's Prize for Arithmetic.

This plan of giving prizes and scholarships (and especially scholarships) is one of the best and most direct ways of assisting the cause we have at heart. It encourages the pupils and teachers alike to strive towards the same object – a *real* education – that education so admirably described by Mrs W. Grey as 'intellectual, moral and physical development, the development of a sound mind in a sound body, the training of reason to form just judgments, the discipline of the will and the affections to obey the supreme law of duty, the kindling and strengthening of the love of knowledge, of beauty, of goodness, till they become governing motives of action.'

Camden School for Girls

The premises in Camden Street, left untenanted by the removal of the North London Collegiate School to Camden Road, had their work assigned to them by Miss Buss. She had removed her school, with *all* its pupils from them; her interest and property in this school, she had presented to the public. The furniture, also her property, she gave to the new Camden School, which was opened in January, 1871, under the superintendence of Miss Buss, with its own head-mistress, Miss Elford.

It is distinct from the Collegiate School, being of a different grade, although it will serve as an introduction and basis to the higher school. It is not intended for a different *class*, as class distinctions are happily unknown in the Camden schools.

But although experience may show that there is little social difference between the pupils of the two schools, yet in a large neighbourhood like Camden Town, there are numerous parents who cannot afford 9 or 15 guineas per annum for school fees. For this reason, the fees in the Lower School are fixed at 4 and 6 guineas annually.

The need for such a school has been proved by its success. It immediately filled with pupils, and now at the end of the first year the premises are so overcrowded, (the pupils exceeding 220 in number) that a neighbouring house has been hired in order that pupils may not be refused. The want of a starting fund has been the principal difficulty in the Camden, as in the Collegiate Schools. Miss Buss' gift of the furniture was the first gift to Camden schools; but according to the Commissioners' estimate, as the school is at present carried on in rented houses, contributions are required for the rent and for the yearly expenditure, until a sufficient sum is collected for the erection of new and suitable premises.

Several appeals have been made in the newspapers by the trustees of the schools, by Miss Cobbe in the *Echo*, and by Mrs. W. Grey in *The Times*. The results have been small: Mrs Grey's two appeals in *The Times*, having obtained the sum of £122. 2s 6d, whilst the £60,000 obtained by Mr Rogers for a boys' middle-class school, in Cowper Street, show no lack of interest or want of funds, where the education of boys is concerned.

A formal application for funds was made to the City Guilds; the only response to this as yet has been from the Fishmongers' Company, which has generously contributed a hundred guineas.

In another quarter, the need of middle-class education for girls has been recognised. The Princess of Wales has sent a cheque for fifty guineas, and has consented that the Camden Town schools should be under her patronage.[2]

These few gifts are all which have as yet been obtained in consequence of public appeals, the rest of the money which has enabled the work to be carried on, has been collected (amounting to £700) by Miss Buss' personal friends; and on this fact a strong appeal may be founded. Friends have gathered round her because they know her and her work; they know that she has the energy and enthusiasm which will carry her through difficulties, and they also know that by assisting her in doubling and even trebling her sphere of labour, many more minds will be brought – if only into passing contact with herself – yet under the plans organised by her for training and study.

The system of education pursued in the Camden School, is intended to fit girls of the lower middle-class for business or domestic life, or to become the elementary teachers of their own children, or of the children of others, and includes a thorough course of English, arithmetic, French, drawing, plain needlework, class singing, physical training, and the elements of natural science.

A public meeting of friends and pupils was held on 21 July 1871, at St George's Hall, at which the late Lord Mayor, (Alderman Dakin) presided; from whom the following letter was afterwards received by the Rev. Charles Lee.

The Camden School for Middle Class Girls

Mansion House, 9 September 1871

My dear Sir,

I have much pleasure in testifying to the value of the above Institution. My own observation on the occasion of distributing the prizes to the successful girls was confirmatory of the good impression I had before received, and increased my desire to see such happy results of the education and training given, extended more widely, and like the City Corporation Schools for Boys, placed beyond the risk of failure in a pecuniary point of view.

This is, I believe, the first school which has been founded with the object of affording to girls similar educational advantages, at the same cost as the Boys' Schools in Cowper Street.

I confess to a feeling of surprise that comparatively so little has been done for the sisters, while the brothers have been so nobly supported, and I think the time has come for a reformation in our custom in this matter, because, besides the desirability of helping the girls by sound elementary knowledge, to be fit associates and assistants of their future husbands, it is good political economy to furnish the super-abundant women of the country with the means of helping themselves, more especially if the assertion in your report be true, that nearly half the women of England are more or less dependent on their own exertions. It is acknowledged that really efficient education cannot be afforded at prices within the reach of those for whom it is most required, without extraneous aid, and, on this account, large endowments have been subscribed in the case of the boys. It is fair to hope and expect that the same benevolence will make suitable provision for the girls.

The great City Companies, as remarked by one of the speakers, on the interesting occasion to which I have referred, are ever ready to lend their aid to the furtherance of any good work. And if you think that my recommendation will in any way assist your application to them, you are at liberty to make use of this letter, and I shall be only too happy to hear of the success of an institution with the objects of which I so entirely sympathize.

I am, dear Sir,
Yours faithfully,
(*Signed*) THOMAS DAKIN,
Lord Mayor

To the Rev. Charles Lee,
The Vicarage, Haverstock Hill.

A resolution was passed 'That this meeting earnestly invokes the assistance of the Corporation of the City of London, of the City Companies generally, and of the great mercantile firms of the metropolis, on behalf of the education of girls, whose parents, though resident in the suburbs, are engaged in the City.'

The standard prizes were distributed; the prize list being necessarily limited, as the school had only been opened in January, at 12, Camden Street, and but few additional prizes had been offered.

There are two scholarships in connection with the Camden School – The Reid Scholarship, value 20 guineas, tenable for one year at Bedford College; and the Frances M. Buss Scholarship, value 30 guineas, tenable for two years in the North London Collegiate School.

It is intended in future to send pupils from Camden School to the Junior Cambridge examinations. A sufficient preparation for this could not be given in this the first year. – Eight pupils, however, were sent last December to the College of Preceptors' Examination, all of whom passed – six taking honours in bookkeeping.

The following additional prizes are offered for this year:

The Vicar's Prize for general diligence and good conduct.
Rev. J. Back's Prize for Scripture.

Mrs. Thorold's Prize for the best specimen of Plain Needlework.

Mr W. Burbury's Prize for Economics.

Miss Clarissa Gregory's Prize for Arithmetic.

Mrs Laing's Prize for the first student in English.

Mrs Garrett Anderson's Prize for acquaintance with the Laws of Health.

These with two scholarships will furnish abundant incentives to study, while the Frances M. Buss scholarship, tenable in the Collegiate School, affords a permanent bond of union between the Upper and Lower Schools. It is to be hoped that many Camden School girls will succeed, either with or without scholarships, in working their way into the Upper School.

Miss Buss also intends to commence in the Camden Schools, a scheme suggested by Mrs Grey, for the training of student teachers. These *student teachers* will take the place of pupil teachers in elementary schools, and will be bound to the Board for three years – to receive payment in the second and third years. This may form a valuable means for the thorough training of teachers.

We turn now to future wants and plans, and it will already be evident that the first want is such a school building for the Camden School, as may bear comparison with the Töchter-Schulen at Zurich, Frankfort, or Cassel, and which, with large rooms for general instruction, as well as a number of class rooms, will sufficiently accommodate the teeming numbers of the Camden School – now crowded into premises in Camden Street – which are only temporary adaptations of three private houses. It is estimated that Camden school and fittings will cost about £5000; but suitable premises for the complete system of middle-class girls education, which is now started, will require from £15,000 to £20,000. We commend the history and present circumstances of the school, to the consideration of all those who have it in their power either wholly to undertake or largely assist the building of this greatly needed school, and thus to contribute to the enlightenment and true education of numerous women of the next generation, who will in their turn become workers and educators.

The situation of the schools in Camden Town is so central, and in the midst of so large a population, that its managers look forward to a succession of schemes in the future. The first plan proposed by Miss Buss, to follow on the building of Camden School, and for which the present furniture may be utilised, is the commencement of a still cheaper school, on the half-time system, as worked in Copenhagen – with evening classes. Under the half-time system, two schools of children may be taught in the same premises, one attending from eight o'clock till one, and another from one till six, with special arrangements as to teachers. Such elder children, if employed in work, might spend the half day in education, for which they could probably afford to pay from 1s 6d to 2s weekly. Should this plan prove successful, these schools would also require a suitable building – such a building as the half-time school in Copenhagen, where 2000 children are educated.

In this programme of the future the claims of the Collegiate School must not be omitted – it also requires a school building in the place of an adapted house. Thus there is the prospect of work for many years, and also the best of opportunities for the generous gifts of those public spirited men and women who are willing to give for the public good.

NOTES

1 A Paper by Miss Mary Gurney, read at the Social Science Congress at Leeds, September, 1871, and re-printed in the Englishwoman's Review, January, 1872.
2 Letter from H.R.H. the Princess of Wales to the Rev. Charles Lee.

SANDRINGHAM, KING'S LYNN, *November 15th*, 1871.

SIR,

I am directed by the Princess of Wales to acknowledge the receipt of a letter signed by you, in conjunction with Dr. J. Storrar, on behalf of the Trustees and Governors of the Institution established in Camden Town, for the promotion of secondary instruction for Girls.

Her Royal Highness fully recognises the importance and great need of an improvement in the education of Girls of the poorer middle classes, and believes that the North London Collegiate School for Girls, with its Lower School, will not only to some extent meet this want, but that it will also serve as a model for similar schools, the establishment of which in other parts of the metropolis and in the country generally it may encourage.

The Princess of Wales, therefore, has much pleasure in acceding to the request that Her Royal Highness would allow these Schools to be placed under her patronage, and has directed me to forward to you the enclosed cheque for fifty guineas, as Her Royal Highness's contribution towards the funds of the undertaking.

I have the honour to be, Sir,
Your most obedient servant,
M. HOLZMANN,
Private Secretary

The REV. CHARLES LEE, M.A.

Emily A. E. Shirreff

The Work of the National Union

(1873)

The objects for which the National Union for improving Women's education was constituted have been briefly set forth in its circulars,[1] now in the hands of many thousands of persons. But this statement would appear not to be sufficient, since we are daily met with enquiries concerning the work we propose to do; even sympathy in this country is half-hearted unless it be claimed for some practical definite course of action. I propose, therefore, to take up one by one the points laid down in the circular, enlarging upon the statement necessarily made so brief and general there; and I trust it will not be difficult to show that a very extensive field of actual work is only waiting for labourers, and that earnest co-operation, money, and sympathy must all be largely given, before so wide an undertaking can hope for any measure of success.

The low condition of girls' education may, perhaps, be assumed to be proved. Here and there a good school, here and there a few good teachers, pure moral aims, but too narrow to exercise any influence, some general notions that instruction should embrace a greater number of subjects now than formerly, but no notion how to make any instruction educational, no method, no thoroughness, no purpose. This state of things has long been but too well known to all who were interested in such questions; but the revelations of the Schools Enquiry Commissioners brought the evil into clear relief, and afforded grounds on which, more than on any private information or opinion, public feeling might possibly be stirred, and public sympathy enlisted. It was upon this fact that Mrs Wm. Grey founded her hopes when she undertook to form the National Union. A reform was obviously needed, the question was how to make that necessity clear to all; and how to bring about the improvement.

For the reformer who, without authority, without command of wealth, or public influence, stands facing a gigantic evil, one course alone offers any chance of success, namely, that of combining with other reformers, seeking them out wherever they also may be grieving in powerless isolation, and bringing them together, till scattered feebleness is changed into the force of union, till single voices swell into a mighty chorus. In England, where men have ever trusted to attain their ends by private effort, it has been thus that every great reform has been carried, and in this manner did Mrs Grey conceive the hope of working the reform of education.

Such concentration of effort has, as we well know, been again and again found resistless in acting upon the Legislature; but our task is a yet more difficult one, that of working upon public opinion, and through public opinion alone; and of stirring up national activity without the aid of legislation. If once a matter can be brought into Parliament and there settled, the struggle, however sharp and prolonged, has a definite aim and end; but reformers who depend on voluntary action alone see no such close to their labours; they need, therefore, far more sustained effort, a far wider circulation of right principles and convictions. Such is the condition of those who seek to improve the education of women; they must depend entirely on the voluntary, long-sustained efforts of private reformers, sustained till new views and associations shall have had time to form; till routine, and habit, and fashion, or whatever other forces replace reason and conviction with the multitude, shall have turned in a new direction and made such education as they have hitherto received, a thing to be ashamed of even by those who may be as little able to understand its real demerits as the majority of women do now. The ignorant and the incapable will still be among us, the important question is whether they shall take the lead or follow it.

Taking then this view of the possibility of reform, Mrs Grey sought to found, not a mere society, but a *National Union*, one that should spread over the length and breadth of the land, gathering strength by centralising scattered forces. And when, the Union having taken shape, its Central Committee proceeded to define what its objects should be, the first was laid down as follows:

'To bring into communication and co-operation all individuals and associations engaged in promoting the education of women and girls, so as to strengthen and combine their efforts; to collect and register for the use of members, information on all points connected with such education.'

The promotion of local committees offers a powerful means of bringing such co-operation to bear. Scattered individuals in different parts of the country corresponding with a committee in London would be comparatively powerless; but let those individuals combine locally, creating a focus of action where their own names or position severally give them influence or authority, or even the mere power of personal exertion, and of reaching those who have more influence than themselves, and let such local bodies correspond with a central committee, and in time an engine of far reaching power will have been created.

The Union promises, as above stated, to collect and register information, but for such a task local co-operation is quite indispensable; it is no less needful also, for collecting funds, for bringing to light either local abuses, or local resources and exertions, which are hidden from public attention. They also help to foster sympathy with an undertaking which is seen to have become a leading interest to so many. Efforts, donations, small beginnings which would otherwise remain unknown beyond a small circle, are revealed through wide organisation to all co-operators in the same field of labour, and those who were strangers to each other before, become comrades in a noble cause, and feel their resistance to the common enemies – ignorance, apathy, and prejudice – strengthened by all the power of numbers and of sympathy. The formation of local committees is therefore an object of constant solicitude, nor, considering how short a time has elapsed since the foundation of the Union, have we any reason to be discouraged at the results. In some places committees or associations for education formed prior to the commencement of our work, in other bodies formed for the purpose of co-operating with us, are now in corporate membership with the Union.[2] The National Association for the Promotion of Social Science, the Society of Arts, the College of Preceptors, the Scholastic Registration Association, have appointed representatives on the Committee; and the London Schoolmistresses' Association has shown that its members are superior to any paltry jealousies or fears of rival interference, that they care more for education than for supposed private interests, by also appointing a representative. We venture then to hope, that even now in the early dawn of our enterprise, something of a new impulse has already been given to the work previously begun, that some breath of new courage and energy has been infused into those who before toiled silently and patiently, hoping little from the aid or sympathy of others.

Public meetings, from which much assistance had been hoped, are unfortunately a costly and difficult means of attracting attention. Several have, however, been held, and men of great position and ability were on these occasions found willing to advocate the cause of women's education, and the method taken by the Union to promote it. It is now also in contemplation to extend the work in the provinces by means of travelling secretaries and lecturers, who will make known the principles of the Union, and organize meetings and local committees. Two gentlemen are already at work in this manner, and others will follow. One of them is giving active service gratuitously; but whether in that manner or as paid officials, we feel sure that men working up a district in which they are known and have some personal influence, will materially assist to make our work known, and to obtain the material help so much needed.

The objects of the Union, as further set forth in paragraphs 2 to 9 of its Circulars, point to the particular work to be done by the wide combination it is hoped to establish. They enumerate eight different subjects (including many branches) to which the efforts of the Union will be directed. Par. 2 pledges it,

'To promote the establishment of good and cheap Day-schools for all classes above those attending the Elementary schools, with boarding-houses in connection with them, when necessary, for pupils from a distance.'

The absence of such schools is one of the most crying, and fortunately one of the most generally recognised wants of the present day. Since the publication of the Report of the Schools Enquiry Commissioners so much has been said on the bad condition of existing schools, that it seems needless to enlarge upon it here. In the paper which forms No. 1 of the present series, Mrs Grey has entered at some length into the consideration of their defects, and has also sketched out a plan by which they might, in many places, be remodelled, and adapted by a system of co-operation to combine the advantages of large classes with small boarding schools. To this paper I must refer the reader, and pass on to the work the Union itself proposes to undertake.

The reason for beginning operations with the class above those attending the elementary schools is sufficiently obvious. The latter enjoy already an advantage denied to all above them. The State, as educators of the poor, inherit the work of the Church; and the Church having always acknowledged that women had souls to be saved, found it inevitable to treat that portion of womankind that fell under their guardianship as if they had also minds to be culti-vated. It was one of those fortunate inconsistencies which lead men further than they think; and those simple parish schools where it was agreed to teach girls to read because it was not right that a mother should be unable to read the Bible to her children, may have done more than many an ambitious scheme to open the way to changes undreamed of by their founders.

The poorer class, then, are provided for, and the wealthy will naturally follow their own fancies, or the fashion of the hour. Their very independence of all help makes them less amenable to reform. But between the two we have the large middle class through all its different gradations, the class whose boys crowd the grammar, and commercial, and endowed schools all over the country, and whose girls are taught anyhow, and often not at all, acquiring scraps of flimsy information with a little bad French and worse music, at a cost, heavy to the parents and utterly insufficient to give fair remuneration to the teachers. To attempt a remedy for this evil is the fixed purpose of the Union. The scheme for schools which, after much study and deliberation, the Central Committee determined to issue, was for day schools only; and for two principal reasons: first, that the combination of home life with class teaching, and with the general training that belongs to acting with numbers under a fixed rule, presents, we believe, the best form of education that can be secured under ordinary circumstances; secondly, because the economy which is so important an object, can only be secured by having schools on a scale which would be objectionable for boarders, even could the much larger outlay for building be encountered. A third reason weighs also with the Union but may not be so generally admitted, namely, the greater fusion of social classes possible in day schools. The spirit of exclusion is carried to absurdity in the aristocracy, and all who think it necessary to imitate them; but the mania for gentility is the very bane of life in the middle classes, and the nearer the shade that divides one grade from another, the greater the fear lest that shade should be overlooked. Independently of all class considerations, such association as we advocate is obviously impossible in boarding-schools; for parents naturally require that their children's mode of living and the general care and arrangements provided for them, should be in proportion to their own means of paying for such advantages. Hence the boarding houses we hope to see in connection with the schools will be adapted to different requirements. But there should be no grades in teaching; that must be first-rate for all. The limit of time is the only one that can be admitted as marking the difference between class and class. For truly there is no gentility in knowledge, no spirit of exclusion in the training that requires all to be seekers for truth, and subject to authority for conscience sake; nor is there much reason to fear that the gentleman's daughter will lose her home refinement because she follows a teacher's demonstration on the same board which is gazed at also by the children of the small shopkeeper. Manners and language, or perhaps I should say intonation, are among the most subtle results of home influence; they belong to habits and associations earlier and more deeply rooted than anything connected with school, and I believe that neither levelling up, nor levelling down will in this matter result from the fusion of classes at school. It has been very widely tried with boys, and the result justifies my remark; and although girls are more imitative, I believe the fact would remain the same. It must also be remembered that in a well-ordered day school, work leaves little leisure for idle communication, and it rests with parents to make the arrangements they think fit to preclude all chance companionship when the classes are over.

The North London Collegiate and Camden Town Schools, established by Miss Buss, and which have for some years attained signal success under her admirable management and tuition, offer the general model of what the National Union would desire to see opened in every populous district in the United Kingdom; nor will it feel that its efforts have had any satisfactory success, till attempts to meet this immense want are set on foot so widely as to ensure that the example must be followed; till towns or districts not possessing at least one such school shall feel that they are in a backward condition which exposes them to contempt. There is fortunately a contagion of good example no less than of bad, though less rapidly communicated; and the more public any course of action is, the greater is the hope that such contagion will be spread.

Some account of the Camden Town Schools has been given by Miss Mary Gurney, in No. 2 of this series, I need not therefore go over the ground again. More recently the Central Committee of the Union has drawn up its own scheme for a public day school in West London,[3] which has won the approbation of some whose opinion has deservedly most weight in educational matters. In one point the Committee has decided on following a bold course hitherto almost untried for a large public school, namely, that of making the school absolutely self-supporting, paying not only its working expenses, but the interest on whatever capital may be needed for its establishment, independent of all gifts or endowments. Upon the success of this plan only, do we found our hope of seeing the wants of the country in any degree adequately supplied. Let it, however, be fully understood that it is on no ground of pride or principle that we repudiate the idea of depending on endowments; but simply because we know that the utmost that could be obtained by that means, would fall far short of what is needed. In spite of all that has been said in various quarters of the disgrace of educating girls of the middle class upon charity, I confess that I should be only too happy if such charity as that which founded Eton and Harrow, Westminster and Rugby, and again extends its benefits to the education of men at Oxford and Cambridge and all other Universities, were extended to girls also; but they have been disinherited too long. Like Schiller's poet, they bring their claim when all rich and rare gifts have been divided long ago among the more ambitious or the more covetous sons of earth.

Their claim indeed will be persistently urged, and we have every reason to hope that, when the reforms now in progress are effected, a fair share of existing endowments; or at least, what the long perversion of public opinion on the subject will force us to accept as a fair share, may yet be awarded to girls; but the utmost will still be inadequate to the want.[4] In such a state of things, the best result we venture to anticipate from any application of existing endowments in aid of the education of girls, would be the foundation in various parts of the country of model schools which should deserve their favoured condition by taking the lead in every improvement, and by the institution of scholarships to enable pupils to carry on their higher education either at the Girton College for Women, or any other institution of the same nature; or in some of the technical schools where knowledge required for their future career may be obtained.

It is not then, because we should be too proud to receive help, but because we are hopeless of obtaining such help as we need, that we determine to try the more independent course, in beginning to found schools in connection with the Union. We base our efforts on the conviction that the present stir for improving the condition of women must force upon many who have been blind to it hitherto, the fundamental necessity of first improving their education; and that the want of good schools must consequently be sufficiently felt to render it possible to raise the necessary funds by ordinary commercial means, as in the case of any other scheme of recognised public utility. Could this method be proved successful, the Union might feel that they had established a principle most fruitful of national benefit; since the same machinery can be applied wherever schools are needed; and we may rest assured that the more widely it is applied, the more, if successful, will grow the habit of resorting to it, till people grow ashamed of not having good schools, when the funds can be obtained by a little exertion and some business arrangements.

Acting then, upon these views, the Central Committee directed all their efforts last year to the establishment of the Girls' Public Day School Company (Limited), whose capital in £5 shares may in time be so extended and applied as to meet the demand for schools wherever it may arise. Up to this time the capital subscribed has enabled the Council of the Company to open two first grade schools, one at Chelsea, which has been at work since January last, under the admirable management of Miss Porter, formerly chosen by the Endowed Schools Commissioners for their Girls' School at Keighley; and another in Norland Square, Notting Hill, which has just now opened under Miss M. Jones, a lady of great experience and ability.

It is evident that the success of a Company means that it shall pay a fair dividend, and this is the problem which in time will we trust be successfully solved. Schools which shall give thoroughly good teaching at a moderate cost, and yet shall be not only self-supporting as regards current expenses, but shall provide some return on the capital expended, must evidently not be expected to vie, either in external appearance or in costly fittings, with establishments on which thousands have been lavished in free gift. In them strict economy must preside over everything but the appliances for teaching and the salary of the teachers. For these there should be no stint, the expenditure would rather be the truest economy; since even in a commercial point of view, the first object must be to make the schools, as far as possible, educationally perfect.

Large schools, have, as before remarked, been proved to be best in point of economy, and the teaching of large classes is also found by experience to be within certain limits, the most efficient, while classes can only be really well organised when the numbers in the schools are sufficient to allow of bringing into one class, only those who are really on the same level of proficiency.

The outline of the scheme of instruction in the Company's school is given in the Prospectus (Appendix II). To many persons the proposed course of studies will probably seem too extensive, but it must be remembered that it is framed to meet the wants of various ages and various conditions, to extend over the whole school period, beginning with little children, to end with young women prepared to enter upon the active duties of life. The age for leaving school necessarily depends upon the circumstances of the parents, and the after-destination of the pupils. A comparatively small number only, those whose means allow of protracting the period of tuition without reference to work, and those who are destined to become teachers, will have the benefit of the advanced classes, the announcement of a few abstruse subjects need not therefore cause much alarm; but in all classes alike the subjects have been chosen with careful reference to the first great purpose of all instruction, the discipline of the mental faculties. All hope of improving the education of women rests on establishing the fact that mental training, as distinguished from mere instruction, is no less powerful in its influence on character than on the intellect. This essential fact is indeed lost sight of quite as much in the education of boys as in that of girls, and if the former are well taught while the latter are neglected, it is only because other motives come into operation. The intellectual training of boys is an investment, and questions of character are left quite in a subordinate category; the education of girls is generally felt to be an unproductive expenditure, and questions of character are supreme. The moral condition of women *is* cared for, but that it should be influenced by their mental condition is not perceived by nine out of every ten who dogmatise on the subject of what it may be right and fitting to allow girls to be taught. One good only results from this wide-spread error, namely, that in dealing with the education of girls we are always driven back to dwell upon first principles. Boys' schools may continue to be built for the primary purpose of training better City clerks, other improvements being incidental; but where girls' schools are founded they must be primarily directed to form more perfect human beings, creatures more apt for the life-tasks the Creator has set to each and all, and incidentally they will be fitter also for breadwinning-toil, should such be their portion. Mere parrot-like acquisition of facts, in any branch of knowledge, can have no influence on conduct, but neither does it strengthen the mental faculties. The whole of Euclid might be committed to memory, and yet the pupil have learned no lesson of reasoning; the results of every science may be acquired by rote and yet no power of observation, no habit of weighing evidence have been gained; just as we daily see that every text from Christ's teaching may be familiar, and yet the clear path of Christian duty be unperceived. Thus errors and shortcomings that careful training would have corrected, continue to flourish under increased teaching, and the opponent of higher culture points triumphantly to the failure, and charges it upon education, when in fact no education has been attempted. As well might men be expected to be fed, by dealing in their daily trade with articles of food, as to learn to observe correctly, and to think clearly, and to act uprightly by heaping up facts in their memory. On the other hand, let instruction be directed to giving habits of accurate observation, of clear reasoning, of patient resolute work under difficulties, of making simple truth the first object, and these mental habits will translate themselves into action, and their worth will be seen to be moral no less than intellectual. The necessity of thus continually laying down the foundation afresh – of proving over and over again, when the better instruction of girls is spoken of, that strengthening the understanding does not weaken the conscience and the affections – that feebleness and ignorance are not essential guardians of the domestic virtues – this necessity must plead my excuse for discussing principles of education at all in a paper like this. It is indispensable at the eve of opening a large school under the auspices of the Union, that there should be no mistake about the principles on which it will be conducted.

Finally, I must notice another objection which may perhaps be made to our proposed course of studies, namely, that it embraces no technical instruction whatever, although a large proportion of the pupils will probably require such instruction for their future lives. The reason for this omission is twofold; first, resting on the material difficulty, or rather impossibility, of giving technical instruction in the manifold forms in which it might be wished for; secondly, on the important principle that all technical instruction requires one and the same foundation of sound mental training, and that when a general school has given that, it has prepared its pupils for all the practical work of life, from common household duties to the study of any special branch of art or trade. The school educates, the technical school instructs; the task of the latter is easy in proportion as the work of the former has been complete.

Some persons may perhaps fear that a Company having once been formed for the financial part of the scheme, the direction of the school may pass out of the control of the Union and degenerate from the original standard; this danger has not been overlooked; but in the constitution of the Company every effort has been made to provide against it. The manner in which this will be done cannot be entered into here, but it may safely be affirmed that in every school founded under the auspices of the Union, certain fundamental rules will invariably prevail, such as, for instance, the public character of the schools admitting no class or denominational distinction.

Religious, unsectarian teaching. The appointment of trained teachers only, whether for head mistress or subordinates.

The formation of a class of student teachers to be trained in the theory and practice of education; the inspection of the school by examiners unconnected with their management, and the presence of women on the board of governors.

All these, which are essential points, and involving important educational principles, are not difficult to lay down for general guidance, it may be affirmed that the Company formed under the auspices of the Union, will establish no schools in which they are not insisted upon.

A rumour has been spread that the Union is hostile to all existing schools; but like rumour in general, this has a root of truth and a large growth of falsehood. Every reformer must needs be hostile to that which he conceives to need reform, and thus the Union is a league against bad schools and inefficient teachers. Those who complain of its hostility, by so complaining, place themselves in that category. The best refutation of an assertion so evidently intended to injure the Union, is the fact already mentioned that the London Schoolmistresses' Association have entered into connection with it, and named as their representative at the Central Committee, Miss Buss, whose name alone is a guarantee. It is undoubtedly our purpose so to rouse public opinion with regard to all the defects of existing systems, that many things which have been accepted will be acceptable no longer; and, for instance, that it will be as impossible to open a middle-class girls' school as a mere genteel speculation, without proper warrant for fitness to conduct it, as it would be to set up one of the old Dame schools on the village green in competition with the National School under its certificated teachers. But in working this most necessary reform, we would be as careful as the nature of things will allow, of those who have made the sad mistake of embarking in a career for which they have no aptitude. We would drive them gradually out of the field it is true, but only by setting the example of good schools in aid of the few already existing; and by spreading knowledge of what the teacher's art really is, and what all who know the true scope of education expect of the educators. When these things are better known it will be seen at once that dilettante schools have no better *raison d'être* in a civilized society than dilettante hospitals or courts of law.

This consideration brings us naturally to No. 3 of the 'objects of the Union,' in which the Central Committee pledges itself 'To raise the social status of female teachers by encouraging women to make teaching a profession, and to qualify themselves for it by a sound and liberal education, and by thorough training in the art of teaching; to supplement training colleges by attaching, where possible, a class of student teachers to every large school, and by such other means as may be found advisable; also to secure a test of the efficiency of teachers by examinations of recognised authority and subsequent registration.'

The two important points insisted on in this paragraph, of improving the efficiency of teachers, and raising their social condition, are to a certain degree indissolubly connected. The low attainments of the teachers, and his or her low standing in society, are reciprocally cause and effect. Society cannot honour the half-instructed governess or the incompetent schoolmistress; nor, on the other hand, will energy, ability, and high character seek a career where little profit, little honour, and no advancement are to be found.

There is no subject, perhaps, on which the British public is more profoundly ignorant than on that of the value of trained teachers, though they might have learned something from the example of the elementary schools. It was thought a hard measure at first when Government grants were refused to any school that was not under a certificated master or mistress. Those who had ruled uncontrolled before encouraged each other in calling this regulation a proof of the interfering spirit of administrative authority; but fortunately it was maintained, and gradually men came to see that the trained teacher brought something more to his or her task than the mere instruction, in which their old rivals might often equal them. They brought a different appreciation of the work to be done, and definite methods of doing it. Thus one immense advantage has been secured to the children of the poorest classes, while all ranks above them, being independent of Government help, and therefore of Government control, have used their freedom to stumble on in the old way, letting any one teach who had a fancy for that mode of earning a livelihood, or who found it, as women so long did, the only one they could embrace without absolute forfeiture of social consideration. The few openings that even now exist for women who wish to earn an independence without manual toil, have been gained slowly, one by one, through successive contests with men who have so long monopolised all lucrative or honourable labour, that they have learned to look upon that monopoly as a law of nature. Formerly no such openings existed at all; to work with their hands, to teach or to starve were the alternatives, and hence it is with the tenderness of a great pity for silent and undeserved suffering, that we must speak of the shortcomings of female teachers. The absurdity of any comparison of their schools with boys' schools is only equalled by its injustice; since not only have all the educational privileges the nation had to bestow been kept possession of by men, but that the latter, when incompetent, could still shelter their incapacity under the dignity of the clerical profession. These are profitless comments perhaps it will be said, but when forced to condemn, it becomes almost a duty to point out by what fatality the condemnation has become inevitable.

It must also be remembered that if the school-mistresses were incompetent the public was ignorant. Even now, it is the cry of a few reformers that calls for a better state of things, not any public recognition of the national disgrace of entrusting the noblest of human vocations to those who have not studied the first principle on which its exercise depends. That education is an art which men cannot learn by merely passing through a university, nor women in the ordinary contact with children, is a fact not yet commonly admitted. How difficult an art it really is, how requiring deep and long preparation, and the exercise of some of the noblest faculties of the human mind, those only perhaps can tell who have made it their life long study, but it seems strange that an amount of ignorance should make people imagine that to train a human creature needs less special preparation than to train a hound or a race-horse.

One better qualified than myself has treated this subject in another number of this series.[5] I will therefore rather glance at some of the social aspects of the question in order to point out how much all members of the Union, and especially all societies in association with it, may do in spreading right views on this most important and most neglected subject.

In the great dearth of occupation for women above the labouring class, teaching has always been a favourite resource, but the casual way in which it has been taken up, has helped to degrade it almost as much as want of capacity. A man prepares for a profession in his early youth, and devotes to it steadily whatever ability he possesses, women have too commonly taken up the teacher's office only in after years as a resource against want, when a father's death, or losses in trade have left them dependent on their own exertions. And what preparation has their previous life been for a career of mental and physical exertion? What success would a man have who should remain idle till thirty or thirty-five, and then begin the work of a profession? It is true that many girls become teachers as soon as they leave school, but their preparation has been as scanty as their prospects are narrow. It is still also an *ad interim* occupation, and human energy will not go forth into such labour. One inevitable disadvantage of women's work as compared with men's, meets us here as elsewhere. Men have marriage and profession, women, (except in rare cases), will have to choose between the two, and the prospect of marriage involving home, and all that is naturally most dear to every human heart remains a near probability for many years of a woman's life, and doubtless deprives her of some of the settled resolution with which a man enters upon the career which will remain his, whatever form his private life may take. This is a natural difference in the position of the two sexes, and a natural disadvantage that women must encounter, but all who wish to improve their education and social position will try to make girls see the truth of things in this respect, and persuade them to prepare themselves for a career of independence, and take up their work as men take theirs, turning their thoughts from possibilities which their own efforts cannot realise, to what may lie before them as the result of their own industry and resolution.

Female teachers taking up work in this spirit will soon receive their need of honour from society; the more the latter is enlightened the more will the teacher's calling be recognised as one of the noblest to which human power can be devoted.

The low teaching power of women hitherto has occasioned this serious material disadvantage to them; that almost if not all, the highest teaching in classes for girls, is given by men. Thus while so few occupations are opened to women, the most honourable and most remunerative part of what might fairly be their own province, passes into other hands. Nor as the case stands at present have we any right to complain. But the members of any profession must of necessity stand comparatively low in public esteem who are systematically excluded from the higher portions of their own work. Let us hope that the pain with which it is recognized that the exclusion is, in great measure at least, unavoidable now, may be the first step towards a better state of things, which shall set aside so humiliating a necessity at some not far distant day.

If it be asked what can members of this Union do towards remedying this state of things, we reply that in a battle against ignorance and false associations, we require the aid of every earnest mind that can see the evil, and have patience to sift the causes.

In this country, where we can scarcely hope to see the law protect society from ignorant pretenders assuming the name of teachers, it is only by the exercise of individual influence that a better system can be introduced. That influence may be exercised in encouraging every means of improving the education of teachers by persuading young women of good ability to adopt the profession resolutely and seriously, and also by upholding socially those who have done so. No law can alter social conventionality, but cultivated women can everywhere in their own home and by their own example discountenance a conventional vulgarism, and help to improve the education of the nation by receiving educators with honour.

It is especially in provincial centres that this influence may be brought to bear, because so much more is there known by everybody, about everybody, that a teacher's antecedents and ability would be far more easy to ascertain than when lost in the privacy of the London crowd. If steadily, and year after year, mothers refuse to take governesses, or to send their girls to school-mistresses who cannot produce their proofs of capacity and merit, and if this action of individuals becomes known till the more timid or ignorant feel it safest to follow the lead, opinion will have produced the same result which abroad follows from the action of Government. Nothing therefore among the many objects the National Union has set forth, will be more earnestly attended to or more perseveringly followed up than this, and in none I repeat is the value of that co-operation it solicits from its members more desirable.

A very important part of the work sketched out in the clause under consideration, is the formation of classes of student teachers in large schools. Only in this manner, we believe, will the great want of trained teachers be supplied. No training colleges for secondary education exist in England, young women intending to devote themselves to teaching, must acquire the art as best they can, and choose what examinations they will go through as a test of their general acquirements, the College of Preceptors alone examining in the theory and practice of education. There are objections of various kinds too long to enter into here against training colleges for this class; but the difficulty of getting money for such expensive establishments would alone be sufficient to make us seek some other method; and that recommended here has met with general approval from persons competent to judge. Miss Buss in the North London Collegiate School, and Miss Beale at the Ladies' College, Cheltenham, have given their sanction to this system, and we hope that ere long the example will be followed; and that every successful educator will be systematically training a band of followers. Practically, every good school always has produced among its pupils a certain number of good teachers, but this plan introduces it as a regular part of the school method, and provides that the theory as well as the practice shall be systematically taught. Members of the Union can scarcely find a more useful or a kinder work to do, than in helping this part of our scheme, by enabling young women of real capacity to bear the expense of remaining at school till this branch of the professional education can be completed.

No. 4 states the wish of the Union to extend the 'existing system of itinerant lecturers on special subjects, for all places not of sufficient size to maintain a permanent staff of efficient teachers.' This is one of many supplementary plans devised to remedy the miserably scanty means of instruction for women, and which more widely extended would doubtless be of very great use. It is only in large educational centres that good teachers can always be found. In small towns there is nothing to attract them; and yet in such towns and from the adjoining neighbourhood classes might often be formed, and would be most welcome could the teaching be procured. Help from a distance therefore is invited, and in many places the plan has worked well. The expense of procuring good lecturers in this manner is, however, a considerable hindrance, and many a small circle must forego the advantage. This is one of the cases in which the Union may be most useful. Some town, A for instance, might require the assistance of a lecturer, but could not raise the funds for paying first class fees for one who should come from a distance, but the Union or some local Committee in the country obtaining information from the Centre, would know that towns B, C, and D, are no less in want of assistance than A, and that being in the same district, or on the same line of railway, a combined engagement with a lecturer becomes practicable, and might induce him to lower the expense for each town considerably. The Central Committee of the Union in the same manner would have the means of information and organisation, so as to meet the wants of small scattered groups, which remain without any natural centre of their own, and thus the want which might have baffled individual effort will be supplied.

No. 5:

'To endeavour to form classes for girls in connection with grammar schools, making the teaching staff available for both.'

And No. 7:

'To promote the increase of the number of girls and women attending the University Local Examinations, and likewise the number of centres for such examinations, and to endeavour to diminish the cost of attending them;' refer to matters of great importance in which the Union can only work through its influence with schoolmasters and mistresses; but here also the value of the accumulated influence, if I may use the word, of a widely spread Association will tell most beneficially. We have undoubtedly on our committee some names of well deserved educational weight, but should such persons write in their individual capacity to the head of a school to urge new schemes or measures of reform, the suggestion would almost certainly be neglected if not resented as an impertinence, but a society formed for the very purpose of reforming girls' education is *ipso facto* authorised to offer advice. The latter may undoubtedly in this case also be neglected or resented, but it will at least be far less likely to meet such a reception; and the wider the association the greater the weight with which it will speak. By the very fact of addressing many in the name of many it creates among those addressed a certain emulation, a dislike to be left behind in the career of reform which others are entering upon, which though not the highest motive for improvement, leads to action, and will probably in time excite the real interest it but stimulates at first. If occasion should arise to appeal to the Universities on the subject of examinations or lectures, or any other form of help they may in future seem disposed to afford, I think few can doubt that an Educational Union which in any sense shall deserve its name of National, will appeal with far more force than individual teachers or managers of classes would do. The Union would represent a collective opinion, and a common want, and might be expected to carry proportional weight.

It is the same with regard to No. 6.

'To endeavour to restore to the use of girls the endowments originally intended for their benefit, and to obtain for them a fair share in the other endowments applied to education.'

The wishes that may be expressed in one or another place where it is hoped that endowments may be given over for girls' education, cannot be so powerful as the collective wishes of all friends of education in all parts of the country, where such endowments exist, urged collectively by the Central Committee of a Union whose branches spread wherever educational work is going on, or educational wants are felt. A committee for urging upon the Endowed Schools Commissioners the claims of girls, existed for some years in London, and had corresponding branches in the country. In Yorkshire and at Bristol these committees have been active and influential, and in whatever direction the Commissioners may in future extend their work, the same method will be pursued in order to combat local opposition and prejudice, and bring favourable local influence to bear. The London Committee has lately assumed the form of a Sub-Committee of the National Union, with which the Provincial branches will correspond, and a wide organization will be kept in readiness for action when required. The Commissioners, as is well known, are most favourable to the claims of women, but in the face of the powerful opposition they often have to encounter, on the old plea of vested interests, it is needful to stir up to their help all the influence we can command in every quarter, and here again, individuals as well as associations can aid the good cause.[6]

No. 8 states it to be the purpose of the Union,

'To aid all measures for extending to women the means of a

higher education beyond the school period; and to facilitate the preparatory and supplementary studies, by forming classes for students and libraries where required, and enlarging the system of instruction by correspondence, already begun at Cambridge and elsewhere.'

And No. 9,

'To assist the establishment of Evening Classes for young women already earning their own livelihood, and to obtain for women, when possible, admission to classes for technical instruction; thus helping them to fit themselves for better and more remunerative employments than are now accessible to them.'

These two clauses relate, partly, at least, to one and the same subject, considered with reference to different classes; namely, that of prolonging the period of education from childhood or early youth to womanhood. They purpose to prevent on the one hand those who have learnt but little, from losing that little, to put them in the way of increasing their store and fitting themselves for better employments than women have been able to undertake hitherto; and on the other, to secure the too large class of girls, whom no necessary labour awaits after school days are over, from wasting in idleness and frivolity some of the best years of their life.

Taking the two clauses in their order we come to No. 8, which points to one of the most important branches of the Union work. The evil it would seek to counteract has perhaps more than any other single cause tended to enfeeble large classes of women and to lower their influence. Nor is the notion, that girls of eighteen have finished their education and that henceforth till they marry idleness is their natural condition, a privileged folly of the wealthy or the aristocratic. The farmer's daughters are as idle as the squire's, and the tradesman, who himself scarcely rescues a few hours from toil, is too commonly content to see his girls aping the fine ladies who come into his shop. The more scanty the previous education and the more narrow the sphere of life, the more offensive is the idleness, since it loses the grace and refinement that prevail naturally in certain stations, and is in more striking contrast with the habits of the men.

At the very period when lads of any class begin whatever is to be the serious occupation of their lives, girls are, if possible, deprived of all steady occupation, and the only wonder is that the mental difference between the two sexes is not greater than it is. The idleness is not of their own seeking, it is far from being always agreeable, but fashion or gentility have decreed it as their portion. Bread winning toil is supposed to be degrading, or is at least submitted to only under the pressure of dire necessity; while the mind is too vacant to turn to mental labour. This is the point to which the Union invites serious attention. Several schemes that have its cordial sympathy have already been set on foot in many places. A Society for Encouraging Home Studies has been working successfully for some years, giving prizes for the best work done, or the best course of reading pursued during the year. Classes for Ladies are established widely in London and other towns, and in some places, such as Clifton, with remarkable success; encouragement being there given to work done as a result of the Lectures. It has been lately decided to open classes of a similar kind under the direct auspices of the Central Committee to begin in some of the suburban districts which are somewhat too remote to allow of easy attendance at lectures in London itself.[7] It is proposed to commence after the summer holidays with courses of lectures on Physiology, to be given by Miss Macomish, a pupil of Professor Huxley, and highly recommended by him for this purpose. Other subjects will subsequently be taken up, all complementary of school studies. The London University and the Cambridge examinations for women are powerful incentives to mental exertion, and though mostly, perhaps, attended by those who look to some future professional career, still many young ladies who would otherwise have done nothing, and have had no idea of what they could do, are yearly induced to work steadily, once this object is put before them. To meet their great difficulties in knowing the right books to use and the right method of working, a system of correspondence has been established, which the Union invites its members, and its branch Committees, to aid and extend. Hitherto in all these things the efforts have been individual, or at most local; but few would doubt that a new spirit would be infused into all such undertakings by the sense of working in unison with others, of co-operating with a large body, acting in various parts of the country with the same motives, and the same purpose. There would be more method in the aims, and in the work; and there would probably often be more economy, both as regards the lectures and the formation of student libraries, if a regular system of correspondence were kept up with the Central Committee, and the many associate bodies. Another effort to aid Higher Education has been the grant of seven scholarships of £25 tenable for one year, to be awarded by the following bodies, the Universities of Oxford, Cambridge, Edinburgh, and Dublin, the Science and Art Department, the Society of Arts, and the College of Preceptors. With the express condition that the successful candidates shall spend the year in studying at some place for higher education, the selection of which shall be submitted for approval to the committee. Only persons intending to be teachers can become candidates for the scholarships awarded by the Society of Arts and the College of Preceptors. Methods of education will form part of the examination by the latter body.[8]

All the attempts mentioned above for aiding the higher education of women, deserve, as I have said, every encouragement; but one institution for the same purpose stands alone in importance and significance for the future – namely, the college for women opened three years ago at Hitchin, and now removed to Girton, near Cambridge. Most people would smile if I ventured to call it a great institution; and yet, with small numbers, small resources, and few friends, it deserves the epithet more than many a richly endowed foundation; for it is great in its conception, as the only attempt made to place the education of women on the same footing with that of men; it is great in being in advance of public opinion, and there is greatness in the energy and determination which have brought it to its present position, and maintained it in the face of discouragement and difficulty.[9] Few undertakings have had so little help from public favour as this college, and yet, if successful, it will assuredly do more than any other yet set on foot, not only to rescue the youth of many women from idleness and frivolity, but to afford a standard for their education. None has existed hitherto, and this is one of the curious facts which marks the contemptuous indifference with which the whole subject has been treated. It has been too trifling, too insignificant a matter to be worth measuring, as important things are measured, by a fixed standard. The first step to remedy this evil was made when the University Local Examinations were extended to girls, and the college carries on the same principle to a higher region.

It may be very generally thought that our university curriculum is not the best for young women to follow, that other branches of knowledge might be pursued with better effect; but we need system even more than knowledge. We need to get rid of the dilettanti character of female education, and to be able to try it by acknowledged tests. The objection against the curriculum will yearly lessen, as the curriculum itself is extended, and public opinion lifts other subjects to a nearer equality of favour with classics and mathematics; but if this were never to happen, the education would still be of the utmost value to women, in giving method and an authoritative aim which for three years at least must govern their studies. The direction of the latter may or may not be changed hereafter, but the leading principle will have taken root, and all idea of applying a fancy standard to the acquirements of women will be at an end; once having in the highest education accepted the same test by which men are tried, it would be imposs-ible to subject them again to inequality of examination. Some thorny social questions may come nearer to a solution in that matter than in any other.

One objection to the college, founded on women's unfitness to bear the strain of such continued application as Cambridge studies imply, has been triumphantly refuted by the fact that during the four years the college has been in active work, no medical attend-ance has been required, yet all who have resided the requisite time have worked for the usual university examinations, not one has failed at the 'little go,' which several have passed in first class, and the only three students who had reached the period for going up to the honours examination passed this severe ordeal most credit-ably – one in mathematics and two in classics. Thus showing that the more arduous form of study had not only been encountered but carried to an issue of unhoped-for success.

The work of the Union in regard to the college is mostly one of sympathy, but it may not be without influence. The only direct aid it could give would be in seeking to increase the number of students, either by combating the prejudice against it, or by aiding the foundation of scholarships to meet the whole or a portion of the expenses of the college course. Every false view of women's education, every prejudice that impedes their attaining a more independent social position, will be found arraigned against this institution; in favouring it we combat them directly and indirectly; we obtain over them a partial victory only at the present moment, but what is far more important, we are preparing new ground for the future when weeds so noxious to true civilization will find it hard to grow.

No. 9 already quoted is, as there stated, the same in principle as the one we have been considering, only dealing with a lower class. The Working Women's College in London is the most successful attempt yet made to supplement the scanty education of girls forced to leave school at an early age to earn their livelihood. This college has been at work for some years, and able and benevolent exertions have never failed in the cause. Evening classes for the same purpose have at different times been formed in many places, and the Union earnestly recommends that this work should be zealously pursued.

The Central Committee has hitherto been hindered partly by want of funds, partly by the scarcity of help, from undertaking any such classes itself, but it is with great pleasure that it has seen the excellent work done in this direction both in Yorkshire and at Birmingham, where ladies devoted themselves with equal ability and energetic benevolence to giving lectures on health and on domestic economy to working women, who attended in large numbers, and expressed in some instances touching gratitude for the help they felt had thus been given to them.[10]

How much good is done morally by so providing occupation and interest for vacant hours, by bringing women of different grades of society together, letting the more favoured learn, through closer contact, what are the trials and temptations of their poorer sisters, letting the latter feel the active sympathy of the intelligent and refined exercised outside any questions of ordinary charity – what, I say, may be the moral benefit of such intercourse it is impossible to calculate.

In these days, when so much deterioration is threatened to the trade of England, owing to the want of trained skill in our artisans, it is most desirable to assist young girls in obtaining such technical instruction as they may require. Schools of design are opened, and in many directions instruction is offered, but means are too scanty, or ignorance too gross to allow individuals to avail themselves of the resource, which would open up a better and more honourable existence to them. Both public and private motives then point to this mode of improving education as most worthy of exertion. The lowest and least remunerative labour must necessarily fall to women if they continue to be lower in knowledge and in skill than the men; opportunities of improvement are now open to all alike, let it be our endeavour as far as possible to enable women to obtain their fair share, remembering how helpless stands many an intelligent girl, away perhaps from any centre of art or cultivation, isolated by her poverty and her ignorance, unless some one points the way and helps her at the outset.[11] It may be that when instruction has done its best, force and injustice may come in to deprive the women of the fruit of their skill, as in the case of the painters on china, when the men insisted that the women should be allowed no painting-stick; but it may perhaps be hoped that the days of such oppression as this are beginning to pass away – at any rate the wider and better the instruction given to women the more difficult will it become to exercise it.

We have now reviewed in succession the various objects which the Union pledges itself to pursue, and it must be apparent that the work so sketched out offers a field for the exertion of as many assistants as can be enlisted to serve in the cause.

School-training of teachers, lectures of many kinds and degrees, endowments, local examinations, student libraries, technical instruction, Girton College, classes for working women – all these demand individual exertion; and each object will be pursued more effectually by that co-operation that the Union invites.

Lastly, individuals and associate bodies, local committees formed as numerously as the needs of the matter and the zeal of the country may prompt, will find work enough in carrying into effect the resolution embodied in the last paragraph of these 'Objects of the Union' – namely: 'to create a sounder public opinion with regard to education itself, and the national importance of the education of women, by means of meetings, of lectures and of the press; and thus to remove the great hindrance to its improvement – the indifference with which it is regarded by parents or by the public.'

When our members are asked what we are going to do, an answer may be ever ready; and it would be strange if some portion or other of that answer should not awake a chord of sympathy in every earnest mind; and sympathy as the first step towards real co-operation – is what we need. Unfortunately, sympathy too often does not go beyond words. We are very commonly told: 'I agree with you, I applaud your endeavour; but I see nothing in which I can assist.' Such wellwishers do not perceive very often the obvious small help of becoming 5s. subscribers! Perhaps they despise such modest assistance; but if they can do no more, let them not think the small sum too minute for usefulness. The subscription was fixed low for the purpose of attracting numbers; because numbers, implying wide ramification, are better for the purpose of the Union than fewer, even though larger subscribers. Some persons wonder why we should require money-help at all, they do not understand our need of funds. Let them ask any one who has had some personal experience of printers' or publishers' accounts, of the cost of getting-up meetings or paying lecturers, or even of such common items as postage and stationers' bills, and they will readily be made to understand that work such as that of the Union cannot be performed without considerable expense. When it is considered further that no extensive work can be carried on without paid secretaries, messengers, office, and committee-room, it will perhaps be granted that subscriptions must be welcome, and that those whose influence can extend no further, will yet do material service, if they use such as they possess in procuring new members and subscribers, which implies, at the same time, circulating the papers, and thereby making the work more and more widely known.

It was for the purpose of assisting this work of influence that the publication of a journal was decided upon 'as a regular organ of communication with branch committees, with associated bodies, and with members generally, as a record of the work of the Central Committee, as a register of all important information sent from different quarters, or collected by the sub-committees, appointed for that purpose; as a medium for correspondence and discussion on all topics connected with the work of the Union, and with kindred work whether carried on in fellowship with the Union or not; on whatever can aid our cause, or whatever offers obstacles to it which closer attention may help to remove.' And we have reason to think that the plan has already worked beneficially.

The journal is also, as stated in the first number, 'The exponent of our educational creed; the means of impressing on the public, line upon line, precept upon precept, the fundamental principles on which all our work is based.'

'Action on public opinion can be effected only by a wide sustained and organised agitation, keeping the questions at issue continually before the public mind, being unwearied in pointing out wrongs, in urging claims, in protesting against neglect, and indifference, and injustice, in recalling forgotten principles; and an agitation of this nature requires an organ to give it expression, and also to afford a field that shall be always open to full and free discussion of the subject.'

The subscription to the Journal for members of the Union has been placed very low, below cost price in fact, for the purpose of inducing all members to become subscribers to this also, hoping especially that the work would by this means be better understood, and attract more intelligent co-operation.

The National Union, in forming which Mrs Wm. Grey worked for months alone, is still a small body, a poor one as we have seen, without power, trusting to no assistance from Government, to no influence of party, and yet hoping to do a great work; and it trusts to accomplish it (as indicated in the concluding paragraph above quoted) by working upon public opinion in every manner and through every channel that can be reached. It must be a work of influence, and therefore far slower and more arduous than one of definite action. To do a given thing may require great ability and energy, but it is more difficult to clear the minds of men of the mists and prejudices which blind them to the fact that the thing ought to be done. It is hard enough also to bring one set, or class of persons, to see that a certain line of conduct is admirable; but it is incomparably harder to bring many different sets to agree in the same view of what is right and expedient. Again, it is not easy to open men's eyes to the value of a certain course, even when arguments of profit and loss can be brought to bear upon the subject; but far less easy is it to persuade them when profit and loss are not in question, or refer to such matters only as human dignity and happiness! And such are the difficulties the Union has to encounter. The benefits to be derived by improving the education of women affect material interests as yet but slightly; many classes of persons must be brought to own the same truth; and the obstacles to its being acknowledged are those very mists of prejudice, that very apathy, to dispel which is more arduous than any active exertion. In the present state of opinion, apathy is stronger than prejudice, comparatively few openly oppose the education of women, but very few have any interest in the matter. If money is so difficult to obtain for girls' schools, it is because parents and the public do not care about them, and they do not care because they are careless and ignorant about education altogether. It is not that wilful injustice is consciously intended to the girls, but simply that education as such, is not valued at all. It is a well known necessity of modern life that boys should have a certain amount of instruction, and the outlay is repaid in worldly success in one form or another; but, as yet, the £ *s. d.* value of girls' education has not been ascertained, hence it is valueless. This same ignorant indifference is at the root of all the defects of boys' education, and it shows itself in the general neglect of professional training for teachers. This ignorance, then, and its accompanying apathy, are what we propose to attack.

In order to do so we must be unwearied in effort, and gain strength from wide spread co-operation. Women especially must work patiently on, helping each other, and rejoicing in the help of the *élite* at least of the other sex, whose generous sympathy has never failed us; while recent events have proved once more how little is to be expected from the justice of the majority! A very small share of ancient endowments or of modern donations will ever be ours, and no position of influence, no free career through which to win an honourable independence, or gratify a laudable ambition, will be conceded without a struggle. Let our first struggle be to increase our own fitness for all we hope to claim. It must ever be remembered that of all the advantages that men have monopolised to themselves, none is of such value and importance as education. The only hope of procuring more remunerative labour for one class, more honourable as well as lucrative employment for another, a more independent position and wider influence for all, is by casting off the old ignorance and with it the old apathy. It is fortunate perhaps that external circumstances over which we have no control, by forcing a much larger number of women than formerly to provide for themselves, have given a new stimulus to the desire for improvement; have made it evident to the most reluctant that women must be unfit for the work that is become so necessary for them, unless they are better instructed. Then the lower motive of gain comes in and will act beneficially in preparing the way for truer and wider views.

If once England could feel the beauty of culture and its bearing on the whole moral as well as intellectual nature, women's education would be prized apart from all money considerations, and educators would be trained and honoured. Till this can be accomplished we can only attack the evil wherever it shows itself in an assailable form, and trust that a country which prides itself upon being practical, will at least recognise ere long that whether or no women would be the better or the happier for their own sake by being differently trained, the men of a nation can only be superficially and mechanically instructed, till the women are so educated as to give a different tone to home life, to the habits and associations of childhood, the pleasures of youth, and the calmer enjoyments of domestic companionship. When some sign shall appear that public opinion is moving in that direction, then, and not till then, will the National Union feel that its work is safe; and trust that new habits, fostering new principles, the path will be cleared for another generation to press forward unfettered in the career of progress.

APPENDIX I

The Objects of this Union are:

(1) To bring into communication and co-operation all individuals and associations engaged in promoting the Education of Women and Girls, so as to strengthen and combine their efforts; to collect and register for the use of members, information on all points connected with such education.

(2) To promote the establishment of good and cheap dayschools, for all classes above those attending the public elementary schools, with boarding-houses in connection with them, when necessary, for pupils from a distance.

(3) To raise the social status of female teachers by encouraging women to make teaching a profession, and to qualify themselves for it, by a sound and liberal education and by thorough training in the art of teaching; to supplement train-

ing-colleges by attaching, where possible, a class of student teachers to every large school and by such other means as may be found advisable; also to secure a test of the efficiency of teachers by examinations of recognised authority and subsequent registration.

(4) To extend the existing system of itinerant lectures on special subjects, for all places not of sufficient size to maintain a permanent staff of efficient teachers.

(5) To endeavour to form classes for girls in connection with grammar schools, making the teaching staff available for both.

(6) To endeavour to restore to the use of girls the endowments originally intended for their benefit, and to obtain for them a fair share in the other endowments applied to education.

(7) To promote the increase of the number of girls and women attending the University Local Examinations and likewise the number of centres for such examinations, and to endeavour to diminish the cost of attending them.

(8) To aid all measures for extending to women the means of higher education beyond the school period; and to facilitate the preparatory and supplementary studies by forming classes for students and libraries where required, and enlarging the system of instruction by correspondence, already begun at Cambridge and elsewhere.

(9) To assist the establishment of evening classes for young women already earning their own livelihood, and to obtain for women, when possible, admission to classes for technical instruction; thus helping them to fit themselves for better and more remunerative employments than are now accessible to them.

(10) To create a sounder public opinion with regard to education itself, and the national importance of the education of women, by means of meetings, of lectures, and of the press; and thus to remove the great hindrance to its improvement, the indifference with which it is regarded by parents, and by the public.

APPENDIX II

Proposed Public Day School for Girls in West London

(1) The Central Committee, in pursuance of one of the objects set forth in the circular of the above Union, namely: to promote the establishment of good and cheap Day Schools for Girls of all classes above those attending the Public Elementary Schools, purpose to begin by establishing such a School in a central position adjacent to Chelsea, Brompton and South Kensington, on the general model which has proved so successful in the North London Collegiate and Camden Street Schools for Girls, under Miss Buss.

(2) In order to reduce as far as possible the cost of a First-class Education, the School will be a large one. It will be divided into three Departments: – 1, Preparatory; 2, Junior; 3, Senior.

(3) The School will be under the general superintendence of a qualified Head Mistress, who will have the same powers and duties as the Head Master of a Public School.
Trained teachers of tried ability will be selected.

(4) A regular system of Inspection and Examination by qualified Examiners will be established.

(5) Pupils may be prepared for the Oxford and Cambridge Local and other University Examinations, and for those of the College of Preceptors.

(6) The School course will include Religious Instruction, Reading, Writing, Arithmetic, Book-keeping, English Grammar and Literature, History, Geography, French, German, the Elements of Physical Science, Drawing, Class Singing and Harmony, and Calisthenic Exercises.

(7) In the Senior Department there will be advanced classes for Ancient and Modern Languages, Literature, and History, Mathematics, the elements of Moral Science and of Logic, Physical Science (especially Physiology as applied to health), Social and Domestic Economy.

(8) Arrangements will be made, if desired, for giving separate Religious instruction to pupils of different denominations.

(9) A Class of Student Teachers will be attached to the School, and special arrangements will be made for training them in the Theory and Practice of Education.

(10)   The School year will be divided into three terms. The Fees will vary from £2. 2s. per term in the Preparatory department to £8. 8s. per term in the higher classes of the Senior department.

These fees will include the use of maps and books of reference, and all expenses for writing and drawing materials.

Instrumental Music, Solo Singing, and Dancing, will be extras, the fees will vary according as the pupil requires elementary or advanced teaching.

(11)   It is proposed that the requisite capital be provided by forming a Company, to be called the 'GIRLS' PUBLIC DAY SCHOOL COMPANY LIMITED.' The Shares to be of £5 each, which may be paid up at once, or in instalments as follows:

> £1 payable on Application.
> £1   „   July 1st, 1872.
> £1   „   Oct. 1st, 1872.
> £1   „   Jan. 1st, 1873.
> £1   „   Apr. 1st, 1873.

The capital will be applied to the hire, purchase, or erection, and the furnishing of School-buildings, a certain proportion being left to form the nucleus of a Reserve Fund. Any profit arising after the establishment of the School, will be applied to the payment of a dividend on the Shares.

In considering applications for entry into the School, and in filling up vacancies hereafter, priority of admission will be given to children of Shareholders, providing that they satisfy the regulations of the School.

(12)   Arrangements will be made to open the School in temporary buildings so soon as a sufficient number of Shares shall have been taken up to guarantee the support of the undertaking. Parents are invited to enter the names of pupils.

(13)   The organisation of the School will be specially directed to meet and correct the defects pointed out in the Report of the Schools Enquiry Commission: – 'Want of thoroughness and foundation; want of system; slovenliness and showy superficiality; inattention to rudiments; undue time given to accomplishments, and these not taught intelligently or in any scientific manner; want of organisation.' Serious endeavours will also be made to train the pupils for the practical business and duties of life.

The want of such a School is seriously felt in the district where it is proposed to found it, namely, in the S.W. District of London. A spot will be selected easily accessible from the stations of the District Metropolitan Railway. After this School has been established, it is proposed that the operations of the Company should be extended to the foundation of Schools in other parts of London, and in the large cities of the Provinces.

APPENDIX III

Associations in connection with the Union

Plymouth.
Hampshire.
Birmingham.
Falmouth.
Guernsey.
Belfast.   } Ladies' Educational
Windsor and Eton.   Association.
Bristol and Clifton.
East London
Wakefield.
Cheltenham.
Cambridge Classes for Women.
Norwich Committee.
Rugby Council for Promoting the Education of Women.
Ladies' Council of Yorkshire Board of Education.
Huddersfield Branch Committee.
Committee at York.
Governesses' Association, Dublin.

NOTES

1 See Appendix. No. I.
2 Appendix III gives a list of all Societies now in connection with the National Union.
3 See Appendix, No. II.
4 In a paper by Charles Roundell, Esq. the following estimate appears, – 'Adopting the principle of calculation adopted by the Schools' Enquiry Commissioners, with respect to boys, and making the necessary allow-

ances, it may be assumed that there are 10 girls out of every 1000 of the population for whom secondary instruction ought to be provided. Upon this assumption there are in England and Wales, according to the returns of the recent census, upwards of 225,000 girls requiring a higher than a primary or elementary education.'

5 *The Importance of the Training of the Teacher*, by Joseph Payne.

6 See notice by Mr Shore in Nos. 2 and 6 of the Journal.

7 See the Scheme in April No. of the Journal.

8 For detail of the Scheme see April No. of the Journal.

9 To Miss Emily Davies is this praise mostly due, she has been assisted, and warmly too, by men as well as women, but her own exertions have been unremitting, and her patient confidence in a better future has sustained others through discouragement. The munificent donation of £1000 by Madame Bodichon, was the beginning of a fund which made it possible to open the college in a rented house; but had her noble example been better followed, it would ere this have been in more appropriate buildings, and nearer to Cambridge, on which it depends for tuition.

10 See reports in the 1st and 2nd Nos. of Journal.

11 The science and art classes in various parts of the country are most valuable, but the Queen's Institute, Dublin, is we believe the only real College we possess for technical training. It is hoped, however, that an Institution for the same nature due to private munificence will ere long be opened in Birmingham.

Isabella M. S. Tod

On the Education of Girls of the Middle Classes

(1874)

The popular axiom, that the mixxle classes are the substance and sinew of a country, and that it is upon them that its prosperity chiefly depends, is one of those truths which are so often repeated, that from familiarity they are apt to lose their force. Limiting the phrase 'middle classes' to that portion of the community which is not only freed from manual labour, but possessed of the taste or means to procure a share of the refinements of life, the axiom quoted is correct. Placed above the atmosphere of mingled suffering and recklessness which poverty creates, and below that of luxurious idleness and self-worship which surrounds great wealth, their very condition compels the exercise of many of the higher faculties of heart and mind, while it also gives them hopes and motives for that exercise. These men and women must of necessity take part in the thousand activities of life, and are summoned to assume many and varied responsibilities. They *must* possess forethought, fortitude, self-control; they *must* learn and practise the lessons of practical wisdom, or they themselves and all around them inevitably suffer. Individual self-restraint, self-reliance, self-culture, are thus, if possible, more requisite in these classes than in any other.

It is, therefore, evident that the education of the young people of this influential portion of society ought to be of a very enlarged and solid character; and, as the first essential for this, that a true ideal ought to be kept in view. We may briefly define education to be the drawing out and strengthening of all the faculties which God has implanted in the soul. The acquirement of knowledge, most important as it is, is secondary to that development of mind which is obtained in the first place by means of that acquirement. What is the real root of the solicitude to obtain or maintain a good system of education for the humbler classes which is so manifest at present in all parts of the empire? It is not that the working man may be able to read his employer's directions, or that the working woman may keep the account of her little household expenses correctly. It goes far deeper. It is because the close connection now seen to exist between ignorance and pauperism and crime has forced the conviction on the minds of all, that the soul left without training *will* deteriorate, and that the teaching which it is wished to give is a most valuable element in that needful training. The ideal thus set before the public mind is negative rather than positive. Yet in a rough way, real, though indistinct, it indicates the appreciation of something higher hidden in the meagre school-work, some valuable moral end to be served by means of the drudgery of spelling and sums. It seems strange that the very men who perceive the importance of instruction in this larger sense for the lower classes frequently overlook it altogether when thinking of their own sons and daughters. Some parents are destitute of any positive aim in the education of their children; they send them to school merely because it is the custom, but have no notion of the necessity of anything more than the most rudimentary knowledge. A larger number look only to the utilitarian aspect of the matter, and insist that both boys and girls shall learn only what in their opinion will be of 'practical' use to them in after-life. This demand for the 'practical' is, in the case of boys, chiefly shown by the requisition made that their education shall be of a 'commercial' character. Fortunately for boys, however, the professions claim a kind of preparation which cannot be narrowed within these limits, and the approval thus stamped upon a more liberal line of instruction prevents the standard for all from falling too low. No such salutary compulsion exists in the case of girls. So far as the majority of parents have any standard of results for daughters, it is only that their manners shall be pleasing, that they shall have such command of 'accomplishments' as may please others, and that they shall have so much surface knowledge as may guard against a display of gross ignorance in society. This vague and slight programme is known by the girls themselves to be all that is wished for, so that conscientious teachers (of whom there are many) find the inertia of the pupils added to the prejudices of the parents, as hindrances to success. This plan of education is also considered to be 'practical' as having respect to a girl's future life. It is hardly necessary to show that, in the case of both sexes, such a narrow and illiberal scheme of education defeats itself, for it ignores the very consti-tution of the mind upon which it is intended to act. The Schools Inquiry Commissioners, after a most elaborate and careful investigation into the present state of middle-class education in England, wrote as follows:

> Much evidence has been laid before us tending to show that indifference and ignorance of the subject on the part of the parents are among the chief hindrances to education at present. Too often the parents seem hardly to care for education at all. Too often they give an inordinate value to mere show. Too often they think no education worth having that cannot be speedily turned into money. In fact, many parents need education themselves in order to appreciate education for their children, and their present opinion cannot be considered as final and supreme.

One of the assistant-commissioners, Mr Bryce, truly says:

> All reform in education should be comprehensive, for the sake of boys as well as girls. The chief cause of every defect is to be found in the indifference of the vast majority of parents, especially of the commercial class, to any education whose direct pecuniary value they do not see. Such indifference is itself the result of a dull and material view of life, of an absence of interest in literature and science, in social and political questions. This is an evil which improvements in female education could not but do much to correct. In a mercantile community only the women have leisure. So far, therefore, from acquiescing in the mental inferiority of woman as the normal state of things, it is really by the female part of such a community that one might expect to see its mental tone maintained; it is there that one would look to find a keener relish for literature and art, a livelier intellectual activity, a more perfect intellectual refinement. To the want of such intellectual interests, and to the dulness of mind which springs from that want, the present defects in our education are due; as it is this very want, this dulness, which a better education is needed to cure and remove.

In every separate grade of schools, from the most fashionable and expensive, down to those which are but little above the State-aided schools, those for girls are distinctly worse, educationally considered, than those for boys of the same grade. The Commissioners say:

> The deficiency in girls' education is stated with the utmost confidence, and with entire agreement, by many witnesses of authority. Want of thoroughness and foundation; want of

system; slovenliness and showy superficiality; inattention to rudiments; undue time given to accomplishments, and these not taught intelligently or in any scientific manner; want of organisation; these may sufficiently indicate the character of the complaints we have received, in their more general aspect.

This indictment sums up the heads of the charges which have long been preferred by thoughtful women against the majority of girls' schools. The ideal of education is a false one; the aims being wrong, the methods are also wrong; and the indifference of parents as to the progress of the girls in serious studies takes away all motive for energy and spirit. This unfortunate state of things tends to perpetuate itself; for women trained under such a system will seldom be able to inaugurate anything better when they become teachers. Yet there are a large number of lady-teachers who are labouring most conscientiously and earnestly in their vocation, with a view to the formation of the moral character of their pupils, and who, if they had the opportunity of learning a better mode of mental training, would eagerly adapt themselves to it. But every earnest teacher finds herself thwarted in her endeavours, both by the direct interference of parents, and still more by the depressing influence upon the girls of the atmosphere of apathy, or even suspicion of study on their part, which surrounds them at home.[1] One lady says, 'If a girl begins to get interested in the schoolwork, and is seen in the evening busy over her theme, her mother comes to me, and says, "Now, Miss – –, you must not make Augusta a blue." If I report that another does not try to improve herself in arithmetic, the mother says, "Well, you know, I am anxious about her music, of course; but it really doesn't matter about her arithmetic, does it? Her husband will be able to do all her accounts for her, you know." Such parents fill children's minds with the notion that their education is not to be of any use to them, and that they need not care whether or not they profit by it, so long as they possess those showy qualities which are supposed to command the admiration of the other sex.' Another remarks that she never heard a parent express the least anxiety for a girl's improvement in any subject except music. The mothers, having themselves been educated under this wretched *régime*, are not so blameworthy as those fathers who have had opportunities of knowing the value of a full and judicious training in developing the mind. But even their sincere affection for their daughters is not often a sufficiently strong motive to overcome the dislike with which average men regard any decided effort to make girls stronger as well as nobler in character. In the caustic language of Mr Bryce,

Although the world has now existed for several thousand years, the notion that women have minds as cultivable and as well worth cultivating as men's minds is still regarded by the ordinary British parent as an offensive, not to say revolutionary, paradox. . . . It is not to refinement or modesty that a cultivated intelligence is opposed, but to vapidity and languor and vulgarity of mind, to the love of gossip and the love of dress.

Whilst urging the claims of girls to an education larger in its scope, and surer in its working, we are haunted by the recollection of one notion which we are aware is often present to the minds of parents, whether they give expression to it or not. They look forward to *all* their daughters marrying, to *all* these marriages being satisfactory, and to the husbands being *always* able and willing to take the active management of everything; neither death, illness, nor untoward circumstances occurring to throw the wives on their own resources. When put before them they must acknowledge that such is not a true picture of life. We shall not stop to discuss whether such a state of things is even desirable. It is sufficient to point out that it does not and cannot exist. Yet they cling to it, and will not prepare their girls for anything else. To have such appearance, manners, and acquirements as will be pleasing to themselves in the meantime, and by attracting admiration may facilitate marriage, is the unavowed, though sole object, which too many seek for their girls. The girl knows it also, and acts upon it. Can anything be imagined more likely to lower the tone of her whole nature? The finer feelings, the moral dignity, which the parents would also desire to see cultivated, thus receive a heavy blow from their own hands. But the plain truth is, that *here lies the great obstacle* to the improvement of the education of women. Parents should remember that they cannot, with a wish, obtain for their daughters exactly the situation in life which they suppose to be most desirable. It is, then, short-sighted to fit them for no other; nay, it is even cruel.

The one essential element, without which reforms of teaching-power, of methods, of subjects, of tests, and all else, can be of no avail, is that these young girls shall be looked upon as human beings with a great unknown part to play in life – as God's subjects, with the talents which He gave them, to be prepared for the work to which He may call them, *not* as colourless, characterless things, of no value, till placed in some relationship to others of their fellow-creatures.

There is but one true theory of education, for men and women alike; just as there is but one religion, but one morality. Experience proves the value of a high ideal in every department of human interests.

It is indeed, in the first place, on the duty of enabling them to *be* whatever Heaven *meant them to be*, that we ground the claim of women to a full participation in the blessings of a liberal education.

But now, as women are not, as a rule, so taught and disciplined as to make the most of their powers, their after-life continually makes demands upon them which they are not able to meet. The consequence is, that gratuitous suffering is often entailed upon them; and considering how much sorrow inevitably falls to the lot of most women, the cruelty of perpetuating any removable part of it is obvious. There is an immediate connection between a cultivated mind and a state of readiness to meet the emergencies of life.

If there is one warning more than another constantly given us by all educationalists, both the philosophical and the practical, it is against the idea of training young people technically or professionally. No matter how valuable professional studies may be in themselves, their introduction into the curriculum, before the broad foundation of liberal studies is fully laid, is deprecated by all. It is important for every one to carry away from the class-room some interest of a kind different from and above his or her probable occupation; something that will help to keep fresh in their own and other minds the recollection that they are men and women, rather than merchants or lawyers, wives or governesses.

But while deprecating technicality in the education of girls during their school and class-room life (and it were well that this were much extended), a weighty consideration regarding their after-life should be kept in view. No observer of society can fail to see that a great change is taking place in public opinion, respecting the employment of ladies. An idea was long cherished with almost superstitious reverence, that work of any kind was degrading to a woman of the refined classes – a remnant, doubtless, of the old heathen notion that work was the duty of slaves, and idleness the privilege of the free. The pressing demands of house-hold cares – more urgent in past times than now, and extending to a higher grade in society – first broke through the practice, and then the theory. Still, anything outside their own households was looked on as a very suspicious occupation for ladies. It is instructive, in looking back at the records of sixty years since, when a great impetus was given to social and literary exertion by the tumult of political excitement, to read of the horror with which many new things were regarded, which seem to us now simple matters of course. Teaching in Sunday-schools, regular visiting of the poor, (at least in towns), efforts at improving the condition of the labouring classes, habits of reading, all which are *now* associated in our minds with the gentlest and most retiring form of the feminine character, were *then* counted as bold and headstrong innovations, contrary to propriety, and destructive of modesty. But the growth of an enlightened public opinion has left such fears far behind, and will assuredly make further progress in the same direction; we cannot 'chain the Future under the Past.' Yet the old prejudice is not dead, it has only entered another phase. It is now conceded that the most dignified and graceful woman may work, earnestly and laboriously, without any diminution of her dignity and grace – only she must not accept any remuneration for it. This is no more than a prejudice, there is no shred of principle underlying it. There is no moral incompatibility between fineness of nature and well-earned reward for work. Nor is there any aesthetic unsuitableness; if there were, the theory would apply as much to all the men who have been helpers and benefactors of the world, who have kindled its highest aspirations, led its deepest thoughts, and provided it with the richest stores of knowledge. We do *not* feel that it is derogatory to the poet to be paid for his poem, to the artist to put a price upon his picture, to the philosopher or *savant* to make business-like arrangements with their publishers, to the professor to charge for admission to his lectures.

In considering the right of women to enter lucrative employments, it is only necessary to show that these are not inconsistent with the high status which theoretically is assigned to women. Practically it is a matter of notoriety that in the lower ranks of life the women work as hard as the men, and at tasks often as noxious and trying, the only difference being that those who are paid at all are paid worse in proportion to their work. Amongst the poorer middle classes the case is much the same, only that paying work is not always as readily found by these women as by those who accept the wages of unskilled labour. But when we reach the classes above these, the circumstances become complicated.

In all that wide circle of persons who have habits and feelings of refinement, but not much wealth, there are thousands of girls brought up amiably, and to a certain extent usefully, but in a manner which leaves them unable to make their own way in the world. It is taken for granted that somebody else will protect and provide for them, consequently they are not taught how to provide for themselves, and hundreds are annually thrown helpless on the world. Every one knows how common a thing it is to see a family who have lived comfortably, perhaps luxuriously, suddenly plunged into poverty by the death of the father. Then, the young ladies, who have spent their time in parties and novel-reading, music and croquet, with possibly a little visiting of the poor, find that 'they must exert themselves.' But how are they to do it? After twenty or thirty of the best years of their lives have been wasted without their having acquired the least aptitude for mental exertion, without having learned that energy and independence were desirable qualities, think what it is for them to commence the exertion of faculties thus weakened by disuse. They have not only to depend on powers so enervated, but they have also to begin the special training needful for the profession by which they must earn their bread. There is, indeed, but one profession open to them, that of teaching, but it is the very last which should be opened to them, for poverty confers no powers for guiding young minds, and parents have no more right to sacrifice a child's mental than its physical health to compassion for another. These poor ladies make an attempt at it, however. They make many blunders, struggling with dire distress the while; sometimes in the scramble picking up a little in the art of teaching and becoming passable governesses, but frequently depending more or less upon grumbling relatives and friends; sometimes sinking slowly in the social scale, dropping out of sight, and starving by inches in some obscure garret. It is not too much to say that men who live up to their income, without making provision for their daughters, and then leave them thus unprepared for a fight with the world, are guilty, not only of gross selfishness, but of actual dishonesty.

But why should those parents who have the prospect of giving their girls what is counted a reasonable provision, suppose it a good thing that they should be incapable of doing anything to support themselves? Work is itself a valuable education, and the possession and management of property exercises and strengthens many qualities well worth a strenuous endeavour. But parents dread the loss of 'gentility.' If such a reputation is only to be had at such a price, is it worth the cost? Yet good social position does not really depend upon uselessness. Here, as in many other cases, a reality is sacrificed to a name. We may hope, however, that with a higher idea of what their daughters are fit for, and the training they ought to get, parents will also adopt wider views regarding their future occupations. In truth, throughout the whole of the middle classes, it should be looked on as a matter of course that girls should be instructed in some business or profession, by which they could acquire a competency, and in which industry, forethought, and ability could obtain their due reward; so that it shall be no longer impossible for a lady to earn ease and comfort, and the means of beneficence, for herself. The family does not lose caste when one boy goes into a merchant's office, and another to the university. Why should the enforced idleness of girls be thought necessary to keep up the status of the rest? Refinement cannot be possessed by proxy. But, indeed, work is no way opposed to refinement; while vacuity and listlessness certainly are. This caste-prejudice, however, is far more easily assailed than is supposed: it is not a fortress to be conquered with difficulty and pain, but a fog-bank to be dissipated by the first breath of wholesome air. A few brave and reasonable spirits could break down its domination anywhere, simply by acting as if it did not exist, and preparing their girls rationally for life.

It is true that many of the occupations best suited for ladies are only being opened slowly, and with difficulty, but the very cause of the delay is the want of those ready and able to take advantage of each step of progress. One objection has been made to this introduction of women into the paying occupations – that it would diminish the number of marriages. It is quite true that it would diminish the number of marriages for bread, and for that good effect alone it would be worth a vigorous effort to obtain it. There would be fewer women who cannot work, and who dare not starve, who are holding on to 'genteel' society by a thread that may be snapped at any moment, and are consequently driven to marry men for whom they care nothing. But that it would lessen the number of marriages for love it is impossible to believe. Nay, as respect is the surest basis of affection, it would be much more likely to increase them.

The great end which we are considering is the true and right education of girls – the training and guidance which will enable them to attain the ideal of their own nature. A part, and a vital part, of this education belongs, in the first place, to the parents, and can be safely entrusted to no other hand – the implanting of religious and moral principle, and the endeavour to lead the young spirit to act in all things according to that rule. But the part of education which comes before the eyes of others, and which must to a great degree be confided to others, is also of the deepest importance. It is to this division of education – mental discipline and instruction – that our attention is now directed. There is a close connection between the two portions; mental power has an affinity with moral power, and though the connection is not by any means invariable, still we have a right to assume that the one will prove an effectual aid to the other. Dr Arnold, speaking of his pupils, said: 'I have still found that folly and thoughtlessness have gone to evil. I am sure that the temptations of intellect are not comparable to the temptations of dulness.'

In selecting out of the great mass of human knowledge, the portions most suitable to be made the medium for the education of girls, there are several things to be borne in mind. It is not the mere acquisition of knowledge that is aimed at, but the invigorating and elevating the mind; therefore we must lay the foundation with what will nerve and strengthen. Every human mind has *some* appetite for knowledge, but the diversity of faculties is great; therefore there must be so much variety, not of details, but of leading lines of interest, as to provide suitable *pabulum* for all. With the exception of accomplishments, the subjects now usually taught to girls are simply the rudiments of those which form a portion of a boy's studies, with a greater or less quantity of unconnected, undigested facts, thrown crudely into the memory, as 'information.' What are usually called 'the English branches' come first – reading, spelling, writing, arithmetic, geography, English grammar, history. Girls are commonly supposed to be deficient in spelling, but we are told that they spell, on the whole, better than boys. Mr Parker, Fellow of Oxford, says that 'if bad spelling, bad grammar, and bad style in English translations were taken into strict account' at matriculation examinations, 'the number of failures would be much increased.' A wider range of reading is needed to improve spelling, which, in a language like ours, is only well learned by the eye. In arithmetic a great change is necessary. This is not only a subject of the utmost practical value in after-life, but it is the first presented to the mind which will task and exercise its powers, and should be taught to girls with particular energy and accuracy, because at present it is the only subject habitually included which compels mental exertion. Treated as a science, not as a mechanical art, its new aspect would repel none but the utterly lazy. The same process would rescue grammar from its present unsatisfactory position. It is usually begun too early, and taught unintelligently. Some knowledge of the English language, and of some other, is required to comprehend grammatical principles, and rules without principles are of little use. Care to prevent solecisms in reading, composition, etc., is enough till the pupil knows something of a second language, comparison being the only certain guide in learning grammar. By geography is generally meant only political geography. Each country is looked at by itself, and the information given is deprived of half its value from its isolation. Physical geography ought to be included, and so much geology as to make it intelligible. History is popular, but it is far too much broken, it being not uncommon to have two or more portions of history in hand at once. Second-rate manuals are also used. The history of one division of time, or of one country, should be learned at once, and that thoroughly, and from a really good author. If so arranged, there is no subject more interesting, or more likely to enlighten and refine the mind.

But something more is needful. Arithmetic and grammar are the only means of real mental exertion yet named, and the latter is as yet incomplete. We look round, therefore, and find that no instrument seems so likely to do the work we want done as the study of Latin. It is generally conceded that the acquisition of at least one language besides our own is a part of all education above the elementary. We cannot rightly understand grammar without it; we do not know the power or the weakness of words without it; whilst there is probably nothing so well adapted to carry the mind fairly beyond our own contracted circle as a knowledge of the thoughts, and the modes of expressing thought, of those who were made of one blood with ourselves, but removed from us in space and time. The French language has its own advantages, and ought not to lose the place it has gained; but is rather useful for conversational purposes, and for the sake of the scientific literature which it contains, than for training. One special argument in favour of Latin is, that there is a large body of well-educated men competent to teach it; and this can hardly be said of anything else, except, perhaps, mathematics. Mr Bryce says: 'Latin is at present the only subject taught with thoroughness.' It thus affords the discipline that we are seeking, especially as the other valuable qualities which attach to the study of language are here found in perfection. We believe that primary instruction in Latin should form an integral part of the education of all. But for those who can continue their course till they are eighteen or twenty years of age, the higher study of Latin brings another advantage. It not only opens up much of ancient literature, but it gives an important clue to the right understanding of the history and literature of modern times; and it renders possible one of the most fascinating of all pursuits, that of philology, which, however valuable, cannot be pursued far in ignorance of Latin.

Some will be alarmed at the suggestion of Greek as a portion of the highest curriculum for girls of the middle classes; but for those who have leisure and vigour of mind, it is well worth consideration whether it ought not to be included in their studies. As a language it is even finer than Latin; to some minds its structure presents fewer difficulties; much of its literature is the grandest this earth has seen.

Language is the first of the humanistic studies, and opens the gates for the next, that of literature. Arnold says of it: 'The study of language seems to me as if it was given for the very purpose of forming the human mind in youth.'

We have already alluded to the special use to be made of French. But wherever it seems likely that girls cannot remain sufficiently long at school to acquire a competent knowledge of any other language, French should be so taught as to include some comparative grammar and philology.

German has a higher value than French, both as a study, and as an introduction to a large part of high-class modern literature.

It seems singular that when speaking of the value of the study of language, our own should follow instead of leading. Our very familiarity with it seems to prevent our proper appreciation of it. As to its structure, and idiomatic peculiarities, they can only be learned by comparison; this systematic study of English, therefore, should go along with the acquisition of another tongue; either Latin or German is best. The analysis of sentences helps the pupil to clearness of thought and precision of language. Composition is essential to a right knowledge of English, as well as to gaining power of expression, but its most forcible claim is its effect in showing the pupil what she really knows, or does not know; how far her ideas correspond to realities, or are clouded with vague fancies, for the saying is still true, that it is 'writing' which makes 'exactness.' Original composition should therefore be required early and late, and carried on constantly and carefully. It is needful, however, that the subjects for themes should be better chosen than they often are. They cannot be too simple and definite to begin with; whilst frequent practice will enable the pupil to express thoughts with accuracy as well as elegance.

The literature of our own language has been too little studied at school. It should certainly be so examined as to awaken an appreciative love for it. The field is too vast for more to be attempted than a sketch of its history and development, with its divisions and their characteristics, and the thorough study of some one or two representative authors. This will stimulate the spirit of self-culture in after years; a thing of unspeakable importance to women, whose often uneventful lives render them peculiarly susceptible to the influences of the books they read.

The opposite side of mental activity to that evoked by language and literature, is that evoked by science. The mind needs both – and, in fact, the humblest education should give a portion of both, while in the higher each should have an ample space. Mathematics are not only the basis for other sciences, but are themselves the best fitted to educate the reasoning faculties, and to erect a standard of fixed law in the mind. This study offers peculiar advantages for the correction of the mental errors to which the neglect of real culture has made women liable, and should form a part of *every* curriculum, its elements at least being taught in all but the merely primary schools.

Wherever the course is so extended as to leave time for it, something should be learned of the sciences founded on mathematics. But all young people should study some one of the natural sciences, for the cultivation of habits of observation and patient investigation, qualities which will be most useful in after-life. The study of logic, and of political economy, are also valuable, not only for mental exercise, but the latter especially for the practical information conveyed.

There still remain to be noticed the two subjects of music and drawing. Music – that is, instrumental music, for singing, though more really useful, gets less attention – is usually allowed to occupy an enormous proportion of a girl's time, without the slightest reference to her tastes or abilities. For those whose talents lie in a certain direction, music is the best form of refined pleasure; but this is attainable without the sacrifice of time necessary to be a brilliant performer. Brilliance is in fact rarely attained by any but those who possess special musical talent. Of course, it is desirable to give all a trial, but a year or two at most is sufficient to test musical capacity. It seems probable that not more than one-third of the young ladies in question should learn more than the outlines of music. The likelihood is that, with less practice but more mental power, the results achieved will not fall short of those now arrived at. A lady, in answer to one of the queries of the school commissioners, seems to have suggested the right solution: 'that music ought to be learned by all as a *study*, by the exceptional few as an *accomplishment*.' For any who have not marked musical talent, the pleasure is too small to be bought at so high a price; for it is the time swallowed up by 'practising' that is the great obstacle to the introduction of subjects which have a direct influence upon the character. Fashion is the idol which insists on this sacrifice. But, as grave studies form the most pleasing characters, public opinion is gradually rectifying itself on this point.

Drawing is not so great a difficulty, for it does not absorb nearly so much time as music; and as fashion is less imperative about it, girls without any taste for it will acknowledge the fact, which they are ashamed to do respecting music. It is even more empirically taught, however. The principles of art should always form a topic of instruction.

It is not meant by suggesting so many subjects that any section of students should attack them all; but it is meant that all should be within reach, so that each mind may find the nurture that suits it.

After the earlier studies have been mastered it may be needful to make a choice of plans. Two or three different courses of study should be arranged, corresponding to the amount of time and money which can be spent. The same principles must be kept in view in each curriculum; each must contain something adapted to strengthen and shape the mind, and something to draw out the natural powers; each must have its literary and its scientific side.

A re-distribution of subjects is a reform imperatively called for. Some are taken up too early – as a rule, those which exercise the memory, with some which cultivate the imagination, and the elements of such robuster subjects as are strictly progressive in their character, should come first. Again, in the more advanced classes, too many subjects are learned at once, and in a broken and disconnected manner. If two or three of the more important are taken at one time (those which make less demand on the mind going on also) and thoroughly learned, a little attention will keep these in mind during the next year or two, when another group is similarly obtaining close and special study. Everything which requires sustained attention should be learned daily whilst it is in hand. No young mind can carry a clear recollection and fresh interest in each lesson over an interval of several days with other things coming in between to distract it. If the plan can be adopted of keeping to one group of subjects at a time, there will be no need for this disheartening confusion.

Next to the obtaining of good teachers, and having a sufficient number of them, the most important thing in actual teaching is to use really good books. Those in general use in ladies' schools are very poor. It is better to take a thoroughly good book, though it was never intended for a school-book, and though it may be in parts beyond the scholars, than to put up with a bald or slovenly manual. A thoughtful book can be explained by a teacher who is fit to teach; or the parts too deep for the pupils can be omitted, and they can be told when to recur to these. Anything is better than the catechism or catalogue style of text-book.

More use ought to be made of examinations, both oral and written. Nothing else can secure that what has been gone over is really comprehended by the pupil. Written examinations in particular are the most thorough test of progress. They ought to be frequent, in all the chief branches of study; thus ascertaining, week by week, and month by month, what mastery over facts has really been obtained, what principles have been grasped, or where there has been failure, and what are the causes of it.

The organisation of institutions for girls' education is the next point for consideration. But the very phrase goes to the root of one of the great difficulties in this matter. For girls of the lower classes, we have schools in each of the British islands, all more or less aided, inspected, and directed by the State. The mistresses, as well as the masters, for these schools also undergo a regular training under government superintendence, and their status and abilities are measured by carefully-bestowed certificates. So far the two sexes are alike; but on looking higher all is changed. While an elaborate network of important establishments for boys and young men, of varied forms, but all acting and re-acting on one another, cover the face of the country, we have only a few scattered and experimental attempts at anything of the sort for girls.

Some remedial agencies are already at work. Of these the most important are the middle-class examinations instituted by the universities. It would be difficult to overrate the good done by the extension of these examinations to girls and women. They have presented a methodical plan of study to conscientious parents and teachers, and have offered a standard to work up to, and a means of proving wherein lies strength and weakness. They also provide a test by which good schools and good teaching may be distinguished from bad.

This test, however, only brings into greater relief the defects of the usual arrangements for teaching. We are going to the root of the matter by insisting upon better schools. Now the preponderant weight of evidence goes to show that morally, mentally, and even socially, large schools are (other things being equal) incomparably better than small. The schools commissioners say –

A special cause of the inferiority in girls' schools, that they are commonly too small, has been noticed above. It is not only that it tends to multiply the number of them unduly, and that it increases the cost, but that, as is well known, small schools are in themselves, as instruments of instruction, commonly inferior to larger ones. A large school can be better classified. . . . In a small school one master must teach several subjects; in a large school each subject of importance may have its proper teachers. Nor are the moral less than the intellectual advantages of a large school. It is easier to create a healthy public opinion. . . . It is easier to neutralise the bad effect of one or two unprincipled scholars. In a small school the classes are too small to rouse emulation, or that other and better feeling which is sometimes confounded with emulation, the sympathy of numbers. Add to this, the pettiness and gossip of the small private school, the more serious evils which are said to prevail in so many boarding-schools, where a girl is at the mercy of her companions, are far more hurtful than such little measure of freedom as is implied in resorting to a public day-school.

From what has been said, it will be seen that boarding-schools are considered as a rule to be less suitable than day-schools as places of education.

'Assuming, as we may fairly do,' say the commissioners, 'that the homes of our middle-class are commonly favourable to the growth and development of the female character, we are ourselves inclined to the opinion, which also appears somewhat to preponderate in the evidence, that in the case of girls more than in that of boys, the combination of school teaching with home influence, such as day-schools admit of, is the most promising arrangement.'

These opinions tend directly to show that it is most desirable to establish large day-schools, of the highest grade, in every considerable town.

This is not the place for entering upon the history of the endowed schools of England. But it is known that many of the endowments were originally intended as much for girls as for boys, and some of these were very wealthy. Here, therefore, is a most important fund, from which could be obtained the necessary means for establishing some of these central schools. Good buildings and sufficient apparatus, good rooms and grounds for recreation, a fund for prizes and scholarships, for payment of examiners, and for keeping up the buildings and apparatus, would start a good school in any suitable locality; especially if the grant were supplemented, as it ought to be, by local subscriptions. Having this excellent *point d'appui*, a first-class principal would have no difficulty in making such an institution worthy of public confidence. University examinations must be made obligatory on such schools. The public would have an interest in them, and some arrangements would be advisable by which influential persons in the neighbourhood, whether appointed by Government or elected by subscribers, should have a share in the management. An ample staff of first-class teachers could be secured in so large a school with lower fees than would be possible in a small school. This economy is of the utmost consequence in arranging for the middle classes; for refinement of thought and desire for culture are by no means measured by income. These large schools would themselves supply a felt want, and they would also do inestimable good by their action on private schools. At present no person or body, however venerable, has a right to inquire where the ladies of the country are educated. By the proposed plan there would be a number of leading schools which the State, by means of the universities, could examine and regulate; and the moral authority of this vivifying and enlightening influence would affect all teaching arrangements.

The need for improvement in the status and qualifications of teachers is the next point we must notice. There can be no doubt that the unintelligent views of education, which have long prevailed, are the cause of that unjust depreciation of teachers from which we have by no means cleared ourselves as yet. There are grades in the teaching profession, as there are grades amongst pupils; but what profession can be accounted liberal if not that which is to give liberal knowledge, and to create liberal tastes and feelings in the minds of the young. The truth is, we of the middle class have lowered ourselves in lowering our teachers.

The acknowledgment, therefore, of the teaching profession as a liberal profession, to be prepared for with the same care and elevation of aim as any other, applies as strictly to ladies who shall adopt it, as to gentlemen. Here, however, with even more force than in any other case, the rule must be observed that professional training shall not even begin till a very broad and sure foundation of solid culture is laid. In other words, that (as in our liberal professions) a university education, or something as nearly as possible corresponding to it, shall *precede* any special training in the art of teaching. If teaching is to be a liberal art, there must be no separation between its students and others. Isolation is the very death of enlightened culture. We are thus brought to the conclusion that the best preparation for the higher teaching which we desire, is that future schoolmistresses and governesses shall receive their education in the same colleges in which girls of the higher and middle classes pursue their advanced studies, with the object of entering upon those liberal occupations which are opening their doors to them, or of cultivating those talents which will render home life more useful as well as more pleasing.

NOTE

1 Sometimes the parents are vigilant in the wrong direction, like one who, on sending his boy to school, wrote to the head-master, 'I desire that Tom shall learn neither geometry, geology, nor geography!'

Mary E. Beedy

The Joint Education of Young Men and Women in American Schools and Colleges

(1873)

The American colonists carried with them their practical English tendencies. They were impressed with a deep sense of the advantages of education, but it had to be got at the least expense.

In the towns and cities they could have schools for boys and schools for girls, but in the sparsely-populated rural districts separate schools were impossible. It was almost more than the farmers could do to pay the cost of one. All the boys and girls within a radius of two or three miles met together in the same school. They were companions and rivals in their pastimes, and it probably did not occur to any one to consider whether there could be any danger in continuing this rivalry in their lessons. In the rapid growth of the population some of these rural centres gradually became villages and towns, but the joint education of the girls and boys went on.

Two leading principles in school economy are, to secure the smallest number of classes, and the greatest equality of attainment between the pupils in each class; and these principles favour large schools rather than numerous schools. Schools affording a higher grade of instruction, and known as academies, sprang up here and there. These were private enterprises, and the commercial aim was to furnish the best educational advantages for the largest number of pupils at the least expense. The teacher wanted to make as much money as he could, and the parents had in general but little to spend for the education of their sons and daughters. The same economical views made these joint schools: fewer teachers were required. These academies, with the district schools I have before

248

mentioned, met almost the entire educational demands of the rural and village population. A few of the more ambitious boys went from these academies to the universities, and a few of the girls went to young ladies' boarding-schools; but these were exceptional cases.

You probably know that we have no men of wealth and leisure living in the country. The soil is owned by the men who work it, and the rich men live in the cities. And I suppose you also know that in any generation of American men the large majority of those who lead in commerce, in politics, and in the professions are the sons of farmers who in their boyhood worked on the farms and went to these rural schools in the leisure season; the wives of these men having had for the most part the same rural training. You can readily see from this that the peculiarities of our rural life, the circumstances that gave these men and women the energy to bring themselves to the front rank of society, were likely to meet with approval. However, joint education was simply looked upon as one of the necessities of our youthful life till about twenty years ago. Men who rose to positions of wealth and honour upon the basis of the education received in these schools did not praise joint education any more than they praised the other natural and frugal habits that attended their rural life. No one had philosophised upon this system, and there was no occasion to think of it. It had simply been the most natural means of meeting a great need. In both the district schools and in the academies the boys and girls did about the same work. They liked to keep together. Now and then a boy went a little farther in mathematics than the girls did, in the prospect of a business career and a life in the city; or he learned more Latin and Greek in preparation for the university. There was no question about difference of capacity or difference of tastes between boys and girls; there was nothing to suggest it. They liked to do the same things, and the one did as well as the other. Forty years ago, in one of the academies near Boston, a number of girls went with a set of their schoolboy-friends through the entire preparation for Harvard University. The girls knew mathematics and Greek as well as the boys did, and formed a plan for going to the university with them. I cannot say whether the plan grew out of a keen zest for knowledge, or out of an unwillingness to break off the very pleasant companionship. Probably from both. The girls did not think there could be much objection to admitting them at the university. They thought the reason there were no girls at the universities was that none had wanted to go, or had been prepared to go. They proposed to live at home; so there would be no difficulty on the score of college residence. However, as their request was new, it occurred to them that a little diplomacy might be required in presenting it; so they deputed the most prudent of the party to do the talking, and imposed strict silence upon the youngest and most impulsive one, from whom I have the story. The girls called upon old President Quincy; they told him what they had done in their studies – that they had passed the examinations with the boys, and wished to be admitted to the university. He listened to their story, and evinced so much admiration for their work and aims that they at first felt sure of success. But President Quincy seemed slow in coming to the point. He talked of the newness and difficulties of the scheme, and proposed other opportunities of study for them, till at length this youngest one, forgetting in her impatience her promise to keep silent, said, 'Well, President Quincy, you feel sure the trustees will let us come, don't you?' 'O, by no means,' was the reply: 'this is a place only for men.' The girl of sixteen burst into tears, and exclaimed with vehemence, 'I wish I could annihilate the women and let the men have everything to themselves!'

This, so far as I know, was the first effort made by women to get into an American university, but the incident was too trifling to make any impression, and I narrate it only as marking the beginning of the demand for university advantages for women. About the same time Oberlin College was founded in Northern Ohio. It grew out of a great practical everyday-life demand. There was a wide-spread desire on the part of well-to-do people for larger educational advantages than the ordinary rural schools provided. They could not afford the expense of the city schools: besides, they wanted their sons and daughters to go on together in their school work; they were unwilling to subject either to the dangers of boarding-school life without the companionship and guardianship of the other. Oberlin College was founded on the strictest principles of economy. It was located in a rural village in the West, where the habits were simple and the living inexpensive. In the third year of its existence it had 500 students, and since the first ten years it has averaged nearly 1,200, the proportion of young women varying from one-third to one-half. There was a university course of study for the young men, and a shorter ladies' course for the young women, which omitted all the Greek, most of the Latin, and the higher mathematics. It was not anticipated that the young women would desire the extended university course, but so far as the two courses accorded the instruction was given to the young men and the young women in common. But the young women were allowed to attend any of the classes they chose, and at the end of six years a few of them had prepared themselves for the B.A. examination, and were allowed upon passing it to receive the degree.

The college authorities did not seem to consider that B.A. and M.A. were especially masculine designations. They regarded them only as marks of scholastic attainments, which belonged equally to men and women when they had reached a certain standard of scholarship. Not many women could stay, or cared to stay, long enough to get these degrees. The 'ladies' course' required nearly two years' less time, and contained a larger proportion of the subjects that women are expected to know. The number of women who have received the university degrees from Oberlin is still less than a hundred, making an average of only two or three for each year. Oberlin sent out staunch men and women. Wherever these men and women went it was observed that they worked with a will and with effect. The eminent success of Oberlin led many parents in different parts of the country to desire its advantages for their sons and daughters. But Oberlin was a long way off from New England and from many other parts of the country; besides some thought it an uncomfortably religious place; negroes were admitted, and it was altogether very democratic, much more so than many people liked. So parents began to say, 'Why can't we have other colleges that shall provide all the advantages of Oberlin and omit the peculiarities we dislike.' Now began the discussion upon the real merits of this economical system of joint education. It had sprung up like an indigenous plant. It had met a necessity remarkably well, and it was only when, its advantages becoming recognised, it began to press itself into the cities and among people where it was not a necessity, that it evoked any discussion. This was a little more than twenty years ago. People who had observed the working of the joint schools were altogether in favour of them. The wealthier people in the towns and cities, who were accustomed to having boys and girls educated apart, preferred separate schools, and thought joint education would be a dangerous innovation; that in the institution adopting it the girls would lose their modesty and refinement, and the boys would waste their time. Leading educators were divided upon this question: those who were familiar with the joint schools were the most uncompromising advocates of that system; those who had known only the schools where girls and boys were educated apart for the most part preferred separate education, where it could be afforded. Not all, however, for many had developed the theory of joint education out of an opposite experience. In girls' schools they had felt the want of adequate stimulants for thorough work. They had seen the strong tendency in girls to fit themselves for society rather than for the severer duties of life; they believed that if girls were associated with boys and young men in their studies, they would not only be better scholars, but that they would remain longer in school, that they would have less eagerness to get out of school into society. And many who were familiar with boys' schools felt the dangers attendant upon the absence of domestic influence, and saw that it might be very largely supplied by the presence of sisters and schoolfellows' sisters. They saw too that the tendencies to a coarse physical development, which are found in an exclusive society of men, might be counteracted by the presence of women. In short, all who were acquainted with joint education gave it their most unqualified approval; while those who knew only the system of separate education were for the most part disposed to favour that, though many of these saw the need of something in girls' schools which the presence of boys would introduce, and something in boys' schools which the presence of girls would supply. The advocacy of joint education was valiantly led by Horace Mann, the greatest American educator, the man who stands with us where Dr Arnold stands in the hearts of English people.

About this time Antioch College was founded in Southern Ohio, and Mr Mann was invited to take charge of it. Its object was to provide educational facilities as nearly equal to those found at the best New England universities as possible, and it was founded avowedly upon the principle that joint education *per se* was a good thing; that it was natural; that it was a great advantage to have brothers and sisters in the same school; that girls were both more scholarly and more womanly when associated with boys, and boys were more gentlemanly and more moral when associated with girls; and that both girls and boys come out of joint schools with juster views of life, and a larger sense of moral obligation.

Other new colleges followed the example of Antioch, and some of the old ones began to open their doors to women. Today the national free schools and public schools in most of the cities of the North educate boys and girls together. In some of the older cities, particularly Boston, New York, and Philadelphia, the schools are for the most part conducted on the original plan of separate schools. The school buildings are not arranged for the accommodation of boys and girls together, and there is still a strong sentiment against the plan, though it is gradually, and I may say rapidly, giving way. In the Western cities, Cincinnati, Chicago, and St Louis, the boys and girls study together throughout the entire course, that is, till they are ready to go to the universities; though in St Louis, and perhaps in the other two cities, there are a few of the grammar schools where they are still apart, the buildings not being arranged for the accommodation of both. The system prevails in the rural schools almost without exception, and almost as generally in the public schools of the towns and cities, with the exceptions that I have mentioned; there are now over thirty colleges and universities that offer university degrees to women on the same conditions as to men. On the other hand, there is still a large number of private schools in the towns and cities which are generally either boys' schools or girls' schools. They are for the most part schools established for teaching the children of some particular religious denomination, for fitting boys for a commercial career, or for giving especial drill for the universities; or, in the case of girls' schools, for giving especial training for society: but the public schools are rapidly drawing into them the children of the best educated families, for the simple reason that they are the best schools of the country.

The oldest universities and colleges still keep their doors shut against women. Harvard, within the last year, has appointed a committee to consider the demand made by women, but their report was adverse. The committee recognised the success of the system elsewhere, but thought it not wise to attempt the change in Harvard.

Michigan University, a free state university, which stands second to none in educational advantages, except Harvard and Yale, and has double the number of students of either of these, admitted women three years ago. And Cornell University, which has as good prospects as any in the country, has just received its first class of women.

I heard it announced with great gravity in the British Association a year-and-a-half ago in Edinburgh, that girls had no difficulty in learning arithmetic, and no one smiled. So completely is this question settled with us, that I think such an announcement would have been received by a public assembly in America with a derisive laugh. Joint schools and colleges have settled the question whether girls can learn not only arithmetic, but also the higher mathematics, logic, and metaphysics, and have established beyond a doubt in the minds of American educators, that in acute perception, in the ability to grasp abstruse principles, the feminine mind is in no wise inferior to the masculine. But the question is still open, whether women have the physical strength to endure the continuous mental work requisite for the greatest breadth and completeness of comprehension. This can be determined only by experiments which shall extend through a longer series of years devoted to study. The records at Oberlin indicate that the young women are no more likely to break down in health than the young men are.

The records of the city schools do not seem to be quite the same upon this point, but the same difference would doubtless appear if the girls were not in school; and this failure in health cannot be attributed to the school work, but rather to the more indoor life of the girls. The Oberlin statistics also indicate that the women who have taken the university degrees have not diminished their chance of longevity by this severe work in their youth. Women have less physical strength than men have, but there seems to be in them a tendency to a more economical expenditure of strength. Their energy is less driving, and there is, in consequence, less waste from friction.

In regard to the social morality at these schools the results are equally satisfactory. At the rural schools boys and girls have almost unrestricted companionship; they have just the same freedom in their home intercourse, but improper or even objectionable conduct is a thing unknown at the schools, and almost equally unknown in the association outside the schools. Brothers and brothers' friends guard the sister, and sisters and their friends guard the brother. In cases where it is necessary for the pupils to reside at the school there is more love-making, but it is mostly repressed by want of time; besides, there are few occasions for meeting, except in the presence of the class, and where there is an acquaintance with so many on about equal terms an especial regard for one is less likely to be formed. The admiration of the boys is sure to centre upon the girls who are nearest the head of the class; but these girls have not time to return it and keep their position, and to lose their position would be to lose the admiration; and the same is true with the boys.

I am sure it would be surprising to any one who is not familiar with these schools to observe to what very practical and common-sense principles all these otherwise romantic and illusory relations are subjected. In this mutual intellectual rivalship the conjectural differences between the sexes, and the fancied charms of the one over the other, are submitted to very practical tests. A disagreeable boy is not likely to be considered a hero in virtue of his assumed bearing and physical strength; nor is a silly girl, by dint of her coquettish airs likely to be thought a fairy with magical gifts. Girls know boys as boys know each other; and boys know girls as girls know each other. Hence the subtle charms that evade human logic find little opportunity to blind and mislead in the constant presence of unmistakeable facts.

In all the time I was at Antioch College no word of disreputable scandal ever came to my ears, and in recent years I have repeatedly heard from young men who were there when I was, that in their whole five or six years they never heard the faintest shadow of imputation against any young woman in the institution. And so stern was the morality, that smoking, beer-drinking, and card-playing were all considered crimes, and banished from the premises.

You have now heard my statement respecting the effectiveness of joint education, and, though it is made from a very extended and thorough acquaintance with the system, I shall not ask you to accept it without the support of other and authoritative testimony. Abundant confirmation of my statement will be found in all Official Reports and in treatises that review this system, while no testimony of a contrary character is anywhere to be found. I will first quote from the published Report of Mr Harris, Superintendent of the Public Schools in St Louis. He is well known to the leading students of German philosophy in all the countries of Europe, and I think I may say in his own country is recognised as standing in the front rank of American educators. No other man has brought so much philosophical insight to the study of our public school system. I quote from Mr Harris's Report of 1871 a condensed summary of the results of this system of joint education as they have developed themselves under his observation and direction. He says:

Within the last fifteen years the schools of St Louis have been remodelled upon the plan of the joint education of the sexes, and the results have proved so admirable that a few remarks may be ventured on the experience which they furnish.

I. – Economy has been secured, for, unless pupils of widely different attainments are brought together in the same classes, the separation of the boys and girls requires a great increase in the number of teachers.

II. – Discipline has improved continually by the adoption of joint schools; our change in St Louis has been so gradual that we have been able to weigh with great exactness every point of comparison between the two systems. The joining of the male and female departments of a school has always been followed by an improvement in discipline; not merely on the part of the boys, but with the girls as well. The rudeness and *abandon* which prevails among boys when separate at once gives place to self-restraint in the presence of girls, and the sentimentality engendered in girls when educated apart from boys disappears in these joint schools, and in its place there comes a dignified self-possession. The few schools that have given examples of efforts to secure clandestine association are those few where there are as yet only girls.

III. – The quality of instruction is improved. Where the boys and girls are separate, methods of instruction tend to extremes, that may be called masculine and feminine. Each needs the other as a counter-check. We find in these joint schools a prevalent healthy tone which our schools on the separate system lack – more rapid progress is the consequence.

IV. – The development of individual character is, as already indicated, far more sound and healthy. It has been found that schools composed exclusively of girls or boys require a much more strict surveillance on the part of the teachers. Confined by themselves and shut off from intercourse with society in its normal form, morbid fancies and interests are developed which this daily association in the class-room prevents. Here boys and girls test themselves with each other on an intellectual plane. Each sees the strength and weakness of the other, and learns to esteem those qualities that are of true value. Sudden likes, capricious fancies, and romantic ideas give way to sober judgments not easily deceived by mere externals. This is the basis of the dignified self-possession before alluded to, and it forms a striking point of contrast between the girls and boys educated in joint schools and those educated in schools exclusively for one sex. Our experience in St Louis has been entirely in favour of the joint education of the sexes, in all the respects mentioned and in many minor ones.

I give Mr Harris's statement as representative of the sentiment of those who are engaged in public school instruction in America. As I said before, in some of the older cities, where the public schools were earliest organised, the joint system has been accepted as yet only partially, and the teachers, who are only familiar with the separate system, generally prefer it. But a very large proportion of the public schools of the country are joint schools, and a still larger proportion of the instructors and managers of public schools favour the system of joint education. Mr Harris's testimony applies to city schools, when the pupils reside at home.

I now quote to you from another authority, additionally valuable inasmuch as it represents the results of this system of education upon young men and women who reside at the school and away from the guardianship of parents.

In 1868 a meeting was called of all the College Presidents of the country, to discuss questions relating to college discipline and instruction. As Oberlin was the oldest college that had adopted the system of joint instruction, a strong desire was felt to secure a critical and comprehensive statement of the results of the system there. Dr Fairchild, the present President of Oberlin, was deputed to make the Report. He had at that time been connected with Oberlin seven years as a student and twenty-five years as professor, and has long had the reputation of being the most accomplished scholar and acute thinker among the Oberlin professors. His statements may therefore be accepted as absolute in point of fact, and as wholly representative of the opinion of those who have conducted the instruction and discipline at Oberlin. But my chief reason for selecting this out of the accumulated published testimony is that it seems to me the best digest of the subject that I have seen.

Dr Fairchild says:

1st. On the point of economy: In the higher departments of instruction, where the chief expense is involved, the expense is no greater on account of the presence of the ladies.

2nd. Convenience to the patrons of the school: It is a matter of interest to notice the number of cases where a brother is followed by a sister, or a sister by a brother. This is an interesting and prominent feature in our work. Each is safer in the presence of the other.

3rd. The wholesome incitements to study, which the system affords: The social influence arising from the constitution of our classes operates continuously and upon all. Each desires for himself the best standing he is capable of, and there is no lack of motive to exertion. It will be observed, too, that the stimulus is of the same kind as will operate in after life. The young man going out into the world does not leave behind him the forces that have helped him on. They are the ordinary forces of society.

4th. The tendency to good order that we find in the system: The ease with which the discipline of so large a school is conducted has not ceased to be a matter of wonder to ourselves. More than one thousand students are gathered from every State in the Union, from every class in society, of every grade of culture, the great mass of them bent on improvement, but numbers are sent by anxious friends with the hope that they may be saved or reclaimed from every evil tendency. Yet the disorders incident to such gatherings are essentially unknown among us. Our streets are as quiet by day and by night as in any other country town. This result we attribute greatly to the wholesome influence of the system of joint education. College tricks lose their attractiveness in a community thus constituted. They scarcely appear among us. We have had no difficulty in reference to the conduct and manners in the college dining-hall. There is an entire absence of the irregularities and roughness so often complained of in the college commons.

5th.　Another manifest advantage is the relation of the school to the community. A cordial feeling of goodwill and the absence of that antagonism between town and college which in general belongs to the history of universities and colleges. The constitution of the school is so similar to that of the community that any conflict is unnatural; the usual provocation seems to be wanting.

6th.　It can hardly be doubted that people educated under such conditions are kept in harmony with society at large, and are prepared to appreciate the responsibilities of life, and to enter upon its work. If we are not utterly deceived in our position, our students naturally and readily find their position in the world, because they have been trained in sympathy with the world. These are among the advantages of the system that have forced themselves upon our attention. The list might be extended and expanded, but you will wish especially to know whether we have not encountered disadvantages and difficulties which more than counterbalance these advantages.

As to the question whether young ladies have the mental vigour and physical health to maintain a fair standing in a class with young men, I must say, where there has been the same preparatory training, we find no difference in ability to maintain themselves in the class-room and at the examinations. The strong and the weak scholars are equally distributed between the sexes.

Whether ladies need a course of study specially adapted to their nature and prospective work? – The theory of our school has never been that men and women are alike in mental constitution, or that they naturally and properly occupy the same position in their work of life. The education furnished is general, not professional, designed to fit men and women for any position or work to which they may properly be called. The womanly nature will appropriate the material to its own necessities under its own laws. Young men and women sit at the same table and partake of the same food, and we have no apprehension that the vital forces will fail to elaborate from the common material the osseous, fibrous, and nervous tissues adapted to each frame and constitution.

Apprehension is felt that character will deteriorate on the one side or the other – that young men will become frivolous or effeminate, and young women coarse and masculine.

That young men should lose their manly attributes and character from proper association with cultivated young women is antecedently improbable and false in fact. It is the natural atmosphere for the development of the higher qualities of manhood – magnanimity, generosity, true chivalry, and earnestness. The animal man is kept subordinate in the prevalence of these higher qualities.

We have found it the surest way to make men of boys and gentlemen of rowdies.

On the other hand, will not the young woman, pursuing her studies with young men, take on their manners, and aspirations, and aims, and be turned aside from the true ideal of womanly life and character? The thing is scarcely conceivable. The natural response of woman to the exhibition of manly traits is in the correlative qualities of gentleness, delicacy, and grace.

It might better be questioned whether the finer shadings of woman's character can be developed without this natural stimulus; but it is my duty not to reason, but to speak from the limited historical view assigned me.

You wish to know whether the result with us has been a large accession to the number of coarse, strong-minded women, in the disagreeable sense of the word; and I say, without hesitation, that I do not know a single instance of such a product as the result of our system of education.

Is there not danger that young men and young women thus brought together in the critical period of life, when the distinctive social tendencies act with greatest intensity, will fail of the necessary regulative force, and fall into undesirable and unprofitable relations? Will not such association result in weak and foolish love affairs? It is not strange that such apprehension is felt, nor would it be easy to give an *a priori* answer to such difficulties; but if we may judge from our experience, the difficulties are without foundation. The danger in this direction results from excited imagination, from the glowing exaggerations of youthful fancy, and the best remedy is to displace these fancies by every-day facts and realities.

The young man shut out from the society of ladies, with the help of the high-wrought representations of life which poets and novelists afford, with only a distant vision of the reality, is the one who is in danger. The women whom he sees are glorified by his fancy, and are wrought into his day dreams and night dreams as beings of supernatural loveliness. It would be different if he met them day by day in the classroom, in a common encounter with a mathematical problem, or at a table sharing in the common want of bread and butter. There is still room for the fancy to work, but the materials for the picture are more reliable and enduring. Such association does not take all the romance out of life, but it gives as favourable conditions for sensible views and actions upon these delicate questions as can be afforded to human nature.

But is this method adapted to schools in general, or is the success attained at Oberlin due to peculiar features of the place, which can rarely be found or reproduced elsewhere, and can it be introduced into men's colleges with their traditional customs and habits of action and thought? Might not the changes required occasion difficulty at the outset and peril the experiment? On this point I have no experience, but I have such confidence in the inherent vitality and adaptability of the system that I should be entirely willing to see it subjected to this test.

I am sorry not to give you a more lengthened account of Dr Fairchild's Report, but the time warns me to hasten.

Respecting economy, school discipline, social order, and the improved character of both young men and young women, and the high scholarship attained by young women, you see that Dr Fairchild's statement fully corroborates my own and that of Mr Harris. He agrees with us that the grade of scholarship of the young men is in no wise lowered by this joint work, but, on the contrary, that the average is higher.

To be definite upon this point, my own opinion is that those marvellous feats of scholarship that sometimes occur in boys' schools are not so likely to occur in a joint school, where a little more of the domestic and social element is found. On the other hand, from a long and close observation, I feel fully justified in saying the average scholarship is higher. There is a more general stimulus for good scholarship. The standard of respectability is somewhat different from what it is in a school exclusively for boys. A boy may secure the respect of his boy-associates by being an adept on the playground or generally a good fellow, but as he is known to the girls only through his class work, he feels more especially bound to make this creditable.

I should like to accumulate authority upon these points, but I must ask you to accept my statement that the opinions I have given you are those held by the very large majority of the educators of the country.

In this system of joint education you see that the difficulty of getting funds to establish schools scarcely appears as an obstacle to the higher education of women. It requires so little more to educate girls along with boys than it does to educate boys alone, and lack of the masculine incentive to study is largely supplied to the girls by class rivalry. The girls like to remain at school, and they like to do as much work and as good work as the boys do; and the boys are equally eager to keep the companionship of the girls, and to keep up the competition in all the departments of the work. There is a mutual rivalry which both enjoy, and the girls work with zest, without thinking whether there is to be any reward beyond the simple enjoyment of their work, without considering whether it will ever bring them any farther returns.

The work of the girls in the joint schools has done much to force up the standard in the exclusively girls' schools. These schools could not afford the disparaging comparison. So the teachers introduce the same studies as are found in the joint schools, and do the best they can to get as good work from their girls. But in most of the girls' schools I have ever visited, the work will not compare with the work of girls in the joint schools.

When Dr Fairchild says he does not know a single instance in which a coarse, strong-minded woman, in the disagreeable sense, has been the product of the Oberlin system of education, it must not be understood that there have been no women of that type at Oberlin, for there have been, and Oberlin has done much to soften them and refine them, but it could not wholly change their natures and previously-acquired habits. Upon this point there is a pernicious popular delusion, and I am at a loss to account for its origin. It is not association with men that developes this type of character. The reverse of this is the case, as Dr Fairchild has indicated. It is true that many highly-intellectual and highly-educated women have been peculiar, have developed peculiarities or idiosyncrasies of character or habit which lessened their companionable and womanly attractiveness, but these women have generally worked by themselves, away from society, apart from the companionship of men.

Joint schools are the most complete corrective of these tendencies. Whatever elevates women in the eyes of men they are disposed to cultivate in the presence of men, and whatever elevates men in the eyes of women they cultivate in the presence of women. There is little danger of careless toilet with young women who are constantly meeting young men; little danger of angular movement, of unamiable sharpness, of egotism, and pronounced self-assertion.

The disagreeable women, the women contemptuously called strong-minded, are women who have not known a genial social atmosphere. Crotchety men and crotchety women are the product of isolation from society, and formerly women could not mount the heights of knowledge except in isolation. The attractive women, the women who seem to have a genius for womanliness, are the women who have been much in the society of men – women at court, women in political and diplomatic circles, women who are familiar with the thought and experience of men, women who talk with men and work with men.

Social intercourse at these joint schools is not of course left to chance. Girls and boys need and get as careful attention at school as in their homes. Usually they enter and leave the school building by different doors, and indeed meet only when they are receiving instruction from the teachers, where they occupy separate forms on different sides of the room. Among the older pupils, at all times, except at the lecture hours, the girls usually have their own rooms and the boys theirs, and no communication between them is possible, except as the teachers choose to grant permission, which is not asked without explaining the occasion. The boys do not appear to care very much to talk to the girls, at least they would not be willing to have it seen that they did. At the boarding-schools the young men and young women usually have their private apartments in different buildings, but meet in a common dining-hall in the building occupied by the young women. Here they arrange themselves as they like, the size of the company and the presence of teachers being quite sufficient to exclude objectionable manners. At the times allowed for recreation the arrangements are such as to preclude for the most part opportunities for young men and young women to meet, though there are very frequent receptions at the homes of the professors or at the general parlours, when they meet as they would at any ordinary social party. At a few of the smaller boarding-schools much more freedom of intercourse has been allowed, and with very admirable results; but this requires great wisdom and care on the part of the teachers, more than they are generally able to give in a large school. Where the pupils live at home no very especial care is required on the part of the teachers, further than would under any circumstances be necessary to secure general good order.

This system of education developes self-reliance and a sense of responsibility, to such a degree that, as I quoted from Dr Fairchild, it is a constant surprise to see how little direction they need. A good many times while I was at Antioch College, young men who had got into disgrace, or had been dismissed from young men's colleges, were sent there to be reclaimed from their bad habits, and it is surprising what effect this home-like association had upon them.

I have already mentioned Michigan University as the best institution that has as yet opened its doors to women. This was done three years ago. For ten years the question had been pending before the trustees. A letter was addressed to Horace Mann, asking for minute information concerning the working of Antioch, and seeking counsel in reference to the advisability of attempting the same plan at the Michigan University. Mr Mann replied, that though he was an ardent advocate of joint education and was satisfied with the results achieved at Antioch, he should be afraid to attempt the plan in a large town, where college residence was not required. This letter settled the matter for the time. The trustees said: 'We cannot endanger the morality of our students, and the reputation of our institution, to accommodate the few women who wish to come. We give them our sympathy, but can at present do nothing more.' But every now and then, with the change of trustees, the question was revived. The men of this new rich State felt ashamed to do so much less for their daughters than for their sons, and they were particularly sensitive to the argument that the privileges of the institution could be extended to the young women with almost no increase in the expenses. Three years ago the opposition found itself in the minority, and a resolution was passed admitting women to all the classes of the university.

The dangers Horace Mann feared have not, and in all probability will not come. Even the young men, who in anticipation dreaded an invasion of women into their realm of free-and-easy habits, now unite in the most cordial approval of the plan. They find a genial element added to their college life in place of a chafing restraint.

The first year only one woman came into the Arts-classes. This bold venturer was the daughter of a deceased professor, by whom she had been trained up to a point a good deal in advance of the requisites for entrance. This enabled her to step at once into the front rank of the class of two hundred young men, who had been in the university a year before her. No sooner was she there than the dread and anticipated restraint on the part of the young men were forgotten, and the most chivalric feeling sprang up in its place.

For a whole year Miss Stockwell was alone in the Arts-classes among seven or eight hundred young men, yet nothing ever occurred to make her feel in the slightest degree uncomfortable. She took her B.A. degree last summer as the first Greek scholar in the university. There are now a hundred young women or more in the various departments of the university. The Professor of Civil Engineering has been in the habit of giving to his class every year a particular mathematical problem, a sort of *pons asinorum*, as a test of their ability. Not once during fifteen years had any member of the class solved it, though the professor states that during that time he has propounded it to fifteen hundred young men. Last year, as usual, the old problem was again presented to the class. A Miss White alone, of all the class, brought in the solution. The best student in the Law school last year was a woman.

I could tell you many other stories of the successes of women in these joint schools, but it would not be safe to conclude from these accounts that the young women in America are superior to the young men; for, as you would naturally suppose, the few women who at present avail themselves of university training, in opposition to the popular notion of what is wise and becoming, are for the most part above the average of the women of the country. I think I may say, however, that girls are a little more likely to lead the classes in the schools than boys are. They are, perhaps, a little more conscientious in doing the work assigned them, and have a little more school ambition.

I quote the following from the Annual Report of the Michigan University for the year ending 1872:

> In the Medical Department the women receive instruction by themselves. In the other departments all instruction is given to both sexes in common.
>
> It is manifestly not wise to leap to hasty generalisations from our short experience in furnishing education to both sexes in our university. But I think all who have been familiar with the inner life of the university for the past three years will admit that, thus far, no reason for doubting the wisdom

of the action of the trustees in opening the university to women has appeared.

Hardly one of the many embarrassments which some have feared have confronted us. The young women have addressed themselves to their work with great zeal, and have shown themselves quite capable of meeting the demands of severe studies as successfully as their classmates of the other sex. Their work, so far, does not evince less variety of aptitude or less power of grappling even with the higher mathematics than we find in the young men. They receive no favour, and desire none. They are subjected to precisely the same tests as the men. Nor does their work seem to put a dangerous strain upon their physical powers. Their absences by reason of illness do not proportionably exceed those of the men. Their presence has not called for the enactment of a single new law, nor for the slightest change in our methods of government or grade of work.

If we are asked still to regard the reception of women into our classes as an experiment, it must certainly be deemed a most hopeful experiment. The numerous inquiries that have been sent to us from various parts of this country, and even from England, concerning the results of their admission to the university, show that a profound and wide-spread interest in the subject has been awakened.

I can say for myself, that I have never known any one who has spent a few days at one of these colleges who has not become a convert to the scheme.

There is in America a strong and constantly growing conviction, that the best plan for educating both boys and girls is for them to reside at home and attend day schools; that this avoids the defects attendant upon the system of governesses and tutors, and also the dangers that are inherent in the congregated life of boarding-schools; and as American families seldom leave home for, at most, more than a few weeks in midsummer, this plan is easily carried out. In accordance with this conviction, the citizens of Boston have recently erected and endowed a large university in the centre of their city, although the time-honoured Harvard stands scarcely two miles beyond their precincts. The Boston University, which starts with larger available funds than those of Harvard, will be opened this autumn, and as a second step in the direction of the popular educational sentiment, the trustees have decided to offer its advantages and honours to young women on the same conditions as to young men.

Mary E. Beedy

There is evidently a disposition in America to open all lines of study to women, and a few women have entered each of the three learned professions, but the time is too short and the number too small for us to be able as yet to generalise upon the fitness of women for professions, or their inclination to choose them.

Most of our women – I think I may almost say all of our women – expect to marry, and most of them do marry. We have not that redundancy of women to trouble and puzzle the advocates of domesticity that you have here; and as fortunes are more easily made, men are not timid in incurring domestic responsibilities. As a consequence of this, the industrial occupations that women seek, other than domestic, are expected to be only temporary, and are such as may be entered upon without much especial professional training, and may be given up without involving much sacrifice of previous study or discipline. I think I may say there is a very general disposition to seek those that will especially contribute to their fitness for domestic life.

This brings me to a peculiar feature of American education – the prevalence of women teachers. In the public schools of St Louis there are forty men teachers and over four hundred women teachers; only about one-twelfth of the whole number are men, and this I think would be about the general average for the cities of the north. The primary schools are taught exclusively by women – most of the grammar schools have only a man at the head of them, and in the high schools there is about an equal number of men and women.

In two of the most successful grammar schools in St Louis there are only women teachers. Recent experiments in placing women at the head of several of the grammar schools in Cleveland, Ohio, give still stronger confirmation of the marked governing power of women as contrasted with men.

Women teachers have been employed in the schools in preference to men as a matter of economy, but underneath this cloak of economy an unexpected virtue has been found. It is now pretty well settled that with equal experience and scholarly attainments women teach better than men do, and that they manage the pupils with more tact; that is, they succeed in getting from the pupils what they want, with more ease and less disturbance of temper.

Where women do precisely the same work as men in teaching, they get less pay. Wages have followed the law of supply and demand. The guardians of the public school treasures have generally not felt at liberty to offer more than the regular market prices for work. But I am glad to say the more enlightened public feeling is beginning to make a change in this respect. A few women are paid men's wages – are paid what they ought to have, rather than what they could command in an open market.

Teaching in America, as I have indicated, is for the most part a temporary occupation; it is chiefly done by young people between the ages of eighteen and thirty who have no intention of making it a profession. The women marry and the men enter other occupations. How much the schools lose by the immaturity and inexperience of the teachers it is difficult to estimate accurately; but that they gain much by the freshness and enthusiasm of these young minds is inquestionable. Young teachers get into closer sympathy with pupils, and can more readily understand the movements of their minds and apprehend their difficulties.

The plan of teaching for a few years is very popular among young people, from the general belief that it furnishes the best possible discipline for a successful life. This experience in teaching is considered valuable for young men, but still more valuable for young women, and many young women who have no need to earn money teach for a few years after leaving school, sometimes from their own choice, but much oftener from the choice of their parents, who wish to supplement the daughter's education with the more varied discipline that teaching affords.

Thus the teaching of women is encouraged from four considerations:

First. According to the present arrangement of wages it is economical.

Second. Women seem to have an especial natural aptitude for the work as compared with men.

Third. The general welfare of society demands that wage-giving industries shall be provided for women.

Fourth. Of all the employments offered to women, teaching seems the best suited to fit them for domestic life, the life that lies before the most of them, and so positive are its claims in this direction that it is being sought as an employment with that single end in view.

A few years of teaching forms so prominent a feature in the education of leading American women, that I could not omit it in any general consideration of this subject.

Note 1 – *The Times* of 3 January 1874, gives the following extracts from 'Circulars of Information,' just published by the United States Bureau of Education: The total number of degrees conferred in 1873 by the Higher Colleges was 4,493, and 376 honorary. One hundred and ninety-one ladies received degrees. Illinois has thirteen Colleges, in which women have the same or equal facilities with men; Wisconsin has four, Iowa three, Missouri four, Ohio ten, and Indiana nine; New York has seven, and Pennsylvania seven.

Sophia Jex-Blake

The Medical Education of Women

(1873)

In the very short time at my command I shall not attempt any exhaustive discussion of the primary question which lies at the root of my subject – the question, namely, whether it is, or is not, desirable that women should be educated for, and admitted to, the medical profession. I can indicate only in the briefest outline the reasons which lead me to answer this question in the affirmative.

In approaching the subject, the first point seems to be to divest the mind as completely as possible of all conventional pre-existing theories respecting it, and to consider it as if now presented for the first time. Let it be supposed that no doctors as yet existed, that society now for the first time awoke to the great want of skilled medical aid, as distinguished from the empiricism of domestic treatment, and that it was resolved at once to set aside persons to acquire a scientific knowledge of the human frame in health and in disease, and of all remedies available as curative agents, with the object that such knowledge should be used for the benefit of all the rest of the race. In such case, would the natural idea be that members of each sex should be so set apart for the benefit of their own sex respectively – that men should fit themselves to minister to the maladies of men, and women to those of women – or that one sex only should undertake the care of the health of all, under the circumstances? For myself, I have no hesitation in saying that the former seems to me the *natural* course, and that to civilised society, if unaccustomed to the idea, the proposal that persons of one sex should in every case be consulted about every disease incident to those of the other, would be very repugnant; nay, that were every other condition of society the same as now, it would probably be held wholly inadmissible. Indeed, I will even go a step further, and say that if any question

arose respecting the relative fitness of men and women for attendance on the sick, the experience of daily life would go far to prove
that, of the two, women have more love of medical work, and
are naturally more inclined, and more fitted, for it than most men.
If a child falls downstairs and is more or less seriously hurt, is it
the father or the mother, the sister or the brother, (where all are
without medical training) who is most equal to the emergency,
and who first applies the needful remedies? Or again, in the heart
of the country, where doctors are not readily accessible, is it the
squire and the parson, or their respective wives, who minister to
the ailments of half the parish? And if women are thus naturally
inclined for medical practice, I do not know who has the right to
say that they shall not be allowed to make their work scientific
when they desire it, but shall be limited to merely the mechanical
details and wearisome routine of nursing, while to men is reserved
all intelligent knowledge of disease, and all study of the laws by
which health may be preserved or restored. I confess that, as
regards natural instincts and social propriety alike, it seems to me
that their evidence, such as it is, is wholly for, and not against,
the cause of women as physicians of their own sex, and it is for
this alone that I am pleading.

To glance at another aspect of the question, I must further say
that I believe few people are aware of the very widespread desire
existing among women for the services of doctors of their own
sex; and yet there are probably few present who have not known
individual cases where severe suffering has been borne, and danger
perhaps incurred, in consequence of the excessive reluctance felt
by some young girl, or woman even of maturer years, to consult
a doctor in certain circumstances, and more especially to tell him all
the facts of her case with the absolute frankness which is essentially
necessary. Doctors have often told me themselves of the extreme
pity they have felt in such cases, and yet I believe that doctors
know, as a rule, less of the facts to which I am referring than
anyone else is likely to do. Of course a lady does not send for a
doctor to say that she will not consult him; and still less, if she
resolves to seek his advice, does she tell him of her difficulty in
doing so. I believe, however, that those who know most of the
matter will most strongly confirm what I am saying; and I am
sure that all will agree that no state of things can be right which,
even in exceptional circumstances, imposes so much pain, and pain
of a kind that ought not to be inflicted, on those who are already
in a condition of suffering. In this case, of all others, there should
at least be a *choice*. If I am wrong in my belief on this point, at

least no harm will be done; if I am right, a quite incalculable benefit will have been conferred.

Even more briefly must I glance at the historical evidence in favour of the medical education of women. Those learned in Greek literature will remember that Homer speaks of medical women both in the *Iliad* and in the *Odyssey*, and that Euripides represents the nurse as reminding Queen Phædra that if her disease is 'such as may not be told to men' there are skilled women at hand to whom she may have recourse. Everyone is aware how common it seems to have been in the days of chivalry for women to be adepts in medicine and surgery, and how frequently the knights wounded in battle were healed in the adjacent nunneries. The midwives and wise women of the middle ages held at least an equal position with the apothecaries and barber-surgeons of the time, and their competition seems to have been so formidable as to drive the male practitioners to seek protection from them, for it appears that in 1421 a petition was presented to Henry V praying that 'No woman use the practise of fysik under the payne of long emprisonment.' Again, in the reign of Henry VIII, we find an Act passed for the relief of irregular practitioners of medicine, 'both men and women,' who were being 'sued, vexed, and troubled by the Companie and Fellowship of Surgeons of London, mynding onlie their own lucres,' the said surgeons having but recently obtained an Act of Incorporation, which they now endeavoured to employ as an engine of oppressive monopoly. Maitland, in his *History of Edinburgh*, also mentions that at the time of the foundation of the Edinburgh College of Physicians in 1681, 'both men and women' were engaged in the 'practice of physic' in that city. I have not time even to enumerate the women whose medical skill has obtained record in history during the past few centuries, but I may mention that no less than three women have held chairs in the Medical Faculty of the University of Bologna, namely, Dorotea Bucca, Professor of Medicine, early in the fifteenth century; Anna Mazzolini, Professor of Anatomy, in 1760; and Maria Della Donne, who was appointed Professor of Midwifery by Napoleon Buonaparte at the beginning of the present century. The Italian Universities have always been freely open to women, and a large number seem to have studied medicine there during the middle ages. In Germany also several such instances have occurred, and considerable numbers of women are now studying in the universities of France and Switzerland.

But even if we had no such historical precedents, and if the special suitability of women for the study of medicine were totally denied, I should still confidently rest my case on my last and most comprehensive argument – namely, the right possessed by every intelligent human being to choose out his or her own life work, and to decide what is and what is not calculated to conduce to his or her personal benefit and happiness. In the words of the late Mrs J. S. Mill, 'We deny the right of any portion of the species to decide for another portion, or any individual for another individual, what is and what is not their "proper sphere." The proper sphere for all human beings is the largest and highest which they are able to attain to. What this is, cannot be ascertained without complete liberty of choice.' Viewed in this light, it is no valid argument to say that women will be happier if excluded from all professions, nor that they will probably make bad doctors; still less that they will find little or no employment when they enter upon practice. Even if every one of these assertions were true, the principle I have cited would remain the same – whether we choose well or ill, wisely or unwisely for our own welfare, we still have an indisputable right to make our choice; and if failure and disappointment ensue, the penalty will be ours also. If women do on the whole make worse doctors than men, they will simply fail in competition with them; if their sister women do not desire their services, they will not obtain practice, and the thing will die out of itself. Where, then, is the need of opposition and prohibition? Here, as in so many other cases, we may safely fall back on the wise words of warning of old, 'If this work be of men it will come to nought, but if it be of God ye cannot overthrow it, lest haply ye be found even to fight against God.'

If, then, it may be assumed that women are at least not to be prevented from entering the medical profession, it is clearly to be desired that they should aim at the same standard, and comply with the same requirements, as all other practitioners of medicine. This is manifestly for the good of the community, and women themselves ask for nothing else. They are quite ready to undertake the ordinary studies, and to rest their claims to practice on their ability to pass the ordinary examinations. They ask for no exceptions and no indulgence; they simply ask that no exceptional hindrances shall be thrown in their way. Two things, then, are essentially necessary,

(1) That they should obtain such an education as shall make them thoroughly competent to take their share of responsibility in the care of the national health; and

(2) that this education should be secured in accordance with the regulations prescribed by authority, that they may be recognised by the State as having complied with its requirements,

and may thus enter upon practice on terms of perfect quality with other practitioners.

The first condition is strictly natural and inevitable; the second, though equally imperative, is in a certain sense arbitrary, or at least artificial.

In the old days before medical practice became a matter of legislation, every doctor could acquire his learning as he liked, and must depend for his success in life solely on the practical results of his subsequent work. In America this is still the case to a very great extent. Every facility there exists for the establishment of medical schools, and of examining boards, on every conceivable principle; and, as all these are recognised indifferently by the State, all have an equal right to grant medical degrees, and to send forth their graduates to compete with all other doctors on terms of perfect equality, there being no further State requirements and no further State recognition. Whether or not this is the best plan I do not propose to discuss; it is self-evident that such a system has great advantages and great disadvantages. It is clear, at any rate, that to the British mind the latter seem to predominate, and hence the careful legislation on the subject in this country. A positive law exists in England to limit the recognised practice of medicine to those whose names are entered on the Government Register, admission to that register being obtainable only through certain specified examining boards. It cannot be too often repeated, as it cannot be too clearly understood, that it is to the existence of this law that all the fundamental difficulties in the way of the medical education of women are due; and that, not because the Medical Act contains any clause excluding women from the profession, but because it vests all power of examination in bodies who seem only too much inclined to wrest and misuse that power for the purpose of effecting such exclusion. The Medical Act says not a word respecting the sex of the practitioner of medicine; it simply lays down certain conditions and requirements, and all who comply with these are *ipso facto* entitled to registration. Two women have so complied, and the names of both appear on the register; so that it is beyond dispute that all women on such compliance have an absolute right to registration.

As, however, many people are not aware how and why it is that two women could do what other women are not now able to accomplish, I must pause a moment to explain the special circumstances of each case. When the Medical Act was passed in 1858 it was expressly provided that any practitioners furnished with foreign degrees, and already in practice in this country, could claim registration, though in future no foreign degrees would be recognised. Dr Elizabeth Blackwell, the first Englishwoman who ever took a medical degree, took advantage of this clause, and, having already graduated in America, her name was at once entered on the register; but the path by which she entered was henceforth closed by the provisions of the Act itself. When in 1860 Miss Garrett desired to enter the profession, she applied for admission to one college and school after another, but with no success, until at length she discovered that the Company of Apothecaries were unable to refuse to examine any candidate who complied with their conditions. She accordingly went through a five years' apprenticeship, attended all the needful lectures, and passed all the prescribed examinations, and at length received the licence to practise, in virtue of which she was admitted to the register. In order, however, to observe the regulations of Apothecaries' Hall, she was obliged to attend the lectures of certain specified teachers; in some cases she was admitted to the ordinary classes, but in others she was compelled to pay very heavy fees for separate and private tuition. Not content, however, with indirectly imposing this heavy pecuniary tax on women, the authorities now bethought them to pass a rule forbidding students to receive any part of their education privately – this course being publicly advised by one of the medical journals as affording a safe way of evading their legal obligations, and thus shutting out the one chance left to women! On such a proceeding I think it is unnecessary for me to offer any comment.

Allow me, then, once more to recapitulate the several conditions which collectively combine to form an apparently inextricable dilemma. The Medical Act makes the legalised practice of medicine impossible to any one who is not registered in the Government register; such registration is obtainable only after examination by certain specified boards; these boards have laid down as a positive condition of examination that students must have studied in certain recognised public schools – it being, moreover, defined, in the case just cited, that it is not sufficient to be taught even by the recognised public teacher, unless such teaching be received publicly and in the ordinary class; and lastly, women are not, so far as I know, allowed admission to any public school in Great Britain, and yet they cannot obtain permission to organise a separate medical school for themselves, or, at least, they are told that the teaching in any such school, however excellent it may be, shall be refused recognition by the examining boards.

I trust that I have given a clear view of the somewhat complicated difficulties of the case; in the few minutes that remain I desire to direct attention to the possible modes of remedy. The difficulties are threefold; depending, that is,

(1)   on the law,
(2)   on the examining boards,
(3)   on the medical schools.

If the conditions were different in any one of these three directions, the present problem might admit of solution. If women were admitted to the ordinary medical schools on the same terms as men, the examining boards could hardly refuse to examine them; if the regulations of the boards were relaxed to the extent of admitting candidates from a new school formed expressly for women, no more would be necessary, for such a school could readily be organised, and might be in complete working order in the course of six months; or, thirdly, if the Medical Act permitted the examination of women by a special board, and their subsequent registration as practitioners, the existing schools and boards might maintain their attitude of exclusion, and yet women could enter the profession on equal terms with men.

At any rate, we confidently trust that whenever a new Medical Bill is introduced, its provisions will be such as to make the present exclusionist policy impossible. It is sufficiently plain that the sole object of legislation on this subject ought to be to give some guarantee to the public that the medical practitioners recognised by law have received an adequate education, and are not unfit to be trusted with the care of the sick, so far, indeed, as such fitness or unfitness can be ascertained by examinations. It is clearly quite beside the scope of any such Bill to establish a monopoly directly or indirectly, and I hope that I have already made plain that it is only by a series of coincidences, which could hardly have been foreseen, that even the present Act can be used as an instrument of such monopoly. No one can wonder that it never occurred to the framers of the law that the medical authorities and the educational bodies could desire arbitrarily to exclude from the profession any candidates who wished worthily to enter it, and who were ready to comply with all the usual conditions of study and examination. Now that it is seen that such a state of things is possible, and now that the injustice which may result therefrom is beginning to be understood, I feel every confidence that in a very short time the needful remedy will be found and applied by the Legislature.

Indeed, this assurance is redoubled by the fact that the proposed action of Government with reference to the medical profession is exactly of the kind which will of itself remove all our difficulties.

Let but the 'One Portal System' be fairly established; let the Government appoint an examining board whose composition shall secure universal confidence; let all candidates who desire to enter the medical profession be admitted to the same examinations; let their papers be identified by numbers instead of names, so that this vexed question of sex may be so far absolutely excluded, and then let all students who are able successfully to pass the ordeal be admitted to registration; and the whole problem which has so long troubled and perplexed us will be solved at once and for ever. In the great scheme of national education the principle of payment by results is becoming daily more and more supreme; let it prevail in this department also.

Every day more and more diversity of opinion is expressed respecting the best mode of medical education. Some say that the old apprenticeship system was the best of all, for under that the student learnt the practical work of his profession under the very eye of his master. Others again maintain that the present system of compulsory attendance at one course of lectures after another – amounting in all to more than a thousand lectures – is the best and only sure means of education. A third party, who know well how perfunctory is such attendance, how frequent the absences except on days when the presence of students is to be ascertained, and how listless and weary the attitude of a majority even of those who are seated on the benches, are inclined to believe that the study at home of the best books on each science, combined with constant attendance on the practical work at hospitals and dispensaries, is the most hopeful of all the modes of education yet devised. I will not pretend to enter on any such discussion; I believe that types of mind vary, and that probably some students could be found who would be respectively most successful under each of the three systems referred to. I trust that the Government, when it takes up this matter, will lay down no such hard and fast rule as is maintained by the present examining boards; I trust that it will have a standard of knowledge fixed by the leaders of the profession, and will appoint thoroughly qualified examiners to see, by examinations both written and clinical, that that standard is attained, and, for all the rest, I venture to hope that students will be left free to gather their knowledge as they choose, uniformity being required in the results alone. If each student examined be desired simply to specify the mode in which he has acquired his information, we shall soon be furnished with statistics to indicate which is really the best method, and it cannot be doubtful that when once this is ascertained the majority of students will desire for their own sakes to adopt it. If, in truth, the present system of

275

lectures is the most valuable, the students who follow it will by their success demonstrate the fact; if, on the contrary, it is found to have been dictated rather by the 'vested interests' of teachers than by the needs of students, it will naturally collapse when its artificial support is withdrawn; and we shall have substituted for it either the old apprenticeship system, or the plan of private study, according to the results that may be obtained from each.

I am inclined myself to think that a somewhat mixed system would probably come to prevail; wherever a man of true intellectual eminence was found to teach, students would no more be wanting than of old; where men of commonplace calibre lectured, those only would attend who found that mode of instruction most suited to their tastes or needs; and probably a large number of students would always prefer to obtain from books the best digested results gathered by the master minds of the profession. But as to such matters of detail I care little to argue. I do not ask for any change in existing arrangements if only women may be allowed freely to profit by them; I do not ask that the regulations or conditions of study should be in any degree modified, if only they be no longer made the engine of an oppressive monopoly.

I hope even in my lifetime that the day will come when the axiom that 'Mind is of no sex' shall cease to be a mere dead letter; when equal facilities of study shall be afforded to all earnest students in connection with the national universities, and all other places of education supported in any degree by public money; but it is not for this that I am now pleading. Whether it is just and fair that women should be taxed in order to supply educational advantages which they are not allowed to share, I leave it to others to decide. I only ask that, if women are to be excluded from all the medical schools that at present exist, they may at least be allowed by their own labour and at their own expense – with such help as may be voluntarily vouchsafed to them – to form and organise a medical school of their own; with the certainty that, on the completion of their studies, due provision shall be made for their admission to the recognised examinations, and for their subsequent registration as legally qualified practitioners, on exactly the same footing as all others who have pursued the same course of study and attained the same standard of professional acquirement.

This is all that is absolutely necessary, and I leave it to the justice of my countrymen to say whether this is too much to ask.

E.T.M.

*An Interior View of Girton College, Cambridge**

(1876)

16 *January* 1876

The first question put by English people to an American Student at Girton College is: 'Why have you left your own country, where public opinion is so advanced on the question of female education, and where Women's Colleges are many, to come here?' The answer we might give is, that the existing Women's Colleges in the United States are little more than high schools, whose status is undefined, whose degrees, when won, mean little or nothing to the public, and whose domestic economy is usually so narrow, and their discipline so onerous, that women accustomed to refined and easy modes of life are unwilling to enter them. Girton College, for the first time in the educational history of England or America, brings women into direct competition with men, under the auspices of an institution of high character and wide reputation, and thus attracts to itself the best young Englishwomen, while the traditions of social refinement and domestic comfort which the college shares with the University of which it is a dependency make a sojourn within its gates possible and delightful to the most fastidious.

For many years a movement has been going on in England having for its object to improve the education of women. The views taken of what the ultimate system of female education might be, do not perhaps always agree. Those who hold that women can only be fairly tested by the educational standard and methods

---

* The following account of Girton College was written for an American Journal by an American lady who was herself for a time a Student of the College. It is reprinted, with the writer's permission, for English readers, as giving a picture of the internal life of an institution still very imperfectly known in our own country. – E.D.

which the experience of ages has shaped for men have aimed chiefly at obtaining the extension of University education to women. The first successful effort in this direction was the admission of girls to the University Local Examinations, which was granted by Cambridge in 1865 and by Oxford a few years later. The effect of this extension was felt in private schools and also in the home training of girls. It gave a much needed sanction and support to definite and thorough elementary training. Many of the best private schools are now organised with a view to sending up their pupils to these examinations, and girls of the best families have been prepared at home and have passed. But these examinations were limited to boys and girls under eighteen. It was felt that much more was needed to place young Englishwomen on a level with their brothers as regards education. At Oxford and Cambridge residence is required under a system of instruction and discipline for a certain period by those who aspire to be graduates of the University. In order to give women an opportunity of fulfilling similar conditions of residence, it was determined to found a college for them, to be connected as closely as possible with the University of Cambridge.

In 1869 a house was hired at Hitchin, about thirty miles from Cambridge. Some of the best tutors of Cambridge, who were interested in the proposed experiment, promised to give the benefit of their tuition, at no small sacrifice of time and comfort. In October, 1869, six women came together at Hitchin and entered upon their new and arduous undertaking. They were but slightly acquainted with even the elements of classics and mathematics, and to their inexperience the modest requirements of the 'Little-go' had a formidable aspect. After a year of somewhat anxious work, a little band of five went up to Cambridge for this, their first, university examination, the Examiners having consented to look over their papers and report upon them according to the university standard. This crisis was successfully passed, and two years later one of the same students was examined in the papers set for the Mathematical Tripos, and her work was pronounced to be such as would have entitled an undergraduate to a place in the Second Class. In February, 1873, two other students were similarly examined in the papers set for the Classical Tripos and declared to be deserving of Honours. Meanwhile a field of sixteen acres was purchased in the parish of Girton, about two miles from Cambridge, and a College building fitted to accommodate twenty-one students was erected. This building is one side of a proposed quadrangle. The funds required for it were raised by loans on mortgage and by public subscription. While the building was in progress undergraduates and dons made it a favourite goal of their afternoon ramble, and many a brick was laid by these as a token of their goodwill. In 1872 the institution was incorporated under the name of Girton College. In October, 1873, the occupation of the new building began, and since then the interest of Cambridge in her foster-child has been more generous than ever.

Great latitude is allowed as to the subjects of study at Girton, but the course taken by most of the students is identical with the Cambridge course – or rather courses – for the university curriculum also gives a wide range of choice. All University regulations as to the preliminary examinations and terms of residence are observed. The examinations take place at Girton at the same time that the students of the university are in their places at the Senate House. Half an hour after the examination questions have been given out to the undergraduates a sealed packet of the same papers is sent to Girton. The examination is held under strict supervision and the allotted time for each paper scrupulously observed. At the close of each day's work the papers containing the candidates' answers are forwarded to the Examiners, who report upon them to the college. In some cases the exact place that the student would have taken if she had been an undergraduate of the University has been reported, in others only the Class, in others again only the fact that the student would have been qualified for Honours. The amount of information given depends on the examiners, who give the favour of their services at the request of the college, not as yet with the formal sanction of the university. At the close of the course, students who are in fact, though not technically, qualified for a university degree, receive from the college what is called a Degree Certificate. The teaching at Girton is at present almost entirely supplied by Tutors and Lecturers or Fellows of various Colleges at Cambridge. Many of the most distinguished members of the university have cheerfully sacrificed their afternoon hours, usually so jealously guarded for purposes of recreation, to lecture at Girton, and have expressed pleasure in the contact with the fresh, enthusiastic minds they found there. How the tuition of the college will ultimately be organised it is hard to say. Its friends can only hope that the future has in store honours for Girton students which will qualify them as first-class teachers, and funds for the college which will enable it to offer inducements adequate to secure the permanent services of such teachers, whether its own members or those belonging to other colleges. The arrangements for lectures are made by the Mistress. Up to the expiration of last Michaelmas Term seven students have taken honours, none as yet higher than second class. For a first class

Girton must probably wait until her students come prepared by the careful training which boys receive from early childhood. Three students have also passed the general examinations for the Ordinary Degree of B.A.

Turning from the constitution of the college to its inmates, one feels it difficult to convey an idea of their vigorous tone without arousing in the imagination of American readers a suspicion of the 'strong-minded' type, which has become so justly odious. Perhaps one may best indicate how false such an idea of Girton students would be by dwelling on their great unconsciousness of any representative character. They never seem to regard themselves as the exponents of a cause; there is rarely any reference made among them to their conspicuous position before the eyes of the public. They are simple-hearted English girls and women, doing work for its own sake, spontaneously and with pleasure, without any of that morbid craving for recognition which is so frequently obtrusive in women's work. Speaking generally, about half of the students look forward to being teachers; not governesses, but teachers and head mistresses in schools. The great Endowed Schools for girls, established under the authority of the Endowed Schools Commission, will doubtless look to Girton for their Head Mistresses, while in turn they will prepare students for her. In the scheme for one of these schools – St. Paul's, London – £700 a year is provided for girls from the school to pursue their education at institutions of superior learning; and at least a large share of this will naturally be spent at Girton. Other schemes have similar provisions. The other half of the students at Girton are working without reference to any special career.

Although the students now come somewhat better prepared, and the kind of 'coaching' they need is now better understood than when the college was started, aspirants for Honours still labour under considerable disadvantage, owing to deficiencies of early training. There is, however, no such pressure as to be injurious to health if reasonable care is taken, and there have been several cases of marked improvement in health and strength during the time spent at the college. What greatly facilitates an English College course for women is the absence of any system of marking at recitations. This allows a Student, whenever she is temporarily out of sorts, to fall below her average of work, or miss her lectures entirely, if necessary, with the knowledge that she can redeem the lost time afterwards. Another feature of Girton life, while it is a condition of first-class work, appears to me also a great safeguard to the nervous, and therefore to the general health of students – I mean the opportunity which each Student possesses of perfect privacy in her own apartments. A bedroom and a study, or one large room combining the two uses, is set apart for each student, and as there are never more than five students on a corridor, there is never such a noise outside the doors as to cause disturbance. This arrangement forms a marked contrast to the provision at Vassar, for instance – where five students have only three bedrooms and one study together.

The internal discipline at Girton is as slight as possible. Students are required to enter their names on the marking-roll three times daily, and to be present at lectures, unless especially excused by the Mistress. They must not accept evening invitations more than on an average once a week; they must not receive visits from gentlemen in their rooms; and they must always be within the college gates by six o'clock in winter, or before dark in summer, except when they are out visiting, in which case notice is given to the Mistress of their destination, and they may be out till eleven. Within these limitations they study, walk, ride on horseback, play cricket and their favourite 'fives,' without let or hindrance. The student's day begins about 7 a.m. At eight o'clock prayers are read in one of the lecture rooms. Between 8-15 and 9, breakfast is on the table. After breakfast the morning hours are devoted to study, which is entirely done in the private rooms. As there is, as yet, no proper library building, the small, though choice collection of books that the college owns, is kept provisionally in one of the three lecture rooms. This is, of course, frequently occupied by lecturers, and books of reference are therefore carried off by students to their studies when needed. These studies are cheerful airy rooms, enlivened with photographs and engravings, flower-pots in the windows, Turkish rugs, bookshelves, etc. In each of them a big table, loaded with papers and text books, denotes the essential character of the apartment. Luncheon is spread between 12 a.m., and 3 p.m., but it is mostly about one o'clock that the students come in for a light repast, of which the rich sweet milk, abundantly supplied, is an important part. After luncheon some hearty exercise is the general desire. Many of the students go off in pairs for an hour's rapid walk – in springtime, or early autumn, over the fields, through hedge and ditch; in winter, when Cambridgeshire fields are half flooded, along the highways. Like most English people, Girton students are ardent lovers of nature, and as soon as spring stirs in the meadows a basket or pail is carried on every student's arm, and comes back from the ramble filled with entomological or botanical treasures. If the weather is bad or if it is necessary to condense a great deal of exercise into a few minutes, a suitable dress is put on, and recourse is had to the gymnasium. The gymnasium is a covered court separate from the college building. It is still destitute of gymnastic apparatus, and is mostly used for 'fives,' a game played with bat and ball, and resembling tennis. In the spring and autumn, lawn tennis, or cricket is preferred to exercise in the gymnasium. These games are played on the grass plots near the college building. The *entourage* of the building, by the way, is rather dreary. The land belonging to the college is mostly let to a neighbouring farmer, and the portion reserved immediately around the college is only provisionally laid out, and almost destitute of trees.

Most of the lectures occur in the afternoon. A student does not have, on an average, more than one lecture a day. The variety of subjects pursued renders the number of those who attend each course of lectures very small, often only one or two persons. At these lectures the lecturer reviews the work done by each student since the last lecture, whether mathematical problems, Greek and Latin compositions, or answers to papers of miscellaneous questions on the subject of study. Any questions which have occurred to the student are answered. Then the lecturer starts off on his lecture proper, usually choosing portions of the subject, or methods of treatment which are not found in the class books in use. Those students who have not taken exercise before their lecture go out after it. In the Michaelmas and May terms many of the students get a ride on horseback, in parties of two and three, before dinner, which is at six o'clock. This meal is always a specimen of good, plain English cooking – abounding in roast joints and puddings. After dinner there is sometimes a little music, College songs in chorus, or a country dance intervenes. Then the nocturnal labours of the students begin. There is always a break of thirty minutes or an hour, caused by the appearance of tea, coffee, or cocoa, which innocent beverages are brought to the student's rooms by the college servants before nine o'clock, or prepared by the students themselves over their open fires at a later hour. This is the moment when hospitality is most practised. One student invites several to her room, and these gatherings take the place of the men's 'wines.' Many are asleep at half-past ten, others burn the midnight oil.

On Sundays most of the Girtonians attend both morning and afternoon service in Cambridge, lunching between at a ladies' reading-room, to which they have access, and where light refreshments are to be found. There is a parish church at Girton, a quarter of an hour's walk from the college, but the students generally prefer the fine services in Cambridge, especially attractive among which are the afternoon sermons in the University Church, always by some distinguished preacher, and the choral service afterward at King's College Chapel.

Cambridge is often visited during the week, also, by the Girton students, either to see friends or for the purposes of their simple shopping. At different times, again, students have gone into Cambridge regularly to attend Professors' lectures, or to study at the University Museums. Once in a while the students devote an evening to charades, a debate, or a Shakespere reading; but it is rare that all can unite to give up an entire evening to amusement.

The college has never been rich enough to afford a chapel, and the only religious exercises are family prayers, conducted by the Mistress, which it is optional with the students to attend. Girton rather labours under the reputation of a bias towards free thought, but fully two thirds of the students have been staunch Church-women. The dress and manners of students at Girton are those of English girls of their class – i.e. the professional and upper-middle. If one student threatens some eccentricity, there is a general outcry by the others. 'Do not let us make too many experiments at once,' they often say. They are asserting their capacity for that thorough education which is the foundation of practical effort in every department of life, and if this experiment succeeds, they are confident that the practical life of women will so expand as to burst the gilded shackles of luxury and fashion by which it is now confined. Girton students, moreover, are, as a rule, much too true to their English nationality to profess any contempt for marriage. There is considerable discussion among them as to the proper fields of activity for women in after-life. One article of faith, however, has brought all these busy students together: the conviction that, whether as scientific specialists, as teachers of the young, as business women, or in a purely domestic sphere, the liberal education which they are gaining must ever be the best preparation for their duties. Such an education is not intended for all women, any more than for all men. To the thoughtful minds of either sex it must be the best succour in adversity, the truest luxury in prosperity.

V. Sturge

The Physical Education of Women

(n.d.)

As we near the close of the century, our ears are filled with the demands of women – noisy, perhaps, but in the main reasonable – for a larger life: a fuller share in the work of the world. There is, however, the danger that, in the rush for fresh opportunities – new spheres of activity – those already possessed may be under-valued and neglected.

The work of improving the physique of the race, and of building up sound and healthy bodies, lies largely with women, yet they are neglecting, almost despising, the opportunity. Those women who are mothers have, of course, the greatest power in this direction; to them is entrusted, in large measure, the physical well-being of the young. But every woman has it in her power to make those around her happier – her little world brighter – by caring for her own body, and developing it to its utmost possibilities.

Half the petty annoyances of daily existence, the numberless small frictions which so often spoil family life, may be traced to the ill health of women. Certain failings – irritability of temper, gloomy demeanour, impatience of others, and numbers more, are the direct result of some physical disturbance. Remarks of this kind are frequent: 'A's temper *is* uncertain, but then, poor thing, her health is not what it should be;' or, 'B is so unreasonable, so difficult to please, but then her nerves are out of order.' We make excuses of this kind for others; perhaps we should make them oftener; but to attribute our own failings to a physical cause – headache is a favourite scapegoat – in no wise excuses us, because, in nine cases out of ten, the headache might have been prevented. We have been guilty of two sins – first: the breach of a physical; second: the breach of a moral law, the result of the first transgression.

284

Taking the larger world, we find a great deal of sin and misery, apparently the result of physical conditions. There are those who say that physical deterioration is the result of moral deterioration, not the cause; and, indeed, the two are so mixed that the point is difficult to decide. Certain is it that many people come into the world with such a miserable *physical* heritage that resistance to some forms of temptation is almost impossible. To such the soul is too often the slave of the body. 'A strong body obeys; a weak body commands.' The physical well-being of individuals and communities is of the first importance: the care of the body should come even before that of the mind; for *ultimately* the brain power of average mankind depends on physique. One-sided education results, sooner or later, in deformity. The ascetic, the pedant, and the circus athlete afford examples of one-sided training carried to excess. In each case we have an abnormal creature, not a well-balanced man. That alone is true education which aims at training every side of the nature – at producing an harmoniously developed being. Now-a-days women have every opportunity for intellectual development; the need for mental training has been recognised and met. The pressing need for physical training is, on the other hand, little understood; only in the last few years has it received serious attention at all. Even now it is said the less girls think about their bodies the better; nature should be left to look after them. Poor nature! she has a bad chance against corsets, and cramming, and indigestible food, and the hundred and one requirements of modern life. Moreover, nature is not the best teacher for members of a civilised community.

Whatever the faults of modern education, no one would seriously propose the abolishing of schools and colleges, or would suggest that girls' *minds* should be left to nature. It is no less a fact, though it has not yet been recognised, that a woman's body, for the first five-and-twenty years of her life, needs earnest, systematic training. On the way in which her body has been treated during those years will depend her own health, and that of her children after her.

I think it possible that the term 'physical education' conveys little to some of my hearers. In its broadest sense, it means the development of every physical power to its greatest possibilities, the production of a truly sane body. Physical education has only just become a science, it has not yet crystallised into a system. The methods must always differ with the needs of the individual; it is impossible to attempt body-training by a set of fixed rules. There are, however, certain broad lines which I should like to indicate roughly with the hope of arousing you to study the matter in detail for yourselves. To put it in Irish fashion, a girl's physical education should begin with that of her mother; the next best thing is for the mother to undertake it from her daughter's earliest years. Until the girl is twelve or fourteen years of age the care of her body naturally lies with her mother; after that the girl's own earnest co-operation is needed. The *aim* must be her perfect health at any cost; every thought should be given to that end. Probably the greatest difficulty will be the physical disabilities inherited by the girl. We must face the unpleasant fact that a tendency to specific disease is the heritage of many girls, a want of tone and vitality that of many more. Perhaps one day the wrong, the deep wrong of transmitting disease to unborn children will be recognised, and no longer permitted: meantime the fact must be faced. The initial step is to discover what special disability the girl in question has inherited; the next to set to work resolutely and in a definite manner to overcome it. A particular example will make clear my meaning. Take the case of a child who has a tendency to lung complaint: all known measures likely to counteract the tendency should be systematically adopted. Chief, perhaps, of these are dry, cleanly air and hygienic clothing. Of course, fresh air and suitable clothing should be given to every child; but in the case I have taken, they should be matters of *constant* thought and attention. In short, the rules of health, with which we are so well acquainted in these days of science teaching, should be applied in every child's infancy; whilst cases of inherited weakness should be carefully studied and fought against.

If it be objected that constant, minute observance of the laws of health involves too much time and trouble, I reply that the building up of a strong little body is worth *infinite* time and trouble. A truly healthy child! Is there any more beautiful sight in the wide world? And is it not often the home of a happy little soul, since it is easy for a child to be good if it is perfectly well? A passage from Kingsley's *Health and Education* will bear out what I say:

Let me ask you, ladies, with all courtesy, but with all earnestness, are you aware of certain facts of which every medical man is too well aware? Are you aware that more human beings are killed in England every year by unnecessary and preventible diseases than were killed at Waterloo or Sadowa? Are you aware that the great majority of those victims are children? Are you aware that the diseases which carry them off are, for the most part, such as ought to be specially under the control of the women who love them, pet them, educate them, and would in many cases, if need be, lay down their

lives for them? Are you aware, again, of the vast amount of
disease which – so both wise mothers and wise doctors assure
me – is engendered in the sleeping-room from simple ignorance of the laws of ventilation, and in the school-room likewise from simple ignorance of the laws of physiology? from
an ignorance of which I shall mention no other case here save
one – that, too often from ignorance of signs of approaching
disease, a child is punished for what is called idleness, listlessness, wilfulness, sulkiness; and punished, too, in the unwisest
way – by an increase of tasks and confinement to the house,
thus overtasking still more a brain already overtasked, and
depressing still more, by robbing it of oxygen and exercise,
a system already depressed?

Now, in the face of such facts as these, is it too much to
ask of mothers, sisters, aunts, nurses, governesses – all who
may be occupied in the care of children, especially of girls –
that they should study thrift of human health and human life
by studying somewhat the laws of life and health? There are
books – I may say a whole literature of books – written by
scientific doctors on these matters, which are, in my mind,
far more important to the school-room than half the trashy
accomplishments, so-called, which are expected to be known
by governesses. Ah! the waste of health and strength in the
young; the waste, too, of anxiety and misery in those who
love and tend them. How much of it might be saved by a
little rational education in those laws of nature, which are the
will of God, about the welfare of our bodies, and which,
therefore, we are as much bound to know and to obey as we
are bound to know and obey spiritual laws, whereon depends
the welfare of our souls.

The importance of definite health rules during childhood cannot
be over-estimated, but they must vary with the individual child.
In rearing plants, we find that the soil and the amount of air and
sunshine must vary with the kind of plant, and our gardening is
successful, in so far as we understand the individual plant needs.
In dealing with children, it is too often the way, where any systematic plan is attempted at all, to apply a set of traditional rules,
regardless of individuality. Yet in the children of one family great
differences are frequently seen. One little girl is dreamy, imaginative, highly nervous; while her sister is the exact reverse – matter-
of-fact, practical, apparently without nerves. The physical needs
of those children are as unlike as their temperaments. The amount
of sleep required, the nature and quantity of food, the daily exercise

needed; scarcely any physical requirement will be the same in both cases. I admit that to make a study of a child's body, and to supply its special needs in the best way *is* a difficult matter, yet all intelligent parents and teachers attempt this for the child's mind. The same deep sympathy with child nature is needed, the same patient observation, and, in addition, some knowledge of the structure and functions of the human body. The hygiene of childhood is, however, too large a subject for this paper. I have only tried to show that a knowledge of the laws of health, and their individual application, is the foundation of all physical education.

I now pass on to a definite method of body training, the training of the body by means of muscular exercise. It is *the* means above all others for producing a fine physique, provided it is taken under hygienic conditions. The desire for muscular exercise is great in children, as in all young animals; it is a physical need requiring satisfaction. During the first years of life, children instinctively supply the need by means, in babyhood, of seemingly aimless muscular actions; later by romping games. These last are, unfortunately, often checked by nurses for the sake of quiet. They do not realise that to insist on stillness from a young child, except for a very short space of time, is positive cruelty; as cruel as to refuse it sufficient food when it is hungry. The results are very similar. Give a child day after day half the amount of food it requires, and it will soon cease to demand even to want a larger quantity: deprive a child, day after day, of constant movement, and it will soon lose its desire to play. In either case, the system has adapted itself to unnatural conditions; a physical need has been thwarted, and physical development seriously hindered. Girls, and we are considering girls today, are especial sufferers from nursery repression. An idea still exists that, while a little boy needs plenty of movement, a little girl should be content with her doll, and the maternal instinct is so strong in the girl, that she readily falls in with this view; and the first serious mistake in her physical education is made. The mistake is continued when school-days begin. Games are an essential part of a boy's school-life, his football and cricket engross him as much as his lessons; a healthy mind in a healthy body is the natural result.

Mrs Grundy rules, or rather has ruled, for her power is on the wane, that games, except of the mildest kind, are harmful for girls. Yet physicians tell us that, during childhood, boys and girls are equally strong, capable of the same exertion. Why then is the difference made? No wonder that school-girls complain so often of fatigue and headache; these are the natural results of long school hours and insufficient exercise. The chief part of a girl's interest and energy frequently centres in her lessons, and in striving to do these well, the duty owed to her body is overlooked; sooner or later both body and mind suffer. If parents and teachers insisted on the daily walk or healthful outdoor game, and regarded its omission as a serious fault, girls would be stronger and healthier, and school-work, too, would be better done. Mind and body must be harmoniously trained, brain cannot be truly developed at the expense of physique.

Here again, I should like to give you an extract from Kingsley:

It is proposed, just now, to assimilate the education of girls more and more to that of boys. If that means that girls are merely to learn more lessons, and to study what their brothers are taught, in addition to what their mothers were taught; then it is to be hoped, at least by physiologists and patriots, that the scheme will sink into that limbo whither, in a free and tolerably rational country, all imperfect and ill-considered schemes are sure to gravitate. But if the scheme is a *bona fide* one: then it must be borne in mind that in the public schools of England, and in all private schools, I presume, which take their tone from them, cricket and foot-ball are more or less compulsory, being considered integral parts of an Englishman's education; and that they are likely to remain so, in spite of all reclamations: because masters and boys alike know that games do not, in the long run, interfere with a boy's work: that the same boy will often excel in both; that the games keep him in health for his work; and the spirit with which he takes to his games when in the lower school, is a fair test of the spirit with which he will take to his work when he rises into the higher school; and that nothing is worse for a boy than to fall into that loafing, tuck-shop-haunting set, who neither play hard nor work hard, and are usually extravagant and often vicious. Moreover, they know well that games conduce, not merely to physical, but to moral health; that in the playing-field boys acquire virtues which no books can give them; not merely daring and endurance, but, better still, temper, self-restraint, fairness, honour, unenvious approbation of another's success, and all that 'give and take' of life which stand a man in such good stead when he goes forth into the world, and without which, indeed, his success is always maimed and partial. Now, if the promoters of higher education for women will compel girls to any training analogous to our public school games; if, for instance, they will insist on that natural and most wholesome of all exercise, dancing, in order to develop the lower half of the body; on singing, to expand the lungs and regulate the breath; and on some games – ball or what not – which will ensure the raised chest, and upright carriage, and general strength of the upper torso, without which full oxygenation of the blood, and therefore general health, is impossible; if they will sternly forbid tight stays, high heels, and all which interferes with free growth and free motion; if they will consider carefully all which has been written on the 'half-time system' by Mr Chadwick and others; and accept the certain physical law that, in order to renovate the brain day by day, the growing creature must have plenty of fresh air and play, and that the child who learns for four hours and plays for four hours, will learn more and learn it more easily, than the child who learns for the whole eight hours; if, in short, they will teach girls not merely to understand the Greek tongue, but to copy somewhat of the Greek physical training, of that 'music and gymnastic' which helped to make the cleverest race of the world the ablest race likewise: then they will earn the gratitude of the patriot and the physiologist, by doing their best to stay the downward tendencies of the physique, and therefore ultimately of the morale, in the coming generation of English women.

One cannot praise too highly out-door games as a means of physical development, but it is not of itself a sufficient means, at least under modern conditions. Bodily development is apt to be disproportionate, one-sided, when the recreative element is the predominant one; games and athletics are pursued for the amount of pleasure derived rather than for their educational value. What sort of mental development would result if a child were allowed to learn only those lessons which pleased it? Similarly, bodily development by means of games is rarely harmonious, because the choice of games has been decided according to personal inclination. Gymnastic exercises, wisely planned and executed, are far more effectual than games in producing a fine and proportionate physique; indeed, taken under proper conditions, they are the best means of all. Unfortunately, the recreative element has crept into gymnastics to such an extent that many of the so-called systems have little educational value, being merely elaborate methods for producing acrobats. Exhibitions of acrobatic gymnastics are common, and they have prejudiced many parents against gymnastics for girls altogether.

But rational gymnastics, based on the laws of the body, and

given for the sake of health, are invaluable. A system of gymnastics which improves all the vital processes, strengthens the action of the heart, increases the chest capacity, aids the digestive organs, and produces a sound and harmoniously developed body – such a system should have a part in a girl's education. Rational gymnastics counteract bad postures, spinal curvature, round shoulders, and the like, to which a girl, by reason of her mobile body, is more liable than a boy. But they do more: they are definite means of improving physique, of making girls sounder and stronger, and, not least result, they counteract nervous tendencies, and tend to produce self-control. There is at the present time a marked want of self-control, a restlessness, a physical indecision, a tendency to nervous disease. Neurotic girls – yes, and women, characterised by nervous movements, uncontrolled ways of sitting, standing, walking, painful self-consciousness, and general want of dignity, are too common. The decided, intelligent, exact movements of the gymnasium invariably produce physical control and repose. Much of the awkwardness, shyness, and tendency to hysteria incidental to girls in their teens, might be prevented by rational gymnastics before that period.

As yet, few even among educationalists understand how much gymnastics *can* accomplish: only those who have studied the effects of physical training would fully accept the statement I have made. The ordinary visitor at a gymnasium remarks on the 'prettiness' of the performance; the school inspector on the *time* of the pupils. That the children look nice and work together – that is all the public asks for – a set of automatic machines; that is the popular idea of a successful class.

Perhaps you will allow me to tell you something of the greatest exponent of physical education that the world has yet seen. I refer to Peter Henrik Ling, founder of the Swedish System of Gymnastics. Ling was born in an obscure Swedish village at the close of last century. He received a very ordinary education at the village school. But in Sweden Scandinavian mythology and the tales of the old Norse heroes are taught to every child, and on Ling, who was an imaginative boy, these made a great impression. As he grew up he was possessed with the dream of a new Sweden, where every man and woman should be strong and beautiful in body, and noble in character. After leaving school, Ling wandered through Europe for eleven years, writing as he went poems and romances, which made him famous. Long before Ling the gymnast was heard of, Ling the poet was known and loved. His idea in his writings was always to inspire his countrymen with love of the beautiful and true, to bring back in some degree the heroic age.

Gradually, however, he came to see that his poems alone could never give back the physique of the Northmen to their descendants. Ling, himself, with his passionate love of physical beauty, was deformed, suffered from spinal curvature. In the course of his wanderings he went to Paris, and there took up fencing, an art in which he became most proficient, and his curvature disappeared. Then it struck him that as one deformity had been cured by exercise, perhaps others might be prevented and cured, and the whole body developed by some system of rational exercise. If so, then he might realise his dream. After years of patient study of Physiology, Anatomy, and Animal Mechanics, Ling began to arrange a system of practical gymnastics. The greatness of the task cannot be estimated; at that time, the effects of movements on the vital organs were almost unknown. Yet Ling collected and arranged hundreds of movements, and every movement in his system has a definite purpose, and a known effect.

The man was before all things a poet, and his gymnastics grew out of his poetical nature. To him, the human body was sacred, it must never be lightly treated, no movement could be allowed which was not founded on the laws of the organism, which would not serve to ennoble and develop the physical nature. For this reason, the work of body training must be in the hands of educated men and women, artists, who should mould their living models with reverent care. In order to carry out this theory, Ling applied to the Government for money to erect a training college for teachers of his system, and, after several refusals, his request was granted. In the early days of his enterprise, he encountered the fiercest opposition, his ideas were misunderstood on every side; but Sweden is a new country for his work. Now, the meanest Swedish peasant can tell you of Ling, and the poorest school has its simple gymnastic apparatus. The Educational Code enacts that four-and-a-half hours every week shall be devoted to the physical training of each child. The improvement in national physique is most marked. A recent visitor writes that in the streets of Stockholm a stooping or a round-shouldered person is rarely seen. The physical training seems, too, to have had its effect on character and manners; another visitor states that the absence of vice of every kind is remarkable, and it has been said that every Swede, be he baron or woodcutter, is a gentleman.

The Swedish system is now well-known in England and America; everywhere it has had the greatest success. The individuality of body training is the underlying idea. 'Each man,' said Ling, 'is the unit by which his strength should be measured.' His followers therefore strive, not at bringing every pupil to the same fixed standard of excellence, but at developing each body to its utmost possibilities. Competitive exercise is therefore discouraged; for what is but a slight effort to one pupil, may be violent exertion to another. The test of training in each case is the health and correct posture of the pupils; not the size and strength of this or that muscle. It is safe to say that if the heart and lungs are cared for, the muscular system will look after itself. Of course, a well-developed muscular system usually follows from gymnastic training, but in itself it is no guarantee of physical soundness: it is, by no means, uncommon to find great muscular strength and at the same time organic disease. Not long ago, a Society was formed for the 'Promotion of Physical Education.' Persons were offered certificates of physical proficiency, who should perform certain feats of strength. For example, a certificate was offered to all who should raise themselves a certain number of times on the horizontal bar. Such a test by itself is absurd; it certainly indicates the strength of the biceps muscle, but not of the whole body. A considerable number of non-Swedish gymnasts suffer from heart-disease, produced by too constant use of the bar, the trapeze, and the vaulting horse. Exercises on these pieces of apparatus are always popular, but they are of a somewhat violent nature, and exert a distinct strain on the heart. Taken among other movements, these are valuable; but when they form, as they often do, the whole of the gymnastic lesson, they are most injurious. Moreover, these particular exercises chiefly affect the muscles of the arms, and those between the shoulder blades: the latter especially become unduly developed by over use, and extremely round shoulders are the result. Go to any ordinary gymnastic exhibition and you will notice this excessive muscular development, amounting in some cases to positive deformity. The gymnasium has produced acrobats, but at the same time, a set of mis-shapen citizens!

The fault of all this lies with the general public, who have as yet no true conception of physical training, and who entrust this branch of education to teachers, many of whom are entirely ignorant of the most elementary physical laws. Gymnastic movements are but means to an end; too often they are considered the end itself. Those of Ling's System are for the most part simple; and though many of them require great skill and physical control to perform them faultlessly, none are showy or acrobatic. The body is trained step by step, by means of carefully graduated exercises; so that at last the pupils execute really difficult movements without strain or undue effort. In short, pupils who have taken a course of Swedish gymnastics reach, in so far as individual defects will allow, a high standard of physical development and control.

In the last few years physical training has done much for English girls; in the future, when it is a recognised part of education, it will do much more. But, before it can become general, there will have to be an awakening to a nobler conception of the human body, a fuller recognition among women themselves of the worth and wonder of the physical self. To make physical education an established fact, it is needed not so much that we follow this or that code of rules, but that we should, each one of us give individual thought to the matter. We are coming more and more to see the unity of life, the dependence of every part of society on every other. Thoughtlessness, indifference, individual irresponsibility do not end with ourselves, for 'Our lives here are mostly in the power of other lives, and each one is bound to be his brother's keeper.' In a very real sense, women have in their keeping, not alone their own lives, but those of their children after them; if the mothers are well and strong, the children will be beautiful with the beauty of health. The physical regeneration of the race is no Utopian dream; we can begin it here and now.

One word in conclusion. The parts of our being are so intimately bound together, the seen and the unseen are in such close contact, that to raise and ennoble the physical self is to raise and ennoble the moral self too. In this lies the highest argument for physical education.

Anne Jemima Clough

Women's Progress in Scholarship

(1890)

Having been asked to give some account of high schools and colleges for women, and especially of their colleges and higher education and its results, I propose first to draw attention to some of the causes which forty years ago or more led to the rise of the higher education of women.

The great stirring of religious and political thought which began soon after the peace which followed the battle of Waterloo, and went on during the next twenty years – in which the Catholic Emancipation Bill was passed and the great Reform bill – and the movement for social reforms and for the improvement of the poor, penetrated into the homes of the well-to-do and those who, though not rich, ranked themselves among the gentry. Women's minds were stirred, and those who were unmarried and living at home without employment became restless. Their brothers had gone out into the world, and their married sisters were busy with their families, and those sisters left at home were too many for the work there. Moreover youth will long for some outlet, some intercourse with the outside world, some great interest to take up.

Most of these young women had had very little training, and knew not how to make plans or to carry out the schemes which floated through their minds. Those who had been more fortunate in their education perhaps felt more strongly the difficulties of running contrary to the opinions and wishes of their relations, and would see more clearly the many obstacles in the way of women who wished to do serious work. Still some found helpers, for did not the brothers come from schools and colleges, and enter into the difficulties of those at home? Dr Arnold's earnestness had moved them in their schoolboy days; they understood and appreciated the difficulties and the aspirations of their sisters. But it was not so with all; some had none to help them or give them sympathy. In the strong, irritation set in; they struggled for they knew not what, they became eccentric and acted unwisely. Others were overtaken by ill-health and became invalids; the battle of life was too strong for them.

But this was not to go on; some took courage. Religion and the enthusiasm of humanity have always been the torches which have lighted up unknown paths for women and given them courage to explore them. The great practical work done by Florence Nightingale moved women who were anxious for some great interest in their lives to venture to seek for it. She prescribed training and discipline, even as she had first sought for these requisites herself before she worked in the Crimea. As the number of women desiring practical occupations increased, the importance of opening out for them more complete courses of education increased also.

Already about 1845 Professor F. D. Maurice opened classes for women at King's College, of which he was Principal, and with the help of Charles Kingsley and other distinguished men he founded Queen's College, which received a royal charter in 1848. In 1849, Bedford College was opened by the exertions of the late Mrs Reid (who had also contributed funds to Queen's College), assisted by friends, and it was connected with University College. These were the first two institutions where higher education was given to women. Miss Beale was, I believe, for a time at Queen's College, and she afterwards became head of Cheltenham College, which has flourished under her management. Miss Buss's private school in London became very important, and set a good example of diligent work in higher subjects. Ultimately she placed it under trustees, thus giving it a public character. The College of Preceptors and the Society of Arts both opened their examinations – the one in 1854, the other in 1856 – but so far the old Universities had done nothing in that direction to assist teachers or schools.

The subject of advanced education was now warmly taken up by Miss Emily Davies. She began to form associations of schoolmistresses, and the local examinations having been granted by the University of Cambridge to boys between the ages of 12 and 18, Miss Davies got up a petition to the university praying that the like examinations might be extended to girls. In 1864 girls were admitted informally to an examination; in 1865 they were admitted by the university as an experiment; in 1867 they were admitted permanently. The School-Mistresses' Association did very important and valuable work in some of our largest towns. They began in London, Manchester, Leeds, Sheffield, and Newcastle, where they first prepared girls for the local examinations; Miss

Buss, who already had her large private school, took the lead in London. New books were much wanted and were now supplied, for boys were working in the same direction. At their meetings the mistresses planned and took counsel together and gave mutual help. They learnt to combine, they were no longer alone, each in her own small sphere, which had been dull and monotonous: they were now becoming part of a system and were gathering strength.

The writer of this article had the pleasure of being present at some of these meetings and of making the acquaintance of many of the members in several towns. Their earnestness and zeal were remarkable, and their power of combining surprising. They were very grateful for sympathy, and very willing to work hard on new lines without much hope of larger remuneration. Their union certainly has given them strength and dignity, and their life has been altered by it. The fact that the University of Cambridge had shown an interest in girls' education by admitting the girls to the local examinations was a great boon to them, it was a bond of union and was something to work for. In 1867 another movement arose. A number of ladies belonging to the northern towns joined together to procure the establishment of high class lectures of an educational character for young women. It was much desired that these should be delivered by university men. This scheme first occurred to me while on a visit at the house of Mr William Smith (the author of *Thorndale*) near London. The kind encouragement of Mr and Mrs William Smith emboldened me to make known my plan to friends in Liverpool and Manchester, and meetings were held there in 1865 and 1866. Friends in Leeds and Newcastle subsequently joined, and in the months of October and November 1867 lectures on the history of science were delivered by Professor James Stuart to audiences amounting to 620. Professor Stuart made the lectures strictly educational by supplying syllabuses and giving questions to be answered, on which he commented. Great was the enthusiasm of the young people, and their elders rejoiced.

While the lectures were going on, the promoters formed themselves into the North of England Council for promoting the Higher Education of Women, as a step towards carrying on these lectures; the first meeting was held in Leeds at the house of the late Dr Heaton, when Mrs Josephine Butler was elected president, and I became secretary. These lectures planned by women were financially a great success; the North of England Council went on for some ten years, and then the work having been taken up, and so many other societies having been formed and developed, both the Council and the organisation of lectures were given up.

One of the most important objects taken up and accomplished

by this Council was the establishment of the Higher Local Examination for women over eighteen years of age. At several meetings
of the Council the subject was warmly discussed. Some objected
because it was to be an examination for women only, but its object
was simply to encourage the intellectual development of women
after they had attained the age of eighteen. There was much
discussion, but finally the Council decided on framing and sending
in a petition to the University of Cambridge asking for such an
examination. This was largely signed, and was presented to the
late Master of Trinity, then Vice-Chancellor of the University, by
Mrs Josephine Butler in June, 1868. It was considered by the
Senate, and the prayer of the women was granted. The first examination was held in London, Manchester, Leeds, and Sheffield, and
women went in and were successful. Surely it was a great point
that women should be able, after they were eighteen, to keep up
their connection with the University. This examination is no
longer confined to women, but can also be taken by men.

In this same year, a very important one in an educational point
of view for women, a college for women, under the auspices of
Miss Emily Davies and other ladies, was opened at Hitchin, and
lecturers came from Cambridge and from London. In the
following year lectures for women were set up in Cambridge,
organised by a committee of men and women members of the
university, or connected with members of the university. In 1871
a residence for women from a distance wishing to attend lectures
at Cambridge was provided by Professor Sidgwick, and I undertook the management in the October term. After four years spent
at Merton Hall and other houses in Cambridge, Newnham Hall
was built and opened in October, 1875. Meanwhile, the college at
Hitchin had grown and had been removed to its present site at
Girton, near Cambridge, and in 1872 Miss Bernard became the
mistress. Students went in for the final examinations of the university informally from both the colleges and with success.

Meanwhile, in 1871, when opportunities for higher education
for women were fairly established, and the desire for it began to
grow, it became most important that schools for girls should also
be improved and multiplied. Mrs Grey and Miss Shireff, who had
both taken part in the discussion on the Report issued by the Royal
Commission on the Education of Girls, now proposed a scheme
for setting up girls' schools. These ladies, with some friends,
formed an organisation, under the name of the National Union for
Improving the Education of Women, and the Public Day Schools
Company was one of the results of this society. The first of these
schools was opened at Chelsea in 1873, and now in the School

Report for December, 1887, it is stated that the Company has 32 schools and 6,185 pupils under its management. The Church of England Day School Company, though only founded in 1883, has at least a dozen schools under its care. There are, besides, many independent high schools and many grammar schools and endowed schools which have been started during the last twenty years. Thus there is a large field for teachers, and our colleges have supplied a great number duly instructed and certificated.

We must now turn to Oxford. In 1879 an association was founded for providing lectures and examinations for women, and two halls of residence were opened – Somerville Hall, under the care of Miss Shaw Lefevre, and Lady Margaret Hall, presided over by Miss Wordsworth, who also lately opened on her own responsibility a small hall, where the terms are lower and the accommodation of a more economical kind: this is called St Hugh's.

At Westfield College, which is situated in Hampstead, students prepare for the London degree. Holloway College was opened last October, Miss Bishop being appointed head, and here also students prepare for the London degree, and also for the Oxford examinations. Queen Margaret's College in Glasgow is also an important institution, and there are three colleges for women in Wales, at Bangor, Aberystwyth, and Cardiff. In Ireland there is the Alexandra College for women, founded by Archbishop Trench and others. The first lady to preside there was Mrs Jellicoe, who worked with great diligence and greatly promoted its success. There is still something to add about the Cambridge colleges. Both Girton and Newnham have increased; Girton has added largely to the original building, and Newnham has built two more halls in its grounds. In 1880, when the second hall was built, the lecture association was dissolved, and the halls and the association were merged into one, under the name of Newnham College. For the first two years after it was built Dr and Mrs Henry Sidgwick kindly presided over the second hall, now called Sidgwick Hall. Miss Helen Gladstone succeeded them.

An event of great importance to the two colleges happened in the year 1881. Being petitioned on the subject of examinations for women the Senate of the University of Cambridge by a large majority agreed to admit women formally to their Honour Examinations, and certificates were granted them in the place of degrees.

A large legacy left by Miss Gamble again enabled Girton to add to its already large accommodation, and Newnham, being full, ventured on erecting a third hall and taking in more ground. This last new hall was opened on 9 June last, on the day on which

Prince Albert Victor came to Cambridge to receive an honorary degree; and on this festive occasion the Prince and Princess of Wales, with the young Princesses, and the newly made doctor, Prince Albert Victor, graciously honoured the college with a visit, and thus gave it their royal sanction and sympathy. Over 170 old students came up to this fête, and with the present students there must have been some 300 to welcome the royal party and to assist in entertaining the guests of the college.

The tables on pages 302–3 show what results have been obtained, in the final examinations of the universities, by the women's colleges at Oxford and Cambridge, and the number of women who have availed themselves of the opportunities given to them there. It should be noticed in addition, that a very large number of students at Newnham and the two Oxford colleges have also worked for the Cambridge Higher Local and Oxford women's examinations, and have been very successful in them. Many hundreds of girls have worked at Bedford College, and at Queen's College, and a large number have obtained the London degree. Westfield College at Hampstead has been open since 1882, and six of its students have already obtained the London degree.

What are the advantages of college life for women, and what are the results in a general way? I have given some particulars about the scholarship of the students, and I will now mention a few other points. Our colleges have gathered together women from very varied homes, from different classes in society, with their special tastes and opinions, and, lastly, from different countries. These women have lived together and studied together as friends and comrades; they have learnt to plan and work together and to carry out schemes among themselves. Their studies have taught them energy and self-control; their examinations have taught them the power of collecting their thoughts rapidly, of putting them into words, and of exercising their memories. It may be that these examinations are too frequent and too severe for some students; still they are no doubt useful as tests, and are bracing to the intellect. On another side we may notice the benefits which come from the games and amusements that go on among the students from their societies and clubs. These all tend to bring the members of the colleges together, and to give brightness and joy to their lives. Music and singing are not neglected, concerts and recitals and also dancing are among the pleasures of the winter evenings. We may add that the college authorities, heads, and lecturers have done their best to promote a high tone in the women's colleges, and, we hope, with some success.

When students leave they still keep up their connection with their colleges, and often visit them. There is an annual dinner at Girton for old students, when some forty or fifty students come from a distance for a happy meeting, and a sight of their old college and old friends, and twice when Newnham has had a festival great numbers of its old members have returned to join in the pleasures of the day.

And now I will add a few words about the work taken up by the students. A considerable number are lecturers in our colleges, a great number are head-mistresses and assistant-mistresses in high schools and private schools; some have opened schools or are private teachers; four at least have taken work in Board schools. Some have gone to the United States, some to India, some to New Zealand, South Africa, Australia, and Japan. Several have taken up the study of medicine, two or three are practising it. Art, literature, and research have attracted others. One has much distinguished herself in the study of Greek art,[1] and has written and lectured successfully on the subject; another has done original work in history, and several are contributors to magazines, and have had some success in novel-writing and poetry.

Lately the women's colleges have joined in forming a small settlement in Southwark, to do work among the pupil teachers in the Board schools, the children belonging to these schools, and among the poorer classes in general in that neighbourhood. Past and present students are engaged in the work, belonging to the Oxford and Cambridge and to the London colleges, as well as many non-university helpers. Funds are annually collected by committees in the several colleges, and a committee representing all the colleges superintends the arrangements and the disposal of the funds. A University club has been instituted, which has its abode in Bond Street, and is useful as a meeting-place for college students. I need hardly mention that many of those who have been with us are happy wives and mothers. Many others are living in their own homes, and we believe are making them brighter by the outside experience they have gained, by the new friends they bring to join the family circle, and by their varied interests. One more society I must mention, the University Association of Women Teachers. Its object is to put head-mistresses and parents both at home and in the colonies into communication with assistant-teachers who have passed university examinations. The honorary secretary is Miss C. Elder, Campden House, Kensington.

But we are not yet satisfied; we hope to add several new professions to those now followed by women. They might be conveyancers (one lady, as is well known, already does this work), analytical chemists, dispensers; they might take up more largely

	Number of Students	Number entered for Final Exam.	Mathematical Tripos Class I. II. III.	Classical Tripos Class I. II. III.	Moral Sciences Tripos Class I. II. III.	Natural Sciences Tripos Class I. II. III.	Historical Tripos Class I. II. III.	Modern Languages Tripos Class I. II. III.	Theological Tripos Class I. II. III.	Ordinary Degree
Girton College, open 19 years	295	153	Part I. 3 19 21 / Part II. 1	Part I. 5 20 15 / Part II. 2 2 1 / Unclassified 11	1 10 5 / —	Part I. 8 15 4 / Part II. 2 3 3	5 5 4	1	1	31
Newnham College, open 17 years	451	166	Part I. 3 17 20 / Part II. 2	Part I. 1 10 6 / Part II. 6 1 / Unclassified 4	5 11 12	Part I. 10 22 6 / Part II. 1 7 1	11 17 4	4 4 3	—	2

	Number of Students	Number entered for Final Exam.	Mathematics HON. Mods. Class I. II. III.	Mathematics FINAL SCHOOLS Class I. II. III. IV.	Classics HON. MODS. Class I. II. III.	Classics Class I. II. III. IV.	History Class I. II. III. IV.	Natural Science Class I. II. III. IV.	Literature Class I. II. III. IV.	Modern Languages Class I. II. III. IV.	Philosophy Class I. II. III.
Somerville Hall, open 9 years	86	—	2	1 1	1 1		2 2 2	1 1	5 4 1	3 7 1 1	—
Lady Margaret Hall, open 9 years	100	—	1 1	—	2		1 1	—	3	1 2 3	2 1

	First Classes	Second Classes	Third Classes
Somerville Hall	12	16	6
Lady Margaret Hall	7	7	4

	First Classes	Second Classes	Third Classes
Girton College	26	74	56
Newnham College	41	89	51

In the Classical Tripos of 1887 Miss A. F. Ramsay, of Girton College, was Senior.

gardening, farming, and some kinds of business. But, whatever they do, they must learn to be painstaking and accurate. Our students, at any rate, have taken a variety of paths. Some women love variety, and perhaps it is good for them, but many have been steadfast workers, as, for instance, our devoted college lecturers, head-mistresses, and assistant-teachers. We feel sure that our cordial fellowship is helpful; may it long continue, and may the bond of union that binds us together and unites us to those who have spent their time and their strength, their anxious thoughts, and labour in building up our communities, be strengthened. All honour to our founders! Their names are many, and we are proud of them. Some have fallen asleep, but their names are enshrined in our memories.

NOTE

1 Miss Jane Harrison.

Millicent Garrett Fawcett

Altissima Peto: An Address to High School Pupils

(n.d.)

I have been invited by the kindness of the editor of *Time* to express an opinion upon the aims and results of High School education for girls. These aims appear to me to be similar to those of all education which is worthy of the name – that is, to train children in such a manner as to make the best of the intellectual and moral capacity with which each has been endowed by nature. The results must necessarily, in every land but Utopia, fall short of this aim. But the fact that we cannot achieve the highest, is no reason for not aiming at the highest. The aim and end of education, whether for boys or girls, and whether in High Schools or elsewhere, I endeavoured a short time ago to picture, as I conceive it, in a short address, here transcribed, to the pupils of the Girls' High School at Clapham.

It must often occur to every intelligent child to wonder why its parents and teachers appear to attach so much importance to the subject of education. It is not obvious, to say the least, what use in after life it will be to know the exact history of the extraordinary excitement at Athens in 415 B.C. caused by the destruction of the Hermæ; to be able to play with decimals and 'imagine solids,' and to have a firm and positive view as to whether Mary or Anne Boleyn were the elder of the two sisters. When any girl so far makes me her friend as to confide doubts of this kind to me, my custom has been to answer that it is not so much the absolute knowledge of facts acquired in education that is of value, as a certain quality, which real knowledge of almost any kind, gives to the mind. Those who will take the trouble to learn anything really well will be delivered, all the rest of their life, from mistaking what they do know for what they do not know. To know what you know, is a security that you will also know what you do not know. I believe it is one of the traditional sayings of Socrates that the result of his learning had been to convince him that he knew nothing. It is one of the principal objects of education to teach people the difference between what they know and what they do not know. The more crudely ignorant any one is, the more daring, probably, will be his assumption; whereas it is proverbial that no one is more humble, in the presence of the vast regions of the unknown, than the men of science who, like Newton and Darwin, can almost be said to have made one special realm of knowledge their own. Of Newton we have the beautiful anecdote which tells how he compared himself to a child who had merely gathered a few shells from the vast ocean of the wonders of the universe; while of Darwin, all the readers of his life will acknowledge the incomparable charm of his deep humility and of his reverence for truth. The exact contrary of these beautiful qualities is the characteristic of ignorance. The man who said he did not know whether he could play the violin because he had never tried was in a very elementary stage of ignorance; he had not learned to distinguish between what he knew and what he did not know. And it must be borne home to every teacher and many students that school work leaves the pupils just where it found them, in this important respect, unless the work gone through is real and hearty. It must not be of the kind described in the little boy:

> And if you asked of him to say
> What twice ten was or three times seven,
> He'd glance in quite a placid way
> From heaven to earth, from earth to heaven:
> And smile, and look politely round
> To catch a casual suggestion;
> But make no effort to propound
> Any solution of the question.

Every one must feel that, however fascinating this little boy was, his education, at the period indicated, had hardly begun. Education, if it is real, means definite, persistent effort, not to excel others, but to gather knowledge; it teaches the value of accuracy, and it will enable those on whom its influence has been exerted to appreciate their own ignorance. I am not sure that it will not do another thing; that is, teach the difference between what can be known and what cannot be known. It is dangerous to be dogmatic as to what, among the vast interests of human life, belong to the things which cannot be known. One of the greatest of men taught, in his day, that physics and astronomy were subjects inaccessible to the mind of man, and that to study them was 'insane, fruitless, and impious.' This error of so great a mind should teach us humility and hesitation before saying that such and such a region of thought can never be conquered by human intelligence. It must not be too readily assumed that the ample page of knowledge, rich with the spoils of time, has been fully unrolled. But the more successful education has been in teaching students the conditions under which knowledge of any subject can be acquired, the less liable will they be to be deceived by the false promises which some people have held out that they will solve the insoluble enigmas which shroud so much of the origin of things, and of the relation between matter and spirit. When, for instance, a lady professes to lift the veil which separates life from death, and seeks to prove the truth of her mission by banging you on the head with a tambourine, in a dark room, or by causing cigarettes to drop from the ceiling or coffee cups to float there, I think if our education has been of any use to us we shall perceive that such things can never advance our knowledge of the spiritual world one iota. 'That which is born of the flesh is flesh, and that which is born of the spirit is spirit.' The grotesque absurdities which are miscalled spiritualism are nothing to the point. The influence, stronger than physical force of really spiritual things, such as mercy, justice, love, and purity, indicate the sources from which we must seek to know more of the inner life of the spirit; and if, in the life of the spirit, we are constantly brought up, just as we are in the physical world, against the blank wall of the unknown, I think we are more spiritually minded when we bow the head in acknowledgment of our ignorance and feebleness, than when we seek to lift the veil from the impenetrable mysteries which surround our life.

Therefore to sum up: the years of education will serve, it may be hoped, not only to give you who are students habits of patient, persevering industry and accuracy, but will help you to distinguish between what you know and what you do not know, and between what can be known and what cannot be known. If your education does this for you it has accomplished a task far more valuable to you than any of the special knowledge you may have acquired.

Other thoughts than these, however, almost necessarily come into the minds of us older women when we stand, as we do today, face to face with a number of the young recruits. Perhaps that word indicates what I mean. I look upon you as young soldiers just about to enter a great fight. Only we do not know, perhaps no one knows yet, which side you will fight upon. That you will fight on one side or the other is certain and inevitable. I mean that the total result of your life's work, when the end comes, will be either to have helped the powers of goodness and righteousness, or the powers of darkness. This is the great strife that is going on everywhere in the world, and in which, whether we know it or not, we are all taking part. In the baptismal service of the Church of England every girl and boy is dedicated at the font, and the promise is made, in the name of the child, 'manfully to fight under Christ's banner against sin, the world, and the devil, and to continue Christ's faithful soldier and servant to his life's end.' And I doubt not that other religious bodies have a somewhat similar form of dedicating their children to the right side in the great warfare of life. But whether this is so or not, it is a strife in which not one of us can remain inactive; and if we could, the enforced quiescence would be in itself a doom more painful than the imagination can easily grasp. One of De Quincey's most terrible dreams pictured such a situation. Some great battle, a strife, an agony was going forward; the day was one of crisis and of ultimate hope for human nature; a greater interest was at stake, a mightier cause than ever yet the sword had pleaded, or the trumpet had proclaimed; and the dreamer had the consciousness that in him lay the power to determine the issue of the battle. 'I had the power and yet had not the power to decide it. . . . I had the power if I could raise myself to will it; and yet again had not the power, for the weight of twenty Atlantics was upon me, or the oppression of inexpiable guilt. "Deeper than ever plummet sounded I lay inactive." . . . Then came the awful sense that all was lost, lost in consequence of this paralysis of the will, which was torture the most exquisite that could be endured.' No wonder that the dreamer added, 'I awoke in struggles, and cried aloud, "I will sleep no more." '

This horrible doom of lying inactive while a battle is proceeding, the issue of which is one of ultimate hope for human nature, is one which exists only in poetical imagination. We must all of us take a side one way or another. It was one of the wise laws of Solon, that any citizen who stood apart and neutral during a period of tumult and sedition should be dishonoured and disfranchised; and in the great battle of right against wrong, reality against shams, truth against falsehood, health against disease, cleanliness against dirt, order against disorder, industry against idleness, we all must take our part, and help on one side or the other. The object of your education is in reality to prepare you to be stalwart soldiers on the right side. Like the gymnastic exercises of the ordinary soldier, your mental and moral powers are now being tried and cultivated, in order that when the time comes 'the faithful soldier and servant' may be an efficient warrior in whatever part of the great strife she finds herself engaged. No one can tell what your marching orders will be. Perhaps the first enemy you will have to contend with will be in your own heart; there may be some tendency to laziness, selfishness, or vanity to overcome. The work that lies nearest is always that which should engage us first, and who so near to us as we ourselves? Just before Trafalgar the great and ever-honoured Nelson issued a series of instructions to his captains concluding in the words: 'As for captains who during the combat are unable to perceive the admiral's signal, they cannot do amiss if they place their vessel alongside a vessel of the enemy.' This direction will serve for us too. 'If, during the combat, we are unable to perceive the admiral's signal, we cannot do amiss if we place our vessel alongside a vessel of the enemy.' The enemy is the many-headed beast: vanity, ignorance, lying, uncleanness, intemperance – all those things, in a word, which degrade and lower mankind, and make the world far less happy and beautiful than it would otherwise be.

The simile I have used of a battle in which we all are soldiers suggests rather too much, I fear, a kind of physical boisterousness which I do not at all wish to recommend. The most efficient soldier against the powers of darkness is often among the most quiet and gentle in outward demeanour. Our object should really be to make what is good and right easier both to ourselves and others; this kind of influence often proceeds, as many of us have been fortunate enough to learn, from those to whom physical conflict would be an impossibility. Who has not known cases in which, from an invalid's couch, has proceeded a powerful compelling influence, supporting whatsoever things are pure, righteous, and of good report? No one needs physical prowess to become a power on the side of goodness; the only thing essential is the heart and will earnestly to strive for truth and right. Any one who has these is a power in the world for goodness, however narrow and limited may be the circle in which she moves.

One hears, now and then, a good deal said about over-work, and I think those who have the charge of education cannot be too careful to avoid its evils. My own feeling is that the most over-worked class in the educational world are the teachers, and I should be very glad to hear that their labour was substantially lightened; but I think they will agree with me that over-work is a less evil than under-work. To see a woman of really able mind and power frittering away her life in trifles, is far more melancholy, to my mind, than over-work. A blind lady, the daughter of a bishop, who began at the age of twenty-four or five to work hard to improve the condition of the blind, was often entreated by her friends not to work herself to death. She had tried the ordinary society life of an upper class family, and invariably replied, 'I am not working myself to death; I am working myself to life.' To the girls whom I see before me, I now appeal to devote themselves, when their schooldays are over, to some worthy and ennobling work which will leave the world better than they found it; and so far from working themselves to death, I think they will find, as Miss Gilbert did, that they are working themselves to life.

Wilena Hitching

Home Management

(1910)

I Introduction

Work *should be the end and aim of education*, for work is the source of all true felicity – it is the *secret of happiness in life* (RUSKIN)

Begin by asking why all girls and boys have to attend school from five to fourteen years of age. Then lead on to the subjects taught in the girls' school, and in a pleasant, chatty style get the girls to name their favourite lessons, and tell why they are so. (The teacher will find that even girls of this tender age manifest keen appreciation of those subjects that will help them most when they leave school.) Then lead them to think which is the most important subject for girls to learn – a subject that every girl can even now take a great interest in – a subject that, when she is older, may become all-important to her, namely, the management of a home.

How proud a girl is of her *doll's* house! How delightful it will be for these girls to have, some day, a *real* house of their *very own* to manage! Do not be content until the eyes of every child in the class sparkle with enthusiasm. Contrast various types of homes – some so comfortable; some, alas! just the reverse. What makes the difference? Not money – for a poor home may be a very happy one – but the disposition of the people and *the way the homes are managed*.

Nobody can manage a home well unless she feels in her heart what a splendid work it is she is doing. The cleverest *men* in the world may make good, wise laws, and strive with all their might to make the nation happy and prosperous; but unless *woman's* work is well done they cannot succeed, for mismanaged homes can never make a happy nation. It is not only good *law-makers* that are needed, but good *home-makers*. In no walk of life is there more need for unselfishness; there is no more self-denying, no more heroic, no more truly lovable person than a good mother. From morning to night, week in, week out, she thinks for others, and looks after their comfort. To the mother in the home, to sisters and daughters, has been given the *most important* and *noblest work in the world* – that of home-making.

Lead the girls to think what makes a happy home, and how it may be recognised. From a happy home goes forth, morning by morning, a happy, healthy, well-cared for father, who, because he has such a comfortable home, is never tempted to spend his evenings in the public-house or club. A happy home means happy children also – healthy-bodied, clear-minded, good-mannered, light-hearted, and fond of fun.

Home management needs not only a woman's loving heart and willing hands, but a *clever brain*. It is not true to say that *any one* can manage a home. The best home manager is the one who begins, when quite a little girl, to fit herself for the work. Ask the girls which of them would like to begin now; to have lessons in school that they can at once carry out in their own homes, and surprise and gladden father and mother. Then when the time comes – and speak of this in a matter-of-fact sort of way – that the girls have homes of their own, what happy, comfortable homes they will be – a credit to themselves, a credit to their town, and a credit to the nation!

Enthusiasm having thus been aroused, the teacher may proceed with the lessons, giving the subject of each beforehand, so as to lead the children to think about and talk over the matter with their mothers. The teacher who gives the lessons in a tactful, sympathetic way creates a bond of union between herself and the parents, and brings out the dullest children in the class in a most wonderful manner. (The writer recalls with pleasure the case of a poor girl, the very per-sonification of dullness, who became a perfect enthusiast in the art of furniture-polishing, and who, after seeing the effect of the polish on the school piano, could with difficulty be restrained from clean-ing and polishing every other wooden article in the school.)

II   Management of the Home

1. Need for Method and Forethought

Much discomfort is caused in very many homes through lack of method, and consequent waste of time. It is *wrong* for mothers and those at home to have housework going on in the evening, when fathers and elder brothers and sisters return after a hard day's toil, and naturally expect peace and comfort. Dwell at much length on this point; lead the children to think of the great number of fathers and elder brothers who are practically *driven* outside, to seek at public-houses, clubs, or music halls the comfort that should be theirs at home. A good housewife is never happier than when she has all the members of her family around her.

Show the school time-table. Lead the girls to imagine what a *school* would be like without one. It is just as necessary to have a working time-table for the *home*, and it is an excellent plan for the young, inexperienced home manager to write one out. Tell the girls that later on they shall make a time-table in their note-books – a good-sized exercise-book, used not only for the Home Management lessons of the first year's course, but for those of the second and third years' courses also. This book should become the property of each girl on leaving school.

No girl has the least chance of becoming a good home manager unless she is orderly and methodical in her work. There must be no rushing about at random, no sitting down and wondering what to do next. To 'run a house' smoothly, the work must be carefully planned beforehand, and carried out, so far as possible, as planned. 'Order is Heaven's first law,' and it must be the home manager's too. If she would avoid hopeless muddle, her rule must be, 'Clear as you go.' There must be one place, and no other, for everything in the house, but more especially in her kitchen.

2. A Day's Housework

Lead the girls to suggest, if possible, every step, and the need for it.

(1)   The great importance of early rising. For a comfortable 8 a.m. breakfast, the mother and girls at home should be down not later than 7 a.m.

(2)   **Before Breakfast** – (i) The fire should be lighted. This is a suitable task for the boys of the home, who should be held responsible for this work, and for the replenishing of all coal-boxes and the cleaning of, at all events, father's boots and their own. No thoughtful man or boy will ever allow his wife or mother or sister to drag heavy coal-scuttles up the kitchen stairs.

(ii) The living-room should be swept and dusted. Breakfast should be a comfortable meal in a comfortable room.

(iii) The children should be roused, washed, and dressed,

313

except the baby, which should be washed later. If big enough to wash themselves – and a careful mother will early train them little by little in this respect – the children are still not too big to appreciate mother's approving glance, following the careful scrutiny of necks and ears of boys, hair of girls, and the teeth and nails of both.

(iv) If there is more than one daughter at home able to help, the entrance or passage, door-bell, and front doorstep should be cleaned before breakfast.

(v) Breakfast should be served punctually, and all members of the family should be required to present themselves in a tidy, *fully-dressed* condition; no girl in curling-pins, no boy without a collar. See if the girls know anything of gongs. Show one; let a child strike it. Lead the children to see what trouble it saves in large houses, and tell them what a breach of good manners it is for even a *visitor* not to obey it quickly. How much more necessary is it to be punctual at breakfast in *one's own home*, where there is often only one pair of hands to do almost all the work!

·   (3)   **After Breakfast** – (i) The breakfast-things should be cleared away on a tray, and the washing-up water put on.

(ii) While the water is being heated, the mother goes upstairs to empty the slops, wash out and frequently 'scald' every utensil, using a special cloth reserved for that one purpose. She notices particularly if all the members of her family – even the little girls – have left their bedrooms just as they ought to be left. Lead the children to offer suggestions, and make the lesson real by using a large doll's bed, or, better still, an ordinary single one. Let a girl take off her boots, put on a night-dress, and pretend to be a girl just getting up in the morning. Let her carefully throw the bedclothes back over the foot of the bed and two chairs placed with their backs to the bed. Lead the other girls to see why all this is necessary; why, unless the day is very foggy and damp, the windows must be opened wide top and bottom; why the night-dress, night-shirt, or pyjamas should be hung over another chair for some little time; why the bed is not made straight away; why the slops should be emptied first thing.

(iii) The breakfast-things should be washed, and the kitchen tidied. The fire should be made up ready for cooking the dinner.

(iv) Mother next puts on a clean apron and cookery-sleeves, and goes to make the beds. Then she takes off her clean apron and sleeves and puts on another apron. Her next work is to take up with carpet-brush and dust-shovel any 'bits' there may be on the carpet. The hair-combings from the tidies she puts on the shovel. Then she dusts the bedrooms, the landings, and the stairs.

(v) The bathroom taps must be rubbed daily, and a careful mother will always put on old gloves for this and similar work. Speak of the need for each member of the family leaving the lavatory basin clean.

(vi) Preparation for dinner. (*a*) Freshly-filled salt-cellars, spotlessly-clean knives, shining forks and spoons, and transparent glasses should be put on a tray all ready; (*b*) table to be properly and daintily laid; and (*c*) dinner, like the breakfast, to be served punctually.

(vii) Washing up dinner-things.

(viii) The fire should be made up for the afternoon, the kettle filled and put on the hob (but not allowed to boil until wanted), and the kitchen and scullery left quite tidy.

(ix) The housewife should now wash and dress herself, and prepare tea. After tea she should wash up, or, better still, let the girls home from school do so.

(x) A good home manager tries to have the evenings for conversation, reading, games, or needlework. (One may be *sure* the home is a pleasant one when the father and mother join in games with the children, and when one sees that after the little ones have gone to bed, the father reads some bright, entertaining story, or extracts from the newspaper, to his wife and elder children while they are busy with their needlework.)

(xi) At dusk the bedrooms should be prepared for their occupants. Leave the windows open a few inches at the top; turn the bedclothes down; supply clean water, unless there is a bathroom which can be used by every member of the family (each having his own towel, flannel, tooth-brush, comb, etc.).

(xii) Give the children their supper; after which undress, wash, and put them to bed. Next get supper ready for the adults. Clear away, and get the firing ready for next morning. It is a good plan to put out on a tray the breakfast-things – cups and saucers, spoons, knives, forks, plates, etc. – ready for morning, and cover all with a clean tea-cloth or towel. Some people lay the *table* ready, and cover all with an old, clean tablecloth; and this is an excellent plan where there is only 'one pair of hands' to do all the work.

Margaret A. Gilliland

Home Arts

(1911)

In recent years there has been a widespread movement to bring the education of our girls into relation with their work as home-makers. The old 'blue-stocking' type, who prided herself on not knowing how to sew and mend, and who thought cooking menial, and beneath her, no longer appeals to anyone. The ideal is developing, and we are learning to regard with pity anyone, girl or woman, who is helpless in a home. But at the same time we no longer share the conception of a woman's whole duty held by our grandmothers. We do not applaud the mother or daugher who spends long hours in the kitchen, or who revels in turning the whole house upside down and inside out in that most bewildering and least methodical of all human inconveniences – the spring cleaning. We have come to see that method and system are better than rule of thumb and guesswork, that housekeeping is as much a science as an art, and that in it, as in all other departments of life, it is brain that tells. We want our girls to grow up into sensible, methodical, practical women, able to direct intelligently and sympathetically the manifold activities of the home – ready themselves to lend a hand if the call come – and imbued with a deep sense of the worth and dignity of all true work, whether it be scrubbing a floor or construing a crabbed Greek chorus.

With this change of ideal there has entered into many of our schools an effort to equip girls for such work. The action of the Board of Education has done much to encourage this aim. But prejudice dies hard, and in too many schools the ideal is still purely intellectual in the strictly limited and scholastic sense, and cooking and domestic economy generally are looked down upon as all right for 'poor dears' or 'duffers,' but waste of time for a really clever girl.

Regarded from the point of view of instruction in home arts, secondary schools for girls fall roughly into four main groups. It should be stated in passing that practically all schools teach needlework, though the vast majority confine such instruction to the junior classes, and generally discontinue it in one of the Fourth Forms.

(*a*) Some neglect the subject altogether, and explain, where they think explanation necessary, that they consider this subject as falling within the province of the home authorities.

(*b*) A section, unfortunately a fairly considerable one, look upon home arts as the Cinderella of the educational family. When a girl positively cannot make progress with ordinary school work she is put into the cookery class. This position is stated with startling *naïveté* by one school: 'A few girls who are backward in intellectual work learn cookery.'

(*c*) An increasing and very important section, including some of our prominent high schools, carry out a very comprehensive and scientific scheme of work as a post-school course, to be taken, either after the girl leaves school, or when she reaches the age of seventeen. It is perhaps not unfair to point out in passing that this group implicitly suggests the theory of (*b*), because a girl of seventeen, if she is really clever, is generally drafted into classes working for University examinations and not into the parallel 'technical form' where a good many of the ordinary school subjects are dropped. Again, a girl of this sort first begins to feel the pressure of outside examinations about this time, and she is not likely to wish to spend several hours a week on subjects completely outside her syllabus.

(*d*) A few schools regard the due and reasonable training of every girl in the duties and needs of home life as one of their gravest and most sacred responsibilities. In these schools, each girl, clever or average, rich or poor, goes through a course of needlework, cookery, laundry, hygiene, dressmaking, and household accounts.

It will perhaps be useful to take these various groups, and give schemes typical of each. (*a*) and (*b*) need little comment. It is true we want our girls to know the joys of real scholarship: to feel the exultation of seeing their way through a stiff piece of mathematical work, to hear the haunting pathos of Virgil's verse, to see the clash and clangour of human emotion, its laughter and its tears, in our great dramatists. We want them to catch the patient spirit of self-sacrifice and dogged perseverance that must characterise true learning, but we must never forget that they are to be women first and scholars afterwards; dutiful daughters and wise, sympathetic mothers, not only college lecturers and high school mistresses. Therefore we cannot regard home arts as outside the aim of the school. Schools that omit all instruction in the preparation for home life, or who, worse still, treat such preparation with hurtful contempt, may, and do, produce fine scholars. But they are doing very little to help our national life, because they are doing nothing to make our girls builders of homes and makers of men. It is worse than useless to expect a girl to get systematic training at home in housekeeping, when you keep her at school each morning from 9.15 to 1.15, expect her to play games, take gymnasium, drawing, and probably music in the afternoon, and give her sufficient home-work to keep her busy all the evening. In most cases I believe such girls grow up with practically no share in the home life, and with no real knowledge of the principles of cookery and housekeeping generally, exiles from all the sweet joys and varied interests of their own home circle.

The third class is of great importance. Schemes of work here are based upon the principle that a thorough training in home arts can be given only to girls who have reached a certain maturity, intellectually and morally. Since in these cases the pupil takes up the subject only when she is free from the claims of ordinary school lessons, the instruction covers a very wide field. One prominent high school in London grants a 'Housewife's Certificate' to students who take their full course in 'Experimental Home Science and Economics'. In schools under this section the syllabus generally indicates lectures and practical work in the chemistry of food and the house, in laundry, practical and scientific, in upholstery, in dressmaking, in nursing, in child study, and in household accounts and – most delightful item – 'how to carry out economies'.

Such schemes are of widespread interest as showing a deliberate and carefully thought-out effort to cope with the question of preparation for home life, and, theoretically, they provide for instruction in every possible department of the home. Thus, the introductory lesson of the first term deals with the 'origin of home,' 'the business of home-making'; subsequent lectures treat of the construction and management of stoves, fuel, the chemistry of water, cleanliness, and cleaning, 'matter, its nature and changes,' cooking, fuel, foods, study of starch, study of wheat, and in the place of Lecture XII stands the one word 'examination'.

There are two other terms of this course dealing with the composition of various food-stuffs. The training for the elementary certificate takes one year – 700 hours' work; for the advanced course a second year of 700 hours is needed.

The 700 hours are thus apportioned:

Divinity	30
Chemistry	100
Cookery	130
Laundry	80
Housewifery	90
Dressmaking	110
Needlework	110
Hygiene	50

In thoroughly considering schemes of this type, one feels that there is a danger of their becoming too comprehensive; of being extensive rather than intensive. One must of course bear in mind the type of pupil who takes a course of this sort. If she has passed through a good high school she will have had several years' experience in the laboratory, and will therefore be able to grasp scientific ideas better than a less carefully educated girl.

In other schools in this group, there is a special course for girls taking only some of the ordinary school subjects. It is practical rather than scientific, and is designed as the beginning of a preparation for home life.

Several large and important schools are doing work of this kind, and it is a very hopeful sign that housecraft is at last recognised as requiring definite and systematic study and teaching. And many a girl who would otherwise be a little at a loss on leaving school, will find in such a course an interest and an ideal that will help her to bridge over those difficult first years when school life, with its manifold responsibilities, interest, and delights, is ended, and full home duties are not yet assumed.

The weak point lies in the fact that the clever girls who are going through the VIth for university scholarships go to college without any knowledge, as far as the school is concerned, of home arts. Surely the promising girl who wants to become a college lecturer or a doctor needs help in this direction. Indeed it is just she who most needs it, and who must get it during school years, if she is to get it at all. College life once begun, there is little to develop home instincts and household skill. In truth there is much to draw away from these activities, and it behoves the schools to remember that the future of the race depends on the mothers of the coming generation. They must not only be scholarly in book learning, but skilled in household arts, ready, when the sacred call comes to them, to take their place as home-makers and home-keepers.

There remains the (*d*) class, schools in which training in the home arts forms an integral part of the curriculum.

These schools nearly always provide for instruction in needlework for all younger children. The effort is to make this as practical as possible and to avoid, therefore, all merely 'sampler work'.

Cookery is generally taken in the Upper IV or Lower V Form by girls of about fifteen years of age. The aim throughout is to teach the children the scientific explanation of processes which they carry out practically in the cookery room. The science course bears upon the chemistry of food, the action of acids, and of heat, etc., and the various processes of digestion.

The strong point of such schemes is that the children really see the same chemical processes under two aspects, at one time in the laboratory with all the conditions of a scientific experiment, at another in the cookery room with all the circumstances of home needs in the way of varied menus and the necessity for securing that 'good digestion waits on appetite'. The weak point lies in the danger lest the one side should gain undue prominence to the unfair subordination of the other. If the science is sacrificed to the practical cookery, the children lose valuable training in scientific method; if the science usurps too much time, the cookery becomes doctrinaire and unpractical. Each must have its due share. The science mistress and the cookery mistress must work in entire harmony and mutual confidence.

Criticism, to justify itself, must be constructive not merely destructive, and I would therefore, with all diffidence, outline a scheme in which the home arts is absolutely an integral part of the school work, taken alike by the brilliant girl, and by her less richly endowed sister, regarded with the respect and enthusiasm accorded to any other branch of study.

One must begin by saying that, except in small schools, the science and cookery mistresses cannot be one and the same person. The science mistress must, however, know a good deal about the practical side of cookery and laundry. The home-arts mistress must know the principal facts of elementary inorganic chemistry and must have studied the chemistry of food.

Another important preliminary condition; the home-arts mistress must be a regular member of the staff, and should, if possible, be in charge of a Form. This gives her and her department standing. She should teach some subject beyond her special work, some elementary mathematics, some English or nature study, it matters not what, so long as there is no suggestion of 'watertight compartments'. If the school is a large one, it is impossible that the mistress should also be school matron and responsible for servants and housekeeping. She must be entirely identified with the teaching staff and take her place in the mistresses' common room like any other specialist. On the character and standing of the home-arts mistress much depends. Her subject has to win its way in the face of a good deal of old-established prejudice. You cannot get the home arts taught just anywhere and by anyone.

Naturally, needlework would commence the course. The little people in Form I begin sewing, and it should be continued throughout the lower and middle school. At first forty-five minutes' lessons would give ample time, later, an hour, and then one hour and a half, or two hours would be necessary. There should not be more than fifteen in a class. This could be planned by sending half the class to drawing and half to needlework one day, and changing the divisions on another day, or one set might take needlework and the remainder science. Small classes are an absolute essential if girls are to develop individuality and self-reliance.

In no class should the children merely practise stitches, all work should be useful and practical, and even first form babies can make very dainty soft canvas dusters which become precious and cherished possessions. Another class of youngsters can make wrappers in which to fold away their work, others learn to cut out and make work-aprons. Flannel stitches must next be taught, and then perhaps a pretty camisole, such as all nice girls love, could be made. Quick deft-fingered girls will be able to work out designs in the studio for embroidery. Science overalls and cookery aprons and sleeves come next. The long wearisome seams become full of interest when the needlewoman is trying how perfectly straight she can machine, and this gives time for simple embroidery on bib and pocket, and this teaches incidentally much about the need for careful consideration of materials and purpose in design.

By fourteen or fifteen all girls should have given proof of fair proficiency in needlework. They would have facility in all ordinary stitches, and they would be able to draft and cut out any simple garment. They can machine a long seam straight, and better still, if the needle break, they know how to put a new one in. Then they can begin cookery, and their work in science at once comes into connexion with it. Up to this point the science course has been correlated with geography and nature study. These girls will have already had two, and in some cases three years' training in science, they will have gone through a course of general elementary science, and, for a year immediately preceding their cookery, they will have studied the chemistry of air and water. During this year they thus gain a knowledge of the fundamental elements from the study of substances within their own experience, i.e. air and water; so dealing with one of the food classes, water.

Science and cookery proceed together step by step. The scheme here deals with milk first, because in it the children can find, by experiments carried out entirely by themselves in the laboratory, all the foodstuffs necessary for life. Experiments on eggs will illustrate the properties of albumen, and thus lead to further work in connexion with meat, which reveals fibrin and connective tissue. The effect of moist heat on these is tried and practical lessons drawn from the results. Thus in the laboratory the children will discover for themselves the properties of milk, eggs, meat, etc. In the cookery room at the same time they will see these principles illustrated from another point of view in the processes of roasting, boiling, stewing, and frying. Starch, sugar, and alcohol, and fermentation generally in the laboratory, at once tell you that bread-making is the subject of the cookery lessons at the time. Processes of cleaning in the housewifery class suggest experiments with certain acids in the corresponding science lesson. The children should do nothing by mere 'rule of thumb'. Science and cookery are mutually dependent, and experiments on meat, eggshell, white of egg, potatoes go on in the laboratory, while on the science bench in the cookery room, the test tube and the retort are ordinary pieces of equipment.

The principles of combustion, flame, coal gas, etc., are taught with special reference to the fire and gas stove in the cookery room. Similarly, by the time the girls reach laundry in the home-arts course, they should be revising in their chemistry the hardness of water and softening agents, and discovering the composition and properties of soap. They would quite naturally make candles and pieces of soap, of course on a small scale. It is not necessary to give more examples. There are abundant points where intelligent correlation will be worked out. Girls find a new interest and a new zest in the work of home when they can thus see the reasons underlying the processes. The 'dull mechanic oar' is transformed, and the daily round of household duties becomes an intellectual occupation based on reasonable and sound principles. And what is of great interest, they go home keen to try fresh methods and eager to apply their new won knowledge. Mothers have come to one school and said, 'My daughter tells me the reason of things I have been doing by rule of thumb all my life.'

Of course neither science nor cookery must be subordinated the one to the other. It must never be forgotten that the science course must train girls in the patient investigation of facts – must in short give them an inkling of what is meant by the scientific attitude of mind. The work should never be allowed to become 'scrappy' and detached; each experiment must follow from some preceding piece of work and itself lead on to further study. It must be remembered, too, that this science cannot be suddenly inserted into a scheme, it must be led up to; it must itself lead on to further study and training. So, too, the home-arts mistress must always bear in mind that she is teaching an art as well as a science, and that it is no use at all to know the scientific principles of the thing if you cannot cook and serve a dinner, if need be. Science and its practical application must go hand in hand, and the girl-housewife must be ready to discover all sorts of labour-saving devices. She must know the 'times and seasons' and the prices of stores, and she must, above all, understand the fundamental ideas of the different food values of ordinary articles of diet. This course should be kept in close touch with the home. The more the mothers and fathers can be interested, the more successful is the work. The 'Saturday morning bake' is a delightful institution, and one which puts to practical test the value of the school training. Home criticism of these experiments should be encouraged. In one school the girls keep a notebook in which all home practice is entered and parental comment added. Of course this needs time, and is only possible where the girls are practically free from the all-absorbing tyranny of home lessons.

The VIth Form should begin dressmaking. They can easily draft and cut out a skirt and blouse, and quick workers would embroider from designs worked out in the drawing classes.

Time must be found for hygiene and for some elementary ideas of home nursing. Household accounts will be taught practically in connexion with the cookery classes, and the buying and keeping of stores in the home-arts department. The great difficulty is how to find time for all this. That it can be done has been proved. Two hours a week, if the work is well organised, and if the pupils are trained to bring that zest and concentration which enables them to get every bit of value out of a class, will be sufficient to work through such a course as that thus roughly outlined.

The value of some such scheme of home arts cannot be overestimated. At our peril we omit it in our schemes of work. It claims a place on intellectual, on physical, and on moral grounds: intellectual, because it is a means of training in scientific method: physical, since it practises in the due co-ordination of hand and head: moral, because it brings into practical prominence the claims of the home, and dignifies the daily round and common task of household duties. In these days of the disintegration of homes, and in face of the undoubted tendency of daughters to drift away from their mothers' interests, it is something to give a girl a zest for the activities of home and a sense of the dignity and intellectual worth of home arts. Many a mother and daughter have been brought into a closer and more sympathetic understanding during the difficult period of the girl's young life by this community of interest in the household round.

To do this is surely supremely worth while, and the home-arts course does this, and more. It is really a preparation for life. Our girls are to be scholars, but they are daughters first, and even the woman destined for professional life and a place in the world's fighting line will some day surely be better for such training; while, if the intimate personal call comes to her to be the guiding spirit of some happy home, she will answer the more faithfully because of her previous school training in home arts. Her husband will find in her not only the merely intellectual companion, not certainly the overworked, harassed housekeeper so familiar to many of us, worried into premature and unlovely middle age by the multitude of unmethodised duties that crowd upon her, but the cultured and cheerful comrade of his life, the gracious and quiet ruler of a home in which things go with that ordered smoothness which is the surest sign of disciplined efficiency, and the sympathetic and understanding partner of the hopes and ambitions which animate him in his work in the great world.

L. M. Faithfull

Home Science

(1911)

There can be little need to insist upon the fact that a girl's time-table in any secondary school is in great danger of being over-crowded. The study of languages, literature, history, and geography, the introduction to elementary mathematics and science, demand of the average schoolgirl all the intellectual effort of which she is capable; in the laboratory, at the piano and over her needlework, she finds the variety and relaxation that she requires, and her day is filled to the full. Those concerned in education are now convinced of the further necessity of giving a girl a thorough training in the science of house-keeping, including, when possible, cookery and kitchen laboratory work, laundry, housewifery, dressmaking, hygiene, home nursing, and the management of business affairs. The problem is, when is this wide field of knowledge to be traversed? between the ages of fourteen and seventeen in addition to the ordinary curriculum? or when the heavier part of the school course is at an end?

In supplementing the very interesting paper written by Miss Gilliland, I am endeavouring to represent the view of those who consider that where the average leaving age is eighteen the study of home science should be postponed till a girl is at least sixteen. At that point in her school life I think she should devote from 650 to 700 hours for one, or preferably two years to the acquirement of this knowledge, bringing a well-trained mind and a sound elementary knowledge of chemistry and physics to bear upon her new studies.

Although I fully recognise that the curriculum must vary in different types of school, yet I consider that the attempt to teach home science as a school subject to girls under sixteen should be avoided whenever it is possible; it can at best be regarded as a painful necessity, inexpedient from every point of view. A girl's strength may easily be overtaxed between the ages of thirteen and sixteen, and yet it is at the age of thirteen that a second language must be learnt in the normal secondary school, the study of geometry and algebra added to that of arithmetic, and this without any reduction of the time devoted to history, literature, and geography.

If in addition to these subjects botany, physics, and chemistry have been taken in successive years, a foundation will have been laid on right lines for the study of home science; and familiarity in dealing with test tubes, in making accurate measurements, and in scientific processes will have been acquired. The girl will go to her kitchen laboratory work, or to her practical cookery, impressed with the need of accuracy, and with a power of analysing results.

It would seem best to defer the correlation of science and cookery for as long as possible. The foundations of a knowledge of chemistry and physics should be built up on a well-ordered system which must not be subordinated from the outset to the requirements of home science. The teaching of science during the school years should be such as to prove equally useful to the pupil who elects to take at a later stage a university course in science and to the pupil who enters upon the home science course. I consider the two hours a week that may be spared from the over-weighted time-table altogether inadequate for the new type of work which some propose to introduce at the age of thirteen or fourteen.

Those of us who desire to confine the teaching of home arts and science to a later stage in the school career, by no means propose to restrict the teaching of this subject to girls of slight mental ability, as is sometimes imagined. There are many schools, especially boarding schools, where the majority of girls have no professional career in view, and will only enter for university examinations if they show distinction in some one branch of knowledge, and are encouraged to pursue it at the university. It has been proved more than easy to induce girls of good ability to take a thorough course in home science towards the end of their school career, and thus equip themselves for home life. It may also be maintained with some justice that girls who have taken this subject as a regular part of their school work from an early age, are less likely to continue it at a later age, when a power of selection is theirs, and when the subject does not offer them the excitement of an undiscovered country.

There seems to me to be only one sound argument against deferring the home science course until the age stated above, namely: that in so doing those girls who proceed to a university education with a professional career in view, will, for the most part, be unable to devote a year to learning how to manage a house.

The distinction, however, between the professional woman and the woman whose education includes a study of home science will tend to disappear, when university recognition has been accorded to the study of home science and the graduate of the future is able to choose a subject for her scientific work from a branch of science specially appropriate to her as a woman.

With the present limited experience of domestic economics as a post-school course in England, it is of interest to note the recent German decree, by which so-called Frauenschule are connected with some of the higher girls' schools. The Prussian Government requires a ten years' course of ordinary instruction to be given, and then recommends a further course of two years to complete the education of those girls who are not entering upon a special professional career, but who may marry or take up social work of one kind or another. During these last two years the girls study social and domestic science as well as literature and art.

B. L. Hutchins

Higher Education and Marriage

(1912)

Higher education and the opportunity for a professional career have been demanded and obtained by a number of women in England in the last half-century. These innovations, as they are regarded, are welcomed by many as affording a much-needed improvement in the economic position and social status of women, but there are others (e.g., twenty years ago, the late Mr Grant Allen; more recently, Mr and Mrs Whetham and Dr Lionel Tayler) who tell us that biological deterioration is the certain result of such a course. Education and the prospect of professional advancement, in the opinion of some observers, will draw women away from matrimony and motherhood, and lower the average fitness of the mothers of the race. If the economic advantage of the individual be put before the biological good of the species, the result can only be disaster. These are weighty warnings, which, if proved to be grounded on good evidence, might cause many of us to reconsider our position. What are the facts? The present paper represents an endeavour to collect such information as exists on the position of the college woman in regard to marriage and motherhood, and to ascertain how far the criticisms indicated are really justified.

It has to be pointed out, however, that when the facts with regard to the college woman are elicited, there remains the by-no-means-easy problem of placing them in a true relation to the position of women generally. It is incorrect, for instance, to compare the marriage-rate of college women with the marriage-rate of women generally. The marriage-rate varies very much in different classes of society, and is usually higher in districts inhabited by the manual working class or the very poor, than it is in districts such as Hampstead or Kensington, with a large proportion of the rich or well-to-do. If we want to understand whether a college career alters the probability of marriage for women, we must institute comparisons, not with the marriage-rate of women generally, but with the marriage-rate of women in the same social class. And this is difficult to ascertain, as there are no marriage statistics of any homogeneous class, but only figures for localities, in any of which classes are always mixed, though one may predominate over another. While there is thus little direct evidence, there is, however, a good deal of indirect evidence which leads us to suppose that in the upper classes a much larger proportion of women remain unmarried than in the manual working class.

Table showing the proportion of single women 'living on own means' and in the general population. England and Wales. 1901.

Aged	Number				Percentage			
	Living on Own Means		General Population		Living on Own Means		General Population	
	Single	Married or Widowed	Single	Married or Widowed	Single	Married or Widowed	Single	Married or Widowed
25	18,817	7,546	941,161	1,828,725	71·4	28·6	34·0	66·0
35	25,651	16,242	382,468	1,681,594	61·2	38·8	18·5	81·5
45 and under 55	29,532	29,179	205,176	1,300,806	50·3	49·7	13·6	86·4
All ages over 20	143,324	216,617	2,941,733	6,938,461	39·8	60·2	29·8	70·2

This table brings out the perhaps unexpected result that among all propertied women, the single form a larger proportion than in the general population, and that at the ages at which marriage is most frequent, the proportion of women who are married is below that of the general population to an even startling degree.

Another means of comparing the prospects of marriage in different social strata is by comparing the proportion of single women in the age group 25–45 in rich and poor districts respectively. In making this comparison we must allow for the numbers of domestic servants who, of course, very considerably augment the proportion of single women in the wealthy residential districts. The following table shows that, even if we subtract all the domestic indoor servants from the single women in the age group (which is over-generous, as a small but unknown proportion of them are certainly married or widowed), the single women in Hampstead, Kensington, and Paddington are a considerably higher percentage than in Stepney, Shoreditch, and Poplar. These districts have been 'selected' only in the sense that they were the first that occurred to the writer as affording a marked contrast of wealth and poverty.

Proportion of single women, and of domestic indoor servants, in every 100 women, aged 25–45.

	Hampstead		Stepney	
	Number	Per cent	Number	Per cent
Single Women	18,366	54·9	7064	17·4
Domestic Servants	5,764	31·9	1544	3·8

	Kensington		Shoreditch	
	Number	Per cent	Number	Per cent
Single Women	21,129	54·4	2990	18·1
Domestic Servants	13,126	34·0	435	2·6

	Paddington		Poplar	
	Number	Per cent	Number	Per cent
Single Women	13,118	45·6	3807	16·8
Domestic Servants	6,911	24·0	668	2·9

It therefore should be borne in mind in studying the position of the college woman that she belongs to, and her position and prospects in life are largely determined by, the conditions of a class in which the prospect of marriage is comparatively small. Mrs (or Miss) Washburn Shinn, writing on the 'Marriage Rate of College Women (*Century*, vol. L., 1895), says that the probability of marriage for a college woman does not reach two-thirds of the average for women generally of the same age, but that probably it does not fall so far below that of her own class. She indicates as one cause of celibacy among college women their tendency to take up teaching as a profession. 'There is no station in life (save that of a nun) so inimical to marriage as that of resident teacher in a girls' school,' owing to the very restricted opportunities of meeting men afforded by this mode of life.

It is doubtful, however, whether there is any need to invoke such occupational restriction as an explanation of the rarity of marriage. There is evidence that marriage is comparatively rare in the whole class. Miss Roberts Smith made a statistical comparison of college and non-college women (Publications of the American Statistical Association, vol. vii., 1900). She obtained records concerning 343 college-bred married women (called Class A) and 313 non-college married women (called Class B) of similar social class and position. It appeared from the figures collected that going to college in some degree delays marriage; only two of Class A

had married under t...
But beyond this age...
proportion marrying at...
is rising progressively in e...
in Class B. This will be ma...

Average age

Married 10 years or less
Married 10 to 20 years
Married 21 years and over
Rise in age at marriage

In 1890 Mrs Henry Sidgwick conducte... ...ne life-
history of some hundreds of women who h...   ...nege career,
and concurrently of a number of their sis...   ...d cousins who
had not done so. The results of this investigation are extremely
interesting, but appear to be little known.[1] It is highly desirable
that the inquiry should be repeated, and thus give an opportunity
of gauging the movement of social forces in a highly select class.

Mrs Sidgwick, among other things, collected particulars as to
the number of girls who had married, in the two groups studied.
Mrs Sidgwick was evidently somewhat startled by the small
proportion married. Among the students only about ten per cent.
had married, among their sisters only about nineteen per cent. It
would be too hasty to infer, however, that 'there is something in
having been at College which tends to prevent marriage.' Save as
a very rare event – which at that time had never occurred – a
woman would not either come to college or remain at college,
after marriage. If a student happened to marry during the years
she had intended to remain at a woman's college, *ipso facto* her
career as a student would usually be cut short. A student is therefore from the nature of the case almost certain to be unmarried up
to the time of leaving college, and thus women students may be
regarded as a selected class – selected as being unmarried up to the
time of their leaving college. Thus the statistics collected did not
give the proportion of women who marry to those who do not,
because in the nature of the case the history of the subjects of
the inquiry was still incomplete. Nor did the statistics give the
proportion of married to unmarried women in the given class of
society at any moment; since, the colleges being at that time a new
development, and having increased from small beginnings rapidly
in a short time, the proportion of young unmarried women to the
whole was greater among the subjects of the inquiry than among

...hat Mrs Sidgwick's figures did enable
...pare the proportionate number of students
...with the proportionate number of their sisters
...ied. To do this fairly and accurately some correction
...ances had to be made.

...would exceed the limits of our space to follow completely
Mrs Sidgwick's careful analysis. Briefly, the facts that emerged
were these: The higher percentage of sisters married was found to
consist in the fact that some of them had married early, at ages
when the students were at college. When the marriage rate was
calculated on the number of students who had left college prior to
the time at which the returns were made, the difference between
them and their sisters became negligible; when the marriages of
sisters under twenty-one were omitted, the rate of marriage from
twenty-one to thirty was slightly in favour of students (see p. 58).
Two inferences emerge from these calculations: firstly, that the
proportion of young women in the professional classes who do
not marry is very large, probably more than half; secondly, that
the spending a few years at college tends to postpone marriage till
the age of twenty-one or more, but makes no difference in the
proportion who ultimately marry.

Results of a very similar nature appeared from analysis of the
proportion of children born to the marriages of students and their
sisters respectively. At the time of collecting the returns, no student
had been married as long as fifteen years. The marriages of sisters
exceeding that duration were, therefore, subtracted. The average
number of children born per marriage was slightly lower among
the students than the non-students (1·53 to 1·81), but the proportion
of childless marriages was also lower among students than among
non-students (viz., 27·6 to 40·0), and the average number of children born per year of marriage was higher for students than for
non-students (viz., 0·36 to 0·29). The higher birth-rate among the
non-students was thus merely apparent, being due to the greater
average duration of marriage.

The deaths of children were so few as to afford no basis for
statistics of any value. The records show that the proportion of
still-births to children born alive was somewhat above the average,
both among students and their sisters; the proportion of deaths
among children born alive to both classes was smaller than ordinary. These facts in no way justify pessimistic forebodings as to
the racial consequences of higher education.

It appears, indeed, not only from Mrs Sidgwick's figures, but
from some of the American researches also, that higher education
is not a factor of great importance in regard to marriage and

motherhood. Miss Roberts Smith's paper, already quoted, shows that her Class B mothers (non-college) had, indeed, a slightly higher total birth-rate than Class A (college). But this was explicable by the fact of Class B being married on an average earlier than Class A. When this was allowed for, Class A had a child to every 5·97 years of married life; Class B to every 6·71 years of married life.

That the marriage rate of college women is very low no one can deny; the point that is often overlooked in discussing the subject is that the low rate is characteristic not merely of college women, but of the whole social class from which they are drawn. Calculations published in an article in the *Overland Monthly*, vol. xv. 1890, p. 444, show that the marriage rate of students from different States of U.S.A. varies much the same as does the general marriage rate; thus, the graduates from Western States marry much more frequently than New York graduates, and more than twice as frequently as New England graduates. Women from co-educational colleges, it may be noted, marry more frequently than those from women's colleges, no doubt owing to the greater opportunities of friendship and social intercourse with men.

It is interesting to note that some American researches on this subject show the educated mother to be quite as capable maternally as – indeed, rather more so than – the woman who has not been to college.

Miss Roberts Smith, in concluding the paper already quoted, states that the general tenor of the replies received by her shows the college woman to have a greater sense of responsibility in marriage and motherhood, to lay more stress on hygienic knowledge, and (what is rather specially interesting, in view of recent biological criticism) to be personally more contented with the conditions of their marriage. Miss Abbott, writing in the *Forum*, vol. xx., 1895, quotes a saying of the late Maria Mitchell, 'Vassar girls marry late, but they marry well.'

In conclusion, I would point out that, while the very low marriage rate disclosed by these researches is undoubtedly a serious matter, those critics are evidently mistaken who have assumed higher education to be the cause of the phenomenon. It is quite evident that the question is one of wider extent and significance. It might, indeed, with more truth be urged that the demand for higher education and wider opportunity has arisen as a consequence of the restricted prospects of marriage in the upper class, though this would not, in my opinion, be the whole truth. The demand in question is due (as I think) principally to a real spiritual awakening, by no means confined to single women, and to a righteous discontent with the ignoble futility of many women's lives, and the parasitism of their economic position.

I would also respectfully urge on the heads of women's colleges, or others whom it may concern, the importance of causing further statistical inquiry to be made into the subsequent careers of college women, collating the results, as in Mrs Sidgwick's inquiry, with corresponding figures for girls of the same social position who have not been to college. The women's education movement is being attacked on *a priori* grounds, and with very little knowledge of the real facts. All who care for that movement and believe its significance to be far greater and finer than the immediate advantage of individual students (great though that undoubtedly is), must wish that it should be defended only on grounds of perfect truth, sincerity, and accurate knowledge. At present our information, though interesting and valuable as far as it goes, is incomplete and somewhat out of date.

NOTE

1 *Health Statistics of Women Students and their Sisters.* Cambridge University Press, 1890. 1s. 6d.

Sir Almroth Wright

Letter to the Editor of The Times *on Militant Suffragettes*

(1912)

To the Editor of *The Times*

Sir, For man the physiology and psychology of woman is full of difficulties. He is not a little mystified when he encounters in her periodically recurring phases of hypersensitiveness, unreasonableness, and loss of the sense of proportion. He is frankly perplexed when confronted with a complete alteration of character in a woman who is child-bearing. When he is a witness of the 'tendency of woman to morally warp when nervously ill,' and of the terrible physical havoc which the pangs of a disappointed love may work, he is appalled. And it leaves on his mind an eerie feeling when he sees serious and long-continued mental disorders developing in connexion with the approaching extinction of a woman's reproductive faculty. No man can close his eyes to these things; but he does not feel at liberty to speak of them.

For the woman that God gave him is not his to give away.

As for woman herself she makes very light of any of these mental upsettings. She perhaps smiles a little at them. The woman of the world will even gaily assure you that 'of course half the women in London have to be shut up when they come to the change of life.' None the less, these upsettings of her mental equilibrium are the things that a woman has most cause to fear; and no doctor can ever lose sight of the fact that the mind of woman is always threatened with danger from the reverberations of her physiological emergencies. It is with such thoughts that the doctor lets his eyes rest upon the militant suffragist. He cannot shut them to the fact that there is mixed up with the woman's movement much mental disorder; and he cannot conceal from himself the physiological emergencies which lie behind.

The recruiting field for the militant suffragists is the half million of our excess female population – that half million which had better long ago have gone out to mate with its complement of men beyond the sea. Among them there are the following different types of woman.

The Different Types of Women

First – let us put them first – come a class of women who hold, with minds otherwise unwarped, that they may, whenever it is to their advantage, lawfully resort to physical violence. The programme, as distinguished from the methods, of these women is not very different from that of the ordinary suffragist woman. There file past next a class of women who have all their life-long been strangers to joy, women in whom instincts long suppressed have in the end broken into flame. These are the sexually embittered women in whom everything has turned into gall and bitterness of heart and hatred of men. Their legislative programme is licence for themselves or else restrictions for man.

Next there file past the incomplete. One side of their nature has undergone atrophy, with the result that they have lost touch with their living fellow men and women. Their programme is to convert the whole world into an epicene institution – an epicene institution in which man and woman shall everywhere work side by side at the self-same tasks and for the self-same pay. These wishes can never by any possibility be realised. Even in animals – I say *even*, because in these at least one of the sexes has periods of complete quiescence – male and female cannot be safely worked side by side, except when they are incomplete. While in the human species safety can be obtained, it can be obtained only at the price of continual constraint. And even then woman, though she protests that she does not require it, and that she does not receive it, practically always does receive differential treatment at the hands of man. It would be well, I often think, that every woman should be clearly told – and the woman of the world will immediately understand – that when man sets his face against the proposal to bring in an epicene world he does so because he can do his best work only in surroundings where he is perfectly free from suggestion and from restraint, and from the onus which all differential treatment imposes. And I may add in connexion with my own profession that when a medical man asks that he should not be the yoke-fellow of a medical woman he does so also because he would wish to keep up as between men and women – even when they are doctors – some of the modesties and reticences upon which our civilisation has been built up. Now the medical woman is of course never on the side of modesty, or in favour of any reticences. Her desire for knowledge does not allow of these.

Inextricably mixed up with the types which we have been discussing is the type of woman whom Dr Leonard Williams's recent letter brought so distinctly before our eyes – the woman who is poisoned by her misplaced self-esteem, and who flies out at every man who does not pay homage to her intellect. She is the woman who is affronted when a man avers that *for him* the glory of woman lies in her power of attraction, in her capacity for motherhood, and in unswerving allegiance to the ethics which are special to her sex. I have heard such an intellectually-embittered woman say, though a man had taken her to wife, that 'never in the whole course of her life had a man ever as much as done her a kindness.'

The Question of Intellectual Equality

The programme of this type of woman is, as a preliminary, to compel man to admit her claim to be his intellectual equal, and, that done, to compel him to divide up everything with her to the last farthing, and so make her also his financial equal. And her journals exhibit to us the kind of Parliamentary representative she desiderates. He humbly, hat in hand, asks for his orders from a knot of washerwomen standing arms a-kimbo. Following in the wake of these embittered human beings come troops of girls just grown up. All these will assure you, those young girls – and what is seething in their minds is stirring also in the minds in the girls in the colleges and schools which are staffed by unmarried suffragists – that woman has suffered all manner of indignity and injustice at the hands of man. And these young girls have been told about the intellectual and moral and financial value of woman – such tales as it never entered into the heart of man to conceive. The programme of these young women is to be married upon their own terms. Man shall – so runs their scheme – work for their support – to that end giving up his freedom and putting himself under orders for many hours of the day; but they themselves must not be asked to give up any of their liberty to him, or to subordinate themselves to his interests or to obey him in anything. To obey a *man* would be to commit the unpardonable sin.

It is not necessary in connexion with a movement which proceeds on the lines set out above any further to labour the point that there is in it an element of mental disorder. It is plain that it is there.

A Fatuous Doctrine

There is also a quite fatuous element in the programmes of the militant suffragist. We have this element, for instance, in the doctrine that, notwithstanding the fact that the conditions of the labour market deny it to her, woman ought to receive the same wage as a man for the same work. This doctrine is fatuous, because it leaves out of sight that, even if woman succeeds in doing the same work as man, he has behind him a much larger reserve of physical strength. As soon as a time of strain comes a reserve of strength and freedom from periodic indisposition is worth paying extra for. Fatuous also is the dogma that woman ought to have the same pay for the same work – fatuous because it leaves out of sight that woman's commercial value in many of the best fields of work is subject to a very heavy discount by reason of the fact that she cannot, like a male employee, work cheek by jowl with a male employer, nor work among men as a man with his fellow-employees. So much for the woman suffragist's protest that she can conceive of no reason for a differential rate of pay for man. Quite as fatuous are the marriage projects of the militant suffragist. Every woman of the world could tell her – whispering it into her private ear – that if a sufficient number of men should come to the conclusion that it was not worth their while to marry except on the terms of fair give-and-take, the suffragist woman's demands would have to come down. It is not at all certain that the institution of matrimony – which, after all, is the great instrument in the levelling up of the financial situation of woman – can endure apart from some willing subordination on the part of the wife.

It will have been observed that there is in these programmes, in addition to the element of mental disorder and to the element of the fatuous, which have been animadverted upon, also a very ugly element of dishonesty. In reality the very kernel of the militant suffrage movement is the element of immorality. There is here not only immorality in the ends which are in view, but also in the methods adopted for the attainment of those ends. We may restrict ourselves to indicating wherein lies the immorality of the methods.

There is no one who does not discern that woman in her relations to physical force stands in quite a different position to man. Out of that different relation there must of necessity shape itself a special code of ethics for woman. And to violate that code must be for woman immorality.

Woman and Physical Violence

So far as I have seen, no one in this controversy has laid his finger upon the essential point in the relations of woman to physical violence. It has been stated – and in the main quite truly stated – that woman in the mass cannot, like man, back up her vote by bringing physical force into play. But the woman suffragist here counters by insisting that she as an individual may have more physical force than an individual man. And it is quite certain – and it did not need suffragist raids and window-breaking riots to demonstrate it – that woman in the mass can bring a certain amount of physical force to bear. The true inwardness of the relation in which woman stands to physical force lies not in the question of her having it at command, but in the fact that she cannot put it forth without placing herself within the jurisdiction of an ethical law. The law against which she offends when she resorts to physical violence is not an ordinance of man, it is not written in the statutes of any State, it has not been enunciated by any human law-giver. It belongs to those unwritten and unassailable and irreversible commandments of religion, ἄγραπτα κἀσφαλῆ θεῶν νόμιμα, which we suddenly and mysteriously become aware of when we see them violated. The law which the militant suffragist has violated is among the ordinances of that code which forbade us even to think of employing our native Indian troops against the Boers, which brands it as an ignominy when a man leaves his fellow in the lurch and saves his own life, and which makes it an outrage for a man to do violence to a woman. To violate any ordinance of that code is more dishonourable than to transgress every statutory law. We see acknowledgment of it in the fact that even the uneducated man in the street resents it as an outrage to civilisation when he sees a man strike a blow at a woman. But to the man who is committing the outrage it is a thing simply unaccountable that any one should fly out at him. In just such a case is the militant suffragist. She cannot understand why any one should think civilisation is outraged when she scuffles in the street mud with a policeman.

If she asks for an explanation it perhaps behoves a man to supply it.

Up to the present in the whole civilised world there has ruled a truce of God as between man and woman. That truce is based upon the solemn covenant that within the frontiers of civilisation (outside them of course the rule lapses) the weapon of physical force may not be applied by man against woman nor by woman against man. Under this covenant the reign of force which prevails in the world without comes to an end when a man enters his household. Under this covenant that half of the human race which most needs protection is raised up above the waves of violence. Within the terms of this compact everything that woman has received from man and everything man receives from woman is given as a free gift. Again, under this covenant a full half of the programme of Christianity has been realised; and a foundation has been laid upon which it may be possible to build higher, and perhaps finally in the ideal future to achieve the abolition of physical violence and war. And it is this solemn covenant, the covenant so faithfully kept by man, which has been violated by the militant suffragist in the interest of her morbid, stupid, ugly, and dishonest programmes.

Is it wonder if men feel that they have had enough of the militant suffragist, and that the State would be well rid of her if she were crushed under the soldiers' shields like the traitor woman at the Tarpeian rock?

The Function of the Vote

We have sufficiently considered her, and with her we have considered the thousands of her sympathisers and subscribers. We may turn now to that section of woman suffragists – one is almost inclined to doubt whether it any longer exists – which is opposed to all violent measures, though it numbers in its ranks women who are stung to the quick by the thought that man, who will concede the vote to the lowest and most degraded of his own sex, withholds it from 'even the noblest woman in England.'

When that excited and somewhat pathetic appeal is addressed to us we have only to consider what a vote really gives. The Parliamentary vote is an instrument – and a quite astonishingly disappointing instrument it is – for obtaining legislation; that is, for directing that the agents of the State shall in certain defined circumstances bring into application the weapon of physical compulsion. Further, the vote is an instrument by which we give to this or that group of statesmen authority to supervise and keep in motion the whole machinery of compulsion.

To take examples. A vote cast in favour of a Bill for the prohibition of alcohol – if we could find opportunity for giving a vote on such a question – would be a formal expression of our desire to apply through the agency of the paid servants of the State that same physical compulsion which Mrs Carrie Nation put into application in her 'bar-smashing' crusades. And a vote which puts a Government into office in a country where murder is punishable by death is a vote which, by agency of the hangman, puts the noose round the neck of every convicted murderer. So that the difference between voting and direct resort to force is simply the difference between exerting physical violence in person and exerting it through the intermediary of an agent of the State.

The thing, therefore, that is withheld from the noblest woman in England while it is conceded to the man who is lacking in nobility of character is in the end only an instrument by which she might bring into application physical force. When one realises that that same noblest woman of England would shrink from any personal exercise of violence, one would have thought that it would have come home to her that it is not precisely her job to commission a man forcibly to shut up a publichouse or to hang a murderer.

One cannot help asking oneself whether, if she understood what a vote really means, the noblest woman in England would still go on complaining of the bitter insult which is done to her in withholding the vote.

A Reply to the Politician

But the opportunist – the practical politician, as he calls himself – will perhaps here intervene, holding some such language as this: 'Granting all you say, granting, for the sake of argument, that the principle of giving votes to woman is unsound, and that evil must ultimately come of it, how can you get over the fact that no very conspicuous harm has resulted from woman suffrage in the countries which have adopted it? And can any firm reasons be rendered for the belief that the giving of votes to women in England would be any whit more harmful than in the Colonies?'

A very few words will supply the answer.

The evils of woman suffrage lie, first, in the fact that to give the vote to women is to give it to voters who as a class are quite incompetent to adjudicate upon political issues; secondly, in the fact that women are a class of voters who cannot effectively back up their votes by force; and, thirdly, in the fact that it may seriously embroil man and woman.

The first two aspects of the question have already in this controversy been adequately dealt with. There remains the last issue.

From the point of view of this issue the conditions which we have to deal with in this country are the absolute antithesis of those ruling in any of the countries and States which have adopted woman suffrage.

When woman suffrage was adopted in these countries it was adopted in some for one reason, in others for another. In some it was adopted because it appealed to the *doctrinaire* politician as the proper logical outcome of a democratic and socialistic policy. In others it was adopted because opportunist politicians saw in it an instrument by which they might gain electioneering advantages. So much was this the case that it sometimes happened that the woman's vote was sprung upon a community which was quite unprepared and indifferent to it. The cause of woman suffrage was thus in the countries of which we speak neither in its inception nor in its realisation a question of revolt of woman against the oppression of man. It had and has no relation to the programmes of the militant suffragists as set out at the outset of this letter. By virtue of this all the evils which spring from the embroiling of man and woman have in the countries in question been conspicuously absent. Instead of seeing himself confronted by a section of embittered and hostile women voters which might at any time outvote him and help to turn an election, man there sees his women-folk voting practically everywhere in accordance with his directions and lending him a hand to outvote his political opponent. Whether or no such voting is for the good of the common weal is beside our present question. But it is clearly an arrangement which leads to amity and peace between a man and his womenkind and through these to good will towards all women.

In England everything is different. If woman suffrage comes in here it will have come as a surrender to a very violent feminist agitation – an agitation which we have traced back to our excess female population and the associated abnormal physiological conditions. If ever Parliament concedes the vote to woman in England it will be accepted by the militant suffragist, not as an eirenicon, but as a victory which she will value only for the better carrying on of her fight *à outrance* against the oppression and injustice of man.

A conciliation with hysterical revolt is neither an act of peace nor will it bring peace.

Nor would the conferring of the vote upon women carry with it any advantages from the point of view of finding a way out of the material entanglements in which woman is enmeshed, and thus ending the war between man and woman. One has only to ask oneself whether or not it would help the legislator in remodelling the divorce or the bastardy laws if he had conjoined with him an unmarried militant suffragist as assessor.

Peace will come again. It will come when woman ceases to believe and to teach all manner of evil of man despitefully. It will come when she ceases to impute to him as a crime her own natural disabilities, when she ceases to resent the fact that man cannot and does not wish to work side by side with her. And peace will return when every woman for whom there is no room in England seeks 'rest' beyond the sea, 'each one in the house of her husband,' and when the woman who remains in England comes to recognise that she can without sacrifice of dignity give a willing subordination to the husband or father, who, when all is said and done, earns and lays up money for her.

Biographical Notes

Dorothea Beale (1831–1906)

Extremely critical of her own education, Dorothea Beale attended Queen's College for Women shortly after it opened in 1848 and began what was to be her lifelong interest in women's education. At Queen's College she became the first mathematics teacher but the appointment for which she is best known, and which she accepted in 1858, was that of headmistress of Cheltenham Ladies College. She convinced students, parents and educators that the education of girls should be taken seriously and was among the small group of women who gave evidence to the Schools Inquiry Commission in 1865. Dorothea Beale was also active in The Headmistresses' Association and helped to establish St Hilda's College at Oxford.

She was a supporter of solidarity among women (and actively involved in the women's suffrage movement) and, on the grounds that it could promote rivalry, was against examinations for girls. Despite her own public role, she saw women's primary function in the private sphere but would not allow that this was an intellectual or educational disqualification.

Main sources are Elizabeth Raikes, 1908, *Dorothea Beale of Cheltenham* (Constable, London); Elizabeth Shillitoe, 1920, *Dorothea Beale: Principal of the Cheltenham Ladies College 1858–1906* (Macmillan, London) and Josephine Kamm, 1958, *How Different From Us: A Biography of Miss Buss and Miss Beale* (Bodley Head, London).

Mary Beedy

While no biographical material can be located on Mary Beedy there is an article entitled 'Girls and Women in England and America' in *The Education of American Girls, Considered in a Series of Essays* edited by Anna C. Brackett, (1874, G. P. Putnam's Sons, New York). In the Preface, the editor describes Mary E. Beedy (whose address is given as 83 Ladbroke Grove, Notting Hill) as a graduate of Antioch who 'has taught for many years in different sections of this country and has had unusual opportunities, for several years, of observing English methods and results'.

Barbara Leigh Smith Bodichon (1827–91)

A prominent feminist pioneer who contributed to many aspects of the campaign for women's rights, Barbara Leigh Smith was encouraged by her mother to work for an improvement in the position of women and by her father to be independent. In 1849 she attended the Ladies College in Bedford Square and soon afterwards founded an experimental school for girls and boys – the first of her practical contributions to education.

In 1854 she questioned the legal disabilities of women when she wrote her pamphlet, 'A Brief Summary in Plain Language of the Most Important Laws concerning Women', which documented the consequences of disallowing married women to own property and which was influential in the formulation of the Married Women's Property Bill. This was followed in 1857 by her essay 'Women and Work' in which she argued that dependency was degrading and that women should be allowed education, occupation – and a decent living.

In 1857 Barbara Leigh Smith married Eugene Bodichon. In 1858 she helped to found the ground-breaking periodical, *English-woman's Review*. A close friend of Bessie Rayner Parkes (editor of the periodical) and of Emily Davies, Barbara Leigh Smith Bodichon was completely committed to the principle of higher education for women and put much of her energy and her income into this particular cause. She was a co-founder of Girton College, Cambridge.

A member of the committee which organised the petition for women's suffrage presented by John Stuart Mill to the House of Commons in 1866, Barbara Leigh Smith Bodichon was one of the best advocates of educational rights for women.

Main sources are Hester Burton, 1949, *Barbara Bodichon 1827–1891* (John Murray, London) and Jacquie Matthews, 1983, 'Barbara Bodichon: Integrity in Diversity' in Dale Spender (ed.) *Feminist Theorists* (The Women's Press, London). See also Candida Lacey (ed.), *Barbara Leigh Smith Bodichon and the Langham Place Group*, 1987 (Routledge & Kegan Paul, London).

Jessie Boucherett (1825–1905)

Recruited in 1858 by a copy of the *Englishwoman's Journal* (purchased in a railway station bookstall) Jessie Boucherett made her way to the office of the periodical in Langham Place and offered her services in the campaign for women's education and women's rights. With Adelaide Proctor she started the Society for Promoting the Employment of Women and with Barbara Leigh Smith Bodichon and Emily Davies helped draft the petition that John Stuart Mill presented to the House of Commons in 1866.

In 1865, Jessie Boucherett revived the *Englishwoman's Journal* and changed its name to *Englishwoman's Review* – which she edited until 1871. Her contribution to women's education ranged from her support for the foundation of Girton to the establishment of a school in London to train women as bookkeepers and clerks.

She wrote many popular articles on and for women, often with the aim of promoting increased employment opportunities and wages for her own sex.

Little is known about Jessie Boucherett apart from the fact that she was a member of a conservative Lincolnshire family. There is some information on her in Frances Hays, 1885, *Women of the Day* (Chatto & Windus, London) and in Helen Blackburn, 1902, *Women's Suffrage: A Record of the Movement* (Williams & Norgate, London).

Frances Mary Buss (1827–94)

The eldest child in a large family which had financial problems, Frances Buss started teaching at school at the age of fourteen, and at eighteen taught in a school opened by her mother. In 1849 she became an evening student at the newly founded Queen's College and one year later was awarded the College Diploma. She then founded the North London Collegiate School for girls and became committed to improving women's education.

She campaigned to have university local examinations opened to girls and gave evidence to the 1865 Schools Inquiry Commission. A friend of Emily Davies, Frances Buss actively supported higher education for women – including medical education. She supported women's suffrage, the anti-slavery movement and the temperance campaign: she sought to have women placed on school boards and boards of guardians.

Concerned that women should be self-supporting, she saw education as a means of providing women with self realisation and a career – and she was active in promoting teacher education to this end.

Main sources are Annie E. Ridley, 1895, *Frances Mary Buss and her Work for Education* (Longmans Green, London) and Josephine Kamm, 1958, *How Different From Us: A Biography of Miss Beale and Miss Buss* (The Bodley Head, London).

Josephine Butler (1826–1906)

Leader of the campaign against the sexual double standard, Josephine Butler came from a politically conscious and liberal household and spent the first of her married years at Oxford where she was incensed by the behaviour of academic men. Upon their move to Liverpool in 1866, she and her husband became involved in the North of England Council for the Higher Education of Women: in 1867 Josephine Butler became the president and in 1868 she took to Cambridge a petition requesting the university to set examinations for women. In seeking 'special' provisions for women, Josephine Butler aligned herself with Anne Jemima Clough and the supporters of Newnham.

In 1868 she also published her pamphlet *The Education and Employment of Women* in which she argued for the opportunity for women to be independent.

With the advent of The Contagious Diseases Acts – first introduced in the 1860s – Josephine Butler put most of her energy into demanding their repeal and, aware of the 'reputation' that she was earning, withdrew much of her public support from feminist causes – including that of women's education – because she did not want to bring the other campaigns into disrepute.

Main sources are E. Moberly Bell, 1962, *Josephine Butler: Flame of Fire* (Constable, London); A. S. G. Butler, 1954, *Portrait of*

Josephine Butler (Faber & Faber, London) and Millicent Garrett Fawcett and E. M. Turner, 1927, *Josephine Butler: Her Work and Principles* (London Association for Moral and Social Hygiene). Also, Josephine Butler, 1898, *Personal Reminiscences of a Great Crusade* (Horace Marshall, London).

Mary Carpenter (1807–77)

In 1829, Mary Carpenter, along with her mother and sister, opened a school for girls; in 1846 Mary Carpenter opened her first Ragged School and in 1850 she published *Ragged Schools: Their Principles and Modes of Operation*. In 1851, convinced of the undesirability of placing young offenders in prison, she published *Reformatory Schools for the Children of the Perishing and Dangerous Classes and for Juvenile Offenders*. Then in 1852 she opened a Reformatory School while she also worked for the Reformatory Schools Act of 1854. Many publications on reformatory schools and the treatment of delinquents followed. A circumspect supporter of women's causes, Mary Carpenter was, however, concerned with some of the difficulties women faced in India and she attempted to set up teacher training colleges in the country as a partial solution. At home, she was an energetic worker for the extension of women's education and was in favour of admitting women to medical degrees.

Main sources are J. Estlin Carpenter, 1879, *The Life and Work of Mary Carpenter* (Macmillan, London); J. Manton, 1976, *Mary Carpenter and the Children of the Streets* (Heinemann, London).

Anne Jemima Clough (1820–92)

Born in Liverpool, Anne Jemima Clough lived in South Carolina in the United States from the age of two until she was sixteen. Back in Liverpool in 1841, she opened a school to help pay off family debts. In 1848 she was able to spend a short time in London at a teacher training school and, four years later, she moved to Ambleside where once again she set up a school.

Her meeting with Emily Davies and Frances Buss was a most significant event in her life and, with their encouragement, she used her experience of the Ambleside school to give evidence to the

Schools Inquiry Commission and to publish a paper in *MacMillan's Magazine*, 'Hints on the organization of girls' schools'.

A founding member of the North of England Council for Promoting the Higher Education of Women (Leeds, 1867), she helped to establish a lecture programme for women and special university-based examinations which could serve as teaching credentials. When undertaken at Cambridge the same scheme developed into Newnham College and Anne Jemima Clough became its first principal.

She was prepared to accept special provisions for women partly because she was aware that women were not nearly as well prepared for university entrance; she also believed that such provision would soon succeed and would be rendered unnecessary. Other commitments include the founding of the Association of Assistant Mistresses and support for the University Association of Women Teachers; she was a firm believer in women's emotional and financial independence.

Main sources are Blanche Clough, 1903, *Memoir of Anne Jemima Clough, First Principal of Newnham* (Arnold, London).

Frances Power Cobbe (1822–1904)

Feminist and journalist, Frances Power Cobbe was born in Ireland into a reasonably affluent family, but on the death of her parents resolved on financial independence rather than be supported by her brother. A friend of Lydia Becker and Barbara Bodichon, her 1868 pamphlet, 'Criminals, Idiots, Women and Minors' was an analysis of (and protest against) the way women's dependence was constructed by men in order to permit male supremacy.

She objected to violence at a fundamental level and was an ardent campaigner against male violence to women; in 1878 she published her pamphlet 'Wife Torture' and she worked hard for the Matrimonial Causes Act of 1878 which allowed a wife to be separated from a brutal husband.

She was equally committed to bringing to an end violence against animals.

Her major philosophical contribution to the education debates was her assertion that women existed independently of men and should be educated to that end.

Main sources are Frances Power Cobbe, 1894, *The Life of Frances Power Cobbe*, by Herself (Richard Bentley, London); for her contribution to legislation against violent husbands see Carol Bauer and

Lawrence Ritt, 1983, 'Frances Power Cobbe confronts the wife-abuse problem in Victorian England', International Journal of Women's Studies, Vol. VI (2) 1983, pp. 99–118.

Emily Davies (1830–1921)

From an early age Emily Davies was critical of the double standard and the privileges enjoyed by her brother. She became a friend of Elizabeth Garrett (a pioneer of women's medical education) and of Barbara Bodichon, and her first campaign was to try and persuade the University of London to open its doors to women. She was quite adamant that she wanted women to enjoy the same education – and professions and privileges – as men. She resisted all pressures for special provision for women.

It was as a result of her efforts that girls were included in the Schools Inquiry Commission and in 1866 she published her book, *The Higher Education of Women.*

She was a member of the committee that drew up the first suffrage petition presented by John Stuart Mill and was a firm supporter of women's rights. In 1869, after much fund raising, she saw part of her dream for women's education come to fruition with the procurement of a house outside Cambridge and a programme of university education which evolved into the establishment of Girton College in 1873.

Partly because of her uncompromising attitude towards special education for women, she was engaged in many controversies during her period at Girton during the 1870s but her commitment to women and education was never in doubt.

Main sources are Barbara Stephen, 1927, *Emily Davies and Girton College* (Constable, London).

Lillian Mary Faithfull (1865–1952)

An early student of Somerville College Oxford (in 1883 when it had only twenty-five students) Lillian Mary Faithfull made her career out of women's education. In 1889 she became lecturer in English literature at the newly established Royal Holloway College and in 1894 she was appointed Vice Principal of the women's department of King's College London, where she remained for thirteen years. It was her ambition to make King's College for

Women a leading force in women's education and in this she was successful.

Lillian Mary Faithfull was a pioneer in the field of domestic science education and the first president of the All England Women's Hockey Association. On the death of Miss Beale in 1906 she took over the Cheltenham Ladies' College, including its teacher training sections.

Millicent Garrett Fawcett (1847–1929)

From twelve years of age (or earlier) when her older sister attempted to enter the medical profession, Millicent Garrett was committed to the campaign for women's rights. Her marriage to Henry Fawcett did not curtail her commitment and as secretary to her blind MP/Cambridge professor husband, her learning experiences and political education were considerably enlarged. She gradually emerged as the major force in the constitutional suffrage movement and in 1890, on the death of Lydia Becker and until 1919 she was the leader of the National Union of Women's Suffrage Societies.

She was a fervent believer in the contribution that higher education could make to the equality of the sexes and came out in support of Newnham rather than Girton, partly because of her husband's interest. But while she found 'special provision' for women acceptable in educational terms she was opposed to special provisions in employment as she thought this would be used against women.

Main sources are Ray Strachey, 1931, *Millicent Garrett Fawcett* (John Murray, London); Millicent Garrett Fawcett, 1924, *What I Remember* (T. Fisher Unwin, London).

Margaret A. Gilliland

No details available.

Maria Georgina Grey (1816–1906)

Born Maria Shirreff, the younger sister of Emily Shirreff, Maria Grey (and her sister) made a substantial contribution to women's education. In 1841 she was married and thereafter played little role in public life until her husband's death in 1864, when she put much of her energy into improving education for women.

Maria Grey sought election to the London Board in 1870: she became active in the Charity Organization Society and in 1871, with her sister Emily, launched the Women's Education Union which in 1873 set up the Girls' Public Day School Company and in 1876 the Teachers' Training and Registration Society. She was concerned to provide low cost but high quality education for girls and enhance the training and working conditions of teachers: the model teacher training college which resulted from much of her effort was named the Maria Grey Training College as an acknowledgement of her contribution.

Her concern for women's education was part of her broader commitment to social justice and to women's right to their own independent lives. Apart from the two novels that she wrote (*Passion and Principle*, jointly with Emily in 1853, and *Love's Sacrifice* in 1868) she wrote a series of articles and pamphlets which included *Thoughts on Self Culture addressed to Women* (with Emily in 1850); 'Is the Exercise of Suffrage Unfeminine?'; 'The Physical Force Objection to Women's Suffrage' and in 1889, 'Last Words to Girls on Life in School and After'.

Main sources are Edward W. Ellsworth, 1979, *Liberators of the Female Mind. The Shirreff Sisters, Educational Reform and the Women's Movement* (Greenwood Press, London).

Mary Gurney (1836–1917)

An original and committed member of the Women's Education Union she was an active and influential supporter of the Girls' Public Day School Company and a member of the Council. A teacher, who published many translations from Italian, French, German and Spanish literature, she was highly esteemed for her contribution to girls' education. She was also a member of the Educational Sectional Committee of the sub-committee of Arrangements for the International Council of Women.

Wilena Hitching

(Headmistress, Meanwood Road Girls' School, Leeds) No biographical material available.

Bessie L. Hutchins

No biographical data available: primarily a writer in the field of industrial history and women's participation. Major work: *Women in Modern Industry* (1915); she also wrote *Conflicting Ideals* and *A History of Factory Legislation* (with Mrs Spencer).

Sophia Jex-Blake (1840–1912)

Sophia Jex-Blake was a woman of good family who was frustrated by the constraints placed upon females, who became a feminist and who spent much of her life trying to ensure that members of her sex were allowed more opportunities – and rights.

In 1858 she overcame parental opposition to attend classes at Queen's College and so outstanding was her performance that she was soon offered a tutorship in mathematics – which her parents would only allow her to take up on condition that she did not accept the pay. On this occasion, as on many others, Sophia Jex-Blake denounced the injustice of the double standard which would only permit women work while they went without the pay.

In her search for worthwhile work, Sophia Jex-Blake attempted to collaborate with Octavia Hill, but the relationship had its difficulties and she was soon on her own again and searching for some useful scheme in which to put her energies. She did entertain the idea of starting a girls' college in Manchester, and with this aim in mind, undertook a tour of colleges in the United States.

On visiting the New England Hospital for Women and Children (and on meeting Dr Lucy Sewell), Sophia Jex-Blake found her vocation and determined to become a medical practitioner. To achieve her aim was to take on the British medical establishment – which she did with verve, and success, though not without difficulties on the way.

Although initially admitted to Edinburgh University her entry was later decreed to have been illegal and she was forced to leave and to acknowledge defeat: from there she attempted to qualify through the agency of the College of Surgeons – but the examiners thwarted her ambition by resigning en masse. After that she gave her attention to the establishment of the London Medical School for Women which came into existence in 1877.

Sophia Jex-Blake later returned to Edinburgh to practise and to found another medical school for women (which ran for a short time). She opened up medical education for women and was a wonderful example of female independence.

Main sources are Margaret Todd, 1918, *The Life of Sophia Jex-Blake* (Macmillan, London).

George John Romanes (1848–94)

A 'naturalist', born in Kingston, Canada, he was a graduate of Caius College Cambridge and a friend of Charles Darwin's. His major works include *Animal Intelligence*, (1881); *Scientific Evidence of Organic Evolution* (1881); *Mental Evolution in Animals* (1883); *Mental Evolution in Man* (1888).

Elizabeth Missing Sewell (1815–1906)

Primarily a novelist and teacher, she published more than forty books, on all subjects – including areas appropriate for school study. Among her novels are *Amy Herbert*, *Margaret Percival* and *Laneton Parsonage*.

Emily Anne Elizabeth Shirreff (1814–97)

Sister of Maria Shirreff Grey, the two collaborated on some early works (*Thoughts on Self Culture Addressed to Women* in 1850, and a novel, *Passion and Principle*, in 1853). Convinced of the importance of education for women – for the role it could play in self realisation as well as vocational training – she outlined her philosophy in 1858 in *Intellectual Education and Its Influence on the Character and Happiness of Women*.

In 1870, she was for a short time Mistress of Girton, but in 1871 she joined forces with her sister to launch the Women's Education Union which was designed to foster the education of girls. She became the secretary of the union and the editor of its journal as well as a staunch supporter of the Girls' Public Day School Company which it founded.

While adamant that the education of girls should be no less intellectually rigorous than that of boys, Emily Shirreff did hold that girls as mothers and educators of young children, had special needs above and beyond those of boys.

Main sources are Edward W. Ellsworth, 1979, *Liberators of the Female Mind: The Shirreff Sisters, Educational Reform and the Women's Movement* (Greenwood Press, London).

V. Sturge

No biographical data available.

Isabella Tod

No biographical data available though a report of a lecture that she gave on 9 January in Belfast, on the admission of women to the Universities is contained in *The Englishwoman's Review*, 1874, pp. 126–7.

Elizabeth Clark Wolstenholme-Elmy (1834?–1913)

From a very early age, Elizabeth Wolstenholme deeply resented the greater educational opportunities enjoyed by her brother and determined to develop better education conditions for girls. Prohibited by her guardians from attending Bedford College for Women, at nineteen years of age she opened a boarding school for middle-class girls and embarked on her career as headmistress, and supporter of women's rights.

In 1865 she helped to establish Manchester Schoolmistresses' Association, read a paper on the needs of teacher training at the Social Science Association in Sheffield, and gave evidence to the Schools Inquiry Commission. In 1867 she played an active part in the formation of the North of England Council for Higher Education. She was also involved in the women's suffrage campaign, in the Married Women's Property campaign and in resistance to the Contagious Diseases Acts.

She married Benjamin Elmy in 1874 and under the name of Ellis Ethelmar she wrote numerous books and pamphlets intended to explain the 'facts of life' and human physiology.

She did not become conservative with age and in 1905 became

one of the staunchest supporters of the Women's Social and Political Union – and of Christabel Pankhurst. She was also an inveterate letter-writer who maintained a remarkable correspondence with many famous feminists and reformers.

Main sources: Surprisingly there is no biographical work on Elizabeth Wolstenholme-Elmy. She is mentioned in many of the biographies of the women with whom she was associated (Josephine Butler, Anne Jemima Clough, Sophia Jex-Blake, Annie Besant) and there is a sketch of her entitled 'A Woman Emancipator: A Biographical Sketch', Ellis Ethelmar, in *The Westminster Review*, Vol. CXLV, 1896, pp. 424–8.

Almroth Edward Wright (1861–1947)

An eminent pathologist, he used his medical training to claim authority on all manner of social issues. Extremely outspoken and self opinionated he was involved in a whole series of controversies. A vehement anti-suffragist and anti-feminist he spoke and wrote continually on these subjects. In addition to the letter 'Militant Hysteria' which he wrote to *The Times* he published a monograph entitled *The Unexpurgated Case Against Woman Suffrage*.

He was most unhappily married.

Index

Camden Town School for Girls,
175, 187, 193–7, 204
Carlyle, Thomas, 148
Carpenter, Mary, 41, 349
certificates, awarding, 47, 74, 95,
103, 114–15, 140, 210, 299
charity funds, state use of, 58, 66,
160, 187–8, 205
Chelsea, public day school, 204,
206, 226–8, 298
Cheltenham Ladies' College,
129–37, 213, 345; constitution,
129–30; examinations, 128–9;
pupils, social class, 125
china painters, female, 76–7, 220
Church of England Day School
Company, 299
Clapham Girls' High School, 305
class size, 174–5
clergymen's daughters, education,
63–4
clerks, instruction of, 172, 207
Clough, Anne Jemima, 95, 175,
349–50
Cobbe, Frances Power, 351
coeducational schools, 84–5,
166–7, 248–66
college education *see* university
education
college life, 116–17, 300–3
College of Preceptors, 201, 217,
218; examinations, 178, 213,
296
college system, 126–9, 165, 183
convents, disappearance, 3
Cornell University, 253
correspondence courses, 216, 217
creative thought, 11

Darwin, Charles, 10, 17, 20
Davies, Emily, 5, 7, 175, 296, 298,
350–1
Delamont, Sara, 7
dependence, female, 20, 236–7
De Tocqueville, Alexis, 75
devotion, female, 15, 20
discipline: mental, 238; university,
116–17

doctors, female, 47, 268–71
domestic science, 316–24, 325–7
domestic service, training for, 52,
54–5
drawing, study of, 242
Dublin University, scholarships,
217
Duffin, Lorna, 7
Dyhouse, Carol, 7

Edinburgh Review, 77
Edinburgh University,
scholarships, 217
Educational Council, 160–1
education, female: control of, 6, 7;
defects, 123–6, 141, 149–51,
153–5, 173, 199, 209, 232–3;
different, 21–2, 42, 99, 101,
258–9; domestic science,
316–24, 325–7; effects of, 26–7,
42–3, 47–8, 80, 223, 238;
financing, 58, 59, 61, 63, 66–7,
160, 164–5, 165–6, 174, 176–7,
187, 189, 204–5; and freedom,
3–4, 79; history of, 138–9,
295–300; in mixed-sex schools,
84–5, 166–7, 248–66; need for,
50, 72–4, 148, 162, 172–3;
opposition to, 2–3, 25, 40;
pressure of, 27–9; purpose of, 5,
25–6, 123–4, 144, 146–7, 148,
171–2, 207, 230; redistribution
of subjects, 243; rudiments,
neglected, 124–6, 141, 233; same
as for men, 5–7, 8, 99, 106, 108,
142, 143, 234–5, 249; separate,
84–5, 166–7, 251, 253, 261; as
sound commercial investment,
176–7; study methods, 141,
207–8, 243; suitable, 5–6, 7–8,
42, 239–43, 253, 258–9; *see also*
equality in education; higher
education; schools; university
education
education reform, 146–7, 199–200,
209, 232
Elder, C., 303
elementary schools, 187–8, 202